NEPALI DIASPORA IN A GLOBALISED ERA

This is one of the first books to explore Nepali diaspora in a global context, across India and other parts of South Asia, South-East Asia, Europe and Australia. It discusses the social, political and economic status and aspirations of the Nepali community worldwide. The chapters in the volume cover a range of themes, including belonging and identity politics among Nepalese migrants, representation of Indian Nepalis in literature, diasporic consciousness, forceful eviction and displacement, social movements and ritual practices among migrant communities. Drawing attention to the lives of Nepali emigrants, the volume presents a sensitive and balanced understanding of their options and constraints, and their ambivalences about who they are.

This work will be invaluable to scholars and students of Nepal studies, area studies, diaspora and migration studies, social anthropology, cultural studies and literature.

Tanka B. Subba is Vice Chancellor of Sikkim University, Gangtok, India.

A. C. Sinha is National Fellow at the Indian Council of Social Science Research (ICSSR), Nehru Memorial Museum and Library, Teen Murti House, New Delhi, India.

NEPAL AND HIMALAYAN STUDIES

This series will bring the larger Nepal and the Himalayan region to the centre stage of academic analysis and explore critical questions that confront the region, ranging from society, culture and politics to economy and ecology. The books in the series will examine key themes concerning religion, ethnicity, language, identity, history, tradition, community, polity, democracy, as well as emerging issues regarding environment and development of this unique region.

Books in the series:

NEPALI DIASPORA IN A GLOBALISED ERA
Edited by Tanka B. Subba and A.C. Sinha
ISBN: 978-1-138-92226-6 (hbk)

GODDESSES OF THE KATHMANDU VALLEY
Grace, Rage, Knowledge
Arun Gupto
ISBN: 978-1-138-94585-2 (hbk)

NEPALI DIASPORA IN A GLOBALISED ERA

Edited by Tanka B. Subba and A.C. Sinha

NEW DELHI LONDON NEW YORK

First published 2016
by Routledge
2 Park Square, Milton Park, Abingdon, Oxon OX14 4RN

and by Routledge
711 Third Avenue, New York, NY 10017

Routledge is an imprint of the Taylor & Francis Group, an informa business

© 2016 Tanka B. Subba and A. C. Sinha

The right of Tanka B. Subba and A. C. Sinha to be identified as the authors of the editorial material, and of the authors for their individual chapters, has been asserted in accordance with sections 77 and 78 of the Copyright, Designs and Patents Act 1988.

All rights reserved. No part of this book may be reprinted or reproduced or utilised in any form or by any electronic, mechanical, or other means, now known or hereafter invented, including photocopying and recording, or in any information storage or retrieval system, without permission in writing from the publishers.

Trademark notice: Product or corporate names may be trademarks or registered trademarks, and are used only for identification and explanation without intent to infringe.

British Library Cataloguing-in-Publication Data
A catalogue record for this book is available from the British Library

Library of Congress Cataloging-in-Publication Data
A catalog record has been requested for this book

ISBN: 978-1-138-92226-6 (hbk)
ISBN: 978-1-315-68506-9 (ebk)

Typeset in Bembo
by Apex CoVantage, LLC

CONTENTS

List of figures	viii
List of tables	ix
Preface	x
Abbreviations	xii
Notes about the contributors	xiv

Introduction   1
TANKA B. SUBBA AND A.C. SINHA

1 Diasporic junctions: an eternal journey of mankind   11
P.K. MISRA

2 Changing paradigms of Nepalese migration and emerging diaspora   18
BHIM PRASAD SUBEDI

3 *Hami Nepali?* Belonging in Nepal and the Nepali diaspora   40
ULRIKE MÜLLER-BÖKER

4 Competing perspectives on the Gurkhas and identity politics in Nepal   55
JENS SEEBERG

5 Mythical entrapment of the self and the notion of Nepali diaspora   76
PRAVESH G. JUNG

CONTENTS

6 The Indian Gorkhas: changing orientation of a diasporic society 93
RAJENDRA P. DHAKAL

7 Diasporic imaginations of Darjeeling: Gorkhaland as an imaginative geography 108
MIRIAM WENNER

8 Writing from the edges to the centre: theorising the fragmented identity of Indian Nepalis 131
ANASTASIA M. TURNBULL

9 *The Inheritance of Loss* and the portrayal of Indian Nepalis 144
GEETIKA RANJAN

10 The making of Gurung cultural identifications in Sikkim 153
MELANIE VANDENHELSKEN

11 Ties to Nepal and diasporic consciousness of Indians of Nepali origin: examples from Bokakhat, Assam 170
TRISTAN BRUSLE

12 Between two worlds: a re-reading of *Brahmaputraka Cheuchau* 188
UTPALA GHALEY SEWA

13 Gurkha displacement from Burma in 1942: a historical perspective 203
TEJIMALA GURUNG

14 Nepalis of Manipur from the perspective of 'cultural collective' 221
VIJAYLAKSHMI BRARA

15 Evicted from home, nowhere to go: the case of Lhotshampas from Bhutan 230
A.C. SINHA

CONTENTS

16 **Lhotshampa refugees and Nepali diaspora**   246
D.N.S. DHAKAL AND GOPAL SUBEDI

17 **Riots, 'residence' and repatriation: the Singapore Gurkhas**   259
HEMA KIRUPPALINI

18 **Dreams of sacrifice: changing ritual practices among ex-Gurkha immigrants in the UK**   274
MITRA PARIYAR

19 **Conclusion**   291
TANKA B. SUBBA AND A.C. SINHA

Glossary   295
Index   299

FIGURES

2.1	Nepal: changing population size	21
2.2	Nepal: changing proportion of population in various age groups	22
2.3	Share of population by ecological regions, 1981–2011	23
2.4	Shift in migration patterns	25
2.5	Share in international migration by ecological regions, 2001–2011	27
2.6	Nepal: regional pattern of international migration, 2001	28
2.7	Country-wise distribution of foreign labour migrants	30
2.8	Women's participation in international migration	31
2.9	Foreign labour migration by district of origin	32
2.10	Conceptualising Nepali territorial mobility: the 'home–reach' model	36
4.1	Nepal's national emblem adopted in 1962	56
4.2	Nepal's national emblem adopted in 2006	57
7.1	Map of proposed state of Gorkhaland as envisioned by the GJM	115
8.1	Kolkata, India. My grandmother at her home	132
8.2	Darjeeling, West Bengal	136

TABLES

2.1	Share of regions in in-migration and out-migration, 1981 and 2001	26
3.1	Absentee households and household members in some wards of Majhigaon VDC, 2008	45
10.1	Ethnic diversity in Yangang	160
13.1	Places and categories of evacuees	214
13.2	Details of serving personnel as evacuees	214
13.3	Details of pensioners as evacuees	214
13.4	Details of civilian evacuees	215
13.5	Evacuees who had no home either in India or in Nepal	215
13.6	Statement showing arrival of Gurkha Evacuees in Motihari Camp up to 29 September 1942	215
15.1	Number of families, huts and population of Lhotshampa refugees	241
15.2	Destinations of male and female Lhotshampa refugees	242
16.1	Verification results of the Bhutanese refugees in Khudunabari Camp by the JVT	250
16.2	Bhutanese refugee population in overseas countries	252
16.3	Resettlement of Bhutanese refugees in the USA	253
16.4	Bhutanese refugee population in Nepal	254

PREFACE

This book is the last of the series on Nepalis living outside Nepal on whom we started working together at North-Eastern Hill University, Shillong in 2001. Although the departments we belonged to did not enjoy the best of relationships, having been born as one and later separated, the two of us met and often discussed the plight of the Nepalis in north-east India in general, and Meghalaya in particular. We were also among the few social scientists in India who had done some research and publication on this community. It is unfortunate that few Indians know about the contribution of the Nepalis to India's security and freedom struggle and even fewer know about the sacrifice and contribution made by them to the development of the north-east region. They are religiously believed to belong to Nepal and many youths of the region consider it their right to harass, destroy their property and even evict them en masse. Organising a seminar on them was thus not a politically correct thing to do in Shillong, but we did it the very first time in 2001 and repeated our feat in 2011.

Our 2001 seminar in Shillong was held with a small fund available under the Special Assistance Programme of the University Grants Commission given to the Sociology Department of our university. The seminar turned out to be more successful than we had anticipated and it led to the publication of *Nepalis in Northeast India: A Community in Search of Indian Identity* (2003). Emboldened by its success, we held the next seminar in Gangtok in 2006 at the all-India level. It was funded by the Indian Council of Social Research and the Government of Sikkim, and supported by Sri D.R. Nepal, Joint Secretary (Home) with the Government of Sikkim and Prof. G.S. Nepal from North Bengal University, who also joined us as editors of the volume. The Gangtok seminar also turned out to be a huge success. Our sincere thanks goes to Sri Pawan Chamling, the Chief Minister of Sikkim, for providing all the financial and logistic support for organising a national-level seminar with more than six dozen papers presented in several sessions simultaneously. We chose some of the best submissions made in English at the seminar and published the second volume on the Nepali diaspora titled *Indian Nepalis: Issues and Perspectives* (2009). We regret our failure to bring out another volume based on submissions made in the Nepali language.

The next logical step we wanted to take was to hold a seminar on the Nepalis at the international level, and for this, we wanted the venue to be Kathmandu so that the intellectual and political elites there could be sensitised about the plight of the Nepalis living outside Nepal, but the country was in utter chaos after 1996 and it would be unfair on our part if we insisted on our friends there to organise it. We also thought that Delhi was another good location, but that would need a lot more funds than we were able to collect for the seminar. Finally, we decided to hold it in Shillong, partly because it was much cheaper to do so and partly because we wanted to prove that the local youths of this hill city can be reasonable and not everyone is itching to evict the Nepalis. Once again, thanks to our friends, well-wishers and the Indian Council of Social Science Research standing solidly behind our mission and making the seminar a grand success. We wish to profusely thank Dr Joshua Thomas of the ICSSR's North Eastern Regional Centre and our own North-Eastern Hill University for giving us all the freedom to indulge in this exercise and even provide financial support for the seminar. Although media attention was missing, we had a very intensive seminar for three days with participants from India, Nepal and several European countries. Some of those who could not make it to the seminar have also contributed to the volume and we thank them for kindly accepting our request.

While putting this volume together, we had several moments of confusion, dilemma and ambivalence about the identity, nomenclatures and the history of the Nepalis. Thus, we do not think that we have given to the people what we think is the last word on them. But it is for others now to take the baton ahead. We have done what we wanted and what we could with our meagre resources and limited knowledge. But, like the previous two books, we are confident that this book will also prove to be a valuable reference material on the community. If this book is discussed, criticised and commented upon by the readers, we will consider our mission to be accomplished.

Tanka B. Subba and A. C. Sinha

ABBREVIATIONS

AAGSU	All Assam Gorkha Students' Union
ABA	Association of Bhutanese in America
ABGL	Akhil Bharatiya Gorkha League
AGP	Asom Gana Parishad
ASEAN	Association of South East Asian Nations
BA	Burma Army
BCP	Communist Party of Bhutan
BFF	Burma Frontier Force
BFM	Swiss Federal Office of Migration
BGP	Bharatiya Gorkha Parisangh
BMP	Burma Military Police
BRCF	Bhutan Refugees Children Forum
CBS	Central Bureau of Statistics, Government of Nepal
CPI(M)	Communist Party of India (Marxist)
CPRM	Communist Party of Revolutionary Marxists
DFE	Department of Foreign Employment, Government of Nepal
DGHC	Darjeeling Gorkha Hill Council
GAESO	Gurkha Army Ex-Servicemen's Organisation
GJM	Gorkha Janamukti Morcha
GNLF	Gorkha National Liberation Front
GSG	Gurkha Security Guards
GTA	Gorkhaland Territorial Administration
ILTA	Indigenous Lepcha Tribal Association
INA	Indian National Army
ITA	Indian Tea Association
JRAI	Journal of Royal Anthropological Institute
JVT	Joint Verification Team
LDC	Lepcha Development Council
MNO	Mongol National Organisation

ABBREVIATIONS

NCO	Nepali Community of Oxford
NPR	Nepal Rupees
NRB	Non-Resident Bhutanese
OBC	Other Backward Classes
OBCA	Organisation of Bhutanese Community in America
OECD	Organisation for Economic Cooperation and Development
RGB	Royal Government of Bhutan
RGN	Royal Government of Nepal
SC	Scheduled Caste
SGA	All Sikkim Gurung (Tamu) Buddhist Association
SGC	Singapore Gurkha Contingent
SGPA	Singapore Gurkha Pensioners' Association
ST	Scheduled Tribe
TMC	Trinamul Congress
UCPN (Maoist)	United Communist Party of Nepal (Maoist)
ULFA	United Liberation Force of Assam
UNHCR	United Nations High Commission on Refugees
VDC	Village Development Council
WOREC	Women's Rehabilitation Centre

CONTRIBUTORS

Vijaylakshmi Brara is a sociologist and is presently Associate Professor at the Centre for Manipur Studies, Manipur University. Her major areas of academic interests are gender, culture and grassroots political institutions. Her research area has been north-east India for over a decade. She is the author of the widely acclaimed book, *Politics, Society and Cosmology in India's North-East*. She has many published articles to her credit.

Tristan Bruslé is a geographer at the National Center for Scientific Research, France. His main interests are international labour migration and diaspora. Recent publications include 'Daily Life, Privacy and the Inmate Metaphor in a Nepalese Workers' Labour Camp (Qatar)' (2012); 'Nepalese Diasporic Websites: Signs and Conditions of a Diaspora in the Making?' (2012).

D. N. S. Dhakal is acting president of the Bhutan National Democratic Party and was an official of the Royal Government of Bhutan before becoming a political activist in 1992. He is currently a senior fellow at the Duke Center for International Development (DCID), Duke University, USA, and has been working in Executive Programmes of DCID on Project Appraisal and Risk Management and Fiscal Decentralization and Local Government since 2001.

Rajendra P. Dhakal is the principal of Kalimpong College, Kalimpong. His research interests include state and society, identity politics and politico-literary narratives. He participated in the US Studies Program 2010 as a guest of the State Department at the University of Massachusetts, Amherst. His PhD was on 'Organisation and Management of Rural Development in India with reference to the Hill Areas of Darjeeling'.

Tejimala Gurung is associate professor at the Department of History, North-Eastern Hill University, Shillong. Her research interests include

Nepali migration, social formation and gender history in north-east India, on which she has several published articles. She has edited (with Sajal Nag and Abhijit Choudhury) *Making of the Indian Union: Merger of Princely States and Excluded Areas* (2007).

Pravesh G. Jung teaches philosophy at the Indian Institute of Technology, Mumbai. Some of his areas of interest relate to identity and belonging.

Hema Kiruppalini was research associate at the Institute of South Asian Studies at the National University of Singapore. Her thesis titled "Travelling Dwellers: Nepalese Lahure in Singapore" was among the pioneering works on the Gurkha community in Singapore. She is also the Assistant Editor of *The Encyclopedia of the Sri Lankan Diaspora*. Her research interests are in the areas of migration, diaspora studies, ethnic conflicts and identity politics in South Asia and South-East Asia.

Ulrike Müller-Böker is professor of human geography at the Department of Geography, University of Zurich in Switzerland, and head of National Centre of Competence North-South program component 'institutions, livelihoods, conflicts'. Her fields of competence include the analysis of institutional dimensions of livelihood strategies, the impact of globalisation processes, local resource-use conflicts, labour migration patterns, nature conservation and development and participation processes focusing on South Asia, Central Asia and Switzerland.

Promode Kumar Misra is retired professor of anthropology at the North-Eastern Hill University, Shillong. He was visiting professor of anthropology at the University of Oregon, Eugene, USA; visiting professor of Indian studies at the University of West Indies, Trinidad; and visiting professor of anthropology at the University of Mysore, Mysore. He is currently national fellow of the Indian Council of Social Science Research at the Central Institute of Indian Languages, Mysore, and founder-president of Anthropological Association, Mysore.

Mitra Pariyar is a PhD candidate at the Department of Sociology, Macquarie University, Sydney, and has just completed an ethnographic research on Nepalese/Gurkha immigrants in the United Kingdom. He has contributed numerous articles to different publications. He is also interested in the issues of race and racism, multiculturalism, militarism, as well as wider diasporic experiences.

Geetika Ranjan is associate professor in the Department of Anthropology, North-Eastern Hill University, Shillong, India. Her major publications are 'Tribe as a Category: Perspective from Within and Without', *The Oriental*

Anthropologist; 'Bidesia: The Saga of Migration, Separation and Loss', *The Eastern Anthropologist*; 'Ethnography of Development: Challenges and Promises', *The NEHU Journal*; and 'From Tribe to Social Integration: Bhoksa Youth and the Challenges of Transformation', *Journal of Social Sciences.*

Jens Seeberg is associate professor at the Department of Culture and Society, Aarhus University, Denmark, and is chair of Platform for Stability, Democracy and Rights at the university since 2011. He has researched in several Asian countries such as India, Bangladesh, Myanmar, Nepal, Sri Lanka and Thailand and has published several articles. He currently heads a major DANIDA-funded project titled 'Nepal on the Move: Conflict, Migration and Stability'.

Utpala Ghaley Sewa was educated in Darjeeling and Shillong. She completed her post-graduation, MPhil and doctorate from North-Eastern Hill University, Shillong, and has worked at colleges in Shillong and Kolkata. She now teaches at the Department of English, North-Eastern Hill University, Shillong. She has published a book titled *Memory as Vision: The Poetry of Thomas Hardy* and contributed chapters to edited volumes and articles in some national journals.

A. C. Sinha was trained in anthropology at the University of Ranchi and in sociology at the Indian Institute of Technology, Kanpur. He conducted field study in Sikkim, Bhutan and north-east India, taught at Gujarat Vidyapeeth, Ahmedabad, the Indian Institute of Technology, Kanpur and Delhi, and North-Eastern Hill University, Shillong. He was Smut Scholar at Cambridge University, UK, and Senior Fulbright Visiting Professor at California University, Santa Cruz, USA. He has authored about a dozen books on politics, nation-building, urbanization, social change, ethnicity and environment, including *Politics of Sikkim* (1975), *Bhutan: Ethnic Identity and National Dilemma* (1991, 1998), *Hill Cities in Eastern Himalayas* (1994), *Bhutan: Tradition, Transition and Transformation* (2001, 2004), *Sikkim: Feudal and Democratic* (2008) and two volumes on Nepalis in India with T. B. Subba. Currently, he is a national fellow of the Indian Council of Social Science Research at Nehru Memorial Museum and Library, Teen Murti House, New Delhi.

Tanka B. Subba is the vice-chancellor of Sikkim University, Gangtok, India. He has authored and edited about a dozen books and over 70 articles on various issues related to the eastern Himalayas. He was the editor of the internationally refereed biannual journal, *The NEHU Journal,* until October 2012 and was a member of the editorial advisory boards of several international journals, including *Contributions to Indian Sociology* (Institute of Economic Growth, Delhi) and *Asian Anthropology* (Chinese University of Hong Kong). His current areas of interest are ethnicity and development, health and disease, politics of culture and identity and diaspora. He has published two books on Nepalis titled *Nepalis in Northeast India: In Search of Indian Identity* (edited with A. C. Sinha) and *Indian Nepalis: Issues and Perspectives* (edited with A. C. Sinha, G. S. Nepal and D. R. Nepal).

Bhim Prasad Subedi is professor of geography and former head of the Central Department of Geography, Tribhuvan University. He has been actively involved in teaching and research at Tribhuvan University. He has published widely on migration and ethnic diversification, livelihood, state structuring and social geography, youth-bulge, exclusion – social or spatial, and population redistribution policies.

Gopal Subedi was born in Bhutan but has spent his early childhood as a refugee in a camp in Nepal. He is currently pursuing his master's degree in medical physics from Purdue University, West Lafayette, Indiana. He takes keen interest in human rights, democracy and international affairs and writes frequently on issues related to them. He is also an active volunteer who aids in facilitating the transition of the resettled refugees in the United States.

Anastasia M. Turnbull is a PhD candidate at the Department of Sociology and Equity Studies in Education at OISE, The University of Toronto in Canada. Her research interests include historical Darjeeling, elderly populations, autobiography and arts-informed life history inquiry and representation.

Melanie Vandenhelsken is a researcher at the Institute for Social Anthropology (Austrian Academy of Sciences). Her current work is on the modes of construction of ethnicity (approached as a cognitive category) in Sikkim, in particular on the role of relations between states, transnational networks and various agencies with ethnic groups in ethnic self-identifications making.

Miriam Wenner is a PhD student at Zurich University, Switzerland. Her thesis, titled 'Contested Spaces – Gorkhaland and the Production of New Geographies of Darjeeling', deals with the contested nature of political authority and sovereignty in Darjeeling. She is equally interested in questions of development and food security in Nepal and the Himalayas generally.

INTRODUCTION

Tanka B. Subba and A.C. Sinha

Human migration is one of the most ancient and global phenomena, as millions of human beings have moved from one place to another due to war, epidemic or other reasons over the centuries. However, statistics shows that this phenomenon has accelerated in the recent past. For example, there were 160 million international migrants in 2000, which rose to 192 million in 2005. About 190 countries of the world are either points of origin, transit or destination of international migrants today. There is a tendency among migrants to move from developing countries to the developed ones, probably for reasons such as better transport, health, employment opportunities and communication facilities. In the process, while developed countries receive inexpensive labour, migrant countries receive income from remittance – a necessary boost to their economy. According to the International Labour Organization (ILO), such remittances increased from US$ 2,000 million in 1970 to US$ 8,000 million in 2000. About a million and a half South Asians migrate every year. Among them, India alone claims to have over 20 million people spread across five dozen countries or so. In the year 2007, the World Bank estimated that the South Asian migrants sent about US$ 40,000 million to their native countries. Out of that figure, India received US$ 27,000 million, Bangladesh US$ 6,400 million, Pakistan US$ 6,100 million, Sri Lanka US$ 2,700 million and Nepal US$ 1,600 million as remittances. However, international migration has also proved to be a disaster for many countries, due to demographic imbalance, resource crunch, opportunity appropriation and so on by incoming migrants and the resultant ethnic conflicts and political disorder.

Human migration and the idea of diaspora

Taking a cue from the extensive presence of people of Indian origin all over the world, Indian scholars and policymakers began to study the history of migrant Indians in Mauritius, Fiji, the West Indies, South and East Africa, the Middle East, Great Britain, Canada, the United States of America, Malaysia, Singapore and elsewhere. Their cultural, societal, political and economic contributions to the host countries were the foci of serious academic concerns. As many of the former British colonies gained independence, Indians tried to reach out to India in search of their roots and cultural moorings. With its reputation as an emerging economic power, India has also tried to reach Indians wherever they were living. This paved the way for what came to be known as diasporic studies.

The idea of diaspora is believed to have originated with the Jews' search for their historical/mythical homeland – Israel – and their desire to return home. The term 'diaspora' has Greek origins[1] and refers to the scattering of seeds as they are sown over a wide area. William Safran considered diaspora to be characterised by dispersal from the original homeland, retention of collective memory, vision or myth of the original homeland, partial assimilation with the host society, desirable commitment to restoration of the homeland and continuous renewed linkage with the homeland.[2] On the contrary, Khachig Tölölyan included the 'immigrant, expatriate, refugee, guest worker, exile community, overseas community and ethnic community in the semantic domain of trans-migration' as being part of the diaspora.[3] A working definition of diaspora was suggested by Nicholas Van Hear as the 'dispersal from original homeland to two or more places; movement between homeland and new host and; social, cultural or economic exchange between or among the diaspora community'.[4] Coming to the Indian situation, Jain's extensive and prolonged study[5] refers to the broadest possible canvas of the diasporic expansion in terms of a civilisational theory of the Indian diaspora.

A migrant community may be defined as diasporic if it has an ethnic consciousness, an active associative life, contact with the land of origin – real and imaginary – and relations with other groups of the same origin spread over the world. According to Judith Shuval, 'A diaspora is a social construct founded on feeling, consciousness, memory, mythology, history, meaningful narratives, group identity, longings, and dreams, allegorical and ritual elements, all of which play an important role in establishing a diaspora reality. At the given moment of time, the sense of connection to the homeland must be strong enough to resist forgetting assimilating or distancing'.[6] Paul Brass finds three sets of struggles influencing diasporic ethnic identities: one, there is struggle within the ethnic group for control over its 'material and symbolic resources', which will determine the group's boundaries and the conditions that will ascertain inclusion or exclusion. Two, there is struggle between ethnic groups as they compete for resources, rights and privileges. And three, there is struggle between the state and the groups which dominate it and the other ethnic groups in the country.[7] A significant feature of all diasporic communities is their linkage, 'real or imaginary', with the motherland. However, the intensity of such links depends on a number of factors such as geographical and cultural locations, physical distance between the host country and the mother country, affordability of the immigrants and cultural continuity and retention of the mother tongue. Further, the diasporic communities consciously maintain a collective memory of their homeland, which provides fundamental ingredients to their identity. Similarly, diasporic communities consciously patrol their boundaries, which works against their assimilation with the host country.

After World War II, when Jews were the worst sufferers at the hands of the fascists, the international community managed to thrust the Jews on Palestine with a mandate to share the same with the resident Islamists. This led to a militant Jewry to converge on Israel and turn it into a garrison state. However, Israel continues to be the holy homeland of the Jews spread all over the world.

With the advent of colonial powers, inexpensive labour was required for the industrial growth of the imperial territories. Thus, the Chinese, Indian, Filipino and Sri Lankan labourers spread far away from the shores of their mother countries. Once the colonial powers declined and new nations came into being, those countries began to look at those labourers as an economic and cultural resource. Conversely, the emigrants too began to look to their mother countries as sources of cultural and literary sustenance. Thus, diaspora became a fashionable idea among the countries that had exported labour to the colonies in the past, and along with Jew and Armenian diasporas, Chinese and Indian diasporas began to be discussed by the middle of the 20th century.

However, the Anglo-Saxon migrants across the globe in Australia, New Zealand, Canada, South Africa and the United States of America are not known as 'diaspora'. Similarly, the Germans in Chile and Argentina, Spaniards in Latin American countries and the Portuguese in Brazil, Angola and elsewhere are not referred to as diasporic peoples. Thus, the idea of diaspora has to do with something more than homeland, i.e. more in relation to the 'Other' or subjugated peoples. For Jews, Africans, Asians,

Palestinians and Armenians, the term actually 'signifies a collective trauma, banishment, where one dreamed of home, but lived in exile'.[8]

Nepali diaspora

The Nepalis, also called 'Gurkhas', are known as a 'martial race' in the colonial literature. But that was not the only reason why they were preferred as soldiers by the British; they were also encouraged to migrate to India for road construction, clearing of forests, agriculture, work on tea plantations and so on. There is a long history of their connection with the British, beginning in 1814, when the British fought against the expansionist Gurkhas and discovered their courage and fighting skills. The Nepalese rulers were initially reluctant to permit the British to recruit the Gurkhas, as they saw the British as their adversaries. But once the Ranas came to power in Nepal, a new phase of friendship emerged between them and the British. They also formally permitted the British to recruit their men, which led to the opening of recruitment depots at Dehradun, Gorakhpur, Laheriasarai, Darjeeling and Shillong.

The Gurkhas were also recruited in armed constabulary and police forces in the provinces of Bengal, Assam and Burma, whereas the 'non-martial Gurkhas' were encouraged to migrate due to their hardworking habits. Subsequently, the British adopted a policy to settle the retired Gurkhas near armed cantonments in north-east India for a variety of reasons. Though India-born Gurkhas, labelled as line boys, were not considered suitable for recruitment to the British Army, they were encouraged to settle on thinly inhabited strategic locations in eastern parts of India. Thus, one finds a concentration of the Nepali-speaking population in the Darjeeling hills, Sikkim, Bhutanese foothills, foothills of Arunachal Pradesh, Patkoi Hills and Burma.

By the end of the British rule in India, there were 10 regiments of the Gurkhas serving in the British Army. When India became independent, six Gurkha regiments opted to remain in India and four opted to go to Britain, who were required by the British for their service in far-flung imperial outposts such as Malaya, Singapore, Hong Kong, Latin America, Caribbean islands and the Falkland Islands. However, with the independence of the British colonies all over the world, the requirement for Gurkha forces was drastically reduced. Thus, at present, Great Britain has just about 2,500 Gurkha soldiers on its roll and the present regime has decided to reduce them further by 500 as an austerity measure. However, the British Gurkhas have recently won the battle for 'one rank one pay' and the right to settle in Britain after superannuation, which may further discourage the UK government from recruiting Gurkhas for their army.

There was a demand in the Nepalese Parliament on March 9, 2012 to stop recruitment of the Gurkha soldiers by the British and Indian armies, as they were seen to be a mercenary force – a view resented by the Gurkha soldiers themselves. In the opinion of a parliamentary panel, 'Nepal's government is put on further loss after the British decided to provide citizenship to Gorkha soldiers, and time has come to evaluate Nepal's foreign policy in regard to Gorkha recruitment'.[9] Incidentally, it was the Maoists who were most opposed to their recruitment in foreign armed forces. Needless to add that remittance from the soldiers in foreign service or post-retirement benefits of the superannuated soldiers has always been a significant source of income to the Nepalese exchequer.

Unlike soldiers in uniform, unskilled Nepalese labourers migrate to India unhindered, facilitated as they are by the Indo-Nepalese Friendship Treaty of 1950. They are engaged invariably in the least remunerative jobs and lead the most deprived life in crowded Indian cities or most isolated frontier posts. They often bring their family members to the place of their work or settlement. They are everywhere in India – in its metropolises, cities, towns, agricultural farmlands, forests, mines, factories, ports, roads, studios, movies and most sophisticated information technology sectors. Their exact number is rarely to be found in statistical data, as they live a submerged life away from the glare of media, politics and organised unions. In course of time, their children are born as legal citizens of India unless they choose to surrender their claims themselves by returning to Nepal or migrating to some other country.

Given the above backdrop, the idea of 'Nepali diaspora' is rather novel for the people of Nepal themselves. For them, going out for earning meant – until the 1950s – going to India, Britain, Singapore, Hong Kong, Malaysia, and so on. With the opening of the West and East Asian countries to Nepalese labour, however, new opportunities have emerged for them. These are, however, not only new opportunities, but also new challenges, as they have no or little knowledge about these new destinations.

As editors of the volume, we do not claim that all those who have migrated to India or elsewhere constitute the Nepali diaspora – not because some of them are averse to the idea of a diasporic community because they may be questioned about their relationship to the place where they live, but indeed many of the criteria of a diasporic community discussed in the earlier section do not fit in neatly with the ground realities of the Nepalis living outside Nepal. There have been attempts in India to underplay their connection with Nepal or not to imagine Nepal as their 'homeland', but elsewhere, the non-resident Nepali associations are active. Since no final word is possible on what a diasporic community is or is not, we have considered all those who have left Nepal for various purposes and for various lengths of time as constituting the Nepali diaspora. In this sense, the word 'diaspora' is certainly not used in its strictest sense as we would have loved to do, but we wonder if any community in the world today can qualify as a diasporic community in the strictest sense of the term. We are also of the view that the Hindi/Nepali word 'prawasi' (meaning, 'living in other lands'), which is often associated with diasporic people, is a poor substitute for the word 'diaspora', but we have used the latter word in the sense of its poor substitute, hoping that someday, we would be able to use the latter word in more precise sense in which it deserves to be used.

About the book

The book begins with the keynote delivered by P. K. Misra, whose work on the indentured labourers from eastern India to Trinidad and Tobago is well known. Misra particularly looks at the adaptive capacities of labourers and their ability to interpret their cultural symbols to their advantage. Although the Nepalis did not constitute indentured labourers per se, they were nonetheless labourers hired for clearing forests, construction of roads or for work in tea plantations. He uses the metaphor of 'junctions' to understand the diasporic society, thereby recognising travel and movement as essential components of diasporic societies.

The next chapter by Bhim Subedi is a comprehensive account of the migration of people from and to Nepal as well as within Nepal over the past four centuries or so. Subedi advocates the 'home-reach' model for a comprehensive understanding of Nepalese migration. He argues that the concept of *ghumphir* (short-term moves, including wandering around) must be separated from the concept of *basai sarai* (permanent and/or long-term migration) and their bi- or multi-locality should not be ignored if we are to understand their movement and the emerging Nepalese diaspora.

Drawing her inspiration from Amartya Sen, in the next chapter, Ulrike Müller-Böker (or Mueller-Boeker) argues that social and territorial belonging of an individual is multi-layered and dynamic. The sense of belonging as a symbolic dimension of social relations and interactions reflects also the need for networks essential for different livelihood strategies. She argues that the previous home becomes important to diasporic people only if they have the concept of returning home, but it becomes less important if they want to leave their home behind in search of 'another' life, as observed among the Nepalis in Switzerland.

In the next chapter, Jens Seeberg draws on de Castro's 'perspectival anthropology' to understand changes in the symbolism of 'Gurkha' in Nepal. Drawing on multiple sources of data, including TV clips and videos from the Internet, he compares different perspectives on 'Gurkhas', mainly those found in colonial discourses and Nepali literary narratives, and he links these to the 'Gurkha Justice Campaign' in the UK as well as to recent politics in Nepal.

Pravesh G. Jung, in the next chapter, makes a strong theoretical engagement with the concept of 'diaspora'. He considers the idea of 'homeland' as central to this debate, wherein the 'home' is understood as a space where one is at peace with one's own self. He has also engaged with discourses around the 'martial' character of the Gurkhas, like Seeberg in the previous chapter. However, Jung not only sees a Nepali entrapped in colonial construction of his character, but also sees others who are engaged in Nepali studies as being entrapped in the same construction.

Relying on Nepali literary and social science sources, Rajendra P. Dhakal takes us through three major phases in the orientation of the Indian Gorkhas in general, and the Gorkhas of Darjeeling in particular. The three phases are the evolution of a common Nepali identity; awakening of and building of an economic, social and political space for themselves; and finally, a phase of assertion of their sense of belonging to India.

The next chapter by Miriam Wenner looks at the demand for Gorkhaland as a 'strategic imaginative geography' and discusses how the Gorkha organisations employ their own mental appropriations of the space and the history of Darjeeling not only to justify their demand, but also to carve out a sense of hope among the masses for their future.

In the next chapter, Anastasia Turnbull presents the pangs of fragmented identity in her account of her personal journey to Darjeeling, which she considers her ancestral 'home'. In a way, the chapter embodies her own search for 'home' and what it means to herself and to those who interact with her.

How neighbouring communities, especially the dominant ones, look at Nepalis in India is discussed in the next chapter by Geetika Ranjan. Based on her reading of *The Inheritance of Loss*, a novel set in Kalimpong in the district of Darjeeling and written by Kiran Desai, Ranjan critiques the novelist on the ethics of the art of fiction writing.

In the next chapter, we move from Kalimpong to Sikkim, where Mélanie Vandenhelsken analyses the construction of Gurung cultural 'self-understanding'. Based on her comparative fieldwork in Gangtok and

Yangang village, she shows how the state's affirmative policies, also being a mechanism of control, triggers conflicts within a community. Additionally, and more importantly, she shows how the means and categories of the state are appropriated by politically marginalised people to claim equal rights and access political representation. This chapter also shows how various relations, in particular, the confrontation between varying political projects and views of cultural 'identity' within the Gurung community, lead to changes in cultural practices.

Next, we move to Assam with a chapter by Tristan Bruslé. Like Subedi and Müller-Böker in this volume, Bruslé brings out the multi-layered identity of the Nepalis in Assam on the basis of his fieldwork in a Nepali settlement in Assam called Bokakhat. He argues that the Assamese Nepalis need not underplay their links with Nepal because those links exist and were stronger in earlier generations than they are now. He supports the view of Hutt that Nepal should be seen as a resource, as a horizon of hope in times of crisis in host lands, and what Indian Nepalis need is a state that grants them equal rights as its citizens, more than an hypothetical transnational form of belonging.

The next chapter is also on Assam, based on a re-reading of a novel titled *Brahmaputraka Cheuchau* by Lil Bahadur Chhetri. This Sahitya Academy award-winning novel describes how the exploitative structure that existed in Nepal is re-enacted in Assam. The relationship between Gumane and Khalal – the hero and the villain – dominates the novel. At the symbolic level, the novel shows how Assamese society has finally accepted the Nepalis as one of their own people.

In the next chapter, Tejimala Gurung describes the sordid condition of the Burmese Gurkha families fleeing Burma across the mountains and rivers to India without food and rest and under constant fear of being bombarded by the Japanese in 1942. The majority of such families who survived the long and treacherous journey were from India, a few from Nepal and the rest from Burma itself. The last category of Nepalis was not acceptable to the king of Nepal on account of their defiled culture and religion.

Vijaylakshmi Brara, in the next chapter, brings out the facts about the scholars not writing about the migrant communities in Manipur although they have been living there since colonial times and have contributed immensely to the development of the state. She shows how even permanent land deeds were issued particularly to the Nepalis of Manipur by the Manipur State Council in 1947, which has now become a source of tension between them and the hill tribes of Manipur, who want such deeds to be nullified by bringing the areas settled by them under the Hill Areas Act, under which the Nepalis, being labelled as non-tribals, cannot hold

INTRODUCTION

land ownership. According to her, the only hope for the Nepalis of Manipur lies in the possibility of the Iroquois-type confederacy.

Next, we have two chapters on Bhutan. Both the chapters describe the circumstances leading to the eviction of the southern Bhutanese people called 'Lhotshampas', who are of Nepali origin and have contributed immensely to the development of Bhutan. Both the chapters show how the Bhutanese operation to flush them out from southern Bhutan was ignored by India and the international community whereas Nepal itself did precious little. The two chapters also bring out the internal weakness of the community such as the lack of experienced leadership. Finally, both the chapters deal with the issues of their recent settlement in Europe and America and how that is viewed with helplessness by the elderly and with excitement by the youths.

In the next chapter, Hema Kiruppalini writes that since 1949 the Gurkha Contingent (GC) has been a part of the Singapore Police Force, and yet their families are not allowed to mingle with the citizens of the country and are repatriated to Nepal on their retirement. Drawing attention to the racial riots that occurred in Singapore during the 1950s and 1960s, this article seeks to assess the role of the Gurkhas as a neutral force in the maintenance of the country's internal security. By providing insights into questions of home, identity and belonging, this chapter argues that the atypical migratory dynamics of the Singapore Gurkhas problematises key concepts of diasporic community formations.

The last chapter by Mitra Pariyar on the UK-settled ex-Gurkhas shows that a true Nepali diaspora has not been able to emerge in the UK due to strict laws of the land. The ex-Gurkhas, the author notes, have acquired the right to settle there after a lengthy fight, but they do not feel 'at home' there because they cannot perform certain rituals and cultural practices the way they practice back in Nepal. Thus, the UK-based ex-Gurkhas fought for a home, but yet the elderly among them are not able to treat it like their 'original home' in Nepal.

Notes

1 Origin, Greek *diaspeirein,* meaning 'disperse', the term originated in the phrase 'thou shalt be dispersion in all kingdoms of the earth' (*The New Oxford Dictionary*, Oxford University Press, 1998, pp. 510–11.) Diaspora originally referred to the dispersal of the Jews outside Palestine during the Greek and Roman periods. All the areas of dispersion created by forced captivity and exile, whose people were often subject to persecution and discrimination, were held together by a common religion, customs and the hope for 'return to Zion', the homeland of the Jewish people (*Encyclopedia Americana*, Vol. 9, 1969, pp. 68–9).

2 William Safran, 1991, 'Diaspora in Modern Societies: Myths of Homeland and Return', *Diaspora*, 1(1): 83–9.
3 Khachig Tölölyan, 1991, 'The Nation State and its Others: In Lieu of a Preface', *Diaspora*, 1(1): 37.
4 Nicholas Van Hear, 1998, *New Diasporas: The Mass Exodus, Dispersal and Regrouping of Migrant Communities,* London, University of California Press.
5 R. K. Jain, 2010, *Nation, Diaspora, Trans-nation: Reflections from India,* New Delhi, Routledge.
6 Judith Shuval, 2000, 'Diaspora Migration: Definitional Ambiguities and Theoretical Paradigm', *International Migration,* 38(5): 41–55.
7 Paul R. Brass, 1985, *Ethnic Groups and the State*, London, Croom Helm.
8 A. K. Sahoo and Brij Maharaj, 2007, *Sociology of Diaspora: A Reader,* Jaipur, Rawat Publications.
9 *The Asian Age*, March 19, 2012.

1
DIASPORIC JUNCTIONS
An eternal journey of mankind

P.K. Misra

The globe has no borders when viewed from outer space. Yet, a closer view begins to show the different geographical regions of the world. When one finally descends on the globe, one begins to realise that one cannot move freely: besides passports and visas, there are several other restrictions for crossing from one territory into another.

It has been confirmed that humankind originated in Africa (Wells 2002), and in a very short span of approximately 60,000 years, they moved and colonised different parts of the world. There were also waves of settlers, one displacing the other, or one blending with the other. In the process, identities of weaker groups were often subdued by the stronger groups, temporarily or forever.

The idea of homeland, and hence the idea of diaspora, is wrapped up in the imaginations and mythologies of the people who moved from their place of origin. But to consider that human beings moved only in search of resources for survival or due to certain natural or man-made calamities is, however, too restrictive of the facts for they are versatile and are also endowed with a sense of curiosity to explore what lies beyond a territory, a sense of adventure, a sense of experimentation and also a sense of aesthetic appreciation. Every society is a rich storehouse of myths and stories about their origin and migration. Human beings travelled amazing distances in spite of the limitations of their knowledge of technology and geography. Certainly, the early human movements raise many fundamental questions about human beings. Disciplines such as archaeology, anthropology, linguistics, paleobotany and paleoecology provide some clues regarding the places and routes they took, what they carried, what they incorporated in their language and culture and what they created.

Irrespective of how far they travelled or what they encountered en route, they often stopped at some junctions before setting out for another destination. Human movement continued even after they learned the art of domestication of crops and animals. Mobility and sedenterisation went hand in hand, as they are dialectically related (Misra 1986: 179–88). Even the indigenous populations of the world are migrants from somewhere at some point of time in their history. But it is important to understand the underlying critical differences between the early human movements and the recent diasporic movements, although both were, to a greater or lesser extent, influenced by jostling for resources, subjugation of 'others' and establishment of domination by one group over others. Diasporic movements, which are essentially characterised by a larger scale than the early human migrations, were a creation of colonial rule. In many ways, colonialism changed the world order by introducing new concepts among the colonised people (Chattopadhya 2012). It challenged national boundaries and induced rapid economic and technological changes.

India and Nepal are neighbouring countries. They have a long shared history in which geography has played an important role. The two countries still have a special relationship in the sense that the movement of people between the two countries is not restricted by any visa regime. The Himalayas, in general, have played an important role in shaping the religious philosophy of the Hindus and Buddhists in India; they are regarded with a certain degree of awe and veneration. From time immemorial, Indian ascetics have been going to the Himalayas for spiritual fulfilment, retreat, introspection and for wisdom. Therefore, it is pertinent to ask, like some Nepali scholars have themselves done, if it is correct to speak about a Nepali diaspora in India.

Studies have shown that voluntary migration of people normally results in improvement of their economy, health and education. It broadens their world view and knowledge. It also improves their survival skills and entrepreneurship by locating gaps in the supply of goods and services in host societies, which, in turn, derive multiple benefits besides getting cheap labour. Migrants add to the social, cultural and linguistic diversity of the host society. The home society too derives benefits through their economic, cultural and political remittances.

Diasporic studies initially referred to the dispersal of Jews, but now, it refers to any people living outside their homeland. The features of a diaspora are dispersal of population from the homeland, retention of imagination of the homeland in collective memory, cultivation of a variety of myths about the homeland, partial assimilation in the host society, wish or hope to return to the homeland, some kind of commitment for restoration of prosperity of the homeland and continued interest in keeping linkages with the homeland. Thus, diasporic studies focus on the role of networks that interconnect relatives, friends, fellow countrymen at home and abroad and float formal and informal associations. Such networks – although at times exploitative of new migrants – provide the much-needed information, provide assistance of various types, facilitate employment, accommodation and fulfil social, cultural and emotional needs.

Anthropological literature is so obsessed with discovering the patterns of social structure that the role of the individual in society does not get sufficient space. Diasporic studies, on the contrary, bring out the innovative and creative aspects of the individual in social formation. Such studies also demonstrate that individuals, in order to meet their aspirations, transcend social and cultural boundaries and establish new networks. In any diasporic movement, the decision of the individual to migrate is of prime importance; he/she assesses the physical, economic, political, social and cultural situations in his place of migration. Such situations are at times not only unfamiliar but even adverse. The case of Indian indentured labourers in the plantations of Trinidad or Guyana is exemplary and instructive; exemplary because Indians had a long heritage of textual and oral traditions to fall back upon while reconstructing their community, and instructive because they negotiated a hitherto untreaded path by deciding to work on contract.

Having made the decision to undertake the journey, they travelled together with strangers, lived with them under agonising circumstances and under strange rules. Their caste, religion, dialect, food habits, universe of rituals or social norms were of no consideration to those who were handling the human cargo. The sole responsibility of the labour contractors was to deliver the 'human goods' safely to the planters and earn their commission. A three-month-long journey in ramshackle ships on rough seas could be traumatic for any human being, particularly for those who had no experience of sea travel, such as those who were indentured from many parts of north and east India. During this perilous journey, they not only became lifelong friends but also established fictive relationships as *jahaji bhai/behen,* which continued for generations. The commonalities they shared were physical features, physical conditions and some aspects of their cultural heritage, both textual and oral. After landing in Trinidad or Guyana, they were assigned to different plantations where living conditions were extremely harsh. They were not allowed to go out of their barracks and mix with fellow *coolis*. Their work was supervised by 'drivers', who were themselves ex-slaves and who had experienced harsher conditions when they were supervised by their white masters. Yet, the Indians successfully reconstructed their community there.

This would not have been possible if they did not have a minimum number of people to form a community away from homeland. They also needed to have some commonality among them, a common adversary and an effective leadership for a community to be created in an alien world. Since they had to survive in an alien and hostile environment, they needed to adapt. They reinforced some aspects of their cultural baggage, discarded some others and created some new ones. In all this, the role of individuals, the quality of leadership and ability to pick up issues for mobilisation and create a consciousness of some kind were important.

The formation of the Indian identity in Trinidad illustrates these points (Vertovec 1992; Misra 1995: 201–26). Approximately 143,939 Indian indentured labourers were sent to Trinidad over close to 70 years (1845–1917). Thus, there were sufficient Indians to form their own community. Since every year new consignment of labourers arrived in Trinidad, they refreshed memories of the homeland and old linkages were reinforced. Gradually, non-Indians were identified as adversaries and strategies were devised to counteract them. In this respect, opting to settle down in Trinidad and obtaining land in lieu of surrendering their right to claim free passage back home was the turning point in their history. Their status suddenly changed from being transient to permanent settlers. This was a point of critical importance. The lands acquired by them became the nuclei for the formation of villages. Coming as they did from peasant backgrounds, they soon made their land productive, which gave them economic stability and helped them move up the social ladder. These material developments cannot be undermined while trying to understand the formation of the Indian community in Trinidad.

The stories of the struggle for independence in India and ruthless suppression by the British not only generated empathy for the homeland but also gave them some degree of confidence to launch their own struggle for their rights and restoration of their traditions in Trinidad. They followed the Gandhian path of non-violence. They organised themselves, launched trade union movements and finally joined the cry for independence of Trinidad. Eventually the country gained independence and they began to participate in the political arena there. The political parties dominated by Indians successfully formed governments several times there.

It has been a long journey from being indentured labourers to becoming full-fledged citizens of the country. In this journey, celebration of life-cycle rituals and religious festivals and development of art forms played an important role in the political mobilisation of Indians. They fought for the right to cremate their dead and organise their marriages according to their own traditions. Their traditional marriages were not recognised as lawful by the government, and hence, children born of such unions were declared as illegitimate. In fact, they were given a 'certificate of illegitimacy' by the government. Hence, the risk the Indian emigrants took by not registering their marriages in the registrar's office was indeed a huge one. In this manner, they made a statement of protest against the state as well as the church, which then were in the dominant position.

They were not simply reproducing Indian cultural practices on foreign soil but were also constantly reconstructing and reinterpreting them. The reconstruction of their cultures was not easy, as they did not belong to a homogenous cultural stock. It depended on what was considered significant in a given context. For example, the Hindu Indians in Trinidad did not find any difficulty in adopting the Christian method of Sunday service for organising their pujas in temples. They even created a pulpit (though it was called *asana,* for the priest to sit on), from where the pundit conducted ceremonies and gave sermons. The devotees sat in front of him on benches, much like in a church. Or, take the case of Kali worship in Trinidad. Since Afro-Trinidadians were identified as adversaries, the Indian deity Kali, who the Hindus worshipped with reverence and awe, could not be of the same colour. Hence, they painted Kali in pink, which is a clear deviation from tradition.

Such cultural strategies connect people, create ideas, mythologies and so on and generate an appropriate atmosphere for action. A culture is reconstructed, a pattern begins to emerge, its boundaries get marked and a feel-good situation is created until some other pressure is perceived. For instance, Indians arrived in Trinidad as indentured labourers, but in course of time, Hindu and Muslim identities emerged, and soon, temples and mosques were erected. Within the Hindu fold, the reformist Arya Samajis, who were opposed to the Sanatanis, emerged, and later, devotees of Kali, Sai Baba and Brahma Kumaris appeared. The Muslims too experienced divisions among Sunnis, Shias and Ahemadias, besides the emergence of a strong group of Islamist purifiers who wanted the Indian Muslims to get rid of their defiling cultural baggage brought from India. This group provided economic incentives to attract followers. In the beginning, the Indian Muslims were caught in the euphoria of purification, but in course of time, they began to feel uncomfortable about giving up their cultural practices and breaking their relationship with other Indians with whom they had even formed fictive relationships. Many of them reverted to their traditions (see de Kruijf 2006: 147–67). This story is not isolated. Culture has the tendency to re-establish its significance over and over again. Culture helps people manage their crisis by explaining and interpreting the complex and often conflicting realities around them.

Coping with the uncertainties of life and ensuring the well-being of people are recurrent issues before any diasporic community, which often devises its own set of mechanisms to handle them. There may be contradictions within them, but each culture has a tendency 'to incorporate competing ideas in distinct and unrelated schemes' (de Kruijf 2006: 364). I cite here one of the most telling examples to clinch the point.

An Indian couple had settled in the USA. Both husband and wife were highly educated and worked as leading scientists in an advanced research institute there. One day, they decided to give the contract of building their house to a leading construction company. But the contractor was not allowed to start the work until they heard from their family priest back in their native place in Bihar, India. The priest, after consulting the almanac and also the horoscopes of his clients, fixed an auspicious date for the *bhumi puja*, which was about two months away from the date on which the construction was to start. The contractor had to wait till this arrangement was made. On the appointed day for bhumi puja, the couple arrived at the site complete with all the paraphernalia for the puja and were accompanied by their friends. The puja was conducted by the family priest live over the iPhone for over two hours. The priest gave all the instructions live from Bihar for the couple to perform the rituals, including the direction in which they should face. There was no taking a chance where supernatural forces were involved, as house construction is a sacred activity back home in India. It had to commence at an auspicious moment as per the *sastra*s so that gods and goddesses watching the event bless the ones performing the sacred activity called *yagna*.

Today, performing life cycle rituals, organising festivals, learning Indian music, dance and other performing arts, erecting temples and mosques are common among the Indian communities settled abroad. It is quite clear that technological development has contributed towards reviving and strengthening the traditional links between 'home' and the diaspora. Information can now be easily transferred from one place to another without any physical movement. This has certainly made diasporic networks more important than ever before.

Once a group of people settle down in a new place, a vibrant interplay of social, cultural, economic and political forces takes place, giving rise to situations in which individuals with entrepreneurship, imagination, aspiration and creativity achieve unimaginable success. While the role of cultural baggage in making them successful cannot be denied here, it will not be wise to underplay the role of individuals either. The largely successful migration and adjustment of Nepalis wherever they migrated shows that they are good at reinterpreting their cultural symbols the way the Indians in Trinidad did. Their eviction from Bhutan and some parts of India's north-east in the 1980s and 1990s should not influence our assessment of them as a diasporic community.

References

Chattopadhya, G. P. 2012. 'Colonialism-in-the-mind', in Gopala Sarana and R. P. Srivastava (eds), *Studies in Social and Physical Anthropology*. Jaipur: Rawat Publications.

de Kruijf, J. G. 2006. *Guyana Junction: Globalisation, Localization and the Production of East Indianness*. Amsterdam: Dutch University Press.

Misra, P. K. 1986. 'Mobility-Sedentary Opposition: A Case Study among the Nomadic Gadulia Lohar', in Joseph Berland and Matt T. Salo (eds), *Peripatetic Peoples,* 21/22: 179–88.

Misra, P. K. 1995. 'Identity Formation in Trinidad', *The Eastern Anthropologist*, 48(3): 201–6.

Vertovec, S. 1992. *Hindu Trinidad: Religion, Ethnicity and Socio-Economic Change*. London: Macmillan.

Wells, Spencer. 2002. *The Journey of Man: A Genetic Odyssey*. New York: Random House.

2
CHANGING PARADIGMS OF NEPALESE MIGRATION AND EMERGING DIASPORA

Bhim Prasad Subedi

Introduction

People have moved from one place to another throughout history and most nation states are a microcosm of such history from various time periods. Nepal is no exception. Whereas large numbers of Nepalese have migrated both within and outside Nepal, the majority have stayed back, with just occasional and temporary or seasonal movements outside their village. Much has been written about those who left their homes for long-term migration, but not much attention has been paid to those who have stayed behind. With very few exceptions, Nepalese migration literature largely revolves around permanent or long-term migration and has failed to incorporate the forms of mobility that are of shorter durations. This chapter seeks to fill this gap in migration studies on Nepal.

This chapter discusses two aspects of Nepali migration. First, it analyses the emerging patterns of migration on the basis of census data on absentees abroad and records of employment from the government of Nepal. Second, it analyses how migration studies have evolved and are conceptualised. In doing so, it treats the Nepali diaspora within a conceptual home-reach framework of their mobility. There are major shifts in the patterns of migration in terms of direction, composition and forms of mobility. Some of these shifts, especially after the 1990s, can be considered as paradigm shifts. Nepalese scholars have paid little attention to conceptualising how mobility has been integral to the functioning of their society. There has been an overemphasis on migration at the expense of overall mobility, particularly the neglect of circulation often referred to as *ghumphir* in Nepali language. It is only through incorporation and understanding of *ghumphir* that the current foreign labour migration and Nepali diasporas can be understood in their proper perspectives.

Data and methods

Decennial censuses carried out by the Central Bureau of Statistics, Government of Nepal and records available from the Department of Foreign Employment (DFE), Ministry of Labour and Employment have been used as the main source of data for this chapter. The first attempt of census-taking in Nepal was made in 1911 though it was primarily a head count. Since then, head counts are available till 1952/54 at intervals of about 10 years. The 1952/54 census being the first 'scientific census', Nepal has been conducting censuses every 10 years since then. The recently conducted 2011 census is the latest in this series.[1]

Despite a long history of international labour migration in Nepal, there is very little data on the magnitude of Nepalese nationals going out to neighbouring countries and abroad, let alone their engagement in various types of activities. The late 1980s marked the new era of overseas labour migration. In the context of labour demands in South Korea and West Asia, amidst low levels of employment generation and consistent increase in labour force in the countries, the government of Nepal decided to promote the employment of its nationals in the overseas countries with the assumption that for 'countries like Nepal, who have been suffering from the serious problems of unemployment and poverty, foreign employment could be an effective medium to avail the opportunity of employment for the benefit of the country and its people' (MoL 1999: 4).

The government of Nepal formally adopted the promotion of foreign labour migration through the enactment of the Foreign Employment Act 2042 (1985). It was first amended in 1992 after the establishment of the multi-party system in 1990.[2] Foreign labour migration is currently governed by the Foreign Employment Act 2007. Accordingly, any institution intending to carry out foreign employment business must register with the DFE with a cash deposit and bank guarantee. These institutions must renew their license every year. Initially, 15 countries were open for foreign employment, and later, other countries were added to the list. The countries initially open for taking in Nepalese migrants included Saudi Arabia, Kuwait, Oman, Qatar, the UAE, Bahrain, Iraq, Malaysia, Hong Kong, Singapore, Brunei, South Korea, Saipan, Macao, Latvia, Kosovo and Israel. At present, the government of Nepal has listed 108 countries for foreign employment.

The DFE is the main source of data on foreign labour migration. It keeps records of those who obtained permission to go abroad for work through private licensed recruiting agencies and/or on an individual basis. Records from the DFE are available from 1994/95. The 1993/94 record combines all those going abroad till then. The total permission records are also available on a monthly basis for recent years.

The context

Before discussing general migration and foreign labour migration, a glimpse of the emerging trends in population change is imperative. The population size of the country is increasing rapidly, and this increase has been even more prominent over the last four decades. Figure 2.1 shows the changing population size in the country. Over the last 50 years, the Nepalese population has increased almost three times, from 9.4 million in 1961 to 26.6 million in 2011. The inter-censal growth rates have been consistent at over 2 per cent per annum between 1961 and 2001. It is only the latest census whose results have shown a sharp decrease in the growth rate, i.e. 1.35 per cent per annum. However, it also shows a large number of absentee people, unlike in the past censuses.

With the increase in population size, its age composition is also changing. The median age is increasing and the population demonstrates the large presence of young people. Figure 2.2 summarises the changes in the age structure of the population over the last 40 years. It primarily sends out three messages. First, a steady decline in the proportion of children's population (below 15 years of age) is evident, e.g. from 40.5 per cent in 1971 to 34.9 per cent in 2011. Second, there is a significant presence of young people aged 15–24 years in the total population. This group of population comprised a little over one-sixth earlier to one-fifth according to the 2011 census. This large presence of youth in the population is commonly referred to as a youth bulge. Third, the share of population below 30 years of age has consistently remained more than 62 per cent, going as high as more than two-thirds of the total population in some censuses. Demographers consider the presence of 60 per cent of the population below the age of 30 and the youth bulge as critical demographic points, where countries face instabilities, upheavals and transformations.

Over the past 40 years, the country has witnessed a clear demographic shift and the census results demonstrate this. Till the 1990s, the population was dominated by the hills, i.e. the largest proportion of population in the

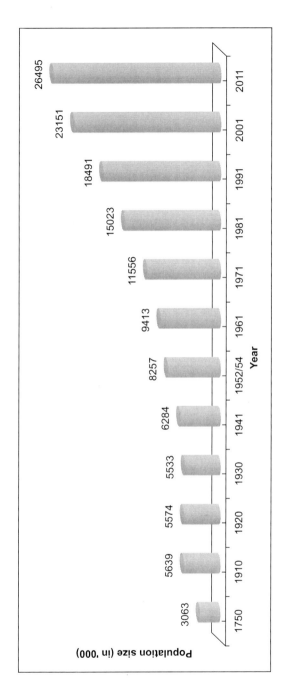

Figure 2.1 Nepal: changing population size

Source: Based on Population censuses of 1952/54, 1961, 1971, 1981, 1991, 2001, and 2011

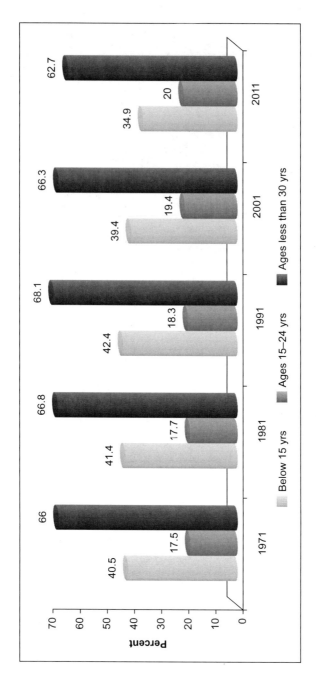

Figure 2.2 Nepal: changing proportion of population in various age groups

Source: Based on Population censuses of 1971, 1981, 1991, 2001 and 2011

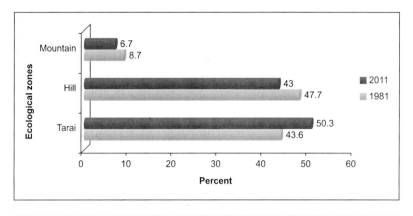

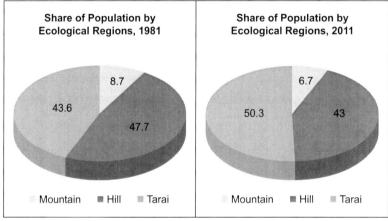

Figure 2.3 Share of population by ecological regions, 1981–2011

Source: Based on Population censuses of 1981 and 2011

country lived in the hills and mountains, representing 56.4 per cent of the total population. By 2011, tarai emerged at the forefront with the largest share in the total population of the nation (Figure 2.3). Physiographically, Nepal's identity is that of a hill country, but demographically, it has changed to a plains country with 50.3 per cent of its population living in the tarai at present. Migration, both internal and international, is largely responsible for this phenomenon.

Emerging patterns of migration

Migration is the most important feature of Nepal's demography, which explains the present spatio-ethnic diversification of the country. The Nepalese are constantly on the move. Some move out for a short period and return to their place of origin while others move out for good. Some important features of their movements are discussed below.

Historical trend

Till about the political unification of Nepal, the movement of people was largely from the north or south to the middle hills and mostly towards the western hills (see Poffenberger 1980). Once these early migrants settled in the middle hills, they followed a pattern of movement towards the east. Figure 2.4 provides a sketch of historical migration patterns in Nepal with four clear orientations over the past three centuries.

First, it shows the entry of various caste and ethnic groups from the north as well as from the south reinforcing population growth in the hills of Nepal. Second, it traces the subsequent pattern of eastward movement, along the hills, together with the process of national unification campaigns of the country by the then rulers. Third, the ecological shift in the movement, i.e. migration towards tarai is apparent after the malaria eradication scheme in the 1950s. This migration took place initially in a planned way, but later, it was rather spontaneous. Fourth, there was an acceleration of rural-to-rural and hill-to-tarai migrations. The latter part of the 20th century was characterised by rural-to-urban migrations on a big scale.

Contemporary internal movement

Over the past 40 years, Nepal's internal migration has, however, been largely characterised by rural-to-rural migration, primarily from the hills and mountains to the plains areas. Further, the comparison of per cent share of regions in out-migration and in-migration between 1981 and 2001 censuses clearly shows the plains as the overwhelmingly recipient area and the hills and mountains as the immensely originating areas (Table 2.1). Albeit to a much lesser extent, the 2001 census also shows tarai as a sending area.

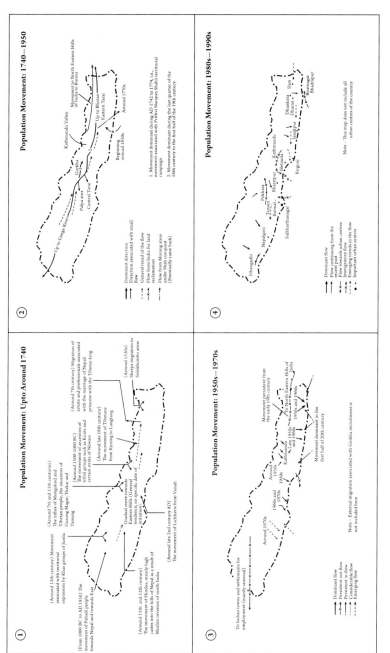

Figure 2.4 Shift in migration patterns

Source: Based on Subedi (1988)

Table 2.1 Share of regions in in-migration and out-migration, 1981 and 2001

Ecological regions	Percent share in			
	In-migration		Out-migration	
	1981	2001	1981	2001
Mountains	5.2	2.3	30.3	17.1
Hills	20.4	20.9	61.3	68.9
Tarai	77.4	76.8	8.4	14.0

Source: Population Census 1981, 2001

International migration

Nepal has a long history of migration to India. Recruitment of the Nepalese in the British Indian Army and police forces further reinforced that process. Up until 2001, India remained the main destination of Nepalese international migrants. The 2001 census records of absentee people from Nepal show that among absentee population, 77 per cent went to India, 14.5 per cent to West Asia and only 8.2 per cent to East Asia and other countries. The 2011 census data are yet to be processed and no reliable information is available about the changing share of countries in receiving Nepalese migrants, but the data available at the DFE indicates the increased share of Nepalese migrants in West Asian and East Asian countries.

Within Nepal, a comparison of the 2001 absentee figure with preliminary results of the 2011 census shows a major change in the regional share of absentees, with the tarai contributing more than 42 per cent in 2011 against approximately 30 per cent in 2001 (Figure 2.5). The share of hills has come down to 52 per cent in 2011 from its overwhelming dominance of over 64 per cent in 2001. This is a shift that challenges the common understanding of the tarai as the recipient region, and not a sending zone, with respect to both internal and international migrations.

The east–west difference is reflected in the distributional pattern by development regions. The total number of migrants going to India decreases with a corresponding increase in their numbers in West Asia and East Asia (Figure 2.6). This is considered to be a reflection of their affordability to go abroad, level of educational attainment and accessibility.

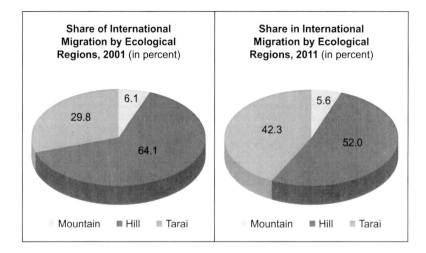

Figure 2.5 Share in international migration by ecological regions, 2001–2011
Source: Based on Population censuses of 2001 and 2011

The figures available from censuses do not allow disaggregation of international migration figures into labour migrants and non-labour migrants. However, it is commonly believed that an overwhelming proportion of international migrants are labour migrants. As noted earlier, the late 1980s marked a new era in Nepal's history of migration. With the promulgation of the Foreign Employment Act 2042 (1985), the government of Nepal formally adopted the promotion of foreign labour migration as its development policy. This adoption was primarily a response of the government to the rapid increase in the entry of young people into the labour market and labour demand in East and West Asian countries, together with the government's inability to create new employment opportunities in the country. Implicitly, this was also considered as a strategy of relieving demographic pressure in the country. By the 1990s, many prospective Nepali labour migrants entered into the external labour market after obtaining permission from the government.

Recent migration of foreign labour

As noted above, foreign labour migration has become a notable feature of Nepal since the 1990s. During the early 1980s, East Asia was the main destination although the number of Nepalese going there was very small.

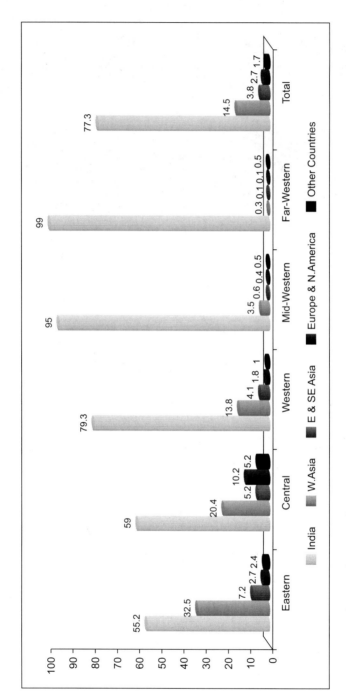

Figure 2.6 Nepal: regional pattern of international migration, 2001

Source: Based on Population census of 2001

By the late 1980s, with the withdrawal of the Korean labour force from West Asian countries, Nepalese labourers got an entry there. Thus, throughout the 1990s, West Asian countries such as Saudi Arabia and Qatar, the UAE and Kuwait became the main destinations. The labour market in Malaysia opened up to the Nepalis in 1999 after it stopped recruiting Bangladeshi labourers. Since 2001, Malaysia has remained the main destination for Nepali labourers and the share of West Asian countries has sharply declined. Nonetheless, the 2010/11 figure from the DFE shows an increased share of Saudi Arabia and other West Asian countries (Figure 2.7). On the whole, outside the Indian labour market, Nepalese labourers are floating mainly between West Asian and South-East Asian countries.

Women in foreign labour markets

Women's participation in international migration has been very small so far. They constituted only 10.9 per cent of the total absentees abroad in 2001 (82,712 out of 762,181). In subsequent years, their participation increased, and according to preliminary results of the 2011 census, they constitute 13.3 per cent of the total absentee population (254,666 out of 1,917,903). This is very small, but the increase in size over the last 10 years has been tremendous. Figure 2.8 shows the increasing participation of women in the external labour markets. The overall increase in absentee population abroad has increased 2.5 times between 2001 and 2011. Of the three ecological regions, the increase in women's participation in international migration has been most evident in tarai (Figure 2.8).

Foreign labour migration

The volume of international labour migration has significantly increased in recent years. The government of Nepal has officially reached out to more than 107 countries for labour work. The latest figures from the national population census show nearly 2 million Nepalese now living outside their country of origin. Figure 2.9 shows the distribution of foreign labour migrants by their district of origin. This figure is based on the flow of labour migrants recorded by the DFE between 16 April 2003 and 15 December 2009, for which district-level data was available.[3]

The overall scenario is that among labour migrants, 47.8 per cent are from tarai, 46.2 per cent from the hills and 6.0 per cent from the mountains. Thus, tarai has emerged as the main labour-sending region. If one considers smaller numbers, labour migrants are from all ecological

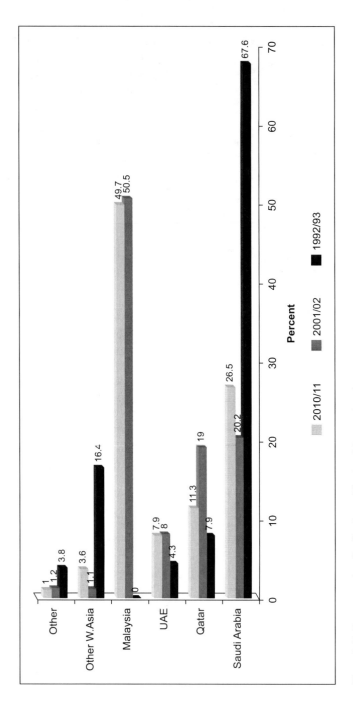

Figure 2.7 Country-wise distribution of foreign labour migrants

Source: Based on data from Department of Foreign Employment, Ministry of Labour and Employment, Govt. of Nepal

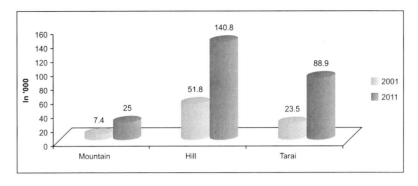

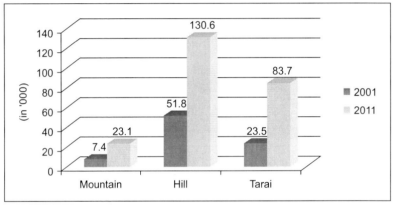

Figure 2.8 Women's participation in international migration

Source: Population censuses of 2001 and 2011

regions, regions of all stages of development and from all 75 districts of the country. It covers all castes, ethnicities and religious faiths. Among the top 10 districts sending labour migrants, 9 are from tarai and only 1, i.e. Tanahu, is from the hills. Dhanusha ranks the highest, followed by Jhapa, Siraha, Morang and Mahottari.

Figure 2.9 is based on combined figures of the documented flow over six and a half years. Lately, annual figures are also available at the district level. On the whole, the distribution pattern remains the same, with the tarai as the dominant migrant-sending ecological region. For example, during 2009/10 (Nepalese fiscal year 2066/67), a total of 223,989 Nepalese officially migrated for labour employment and all the top 10 labour-sending districts were from tarai, with Mahottari pushing Dhanusha to the second position. Jhapa, Siraha and Morang came third, fourth and

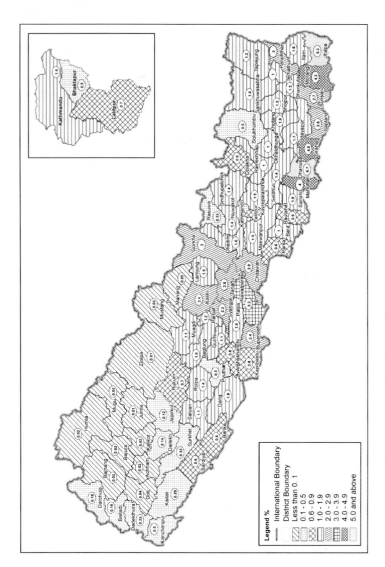

Figure 2.9 Foreign labour migration by district of origin

fifth respectively, which means the top five remain the same in both these data sets.

The dominance of the plains was obvious among those going for foreign labour employment during 2009/10. Out of the total labour migrants, 55.6 per cent were from the plains, 39.2 per cent from the hills and only 5.2 per cent from the mountains. While this distribution is a reflection of the distribution of population itself, there is clearly an over-representation of the plains and under-representation of the hills and mountains. On the contrary, the hills were overrepresented and the tarai under-represented in the past.

No preference to particular countries is evident. Malaysia ranks the top, with the largest number of Nepalese going there, followed by Saudi Arabia, Qatar, the UAE and other countries. In a relative sense, the proportion going to West Asian countries, primarily Saudi Arabia, Qatar and the UAE is higher from the hills than from the tarai and the mountains.

Paradigm shifts in Nepalese migration

In recent history, two major turning points are noticeable in migration from Nepal. The first is the planned migration to tarai in the late 1950s and early 1960s. This was characterised largely by household migration and migration from rural hills to rural tarai. This entailed changes in the size of the population and the direction of movement, but, by and large, there was continuity in the ways of earning livelihood, the sociocultural life and the kinship network. The second turning point is that of external labour migration in the late 1980s and 1990s. The change in migration pattern in the 1990s is, so to speak, paradigmatic.

First, contrary to common belief, India is not the only recipient of Nepalese labour migrants. Second, it was rather difficult for such migrants to get passports and visas from many receiving countries. Third, they migrated to places having languages, cultures and religions different from their own. Fourth, working in many countries was more difficult and expensive than working in India. Fifth, migration has not only led to residential but also occupational change. With few exceptions, Nepalese labour migrants are more into non-agricultural employment than ever before. Sixth, the direction of migration is from rural to urban unlike the dominance of rural to rural migration in the past. Seventh, the movement for labour recruitment, which had emerged as an important form of territorial mobility in eastern Nepal during the British Indian period (see Subedi 1993), has again become widespread. Unlike *lahure* employment, which is largely limited to specific ethnic groups, this new form of employment has no barriers of caste, ethnicity and religious faith. Eighth, migration is individual-based rather than a mix of individual- and household-based, as in the case of internal migration. Ninth, there is also a shift from an absolute male dominance to some share of women in the external labour market – not as a dependent, but as the main breadwinner. Finally, the stream of migration for external employment is more tarai-dominated than hill-dominated.

Conceptualising territorial mobility and diaspora

Social science researchers in Nepal have been rather shy about conceptualising territorial mobility within the broader framework of societal functioning and its role in linking Nepalese society with the outside world. Migration is the dominant terminology used, irrespective of whether it entails permanent residential change or temporary movement or sojourn or seasonal labour migration. This is despite a clear divide in the Nepali language between long-term migration as *Basai sarai* and short-term migration as *ghumphir*. Most research on migration in Nepal has failed to bring out this difference clearly. That the majority of these movers retain their foothold at 'home' or the place of origin, maintain their spatial identity based on the place of their origin and do not always want to abandon their social network despite staying away for long has largely been overlooked in the studies carried out by Nepalese researchers on migration, as is evident from the following paragraphs.

Nepal hardly dealt with migration as a research topic till the 1960s. Whatever scholarly attention was there was limited to historical references to how, when and from where various caste/ethnic groups originated and where they have settled in the country. Karan (1960), writing about the physical and cultural geography of Nepal, argued that Nepal was primarily populated through large-scale migration from China and India. Likewise, Regmi (1961) refers to the links the Nepalese had with India and China, but he also notes the policies of the government of Nepal about settling the hill Nepalis in tarai regions.

The 1970s marked the beginning of proper social science research in Nepal on migration. A group of scholars affiliated to the Centre for Economic Development and Administration (CEDA) and the Centre for Nepal and Asian Studies (CNAS) carried out research and published articles on migration. Rana and Thapa (1974) discussed the magnitude, scope, causes and consequences of migration in Nepal while Kansakar (1974) traced the history of migration and Elder et al. (1977) discussed the planned resettlement in Nepalese tarai. Likewise, Dahal, Rai and

Manzardo (1977) showed the link between land and migration in far-western Nepal. They also mentioned the *reversible* and *irreversible* forms of migration. However, these dimensions of migration were not carried further.

The 1980s witnessed the proliferation of research on migration. The census was the main source of data for the researchers (see New ERA 1981; Kansakar 2003; Dahal 1987; Subedi 1988; Gurung 1989). Special surveys focusing on migration were carried out to understand the causes and consequences of rural-to-rural migration and some of these were theoretically grounded on Marxist philosophy (see Conway and Shrestha 1981; Shrestha 1989; Thapa 1989). In the meantime, the government expressed its concerns about addressing internal and international migration issues. First, it constituted a task force to study and make policy recommendations on internal and international migration in Nepal (see Gurung 1983). Second, the government published a separate volume on migration statistics, extracting data from the Demographic Sample Survey of 1986/87 (see CBS 1988).

In the 1990s, research works on migration took place on three fronts. First, the publications using census data continued (CBS 1995; KC 1998). Second, a national survey of migration was carried out, covering internal and international migration using the conventional definition of lifetime migrants (KC et al. 1997). Third, a study was carried out questioning the validity of transnational application of the concept of migration and an attempt was made to conceptualise and categorise territorial mobility from the perspective of traditional society (Subedi 1993). How the traditional society viewed mobility in its entirety was discussed in detail through the identification of two forms of mobility, namely, basai sarai and ghumphir. This refocused on the role of migration in the development of Nepal and recaptured data on migrants having dual locality since both locations could be extensions of home.

The first decade of the 21st century witnessed further proliferation of migration studies. Some continued to analyse census data on migration (KC 2003), while others used data on migrant workers going abroad (Subedi 2003) and Nepali migrant workers in India (Upreti 2002; Neupane 2005; Thieme 2006), Japan (Yamanaka 2000), Indian labourers to Nepalese tarai (Mishra et al. 2000) and others (NIDS 2009). Specific studies on vulnerabilities of women migrant workers (POURAKHI 2008), migration and remittance (Thieme and Wyss 2005) and human trafficking, migration and HIV/AIDS (WOREC 2002) are a few examples of studies during the first decade of the present century.

Now that migration has become a global phenomenon, more and more Nepalese are migrating both within Nepal and to the outside world. Many Nepalese international migrants do not want to abandon their ties with Nepal. The Network of NRN (Non-Resident Nepalese) is an expression of its vibrancy. There are conceptual and methodological difficulties in explaining their identity from the perspectives of those who have stayed on in Nepal and the debate continues. However, in trying to understand this diaspora and its dynamics, migration needs to be conceptualised in a comprehensive way so that it captures all temporal and spatial forms of mobility and the interaction between 'home' and 'reach' rather than considering mobility within the origin–destination matrix. As Figure 2.10 shows, home and reach are not independent identities, but are part of a network of movers and stayers. The interaction between home and reach makes the society alive and vibrant. The prolonged stay in the reach may turn it into a 'new home' for some, but for others, it may still continue to be a reach only. It depends upon the success or failure of the people who have moved out. Even in case of success, the general opinion is that 'home' means a great deal and maintaining a foothold at 'home' one way or the other remains crucial for the migrants.

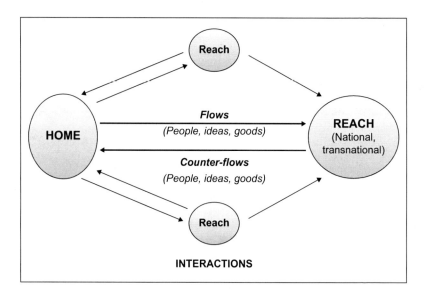

Figure 2.10 Conceptualising Nepali territorial mobility: the 'home–reach' model

Conclusion

To understand the entire mobility dynamics in the country and outside, we need to examine the concepts, methods and data utilised so far in migration research very carefully. We need to assess whether or not the concepts of migration based on Western societies fit in with the Nepalese society. We also need to conceptualise migration more comprehensively, and consider the increasing evidences on dual locality or multi-locality presence of people in recent years to enrich our understanding of migration. The concept of 'diaspora' also needs to be looked at from such perspectives.

Migration is central to Nepal and over the years several shifts in migration pattern have been noticed with regard to direction, scale, purpose and composition of migrants. Some such shifts show major departures from earlier patterns, such as the one from 1990s, as the migrants are going to non-agricultural sectors. They are also venturing into places with unfamiliar environments, languages, cultures, religions, laws, etc. With the active facilitation by the Nepal government they are there in almost every country in the world, albeit mostly in menial jobs. This is indeed a paradigm shift in the history of Nepalese migration.

Notes

1 Some of its results have been published recently. However, more details are yet to be made public.
2 The earlier Act has been totally revised in 2007. The current foreign labour employment process is facilitated by the Foreign Employment Act 2064 (2007). This Act was authenticated on 5 September 2007.
3 The officially recorded total labour migrants during this period were 867,979. This figure refers exclusively to those going abroad (outside India). Concerned authorities estimate that an equal number may have gone abroad for labour work unofficially during this period.

References

Conway, D. and N.R. Shrestha. 1981. *Causes and Consequences of Rural to Rural Migraation in Nepal*. Indiana: Indiana University, Ford Foundation and Rockefeller Foundation.

Dahal, D.R. 1987. *Nepali Emigrants in India*. Kathmandu: Centre for Nepal and Asian Studies.

Dahal, D.R., N.K. Rai and A. Manzardo. 1977. *Land and Migration in Far-Western Nepal*. Kirtipur: Institute for Nepal and Asian Studies.

Elder, Joseph W. et al. 1977. *Planned Resettlement in Nepal Tarai: A Social Analysis of the Khajura/Bardia Punarvas Projects*. Kathmandu: CEDA/INAS, Nepal and University of Wisconsin, Madison.
Government of Nepal. 1999. *Profile of Foreign Employment in Nepal*. Kathmandu: Ministry of Labour.
Gurung, H. B. 1983. *Internal and International Migration in Nepal*. Kathmandu: National Commission on Population.
Gurung, H. B. 1989. *Regional Patterns of Migration in Nepal (Papers of the East West Population Institute 113)*. Honolulu, Hawaii: East West Center.
Kansakar, V. B. S. 1974. 'History of Migration in Nepal', *The Himalayan Review*, 5(6): 58–68.
Kansakar, V. B. 2003. 'International Migration and Citizenship in Nepal', in Cental Bureau of Statistics, *Population Monograph of Nepal*, Vol. II, 85–120. Kathmandu: Central Bureau of Statistics, Nepal.
Karan, P. 1960. *Nepal: A Physical and Cultural Geography*. Lexington: University of Kentucky.
KC, B. K., B. P. Subedi, Y. B. Gurung, B. Acharya and B. R. Suwal. 1997. *Migration Situation in Nepal*. Kathmandu: Ministry of Population & Environment and United Nations Population Fund.
KC, B. K. 1998. *Trends, Patterns and Implications of Rural to Rural Migration in Nepal*. Kathmandu: Tribhuvan University.
KC, B. K. 2003. 'Internal Migration in Nepal', in Central Bureau of Statistics, *Population Monograph of Nepal*, Vol. II, 121–68. Kathmandu: Central Bureau of Statistics.
Mishra, C., L. P. Uprety and T. R. Panday. 2000. *Seasonal Agricultural Labour Migration from India to the Nepal Tarai*. Kathmandu: Centre for Nepal and Asian Studies.
Neupane, G. 2005. *Nepalese Migrants in Delhi*. Kathmandu: Centre for Development Studies.
New ERA. 1981. *Study on Inter-regional Migration in Nepal*. Kathmandu: National Planning Commission.
NIDS. 2009. Nepal Migration Survey. Kathmandu: The World Bank.
Poffenberger, M. 1980. *Patterns of Change in the Nepal Himalaya*. Madras: Macmillan.
POURAKHI. 2008. *Addressing Vulnerabilities of Women Migrant Workers to HIV & AIDS*. Kathmandu: POURAKHI.
Rana, R. S. and Y. S. Thapa. 1974. 'Population Migration: Nature and scope', in D. A. Upadhyaya (ed.), *Population and Development in Nepal*, pp. 43–77. Kathmandu: Centre for Economic Development and Administration.
Regmi, D. 1961. *History of Nepal*, Vol. II. Calcutta: Firma K. L. Mukhopadhyay.
Shrestha, N. R. 1989. 'Frontier Settlements and Landlessness among Hill Migrants in Tarai', *Annals of the Association of American Geographers*, 370–89.
Shrestha, N. R. 1990. *Landlessness and Migration in Nepal*. Boulder, Colorado: Westview Press.
Subedi, B. P. 1988. 'Continuity and change in population movement: The case of Nepal', *Population Geography [Also Reprints of the East-West Population Institute, No. 151. Hawaii]*, 10, 28–42.

Subedi, B. P. 1993. *Continuity and Change in Population Movement: From Inside a Rural Nepali Community.* Ann Arbor, Michigan: University Microfilm International, UMI.

Subedi, B. P. 2003. 'International migration from Nepal: Emerging patterns and trends', in Y. Ishikawa, *A Comprehensive Study of Migration Changes in Asia and Pacific Region,* pp. 252–72. Kyoto: Japanese Society for Promotion of Sciences.

Thapa, P. 1988. *Nepal: Socio-economic Change and Rural Migration.* New Delhi: Vikas Publishing House.

Thieme, S. 2006. *Social Networks and Migration: Far-west Nepalese Labour Migrants in Delhi.* Berlin: LIT Verlag.

Thieme, S. and Simon Wyss. 2005. 'Migration Patterns and Remittance Transfer in Nepal: A Case Study of Sainik Basti in Western Nepal', *International Migration,* 43(5): 59–98.

Upreti, B. 2002. *The Marginal Migrants: A Study of Nepali Emigrants in India.* Delhi: Kalinga Publications.

WOREC. 2002. *Perceptions of Grassroot People about Human Trafficking, Migration and HIV/AIDS.* Kathmandu: Women's Rehabilitation Centre.

Yamanaka, K. 2000. 'Nepalese Labour Migration to Japan: from Global Warriors to Global Workers', *Ethnic and Racial Studies,* 23(1): 62–93.

3

HAMI NEPALI?

Belonging in Nepal and the Nepali diaspora

Ulrike Müller-Böker

Introduction

In order to understand the lifeworlds of people living in a diaspora, it is helpful to shed light on how the sense of belonging is constructed within their country of origin – in this case, Nepal – and how it changes in a multi-local life context.

I argue in line with Sen (2006) that people's sense of belonging is multi-layered and varies according to the life context (also Sinha 2009). First of all, the human sense of belonging not only has a social dimension, but also a territorial one: the sense of belonging to a specific place. Social belonging relates to any form of social entity and concerns the symbolic dimension of social relations and interactions,[1] which vary in the course of societal transformation and changing life contexts. Kasarda and Janowitz (1974), for example, highlight the progressive loss of significance of belonging to a local community in a modernising and globalising world. Giddens (1991) even suggests the emergence of a single, more or less universalistic, cosmopolitan belonging, whereas Pollini (2005) has noticed, based on surveys conducted in diverse geographical regions, more of a change in the structure and configuration of socio-territorial belonging than its loss of importance. Senses of belonging, which refer to multiple social collectivities such as movements, unions, organisations and so on gain importance and are not necessarily any more territorial.

In the case of migration or displacement-induced mobility, people are no longer rooted to one single place. They live and have different engagements, obligations and affiliations in at least two – and often more – places, and experience multi-local livelihoods (Thieme 2008). Their sense of belonging changes, and more complex and nuanced constructions and governmentalities of belonging emerge (Erel 2011).

Othering is one component of the two-way process of bordering and the construction of 'we-ness'. The term is rooted in postcolonial studies.[2] Spivak (1985) points out the juxtaposition towards the other, which constitutes the self, and Jensen (2011) defines othering as the discursive processes by which powerful groups define subordinate groups in existence in a reductionist way. However, this process also happens in the reverse. There are also bordering and othering discourses and practices of subordinate groups in relation to dominant groups, i.e. the rich, the suppressors, but these are usually less powerful and are made with less self-assertion.

Keeping these key terms and concepts in mind, I give here some glimpses of regional, ethnical, caste-based and national senses of belonging, which I observed in Nepal and in two Nepali diasporas – in India and in Switzerland. My questions are: To which societal and regional entities do they imagine they belong to? Who are 'the others' within the country? And does this sense of belonging change in the diaspora?

Glimpses of ethnic, caste-based, regional and national senses of belonging in Nepal

Prithvi Narayan Shah, the Gorkha ruler who 'unified' by the end of the 18th century, a number of small kingdoms into the kingdom of Nepal, termed this new entity as *sabai jatko phulbari* – a flower garden of all castes and ethnic groups – referring to Nepal's social, cultural and linguistic heterogeneity. In the sequel, the ruling elites of the once Hindu kingdom tried to bring a hierarchical order into this heterogeneous social fabric by institutionalising a national caste system. In addition to the existing caste groups, each of the various ethnic groups was assigned a specific position.[3] Even today, Nepal's political concept of inclusive development is coined by a strong emphasis on caste affiliation and ethnicity,[4] as the new target groups of disadvantaged or socially excluded groups (i.e. Dalits, ethnic groups)[5] refer to and reproduce the caste or ethnic origin. Whereas earlier, issues of ethnicity and social disadvantage could only be alluded to indirectly, ethnic activism and Dalit movements made rapid strides and gained strong political influence (Whelpton et al. 2008: xvii). The emphasis on discriminated castes and ethnic groups and the related bordering and othering of the dominant groups suggests that these strong social categories shape the senses of belonging, even today, in Nepalese society. However, I hypothesise that people's sense of belonging is multi-layered and relates to their life context.

ULRIKE MÜLLER-BÖKER

Impressions from fieldwork in Nepal during the 1970s and 1990s

To start with, I revisit three research sites, where I worked during the 1970s and 1980s. This was when Nepal was a Hindu kingdom, when it held itself responsible for the country's modernisation, but simultaneously, used the concept of Hinduism as an instrument of power and empowerment for the country's elites.

During the 1980s, I worked in Gorkha, the place of origin of Prithvi Narayan Shah. Gorkha, with its old palace and famous temples is, even today, widely held to be the heart of the nation. In Gorkha, many people emphasised this peculiarity of their place. There was no other place I visited in Nepal where I met people who celebrated the king's and queen's birthdays as enthusiastically as in Gorkha. The song '*Hami Nepali, hami Nepali*' was chanted with persistence. Hundreds of people participated in Dasai celebrations in and around the palace, choreographed by the royal priests and high-ranking members of the Royal Army, and symbolising not only the power of the goddess, but also of the Hindu kingdom (Unbescheid 1986). Dalits were widely excluded from these public events, although Dalit musicians played their instruments and their traditional role during these Dasai celebrations.

Of course, not everybody was in favour of these events and demonstrations of national identity and adoration of the royal family. I remember a meeting of the Lyons Club of Gorkha, where only a handful of men were present because the majority of the club's members were in jail. They had been arrested because of their involvement in strikes and rallies against the state's school policies, and, in general, for demanding more democracy in Nepal. Even in opposition to the state, their political goals were directed towards improving the state, reflecting their sense of belonging to the whole country.

Who lives in the region of Gorkha? The majority are Nepali-speaking hill castes to which the Shah's Thakuri caste also belongs. A number of Newars also live at the Gorkha bazaar.[6] I perceived the ethnicity of these Newars to be rather weak. Most of them did not speak Newari and the term 'Newar' was never used (Müller-Böker 1986). It seems that despite different ethnic backgrounds and opposing political positions, many people in Gorkha had a strong sense of belonging to the nation, and some also to the king, and the symbolic significance of the people's locale shaped their sense of belonging.

Before my research in Gorkha, I worked in Newar settlements in Kathmandu Valley (Müller-Böker 1988), where a very strong sense of belonging to their ethnic group and a strong othering, especially towards the Gorkhali or Parbate, were noticed. Newars, for example, often highlighted how Gorkhalis had violently conquered the Kathmandu Valley and were, therefore, its illegitimate rulers. In Thimi, where I stayed for several months, I frequently received well-meant advice on how to deal with Bahuns and Chhetris. Despite strong emphasis on being Newars, they are not a homogenous ethnic group, but a highly segmented social entity, more or less divided along caste, religion and class lines.

Similarly, the Chitwan Tharus, the subjects of my research later in the 1990s, represented themselves as an indigenous group with a strong ethnicity (Müller-Böker 1993). Oral history and old travel reports reveal that they lived relatively undisturbed in this malaria-affected lowland region. It was only in the 1950s that the malaria eradication and resettlement programmes of the Nepal government were implemented and migrants from the hills came in large numbers. This undisturbed past was termed *satjugi* (i.e. the Golden Age), and frequently, the statement rang out: 'In *Satjugi*, everything was better'. The Tharus call the immigrants from the hills, 'Pahariya'. They frequently state that they were pained by the confrontation with the immigrants. The general consensus – even among the wealthy Tharu landlords – was: 'The Pahariyas look down upon us, they are doing much better than we are!' At the same time, Tharu elite families started to adopt typical religious practices such as Hindu pujas and engaging more and more Pahariya Brahmins for certain rituals, and giving up certain vocations such as keeping pigs, which is considered impure by their Hindu neighbours. Nevertheless, they pointed out that they could never correspond to the Hindu ideal. Their attitude towards the Bahuns and Chhetris, as the representatives of Hinduism, was thus extremely ambivalent. On the one hand, they were collectively regarded as bloodsuckers of the poor, while on the other hand, they were collectively idealised as the more pure and the more competent people than themselves.

The foregoing discussion indicates that in different locales and societal constellations, different imaginations of belonging occurred. In Gorkha, I observed that, despite different ethnic backgrounds and opposing political positions, many people had a strong sense of belonging to the nation. I assume that the symbolic significance of their locale shaped this sense of belonging. The rural Newars were stuck in a world of their own. As the 'rightful' inhabitants of the Kathmandu Valley, they considered the king and state as superimposed (Gellner 1997). Also the Chitwan Tharus put a strong emphasis on ethnicity. But being labelled as backward and underdeveloped, Tharu leaders attempted to live up to Hindu norms and values.

Many things changed in the three sites of my fieldwork. Gorkha was a stronghold of the Maoist rebels during the decade-long armed conflict. In Chitwan, the Tharu ethnicity metamorphosed into the Tharu movement, claiming to be the indigenous people of Tarai and fighting for a separate identity within the Madheshis (Sheppard 2009; Mathema 2011). This movement is one of the most influential movements in contemporary Nepal. In contradiction, the strong sense of Newar identity did not motivate them to implement ethnicity-based political actions.

Belonging in two Nepali diasporas

In the following section, I want to elucidate how the sense of belonging is constructed in two different Nepali diasporas.

Nepali diaspora in Delhi

The following insights derive from our research in a few hamlets of Bajhang and Bajura districts of the Far Western Development Region, where migration to Delhi, the capital of India, has been practised for generations and is a key livelihood strategy.[7] The far-western part of Nepal is extremely impoverished even by Nepalese standards and isolated from mainstream development, far away from major centres of innovation and services and national and international politics. The villages of the area have been affected by the armed conflict between the Maoists and the state.

The majority of the population covered by our research belongs to the Hindu high castes, which are distinctly separate from the 'impure' castes (Cameron 1998; Müller-Böker 2003). Furthermore, the daily life of the communities is governed by many strict rules of interaction, which are more stringently practised than in other parts of Nepal. Caste affiliation determines social and economic practices and livelihood strategies. *Jat* (caste) and *thar* (patri-clan) also govern marriage relations. The most important relationship between high caste and low caste households is the traditional patron–client system, which has been in existence for generations.

Chhetri, Bahun, Thakuri, Kami and Sarki have their own hamlets. People mostly refer to *thar, jat* and their hamlet while using the term, 'we'. In addition, married women emphasise bonds with their natal home (*maiti*). Although people maintain a wide variety of interactions in everyday life, holding membership in a political party, taking part in communal activities, practising *padima* (reciprocal help) and so on are linked by the patron–client system.

Beside the hamlet and kin networks, people frequently express their belonging to the region Channa, a watershed comprising two Village Development Councils (VDC). References to the district or the Nepalese state were mainly made concerning the district capital's lack of infrastructure (high schools, hospital etc.) or concerning the presence of the Nepalese Army (permanently in the adjacent national park, and occasionally, during armed conflict). Many of them have never visited Kathmandu, the capital of Nepal.

But strong ties exist with India. In the whole of Nepal, particularly in the villages of investigation, it is common for men, partly accompanied by their wives and children, to seek work in India, leaving their extended families and relatives in the villages behind.[8] People from the Channa region go time and again to work in India, either to Delhi, Bangalore or Uttarakhand (Upreti 2002; Bruslé 2008). A complete household survey for three wards of Majhigaon VDC conducted in 2008 by M. Junginger reveals that 51 per cent households prefer India, especially Delhi, as their primary destination of labour migration. A further 12 per cent of the households have chosen to settle in the tarai, while 16 per cent have family members migrating to at least two different destinations (within Nepal and abroad). The remaining 21 per cent did not migrate at all. Yet, most of the latter still looked back on various kinds of migration experiences in the past. At the time the data were collected, a large number of people (see Table 3.1) were not present in the village, as most of them stayed permanently or for a certain period in Delhi.

The life of the majority of people oscillates between at least two different localities with specific – sometimes, rather unrealistic – time horizons. I argue that the intensity and simultaneity of these cross-border activities lead to the emergence of transnational social spaces (Portes et al.

Table 3.1 Absentee households and household members in some wards of Majhigaon VDC, 2008

%	Number of absentees	Absentees
18	14 out of 76	Complete household
63	100 out of 158	Male adult
40	67 out of 169	Female adult
50	81 out of 148	Male children
31	41 out of 132	Female children

Source: Household survey 2008 by M. Junginger

1999; Pries 2001; Vertovec 2001, 2003) and a multi-locality of livelihoods (Thieme 2008).

About the Nepali diaspora in India, migrants rely on village-based networks to establish themselves in the urban environment, mainly to get work, obtain loans, find accommodation and access medical care. Therefore, people from one village usually choose the same destination (Pfaff-Czarnecka 1995; Thieme and Müller-Böker 2010). During fieldwork in Delhi, Thieme observed that male relatives constantly arrived in search of a job in the city, or family members came for medical treatment. In such cases, relatives and friends in Delhi are obliged to provide support and shelter to them. Migrants occupy a distinct niche in the labour market. Men work as watchmen and car cleaners, women as domestic workers. Among the men, jobs are arranged by, or taken over from, friends or co-villagers or have to be 'bought' from a predecessor. Access to seed capital is a crucial precondition in the migration process. Either a loan is taken from wealthier families in the village or by taking part in a *chit* (rotating savings and credit group) or from a village-linked financial self-help organisation, the *society* (Thieme and Müller-Böker 2004). Next to saving and lending money, the societies also form social networks, providing jobs and support in Delhi.

In Delhi, Thieme came across one society established by women.[9] It was based on kinship network and the majority of women belonged to the Chhetri caste. A few Dalit women were also members. Their families were traditionally related to the high-caste families by the patron–client system. All women emphasised that it would be impossible to have a society with the same caste composition like in the traditional setting of the village. The patron–client system and the social exclusion of Dalits as such were not challenged, but the rules in force in the village had been newly interpreted in the diaspora.

Migration is an old established social practice. The older men know Delhi from their childhood, as they accompanied their fathers or grandfathers to this city. Some spent almost all their life in Delhi and went home only once in a year, or even less frequently. But they saw themselves forced to stay in Delhi and wanting to go back to Nepal. Both men and women expressed a strong sense of belonging to their villages and they are nostalgic about the fresh air and clean space in their villages. They dream of going back and never returning to India. Therefore, if migrants want to return sometimes, they have to maintain their home networks.

A number of them planned to buy land in the Far-West Nepalese tarai (lowland). For those who already purchased land, migration patterns have become even more diverse, having now another focal point in the tarai (Poertner et al. 2011a). Even in the tarai, village-based social ties are very strong. For example, the vast majority of migrant households in Bajhangi Tole in Dhangadi (Kailali District) originate from the Channa region. Kinship and village networks established by a few pioneer settlers have channelled migration to Bajhangi Tole. These networks even advertise internal migration destinations and act as brokers for land. Hence, when one asks the Bajhangi people about social ties, they refer first and foremost to people from the respective village and region of origin. As most of them have close relatives in Bajhang, the social and emotional connection to Bajhang remains close. Apart from the strong ties to 'home', which are manifested in social relations, landholdings, visiting and communication practices, the households in Bajhangi Tole also have noteworthy social connections in India, Kathmandu[10] and in other parts of the far-western tarai.

The migratory practices over generations extended the social – and with it, the spatial – network of kinship from Bajhang to India, tarai, Kathmandu and a series of other places. A similar pattern of 'intergenerational multi-locality' in eastern Nepal has been described by Subedi (1993). The 'historical depth' of such spatial kinship networks seems in both cases to be considerable. Even after generations, the ancestral home and inherited land are perceived as a form of insurance in times of crisis and symbolises the potential return of the migrants. The sense of belonging is affected by this multi-local life experienced in Delhi, in the home villages, in the mountains and in the tarai.

When people migrate from one locality to another, the subjective and emotional attachment to a locale – the sense of place (Cresswell 2004: 7) or territorial belonging, which they develop over a long time, is left behind and cannot simply be transported to a new locality. Following Conway (2005), we assume that the sense of belonging to 'home' can be as influential as the metropolitan structures, in determining life spaces in which migrants and non-migrating family members live. This transforms the meaning of 'home'. Ties to the previous home – often referred to as the 'real home' – fuel the retention of a 'return mythology'. However, the members of subsequent generations, who grew up in the diaspora, have different rootedness to the village of origin than their parents' or grandparents' generations. A certain de-rooting of the second or third generation reduces the attachment to the land and house where they originally came from.

The caste and kinship system is the most important social framework in the migrants' home society as well as in the diaspora. In the new locale, migrants have to restructure a part of their life paths. For example, women follow the traditional patrilineal and patrilocal family networks for recruiting other women to their society, but introduce new patterns of interaction by allowing Dalit women in the society. Another example of new forms of networking is the foundation of a Migrant Nepalese Watchmen Labour Committee on 1 May 2005 and facilitated by one of our testing projects conducted by South Asia Study Centre, an NGO with focus on people from Far-West Nepal (Thieme et al. 2005). The sense of belonging now is to a new, labour-oriented social collectivity and no longer to a village-based kinship.

In the example I gave from Far-West Nepal as well as in the diaspora, social networks based on caste, kin and the village of origin are very important. Do people have in this multi-local setting a sense of belonging to Nepal? Empirical evidence clearly points out that national identity is very important from the perspective of the migrants. India is seen as a hegemonic power exploiting Nepal. The fact that some Bajhangis in the tarai (Poertner et al. 2011b) decided to return to Nepal to make a 'Nepalese' education possible for their children indicates that in Far-West Nepal, a sense of belonging to Nepal is pronounced. On the contrary, they stress on the difficulties they face in India because of their nationality.

A sense of belonging is also expressed when people emphasise their migration practice or their multi-local life. For generations, people have shared the experience of oscillating between different lifeworlds. The aspects of life 'here' and 'there' – whether perceived from the migrant's starting or destination point – are regarded as complementary (Vertovec 2003: 11).

Nepalese diaspora in Switzerland

Let me end with a few observations from another part of the world – Switzerland.[11] Only a few Nepalese migrate to Europe. From the estimated seven million Nepalese living outside Nepal, only 3.9 per cent are in Europe (NIDS 2011: 45), and of this, only a very small number lives in Switzerland. In 2010, the Swiss Federal Office of Migration (BFM) registered 497 Nepalese as part of Switzerland's permanent foreign residential population. According to the presidential department of the city of Zurich, 29 (in 2010) and 34 (in 2011) Nepalese lived in the city of Zurich.[12] One can assume that in addition, a good number of 'irregular' Nepalese live in the country.

Who are these Nepalese in Switzerland? Migration patterns vary from legally immigrated well-established migrants to 'irregular' migrants. I classify well-established Nepalese as those who have received a Swiss residence permit and a work permit. Some of them are highly skilled persons, who have been – in times of a less restrictive immigration policy – successful in getting a good position in the Swiss labour market. Others married a Swiss partner or a Nepalese with a Swiss residence permit. A small group stays in Switzerland with a student visa. The other extreme, from the legal point of view, has persons without proper residence permit. They usually seek asylum and receive a temporary permit. Others overstay on a tourist or artist visa, become 'sans papiers' or apply for asylum to prolong their stay (Meier 2008).

In general, all migrants have more or less a good education and socio-economic background, as considerable financial and social capital is needed to migrate to European countries. A majority of migrants belongs to the high castes (Bahun-Chhetri-Newar). However, how they entered Switzerland determines the different categories of residence permits. The Swiss government determines the legal status, which is very crucial for their daily life and life perspective, for their security and income opportunities. Asylum seekers have – under certain conditions – the right to work, but irregular migrants normally depend on informal, low-paid and insecure jobs. Many people with limited permit in terms of duration or without any permit somehow legalise their situation. For example, a young man came to Switzerland as a student. Later, he applied for asylum, and finally, he married a Swiss woman. Through this marriage, he received a residence permit, which allowed him to work and study. But there are also examples of those abandoning the dream to stay in Switzerland!

Asylum seekers and irregular migrants do not have the possibility to visit Nepal or to invite family or friends from home whereas most of the well-established migrants regularly visit their families in Nepal and host guests from Nepal quite frequently. But all share the experience that the expectations of their relatives and friends in Nepal concerning financial support and gifts are very high. This can be an enormous economic and psychological burden for people without a job or with a low-paid one. It is not easy to save money, and many do not tell their relatives at home what they are really doing because they feel ashamed to do so.

A majority of them underline the importance of regular contacts with other Nepalese. The well-established Nepalese and their Swiss partners have known each other very well for a long time. The Swiss Nepalese Society is an important institution for them. Also, the less established Nepalese socialise frequently, and newcomers stay in the same flat as compatriots. However, a divide between the established Nepalese and the newcomers is noted. This divide has to do with the legal status in Switzerland, coupled with income disparities. Both groups maintain contacts with other Swiss people and foreigners. The irregular migrants, in particular, depend on contacts to find jobs, support, and sometimes, a Swiss marriage partner.

In Switzerland, belonging to a specific ethnic group, caste, village or town in Nepal is not important. Although the relation with home is maintained, the Nepal-based social networks are no longer crucial in order to manage daily life in the diaspora. Only a strong sense of belonging to different social milieus in the Nepalese diaspora ensures their survival, success and legal status.

Summing up

The different examples from Nepal and Nepali diasporas illustrate that social and territorial belonging of an individual is multi-layered and dynamic. Belonging to a specific ethnic group or caste can be an important component in the construction of a sense of belonging, but not always. The example of Gorkha shows that the high symbolic significance of this place and its historical anchoring has enhanced the sense of belonging to it. In diaspora, the emphasis on the 'home' becomes especially strong if people have the concept of returning home, but it becomes less important if people want to leave the home behind in their search for 'another' life.

The sense of belonging as a symbolic dimension of social relations and interactions also reflects the needs for networks essential for different livelihood strategies. In the example I gave from Far-West Nepal, social networks based on caste, kin and the village of origin are very important in the diaspora. Correspondingly, the home, family and the village are emphasised as an anchor point of belonging. In Switzerland, these social networks are not any more crucial in order to manage their daily life in the diaspora.

In general, belonging to an economically and socially determined stratum of a society is a crucial element of the sense of belonging. However, strong ethnicity can cover up this element, as we saw among the Newars and Tharus. In the Swiss diaspora, the Nepalese migrants stressed themselves that different social milieus were developed and shaped by Swiss government rules.

The territorial sense of belonging always has multiple scales. Especially, in a difficult and strange environment and in small but heterogeneous diasporas, the sense of belonging to a village is no longer important. The sense of belonging comes into being when people emphasise their migration practice, their multi-local life and what they have in common as migrants.

Notes

1. Pollini (2005: 499) distinguishes attachment, loyalty, solidarity and the sense of affinity or 'we-feeling' as components of social belonging.
2. Said, one of the best known exponents of postcolonial writing, for example, wrote of an imagined geography, which constructs the Orient as the 'other' in a reductionist, distancing and pathologising way (1995/1978).
3. In the *Muluki Ain* (the national code) of 1854, the Rana rulers codified in detail the national caste system (Höfer 1979).
4. Ethnicity, production, reproduction and transformation of social boundaries or ethnic groups, is a two-way process that takes place across the boundary between 'us' and 'them' – internal and external defined (Jenkins 1994: 199).
5. The terms *adivasi, janajati, mulvasi* and *bhumiputra* are used and defined as 'those ethnic groups or communities who have their own mother tongue and traditional customs, distinct cultural identity, distinct social structure and written or oral history of their own' (National Foundation for Indigenous Nationalities Act, 2002).
6. It is said that Prithvi Narayan Shah called Newar artisans, architects and traders to Gorkha in order to construct the palace and to develop trade.
7. The fieldwork for this study was carried out in Far-West Nepal and Delhi between 1999 and 2010. At first, a participatory rural appraisal and a household survey were conducted in several villages of the Bajura and Bajhang districts in the Far Western Development Region (Müller-Böker 2003). From 2002 to 2004, Susan Thieme conducted fieldwork in Delhi, where the migrants from the villages of investigation in Far-West Nepal were approached (Thieme 2006). In 2008 and 2009, Junginger revisited the villages in Far-West Nepal. The research was funded by ProDoc (SNSF) and the NCCR North-South (SNSF and SDC).
8. India hosts the largest number of Nepali workers anywhere in the world. Official figures are not available because there is no system of visa or work permit between the two countries. There are several estimates, ranging from 1.5 to 3 million, including a large number of girls and women trafficked from Nepal to India (NIDS 2011). Also see Adhikari and Gurung (2009).
9. Generally, men dominate such societies.
10. The significance of Kathmandu arises primarily from the practice of families sending their sons there to study.
11. The results are based on the qualitative study (MA thesis) of Nina Meier (2008) and my various interactions and observations.
12. www.bfs.admin.ch/bfs/portal/de/index/themen/01/07/blank/data/01; www.stadt-zuerich.ch/content/prd/de/index/statistik/bevoelkerung/bevoelkerungsstand/nationalitaet (accessed 15 May 2012).

References

Adhikari, J. and G. Gurung. 2009. *Migration, Security and Livelihoods: A Case of Migration between Nepal and India*. Kathmandu: NIDS, NCCR North-South.

Bruslé, T. 2008. 'Choosing a Destination and Work: Migration Strategies of Nepalese Workers in Uttarakhand, Northern India', *Mountain Research & Development*, 28(3/4): 240–47.

Cameron, M. M. 1998. *On the Edge of the Auspicious: Gender and Caste in Nepal*. Urbana, Chicago: University of Illinois Press.

Conway, D. 2005. 'Transnationalism and Return: "Home" as an Enduring Fixture and "Anchor"', in R. B. Potter, D. Conway and J. Phillips (eds), *Experiences of Return: Caribbean Perspectives*. London: Ashgate Publishers.

Cresswell, T. 2004. *Place: a Short Introduction*. Malden, MA: Blackwell.

Erel, U. 2011. 'Complex Belongings: Racialization and Migration in a Small English City', *Ethnic and Racial Studies*, DOI:10.1080/01419870.2011.574715.

Gellner, D. N. 1997. 'Caste, Communalism, and Communism: Newars and the Nepalese State', in D. N. Gellner, J. Pfaff-Czarnecka and J. Whelpton (eds), *Nationalism and Ethnicity in a Hindu Kingdom*. Amsterdam: Harwood Academic Publishers, 151–84.

Giddens, A. 1991. *Modernity and Self-identity: Self and Society in the Late Modern Age*. Cambridge: Polity.

Höfer, A. 1979. 'The Caste Hierarchy and the State in Nepal: A Study on *Muluki Ain* of 1854', *Khumbu Himal*, 13(2): 25–240.

Jenkins, R. 1994. 'Rethinking Ethnicity: Identity, Categorization and Power', *Ethnic and Racial Studies*, 17(2): 197–223.

Jensen, S. Q. 2011. 'Othering, Identity Formation and Agency', *Qualitative Studies*, 2(2): 63–68.

Kasarda, J. and M. Janowitz. 1974. 'Community Attachment in Mass Society', *American Sociological Review*, 39: 328–39.

Mathema, K. B. 2011. *Madheshi Uprising: the Resurgence of Ethnicity*. Kathmandu: Mandala Book Point.

Meier, N. 2008. *Same but Different: Experiences of Nepalese Migrants in Switzerland Holding Different Resident Status*. Diploma Thesis, Department of Geography, University of Zurich.

Müller-Böker, U. 1986. 'Die Übernutzung der natürlichen Ressourcen in Gorkha: Soziale und ökonomische Ursachen', in B. Kölver (ed.), *Formen kulturellen Wandels und andere Beiträge zur Erforschung des Himalaya*, Nepalica 2; Sankt Augustin: VGH, 393–414.

Müller-Böker, U. 1988. 'Spatial Organization of a Caste Society: the Example of the Newar in the Kathmandu Valley, Nepal', *Mountain Research and Development*, 8(1): 23–31.

Müller-Böker, U. 1993. 'Tharus and Pahariyas in Chitawan: Some Observations Concerning the Question of Multiethnicity of Nepal', in G. Toffin (ed.), *Nepal: Past and Present: Proceedings of the Franco-German Conference*. Paris: Arc-et-Senans, CNRS, 279–93.

Müller-Böker, U. 2003. 'Livelihood Strategies in the Buffer Zone of the Khaptad National Park', in M. Domroes (ed.), *Translating Development: the Case of Nepal*, pp. 166–77. New Delhi: Social Science Press.

NIDS. 2011. *Nepal Migration Year Book 2010*. Kathmandu: NIDS & NCCR North-South.

Pfaff-Czarnecka, J. 1995. 'Migration Under Marginality Conditions: the Case of Bajhang', in INFRAS & IDA (eds), *Rural-urban Interlinkages: a Challenge for Swiss Development Cooperation*, pp. 97–108. Zurich, Kathmandu: INFRAS.

Poertner, E., M. Junginger and U. Müller-Böker. 2011a. 'Migration in Far West Nepal: Intergenerational Linkages between Internal and International Migration of Rural-to-Urban Migrants', *Critical Asian Studies*, 43(1): 23–47.

Poertner, E., M. Junginger and U. Müller-Böker. 2011b. 'Migration in Far West Nepal: Challenging Migration Categories and Theoretical Lenses', *Critical Asian Studies*, 43(4): 661–65.

Pollini, G. 2005. 'Elements of a Theory of Place Attachment and Socio-territorial Belonging', *International Review of Sociology*, 15(3): 497–515.

Portes, A, L. E. Guarnizo and P. Landolt. 1999. 'The Study of Transnationalism: Pitfalls and Promise of an Emergent Research Field', *Ethnic and Racial Studies*, 22(2): 217–37.

Pries, L. 2001. The Disruption of Social and Geographic Space: Mexican–US Migration and the Emergence of Transnational Social Spaces', *International Sociology*, 16(1): 51–70.

Said, E. 1995 [1978]. *Orientalism*. London: Penguin Books.

Sen, Amartya. 2006. *Identity and Violence: The Illusion of Destiny*. New York: W.W. Norton.

Sheppard, J. 2009. 'Federalism in Nepal: a Tharu Perspective', *Contributions to Nepalese Studies*, 36(2): 213–37.

Sinha, A. C. 2009. 'Introduction', in T. B. Subba, A. C. Sinha, G. S. Nepal and D. R. Nepal (eds), *Indian Nepalis: Issues and Perspectives*, pp. 3–27. New Delhi: Concept Publishing Company.

Spivak, G. C. 1985. 'The Rani of Sirmur: an Essay in Reading the Archives', *History and Theory*, 24(3): 247–72.

Subedi, B. P. 1993. Continuity and Change in Population Movement: from Inside a Rural Nepali Community. Ann Arbor: UMI University Microfilms International.

Thieme, S. and U. Müller-Böker. 2004. 'Financial Self-help Associations among Far West Nepalese Labour Migrants in Delhi, India', *Asian and Pacific Migration Journal*, 13(3): 339–61.

Thieme, S., R. Bhattrai, G. Gurung, K. Kollmair, S. Manandhar and U. Müller-Böker. 2005. 'Addressing Nepalese Migrant Workers' Needs', *Mountain Research and Development*, 25(2): 109–14.

Thieme, S. 2006. *Social Networks and Migration: Far West Nepalese Labour Migrants in Delhi*. Münster: LIT.

Thieme, S. 2008. 'Sustaining Livelihoods in Multi-local Settings: Possible Theoretical Linkages between Transnational Migration and Livelihood Studies', *Mobilities*, 3(1): 51–72.

Thieme, S. and U. Müller-Böker. 2010. 'Social Networks and Migration: Women's Livelihoods between Far West Nepal and Delhi', *European Bulletin of Himalayan Research*, 35/36: 107–21.

Unbescheid, G. 1986. 'Göttliche Könige und königliche Götter. Entwurf zur Organisation von Kulten in Gorkha und Jumla', in B. Kölver (ed.), *Formen kulturellen Wandels und andere Beiträge zur Erforschung des Himalaya*, pp. 225–47. Nepalica 2; Sankt Augustin: VGH.

Upreti, B. C. 2002. *The Marginal Migrants*. Delhi: Kalinga Publications.

Vertovec, S. 2001. 'Transnationalism and Identity', *Journal of Ethnic and Migration Studies*, 27(4): 573–82.
Vertovec, S. 2003. Migrant Transnationalism and Modes of Transformation. Working Paper Nos 03–09m, Oxford, Berlin: Center for Migration and Development, Princeton University.
Whelpton, J., D. N. Gellner and J. Pfaff-Czarnecka. 2008. 'Grasping Ethnicity in a New Political Context', in D. N. Gellner, J. Pfaff-Czarnecka and J. Whelpton (eds), *Nationalism and Ethnicity in Nepal,* pp. xvii–xlviii. Kathmandu: Vajra Publications.

4

COMPETING PERSPECTIVES ON THE GURKHAS AND IDENTITY POLITICS IN NEPAL

Jens Seeberg

Before the Constituent Assembly of Nepal was dissolved after the failure to produce a new constitution by 27 May 2012, the then Parliamentary Committee on International Relations and Human Rights published a draft report, entitled 'Nepal's Foreign Policy in the Changed Context'. The report, which was endorsed by all political parties in the Constituent Assembly, was concerned with the autonomy and dignity of Nepal and it recommended a thorough revision of a number of international treaties, including the tripartite agreement between Nepal, India and the United Kingdom from 1947, which established the post-independence framework for recruitment in Nepal of Gurkha soldiers serving in the British and Indian armies. The document stated that 'working for foreign military power(s) has not been a matter of great pride for the nation'.[1]

This careful wording had two implications. The first was that the Gurkha tradition continued to be viewed as a national symbol, albeit – and this was the second implication – it had become a negative symbol, one that was not invested with national pride. Because of this latter point, the committee recommended that the recruitment should be brought to a stop. Given the substantial income through the remittances and pension schemes generated by former and present Gurkha soldiers, this recommendation implied a conflict between economic versus symbolic capital generated by the Gurkha institution. In this paper, I explore the Gurkha institution as a symbol and return to the issue of the economic benefits versus perceived symbolic cost to the nation.

On symbols

Associated with the unification of Nepal under the Gorkha kingdom, and popularly projected in both national myth and globalised tourist imagery, the Gurkha soldiers in the British, and later, the 'Gorkhas' in the Indian Army have been a national symbol in the past, in spite of the historically dubious and erroneous construction of the very term (e.g. Kochhar-George 2010, and many others). While it is straightforward to identify the

Figure 4.1 Nepal's national emblem adopted in 1962

IDENTITY POLITICS

Figure 4.2 Nepal's national emblem adopted in 2006
Source: http://www.hubert-herald.nl/Nepal.htm.

Gurkhas as a symbol, it is more complicated to answer the question: 'a symbol of what'?

Symbols are capable of generating emotions in an audience that other forms of communication cannot. As Turner pointed out, symbols are triggers of social action due to their properties, such as 'multivocality, complexity of association, ambiguity, open-endedness, [and] primacy of feeling and willing over thinking' (Turner 1975: 155). Symbols are necessary tools for nation-building, but the importance attached to and the degree of identification enabled by any given symbol may vary considerably in multi-ethnic nation states, as has been shown in the case of the rainbow as a symbol for post-apartheid South Africa (Bornman 2006), where the new symbol seemed to be more important for those ethnic groups who had suffered most under the old regime.

While, for many Nepalis, the *khukuri* is primarily a practical cutting tool, it is *also* a metonymic extension of the Gurkha regiments. As such, it was a key element of the national emblem prior to introduction of the new national emblem in December 2006.

The change of the national emblem is an indication of the importance of symbols in general, and of national symbols, in particular. The

57

former coat of arms of Nepal, Figure 4.1, adopted in 1962, portrayed two 'Gorkhali' soldiers, one carrying a khukuri in addition to the bow and arrow, the other carrying a rifle, and with two khukuris placed together with two Nepali flags and the footprints of Gorakhnath, the guardian deity of the Gurkhas. The new coat of arms, Figure 4.2, has neither military nor religious references. Instead, it can be interpreted as a symbol of national unity, emphasising (blue) mountainous, (green) hilly and (yellow) plains regions and the respectful coexistence of both sexes, along with an inscription that translates as 'Mother and motherland are greater than heaven'.

While it has maintained some national symbols – the Himalayas and the Rhododendron flower – it has replaced the soldiers with the joining hands of a man and a woman. Masculine and aggressive symbols of khukuris and Gorkhalis have been replaced by feminine and peaceful symbols of motherhood, flowers and gender equity.

As Peirce has pointed out, a sign – such as a symbol – is only a sign if it is interpreted as such by somebody; in this sense, the meaning of a symbol is attributed by the interpreter ('interpretant', in Peirce's terminology) (Peirce 1931, 2.228). Peirce's semiotics goes well with Turner's concept of multivocality in terms of pointing to the fluid nature of symbols. By their very constitution, they render themselves open to different and potentially conflicting interpretations. Yet, symbols are as 'real' as any other object. They should not be mistaken to be ontologically vague in spite of their multivocality and their dependency on the existence of an 'interpretant', because this multivocality can be analysed systematically and with a sufficient degree of precision for the analysis to be a relevant contribution to our understanding of political debates and social dynamics in contemporary Nepal. Here, I shall adopt an approach that is partially inspired by what de Castro has called 'perspectival anthropology', based on 'controlled equivocation', namely, the study of 'the referential alterity between homonymic concepts. Equivocation appears here as the mode of communication par excellence between different perspectival positions' (Viveiros de Castro 2004: 5). He refers to Simondon's notion of *transduction* to capture the process of 'inversion of the negative into the positive' that 'determines the non-identity of the terms, that which makes them disparate' (quoted in Viveiros de Castro 2004: 20). In what follows, I shall compare different perspectives on Gurkhas (and their 'perspectival' homonyms, 'Gorkha' and 'Lahure'), from which interpretants have attributed meaning to the Gurkha as a symbol of great historical importance for Nepal, and therefore, also of considerable significance in current debates over national identity in the 'New Nepal'. Apart from existing scholarly literature on the subject, my empirical material is constituted by contributions to the Gurkha discourse in the form of books, newspaper articles, blogs, TV clips and videos available on the Internet, spanning a period from the 1960s to the present. They represent a number of distinct perspectives on the Gurkha, namely the 'postcolonial' perspective, the 'Nepali literary' perspective, the perspective of the (British) Gurkha Justice Campaign and the perspective of the Mongol National Organisation (MNO).

The postcolonial discourse

It is a trivial but necessary point that the creation of Gurkha regiments as part of the forces under, first, the East India Company, and subsequently, under the British Crown was a colonial invention. It served the dual purpose of providing cheap and reliable soldiers to the colonial army and weakening the military power of Nepal (Rathaur 2006), and it reduced the risk of armed resistance to the king within Nepal. A number of scholars have provided insights into the colonial discourse on the Gurkhas and its remarkably stereotypical expressions in almost verbatim repetitions of legends of braver-than-brave Gurkha soldiers. It is not my intention or purpose to doubt – or discuss – the potential truth value of these legends. What interests me here is the way these stories are composed and combined into an overriding discourse that has produced a particular set of values invested in the Gurkha symbol.

I shall present one example of such discourse presented in the popular media. It illustrates a remarkable continuity and resilience of the discourse. It is from a 1992 documentary on the Gurkhas as part of a series on 'Special Forces' on the Discovery channel. The portrait of Gurkhas depicted in this 25-minute-long film is typical of the postcolonial discourse in its near-exclusive British Army perspective on the matter. Apart from two brief fragments with ex-Gurkhas and a brief fragment with a 17-year-young potential recruit, the story is exclusively narrated by British officers and it echoes the classical colonial Gurkha literature. For example, the idea of 'martial races' that was originally a specific articulation of 19th-century European racial theories and in line with the overall colonial project is, in this movie, reflected in statements such as the following, offered by Brigadier General Timothy Glass, who speaks about new Gurkha recruits: 'On first encounter, they are very straightforward, they are very good-natured, they've got a nice sense of humour. Very quickly you discover they are also extremely hardy and stoical, and really, it's that quality of stoicism, their ability to endure . . . they tolerate the circumstances that they find themselves in very readily and very naturally and make perfect soldiers in this sort of respect' (Cerre 1992, 15:48–16:20), and the narrator continues: 'The ferocity of Gurkhas in combat is something that can't be taught. It's an instinctive trait that can only be refined in training and that is rarely displayed and never bragged about' (Cerre 1992, 18:44–19:00).

Caplan (1991), in his review of the British military writings on the Gurkhas, notes that even if this particular colonial discourse essentialises the Gurkhas, it differs from the orientalist discourse identified by Inden (1990) in that it places itself firmly in the camp of romantic-idealist approvers to the exclusion of the position of the utilitarianists and their disapproval of everything Indian (or Nepali, in this case). Caplan identifies three constant figures in the discourse, which are remarkably stable in the literature, namely 'martiality', 'bravery' and 'loyalty'. These figures establish the Gurkhas as, on one hand, having the same kinds of qualities that British officers see in themselves, and on the other hand, as dependent upon the leadership of British officers to whom this loyalty is to be demonstrated. In the Discovery channel film, this point is driven home by Colonel Nigel A. Collett, who says about the new recruits: 'Our [newly recruited Gurkha] soldier is still very much of an unsophisticated . . . ehm . . . hill . . . ehm . . . phenomenon. He's the sort of man who's had, perhaps, five or six years' education in his school, he's spent his entire life marching up and down, running up and down the hills of Nepal, the mountains of Nepal, and when he comes to us, he's much more of a raw material than his British counterpart' (Cerre 1992, 13:01–13:29). In this representation, in the case of the Gurkha tradition, the colonial project seems to have been continued seamlessly into the postcolonial era as a 'civilising mission'.[2]

The postcolonial discourse does, to some extent, also recognise the context of poverty as an important motive behind the decision to pursue recruitment. The exception to exclusively presenting the British perspective on the Gurkhas in the film is provided in a brief (17 seconds) interview with a young potential recruit, Gorman Gurung. He says, 'I want to become a "Gurkha" because they are going to the army, then they earn money, you know. And they buy some land and they help their father and mother. So I also think about that, you know' (Cerre 1992, 7:51–8:08). According to the voice of the army, personalised by Lieutenant Colonel Paul Gay in an interview in the same film, this is a *double plus*: 'They are subsistence farmers, hill farmers. A lad comes from a small homestead. Around it, there's some fields which his father owns. He works these fields and attempts to produce sufficient food to feed themselves for the year. Now, if you take a boy off their family, as it were you give them a double plus. It means there's one less person to feed, and also that person is in a position to send money home to contribute towards the family' (Cerre 1992, 6:36–7:07). There is little reflection here about the potential 'minuses' that may be involved for the recruit and his family, and curiously, this acknowledgment of poverty as the main driving force seems never to give the British voices in this film cause to question the notion of loyalty to the British Crown.

Nepali narratives

By comparing the postcolonial discourse with Nepali literary voices, it becomes clear what the former discourse silences.[3] Native Nepali literary voices about the *lahure* (i.e. Nepali term for those who went to Lahore in present-day Pakistan for recruitment) provide a very different portrait than the stereotypical image that is constructed in postcolonial discourse. In Daulat Bikram Bishta's short story, 'The Andhi Khola' (Bishta 1993), the protagonist, Gangi sees a small group of young Nepali men passing her on their way to a recruitment centre in India. The episode throws her 25 years back in time to when she was 19 and her loved one left her to go to war for Britain against Germany, not because of a stance in the conflict, but driven by poverty: 'Gangi was still trying to think of some way to cheer him up when he announced, "Tomorrow I am going to sign up in the war against the Germans". Gangi felt as if she had tumbled down a waterfall. Without giving her any chance to question him, he set off for the village. Then Gangi was gripped by fear – that day his voice lacked its usual jocularity. She cast around for hope, but the more she did so, the more she became convinced – he was going to the war, for sure. His land was in a rich man's hands; his livestock were all mortgaged. He was not prepared to wrestle with poverty every day of his life' (ibid.: 233–34). When recalling the events, Gangi's agony is exacerbated by her memory that as a child, she had mocked him about his family's poverty. Twenty-five years after his enrolment, waiting in the darkness of the night, long after the small group had disappeared over the hilltop and into unknown land, she keeps watching for his return.

The story focuses on the feelings of those who are left behind by the *lahure* and the disruption of life in Nepal created by this long-term and uncertain absence. While present-day means of communication has considerably changed the modalities of this kind of uncertainty, Bishta's story points to the price the families of recruits have to pay in terms of disturbance of actual or potential family ties as well as emotional hardship. This focus is far from the 'double plus' described in the postcolonial discourse, where emotions other than loyalty to the crown have no real significance.

The theme of guilt is the topic of Sikkim-born Shiv Kumar Rai's short story, 'The Murderer' (*Jyanmara?*), originally from 1968 (Rai 1993). Burma war veteran Ujirman has returned to his village. His traumatic war experiences are symbolised by the loss of three fingers that were cut off in a fight against Japanese soldiers; he does not know whether they were cut off by his opponents or by himself in the heat of the fight and he didn't notice until he returned to the camp, after which he was hospitalised for a month. Back in his village, he is known for his hunting skills. He marries a young woman who is the object of admiration and desire among the men in the village. One day, he mistakes police officer Bhalu for a bear and shoots him. During the ensuing court trial, it is revealed that Officer Bhalu and Ujirman's wife had an affair, which was known to everybody but Ujirman, and that in an argument the same morning as the incident took place, Ujirman had a quarrel with his wife in which he had said he would shoot a bear (*bhalu*). While the judge was hesitant to convict him on this circumstantial evidence, Ujirman suddenly gives a false confession that he shot the adulterer on purpose and breaks out in a hysterical laughter.

Hutt suggests that Rai wants to convey 'that the old Gurkha has decided to accept imprisonment honourably, not for the crime of which he stands accused, but for the life of killing and violence he led before his retirement' (Hutt 1989: 26). An alternative interpretation of the story would be that the events in the village constitute a repetition of the traumatic events in the war and that Ujirman returns to his village as a changed person because of these traumatic events. The rendition of his killing as a hallucination – he believes he has shot a bear – and the ending, where his hysterical laughter is mixed with the self-punishment involved in assuming guilt for something he did not realise that he did, seem to be a doubly critical comment *both* on the very killing in war on somebody else's behalf *and* on the personal price that the ex-Gurkha has to pay after return to his home country. Hence, Rai seems to see the Gurkha as a 'murderer' – therefore, the title of the short story – but as a murderer followed by a question mark, since he has little control over the circumstances that made him commit it. The story also points to the inherent ambivalence in Nepal towards the Gurkha tradition, represented by the ambivalent judge in the story.

A more direct reference to the cruelty of war is provided in the classical feminist novel by Parijat Tamang,[4] *Blue Mimosa* (Parijat 1972), which is partially based on her interviews with ex-Gurkha soldiers (Hutt 1989: 26). The novel tells the story of a former Gurkha who falls in love with Sakambari, the younger sister of his best friend and 'drinking brother'.

Being old (at the age of 46) and alcoholic, he is unable to convey his feelings, and more importantly, to understand them. Thus, he is thrown into flashback experiences where he sexually and emotionally molested three Burmese women during the World War II campaign in Burma. These crimes transformed him into an emotional amputee and he is unable to engage in meaningful emotional bonds after his return to Nepal. When he eventually tries to show his feelings by clumsily forcing a kiss onto Sakambari's lips, not only is he rejected, but he also 'infects' her with the 'disease' created within him by his deeds during the war, and she falls ill with an incurable disease that eventually kills her: 'I have killed Sakambari. In broad daylight, I raped Sakambari. Bari died proving the emotion of my true love a rape. It is my history' (Parijat 1972). The novel depicts the Gurkha's participation in the war on behalf of the British as meaningless, but it also points to the general feeling of meaninglessness and alienation that he experiences. While the story may be read as a general commentary on gender roles and alienation in Nepal in the 1960s, the author also – as pointed out by Hutt (1989: 26) – had the intention to influence the public perception of the lahure in Nepal. A corrective point is also taken up by Onta (1994), who analyses Gurkha soldiers' letters from the field during World War I and points to the dehumanising effects of the postcolonial discourse.

The above examples are by no means exhaustive of depictions of lahure in Nepali literature, but they suffice to establish a contrast to the glorifying portrait so powerfully painted within the postcolonial discourse. This contrasting picture speaks of broken families, emotional suffering and damage to people who are or have been engaged in war – types of damage that influence social competences and relations long after the fighting has seized. Hence, while the literature questions these consequences through explorations of the psychological and social dimensions of the lahure tradition, they also place these people in the context of Nepal at the time of writing. The literary exploration of gender relations in connection with the absent or returning Gorkha soldier introduces a female perspective on the exclusively male-oriented postcolonial discourse. By choosing these literary contributions, I wish to show that at least the literary Nepali elite has challenged the postcolonial discourse for many years; hence, there is nothing new in the ambiguity with which the Gurkha tradition has been viewed in Nepal – at the same time, feared and admired, projected as male heroes and suspected of immoral and emotionally crippling actions. However, the individuals who have left for Foreign Service have rarely been condemned; when not projected as heroes, they have been considered as victims of larger colonial and postcolonial forces.

By excluding Nepali narratives that demonstrate pride in the Gurkha tradition among the ex-servicemen community, I intended to provide a contrast to the dominant discourse to point to other dimensions of the Gurkha as a symbol. Whereas the postcolonial discourse attributed male values of martiality, bravery and loyalty, the literary Nepali voices attributed notions of pain, deprivation and loss – of limbs, mental health and sociality. These latter attributes are not necessarily refuted in the postcolonial discourse – they are merely silenced – whereas another attribute of the Gurkhas is fiercely contested – the question of whether or not they may be understood as a type of mercenaries.

The mercenary debate

The mercenary debate is highly emotional and decidedly political. The position that Gurkhas are to be understood as mercenaries has most forcefully been promoted by then Maoist deputy leader, and later, prime minister of Nepal, Baburam Bhattarai, who, shortly after the Maoist Party's election victory in 2008, was quoted on the following statement: 'The obnoxious practice of citizens joining foreign armies as mercenaries will be stopped' (Brown 2008). This was not a new call from the Maoist position. Prior to the insurgency, the Maoist opposition to the Gurkha tradition had been regularly aired, and during it, there were newspaper reports of Indian 'Gorkha' soldiers having been abducted (Sarkar 2005) and rumours of Maoist youths having infiltrated the Gorkha recruitment camp in Pokhara (Harris and Smith 2001). The debate goes back, at least, to the tripartite agreement allowing India and the UK to 'maintain the Gurkha connection' when the then prime minister of Nepal, Padma Shumsher Rana, approved the proposal only if his young subjects would not be 'looked upon as distinctly mercenary' (Adhikary 2012).

'Mercenary', derived from Latin 'merces' ('wages' or 'pay') means 'one that serves merely for wages; especially: a soldier hired into foreign service', according to the Merriam-Webster online encyclopaedia (2012). The ambiguity of classification of the Gurkhas as mercenaries is immediately visible: they are soldiers hired into foreign service, but is it *merely* for wages? Encyclopædia Britannica online (2012) defines a mercenary as a 'hired professional soldier who fights for any state or nation without regard to political interests or issues'. The Gurkhas are hired professional soldiers, who *do not* fight for *any* state of nation – only for the British (or, as it were, Indian, albeit eventually as Indian citizens) – but who do so without regard to (Nepal's; their own) political interests or issues. There are certainly 'mercenary dimensions' to the (British) Gurkha tradition – they serve a foreign country, they do so primarily out of economic motives – and there are 'non-mercenary dimensions' – they serve only one specific country; they sign contracts of a duration that would not apply to mercenaries in general; and they obtain social benefits and recognition that would not apply to mercenaries otherwise. Furthermore, important symbols are involved; they swear loyalty to the flag and to the British Crown, thereby indicating that they could not be purchased in the same way by any other country.

Voices within the postcolonial discourse clearly emphasise the latter aspects when dismissing the mercenary label as wrong, as illustrated by this quote from the Discovery channel film discussed previously: 'Above all, the Gurkhas have been fiercely loyal to the Queen and the British army for nearly 200 years of distinguished service, not as detached mercenaries or cheap soldiers but as professional members of an extended military family. They swear to serve for a minimum commitment of 15 years' (Cerre 1992, 4:44–5:02).

However, while what I have called the postcolonial discourse is unified in the praise of Gurkha bravery and loyalty to the Queen, it is ambivalent in its use of the term 'mercenary'. Even within the Discovery channel film, the initial rejection of the mercenary label is somewhat contradicted by the following statement: 'The Sultan of Brunei likes to have them [i.e. the Gurkhas] around so much, he personally pays the British Government the costs of keeping a regiment of Gurkhas in Borneo at all times to help protect his Sultanate' (Cerre 1992, 3:52–4:05).

A 1995 BBC documentary written by Ian Wooldridge points to this central contradiction in this remarkable way: 'Foreign tourists are entitled to be baffled. The Tower of London. The Crown Jewels guarded by diminutive mercenaries from a distant shore' (Wooldridge 1995). It is as if this particular opening of the film captures the entire colonial history, encompassing as it does the loyalty to the Crown, its contradiction in the concept of mercenary, the colonial paternalism embedded in the use of 'diminutive' and the spatial and geopolitical distance between the colonial centre and the colonised 'other', despite the fact that Nepal was not a British colony.

While the 'mercenary label' in the above example may at least partially have been used for its dramatic effects, a different example – that of a company called 'Gurkha Security Guards' (GSG) – leaves little doubt as to the relevance of the label. Listed at the website of GlobalSecurity.org along with companies such as Blackwater Security Company that has provided mercenaries to US forces in Iraq and Afghanistan, GSG was established in 1989 by two ex-soldiers who had fought in the British

Army during the Rhodesian war. They were joined by Major John Titley, a British Gurkha regiment officer, who subsequently was instrumental in terms of recruitment of Gurkha soldiers in Nepal (Vines 1999). Engaging in various security operations such as protecting the diamond industry in Angola, the case of GSG illustrates that the line between security services and mercenary activities may sometimes be thin and may depend entirely on the needs of the client. Hence, they were engaged to train the Republic of Sierra Leone Military Force in 1995 during the civil war in the country – an engagement that ended with the killing of 21 troops, including five Gurkha 'mercenaries', in a single incident on 24 February 1995 (ibid.: 130).

The GSG may be an extreme case, yet it does lend some weight to the position in the mercenary debate that, in fact, considers Gurkhas as mercenaries. It presents a case that is undoubtedly and objectively mercenary in nature. It is more clear-cut than the British Gurkhas. Recalling the multi-vocal nature of symbols and the role of the interpretant in ascribing meaning to Gurkhas perceived as a symbol, Gurkhas in the British Army may or may not be perceived to be mercenaries. They constitute a paradigmatic case of 'transduction': seen from Britain, the Gurkhas are not mercenaries since they are loyal to the Crown. Seen from Nepal, this is precisely the reason that they are. Therefore, the mercenary debate simultaneously attributes the values of glorious loyalty and national shame to Gurkhas as a symbol, albeit from opposite sides of the postcolonial divide. The lahure-sending communities and institutions within Nepal may be trapped between these two positions. Perhaps, this is best expressed by Mahendra Lal Rai, general secretary of the Gurkha Army Ex-Servicemen's Organisation (GAESO), who said: 'We do feel like mercenaries fighting for foreign armies, but who can deny our economic reality, our compulsions? We are caught between pride and practicality' (quoted in Mukherjee 2008).

The Gurkha justice campaign

The history of the Gurkhas is an intricately woven tie of interdependencies and values shared and distributed between Nepal and the UK, and with battlefields linked globally to this initial tie. In spite of the limited annual recruitment, the number of ex-servicemen has accumulated over the years and the conditions they are given by the British state have a direct impact on lahure-sending communities in Nepal. The fact that the story of the Gurkhas is not only one of bravery in the battlefield, but also that of cheap and reliable military labour and racial discrimination in the

British Army led to the involvement of the human rights law firm, Howe & Co., in a series of court cases that sought to establish equal rights for Gurkhas serving in the British Army as well as ex-Gurkhas in terms of pensions and other entitlements (Kochhar-George 2010). This fight for equal rights turned gradually into a very spectacular and successful public campaign after the involvement of Peter Carroll (2012), a politician belonging to the Liberal Democratic Party in the UK. There are, no doubt, different ways to read Carroll's book about the campaign, but one possible reading is to see it as a story of how an effective campaigner brands himself through a just course, spearheaded by actress and daughter of a Gurkha soldier, Joanna Lumley, thereby not only convincing the British government to change its stand and eventually grant 'Gurkha' soldiers and their immediate families the right to settle permanently in the UK after end of service, but also giving rise to the company, 'Peter Carroll Associates' under the motto, 'Campaigns that change your world'. This is, however, not the place to go into a detailed analysis of the campaign. What interests me in this context are two issues, namely, the slight change of symbolic value of the Gurkhas promoted by the campaign and the impact of its success on political discussions in Nepal.

Joanna Lumley, in numerous media appearances, used her star quality to stress the bravery of the Gurkha soldiers. The campaign very deliberately moved on two fronts, one moral, and another emotional. The moral front was established on a platform of national disgrace and shame that retired Gurkha soldiers were not allowed to settle in the UK. The simple claim was that they had risked their lives for the country, but they were being discriminated against in comparison to retired servicemen from Commonwealth countries. This move effectively turned the highly praised soldiers into victims of discrimination, a status that was carefully staged in displays of former soldiers who had been awarded medals – notably, the Victoria Cross – and had lost limbs fighting for the country, and whose legendary stories were interspersed in many media appearances. As a communication strategy, this was extremely successful, and an attempt by the British government to limit settlement rights to Gurkhas who had retired after the Gurkha HQ was shifted from Hong Kong to the UK in 1997, as well as another attempt to establish a number of hard-to-meet conditions to be fulfilled in order to enjoy the rights, fell flat in the face of the effective campaign. When, finally, the British government gave in and in 2009, granted the right to settle in the UK to all former Gurkhas who had served four years or more, Lumley and Carroll made their first ever visit to Nepal. Even in the chapter of Carroll's book that deals with this visit, Nepal and the Nepalese are strangely absent, whereas many pages are dedicated to organising the media coverage, how to hire an airplane in Nepal and the anxieties that accompany the inexperienced traveller who has to manage the risk of being infected with parasites during his morning shower or having to protect Lumley from the excited mob outside the airport. While nobody should be blamed for not having much travel experience, it is a bit discomforting to read that, according to Carroll, Nepal is so poor that 'a bus driver in Nepal might be lucky to earn £300 [NPR 38,000] a month' (Carroll 2012: 157). Such luck is rarely seen among bus drivers in Nepal. Carroll mentions this in the context of Gurkha veterans in Nepal receiving £30 per month from the Gurkha Welfare Society and asks, 'Can that be right?' Furthermore, to return to Nepal after service is projected as a kind of punishment for the retired Gurkhas, as in this quote: 'back in Nepal, where we as a country [the UK] *condemn* thousands of retired Gurkhas to live in poverty and in conditions that we would find totally unacceptable, medals are still worn with an immense amount of pride' (ibid.: 46, emphasis added).

The Gurkha Justice Campaign focused on the right to settle in the UK, but not on the right to equal pension. The two are, of course, related since the 1997 cut-off point applies in the case of pensions. Former Gurkhas who have retired after 1997 are entitled to the same level of pension as their British counterparts, whereas those who retired prior to 1997 are only entitled to one-third of the pension of British veterans on the grounds that living costs are much less in Nepal, and only if they have served for 15 years.[5] Hence, even if the Gurkha Justice campaign triumphed in obtaining the right for pre-1997 veterans to settle in the UK, ex-Gurkhas who receive the comparatively lower pension are likely to find it difficult to manage financially in Britain, and Lumley and Carroll were subsequently attacked for not having taken this aspect sufficiently into account and for being morally co-responsible for the appearance of helpless ex-Gurkhas who began to appear in the UK and who had not been sufficiently prepared for living conditions in the country – an allegation that Carroll rejected at a press conference by stating that he personally had not believed that they would have been able to win a combined (i.e. settlement rights *and* pension rights) campaign and that he was asked by the Gurkha community to work for their settlement rights. Seen from the UK perspective, and certainly, from the perspective of the campaign, the right to settle in the UK was unequivocally good, whereas to have to live in Nepal was considered negative. However, in Nepal, the change from temporary migration to permanent Nepali diaspora in the UK could be considered a further loss to the country. Ironically, the mercenary debate could now be taken one step further. In the UK, the very granting of such rights – in continuation of distinctions such as the Conspicuous Gallantry Cross and the Victoria Cross – proved that Gurkhas were not mercenaries, whereas as seen from Nepal, the hard-won permanence of shifted loyalties could strengthen the argument that, perhaps, they were.

Gurkhas, *Janajati* and national identity politics

Linked to the British colonial politics of 'race' and its conflation with caste and ethnic groups in Nepal, the colonial construction of the Gurkhas has, over time, also gained political importance as an identity marker for those ethnic groups that were originally defined as 'martial' by the British, such as the Gurung, Limbu, Magar and the Rai. These ethnic groups have been referred to as *adivasi janajati* since the formation of Nepal Janajati Mahasangh in 1990. As pointed out by Hangen, while this has been part of the political discourse in Nepal, this label has also been challenged by some, including the Mongol National Organization (MNO) established by Gopal Gurung, who rejected the term due to its etymological base in 'jati', or caste, and who preferred the concept of 'race' instead (Hangen 2006). The MNO adopted the concept of 'Mongol race' as a common political identity across the same ethnic groups that the British identified as 'martial races' in their construction of the Gurkha soldier tradition. It claims that these groups constitute a 'Mongol race', which is racially distinct from the 'Aryan race', and that the former is *mulbasi* (indigenous). Such claims are, of course, intensely contested and constitute parts of present-day Nepali identity politics, but they also remind us of the power of symbols. By defining the ethnic groups as a Mongol race, Gopal Gurung was able to define his fight against inequity and discrimination in racial terms as a fight against apartheid. How groups of people are labelled, and which values are attributed to them, is of huge political significance. For MNO, the political vision was to create an umbrella political organisation for all the ethnic groups in Nepal.

Hangen (2010) has described the creation of MNO in detail and mentions the importance in that connection of a document entitled *Hidden Facts in Nepalese Politics*, written by Gopal Gurung in 1985, which led to his arrest and imprisonment during 1989–90. The document has been widely distributed by MNO supporters as well as by the Kathmandu-based 'Mulbasi Mongol Rastriya Yuwa Sabha' (Hangen 2010). In this document, which predicted the armed conflict in Nepal, Gurung attacked symbolic representations, such as popular festivals that were seen to represent the Hindu kingdom. The Hindus constituted a minority group of oppressors as opposed to the 'Buddhist Mongol race', which, he claimed, constitutes 80 per cent of the population (Gurung 1994). I mention this, not because I believe these figures are 'true',[6] but because the discussion of the Gurkhas is embedded in this larger contestation of what constitutes Nepal, who are the different Nepalese groups and what are Nepali symbols.

Gurung's political manifesto deals with the 'Gorkhas'[7] at length and creates an overlapping identity between the ethnic groups and the Gurkha soldiers; he even talks of 'the Gorkha race'. On the one hand, he replicates the themes of bravery, loyalty and martiality prominent in colonial discourse (Caplan 1991); on the other hand, he sees them as victims of a tripartite conspiracy, where they were exploited by the British, who historically have granted them very poor conditions in comparison to their British counterparts; they were repressed in the north-eastern states of India, where the 'Mongol race' constitutes a majority, and they were marginalised in their own country under the autocratic kingdom. Gurung writes: 'when I travelled extensively in Nepal to the villages of Tamu (Gurung), Magar, Sherpa, Tamang, Tharu, Dhimal, Limbu, Rai, Koch (Rajbansi), and studied their condition and unwritten history, to my dismay, I found these people neglected in every respect in every part of the nation. Some households were always under the yoke of poverty and they were always in debt even though their five or six family members were serving as mercenaries in foreign countries' (Gurung 1994). He defines 'Gorkha' soldiers as 'mercenaries' and the practice of joining the 'Gorkha' armies as one of deprivation of opportunities (e.g. for education) within Nepal and depletion of the Mongol villages: 'Our Mongol youths join the army after 17 years of age because of their poverty. They are deprived of a smooth academic life and they carry the impression of army life from their forefathers. They are exploited in all fields. They are made to stand in a vacuum of no hope, no future, but only to leave or migrate elsewhere. They have no alternative but to join the foreign army' (Gurung 1994). The manifesto of MNO clearly recommends that the recruitment should be stopped.

The political campaign of the MNO and that of the Gurkha Justice Campaign are entirely different in their objectives, but they share perceptions of the soldiers on two dimensions: (1) both describe the soldiers in a language that constitutes a direct continuation of the originally colonial perception of these 'martial races' and the related connotations of outstanding bravery, exemplified by anecdotes of individual hero soldiers; and (2) the soldiers are, at the same time, victims of intolerable discrimination within the British Army – even if the two positions do not agree on the nature of this discrimination. They arrive at opposite conclusions – one, that social justice means that Gurkhas should stay in

Britain permanently, the other, that they should never leave Nepal in the first place, but stay and be a part of a combined Mongol fight for social justice within the country.

Symbolic versus economic Gurkha capital

Let me now return to Turner's understanding of the symbolic properties of symbols. By observing the meaning attributed to the related concepts of Gurkha/Gorkha/Lahure from different perspectives, we have been able to discern their important differences. From a British postcolonial perspective, they are extraordinarily brave, diminutively British, extremely loyal, exclusively male, socially amicable, 'natural soldiers' and fierce in combat; the Gurkha Justice Campaign builds on these qualities to address that they are, simultaneously, victims of discrimination; much of this is echoed by MNO, which adds the labels of mercenaries, victims of poverty and being deprived of educational opportunities; the Nepali literary perspective, in contrast, focuses on emotional pain, negative social impact at home and war-related trauma; and the Maoists see the institution as a shame to the nation. Recalling Turner (1975: 155), this is indeed a multivocal complex of associations, both ambiguous, open-ended, and certainly emotionally laden, and open to Peircean interpretants from very different political quarters for sometimes overlapping, sometimes opposite and conflicting, readings and emotions.

In this chapter, I have pursued anthropology as a discipline of translation between different perspectives, but not translation that assumes identity of meaning. On the contrary, it has been an analysis of 'transduction' as discussed above – an effort to unfold different and conflicting perspectives on the Gurkha/Gorkha/Lahure tradition. The implication is that the Gorkhas (Nepali perspective) are not the same as the Gurkhas (British perspective), and they never were. In the process of defining the 'New Nepal', this difference of perspective has become a significant contested symbol of and to the country. The possible decision to entirely stop the recruitment may seem a logical next step. The UCPN (Maoist) leadership has often called for an end to the institution, linking it to mercenary activity due to the involvement of Gurkha regiments in contested wars such as in Iraq and Afghanistan, and, as mentioned in the introduction to this chapter, an all-party parliamentary committee in a draft report had recommended that recruitment in Nepal to Gurkha regiments abroad should be stopped.[8]

The draft report stated that the out-migration of about two million youths to countries other than India in search of livelihood opportunities was a serious problem to the country, even if remittances provided a substantial income to Nepal in general. Given this figure, the annual number of Gurkha recruits – in 2011, a total of 176 male recruits entered the British Army (Adhikary 2012) – seems insignificant. Yet, the recruitment of Gorkhas was given substantial importance in the document, not because of numbers, but because of its symbolic value. The report said: 'Although, principally, the operation of foreign policy in Nepal adopts a non-alliance policy, the provisions of the Nepali Gorkha recruitment centres in Britain and India have raised serious questions over Nepal's national integrity. The current situation demands that, to improve national pride, Nepal's foreign policy must give an appropriate alternative to the existing policies' (Parliamentary Committee on International Relations and Human Rights 2012).

Gurkhas have, over time, contributed considerably to the economic status of their families and hometowns in Nepal. Even if the annual recruitment is small, an estimated 25,000 ex-Gurkhas retired from the British Army generate an annual £87 million, or more than NPR 112 crore annually, and annual remittances from India are around 10 times this amount. Ironically, the success of the Gurkha Justice Campaign in Britain leading to the right for ex-Gurkhas to settle in the UK has added to the impetus to end the tradition. The report reads: 'With the decision of British Government to provide citizenship to the Gurkha recruits, Nepal is further losing from the decision, and needs to review its foreign policy regarding Gurkha recruitment (ibid.)'. Following the achievement of the right to settlement, a large number of ex-Gurkha families have left Nepal for the UK, leading to a drying up of remittances. In the case of old-age pension, it may only suffice to cover daily living costs in the UK, and therefore allowing more ex-Gurkhas to settle in the UK rather than leading to an increase of remittances to Nepal.

The question is how to weigh the economic loss against the symbolic gain inherent in a move to end the Gurkha tradition. Views are clearly divided on the issue whether the economic gains for Nepal outweigh the importance of the Gurkhas as an unwarranted national symbol. According to Baral, 'Economic benefits far outweigh the political considerations being mooted, especially in a country in transition . . . ' (quoted in Adhikary 2012). Baral finds the timing of debating the issue wrong, since Nepal is in a state of transition. Whether or not one agrees with this, timing *is* an issue, but symbolic and financial economies are not synchronous. If a substantial flow of remittances continues to be generated by the existing cohorts of Gurkha soldiers in the decades to come, a phased closure that also takes the interests of the involved ethnic groups into account may provide quick symbolic returns while only leading to a slow drying up of the financial benefits. On the contrary, if remittances are, in fact, drying up quickly due to the newly won rights of British Gurkhas, the tension between the symbolic and economic dimensions may diminish.

Notes

1 The draft document, which created a public stir, was subsequently removed from the website of the Parliamentary Commission and was no longer publicly available at the time of finalising this chapter.
2 The perspective Collett represents has also been reproduced in an essay on 'The British Gurkha Connection in the 1990s' (see Collett 1994).
3 My intention here is not to give a comprehensive overview of the subject of foreign army recruitment in Nepali literature – indeed, my discussion below is based on a selection of Nepali literature available in English.
4 A pseudonym for Bishnukumari Waiba.
5 In 2010, Gurkha veterans in Britain lost their case for an increase of pension for pre-1997 veterans at the High Court. The case was subsequently presented at the European Court of Human Rights.
6 Nor do I believe that it is 'true' when, e.g. CIA World Factbook claims that 80 per cent of the population is Hindu. https://www.cia.gov/library/publications/the-world-factbook/geos/np.html. Religious and ethnic identities may be more fluid than a simple census can capture (Gellner 2012).
7 'Gorkha' is spelled with 'o' in this section in accordance with the English translation of the original document. Generally, I have used 'Gorkha' to refer to Nepali soldiers (or soldiers of Nepalese origin) in the Indian Army, and 'Gurkhas' to refer to Nepalese soldiers in the British Army.
8 I am grateful to Mr. Avash Piya for partial translation of the report. However, it should be noted that the translation is unofficial and has not been sanctioned in any way by the Parliamentary Commission or otherwise. When the Constituent Assembly was dissolved, the document itself lost its status and can now be considered a document of historical interest. However, as such, it does represent a strong concern about the continuation of the Gurkha institution in its present form.

References

Adhikary, Dhruba. 2012. 'Maoist Nepal to End Gurkha Tradition', *Asia Times*, January 20.
Bishta, Daulat Bikram. 1993[1968]. 'The Andhi Khola', in M. Hutt (ed.), *Himalayan Voices: An Introduction to Modern Nepali Literature,* pp. 231–35. Berkeley: University of California Press.
Bornman, Elirea. 2006. 'National Symbols and Nation-building in the Post-Apartheid South Africa', *International Journal of Intercultural Relations,* 30(3): 383–99.
Brown, Martyn. 2008. 'Gurkhas Face Ban from British Army', *Daily Express*, May 29.
Caplan, Lionel. 1991. ' "Bravest of the Brave": Representations of "the Gurkha" in British Military Writings', *Modern Asian Studies,* 25(3): 571–97.

Carroll, Peter. 2012. *Gurkha: The True Story of a Campaign for Justice*. London: Biteback Publishing.
Cerre, Mike. 1992. *Gurkhas in Special Forces*. Discovery Channel.
Collett, N. 1994. 'The British Gurkha Connection in the 1990s', in M. Hutt (ed.), *Nepal in the Nineties: Versions of the Past, Visions of the Future*, pp. 98–105. New Delhi: Oxford University Press.
Encyclopedia Britannica online. 2012. mercenary 2012, http://www.britannica.com/EBchecked/topic/375662/mercenary. Accessed on 31 May 2012.
Gellner, David N. 2012. 'Fluidity, Hybridity, Performativity: How Relevant are Social Scientific Buzzwords for Nepal's Constitution Building?', in C. Mishra and O. Gurung (eds), *Ethnicity and Federalization in Nepal*, pp. 91–102. Kathmandu: Central Dept of Sociology/Anthropology, Tribhuvan University.
Gurung, Gopal. 1994. *Hidden Facts in Nepalese Politics*. Translated by B. D. Rai. 4th ed. Kathmandu: Gopal Gurung.
Hangen, Susan I. 2006. 'The emergence of a Mongol Race in Nepal', *Anthropology News*, 47(2): 12.
———. 2010. *The Rise of Ethnic Politics in Nepal: Democracy in the Margins*. Routledge Contemporary South Asia Series No 25. London/New York: Routledge.
Harris, Paul, and Michael Smith. 2001. ' "Maoist rebels" Joining Gurkhas in Plot to Destroy the Brigade', *Telegraph*, January 18.
Hutt, Michael. 1989. 'A Hero or a Traitor? The Gurkha Soldier in Nepali Literature', *South Asia Research*, 9(1): 21–32.
Inden, Ronald B. 1990. *Imagining India*. Oxford: Basil Blackwell.
Kochhar-George, C. S. 2010. 'Nepalese Gurkhas and Their Battle for Equal Rights', *Race & Class*, 52(2): 43.
Merriam-Webster online. 2012. *Mercenary* 2012, http://www.merriam-webster.com/dictionary/mercenary. Accessed on 1 April 2012.
Mukherjeee, Krittivas. 2008. 'Pride or Money – Nepal's Gurkhas at Moral Crossroads', *Daily Times*, April 25.
Onta, Pratyoush. 1994. 'Dukha During the World War', *Himal*, 7(6): 24–29.
Parijat. 2010[1972]. *Blue Mimosa*. Translated by Tanka Vilas Varya. Kathmandu: Orchid Books.
Parliamentary Committee on International Relations and Human Rights. 2012. Nepal's Foreign Policy in the Changed Context (Draft). Kathmandu.
Peirce, Charles Sanders. 1931. *Collected Papers of Charles Sanders Peirce*. Harvard: University Press.
Rai, Shiv Kumar. 1993[1968]. 'The Murderer' (*Jyanmara?*), in M. Hutt (ed.), *Himalayan Voices: An Introduction to Modern Nepali Literature*, pp. 224–30. Berkeley: University of California Press.
Rathaur, Kamal Raj Singh. 2006. 'British Gurkha Recruitment: A Historical Perspective', *Voice of History*, 16(2): 19–24.
Sarkar, Sudesha. 2005. 'Nepal Ultras Abduct 14 Gorkhas of Indian Army', *Deccan Herald*, January 16.
Turner, Victor. 1975. 'Symbolic Studies', *Annual Review of Anthropology*, 4: 145–61.

Vines, Alex. 1999. 'Gurkhas and the Private Security Business in Africa', in J. Cilliers and P. Mason (eds), *Peace, Profit or Plunder. The Privatisation of Security in War-Torn African Societies,* pp. 123–40. Halfway House: Institute for Security Studies.

Viveiros de Castro, E. 2004. 'Perspectival Anthropology and the Method of Controlled Equivocation', *Tipití: Journal of the Society for the Anthropology of Lowland South America,* 2(1): 1.

Wooldridge, Ian. 1995. *The Gurkhas.* London: BBC.

5

MYTHICAL ENTRAPMENT OF THE SELF AND THE NOTION OF NEPALI DIASPORA

Pravesh G. Jung

The discourse on diaspora finds its origin within the orthodox boundaries of Jewish experience, and as Cohen holds, the term, in its classical use was, in fact, only used in its grammatical singular form (Cohen 2008: 1). This singularity was, of course, lost by the 1970s due to a systematic project of expansion that aimed at expanding the denoting power of the term to accommodate groups other than the Jews under the diaspora banner, and the term 'diaspora' began to appear in its plural form, denoting – apart from the Jews – the Africans, Armenians, the Irish, and then later, the Palestinians. This expansion in the extension of the meaning of the term was justified, and its use augmented, on the rationale of an experience of victimhood that, though had its origins in the traumatic experience of displacement brought about through force, exercised in a medium of oppression, was nevertheless held to be shared by other diasporic groups in question as well (Cohen 1996: 512). Thus, in the early phase of the expansionist project, if on the one hand, the accentuation of the idea of victimhood unified the various diasporas despite their diverse sociopolitical and economic reasons that had historically provided the impetus for their respective dispersion from their places of origin, it also, on the other hand, institutionalised the Jewish diaspora as a paradigmatic case of a diaspora by virtue of marking the Jewish displacement and their experience of loss as a defining criterion of a diaspora.

A review of available literature makes us aware that by the beginning of the 1980s, the term 'diaspora', which was till then, a term with fairly defined boundaries in its usage, started to lose its demarcating marks and soon gave way to academic vagueness that emerged due to the expansive academic orientation, which, in its second wave during the 1990s, intended to further expand the defining boundaries of the term to include displaced groups other than the ones named earlier, as being legitimately marked by the adjective, *diasporic*. This second phase of the expansionist project created ripples within the discourse on diaspora by challenging the very contours of the meaning of this hitherto more or less demarked term, consequently forcing scholars of diaspora to reimagine the idea of *diaspora* and the notion of the *diasporic*. The challenge posed by this reimagining of the conceptual boundary of the term 'diaspora' was precisely to maintain *some* boundary that could demarcate a legitimate usage of the term so as to retain the meaningfulness of the term itself. Thus, the looming fear among some scholars of diaspora was that an overzealous expansion of the term might simply render the term hollow, depriving it of any connotative powers, and thus, robbing it of all significance. Therefore, the efforts of scholars such as James Clifford, Khachig Tölölyan, Robin Cohen, William Safran, to name a few, have been steadily directed towards reimagining the extended space signified by the term 'diaspora', so that it remains meaningful, and yet, more inclusive than its orthodox predecessor. One must cautiously note that this task of reimagining the conceptual boundary of the term is not so much a move to retain the purity of the concept of diaspora, but rather, a move to legitimise and provide some stability to the term. For instance, Tölölyan's addressing the danger of the term as 'becoming a promiscuously capacious category' when 'taken to include all the adjacent phenomena to which it is linked but from which it actually differs in ways that are constitutive (and his efforts to) in fact make a viable definition of diaspora possible' (Tölölyan 1996: 8) is an attempt in this direction. The legitimacy of this effort can be seen if one agrees that a predicative term, after all, in its usage as a presentational tool, requires some bone and cannot afford to be mere tongue, for it requires some form of rigidity too, unless one is to hold that all symbolic presentations are mere linguistic representations with no ontological basis. Working on Safran's list of indicative features of a diaspora, the 'consolidated list of the "common features" of a diaspora, drawing on the classical tradition' that Cohen provides us, or his categorisation of diaspora into Weberian *ideal types* as a tool to classify diasporas, 'by using a qualifying adjective (like) – victim, labour, imperial, trade and deterritorialized' to qualify a diaspora to aid us in the 'typologizing and classifying various diasporas, not by ignoring what they share in common, but by highlighting their most important characteristics' (Cohen 2008: 15–16) are attempts made in the hope of stabilising the sense of the term 'diasporic' in its more evolved and recent accommodative *avatar*.

This brief tour of the history of the term 'diaspora' and the emphasis on the expansionist project is of importance here because the very construction of the category of the Nepali diaspora, if it is constructed at all, must hinge itself precisely on to the framework of the expansionist project made available by the scholars of diaspora. This is to argue that the very possibility of the category of *diasporic* Nepalis, if there can be one, must see itself situated within the expansionist project and as essentially partaking in an extension or appropriation of the expansionist meaning of the term, 'diaspora'. This acknowledgement of the rootedness of the possibility of the diasporic Nepalis can be historically argued for since we do not find the idea of 'Nepali diaspora', either in *etic* or *emic* discourse about the Nepali population outside Nepal until the 1990s. Further, it can be seen that most of these claims of being diasporic after the 1990s are still largely confined to *emic* claims.[1] Further, the claims of the category of a Nepali diaspora 'go hand in hand with the surge in international labour migration that emerged from the end of the 1990s onwards' (Bruslé 2012: 4). The 1990s marked their large-scale migration to other countries apart from India, in various capacities. However, without even any hint of privileging the *etic* over the *emic* on my part, it must be acknowledged that mere *self-declared claims* of being diasporic does not legitimise the attribution of the predicate *diaspora* to the corpus of the immigrated population as this move of legitimisation would simply fail to recognise that the politics of recognition requires the *significant other* to acknowledge that predication as a legitimate one, too. A failure to recognise this demand of politics of recognition would allow *any*-body to become *any*-body, resulting in a collapse of all sensible structures of meaningful social predications. Thus, the fundamental question that emerges here is – *is a Nepali diaspora possible within the expansionist's project,* and as a corollary, *is it possible to talk of a Nepali diaspora legitimately within the diasporic discourse?*

Notwithstanding the postmodern critique of the discourse on diaspora, which has a tendency to celebrate the state of being diasporic in stark contrast to the orthodox paradigmatic lament of victimhood evoked in one's imagination of the Jews, the notion of a 'homeland' has remained central, though in various shades, to the very notion of diaspora throughout its interesting history. For instance, though Cohen's list of the 'common features' of a diaspora are not to be taken as a set of essences of a diaspora, and are more to be seen through the lenses of what the Austrian philosopher, Ludwig Wittgenstein called *family-resemblances*, it is nevertheless important to observe that central to Cohen's listed 'common features' of a diaspora is the idea of a space called 'homeland'. It would be hard to miss noticing that this space is also central to all the five *ideal types* of diaspora, as categorised by Cohen, though he emphatically stresses that 'homelands have to be considered as multifaceted, historically contingent and socially constructed entities' (2008: 123). Likewise, even Gabriel Sheffer's proposed criteria for the identification of diaspora (1986), though arguing for an expansion of the meaning of the term 'diaspora' to include other diasporas apart from the Jewish diaspora, nevertheless maintains the centrality of the notion of homeland. In fact, it is hard not to see that even those who have contested the rigidity of the demand of a homeland in terms of a geographically marked space such as a home-nation for a legitimate predication of being diasporic, have consequently argued for an alternative and a more accommodating notion in its place, rather than completely doing away with the notion of a 'homeland'. The same point can also be emphasised with reference to the notion of 'dispersion', a notion that is central to the notion of diaspora. The notion of 'dispersion' essentially marks the diasporic with a necessary movement, thereby demanding a space that enables movement *from* and *to*. Notwithstanding the differences of opinions that lie in the marking of the contours of this space and the christening of this space, the necessity of this space is what, I believe, underlies all discourses on diaspora. That is to argue that the necessity of this space is a *formal* condition for any discourse on diaspora.

Thus, though one can argue for more fluid notions that signify the space designated by the terms *home* or home-*land*, one cannot do away with the notion completely. Thus, for instance, in an attempt to explore the possibilities of queer female diasporic subjectivity and to challenge the conventional routes of framing diasporas, Gayatri Gopinath (2005) does not wish away the notion of this space while capturing and moulding the production of the complexity of relations that can be grasped between the notions of sexuality of queer people, though this space may no longer have the ontological status of the nation to which one longs to return, or the notion of an original nation state. The inevitability of this space emerges due to the demand for a locus that can harbour, hinge, mobilise and provide the grounds for both the notion of *hope* and the feeling of *alienation* that is central to both the notions of *displacement* and *diaspora*.

The idea of a homeland can, thus, be understood in a formal manner as the space that defines the locus of one's repository of both longing and alienation. It is the encountering of this space that enables one to encounter oneself as fragmented from the 'host-land' and provides the fragmented self an individuated identity that enables one to see oneself as being not merely *distinct,* but also *different*. The notion of *home* can thus be seen as characterising this space as that where the self is at one with itself and as opposed to the conditions that bring about the fragmentation of the self. Thus, the idea of *home* provides a sense of comfort and freedom to encounter one's self as oneself. Further, the notion of diaspora, in all its shades, not only necessitates the fragmentation of the self from its surrounding selves to materialise the awareness of one being *different*, but also calls into play the possibility of the space of the *homeland* precisely because the fragmentation of the self is mediated through the encountering of significant others that forces the self to realise its own self so as to contrast it with other selves. It is this space of the homeland that provides the possibility to the self to encounter its own self as well. It is for this pivotal reason that the formal condition of 'homeland' appears as a constitutive constituent of the notion of diaspora, though the notion need not entail the signification of a concrete spatial entity such as a nation state, or a land of origin.

To further explore the nature of this space and its essential characteristics, I take a slight detour here to highlight Vijay Mishra's neologism of 'imaginary diasporic', which draws its sustenance from the works of Jacques Lacan and Slavoj Žižek, as a welcoming aid to help me drive my point home. Mishra predicates the attribute of 'imaginary' to the notion of diaspora, where the term 'imaginary' entails both in 'its original Lacanian sense . . . and therefore characterised by a residual narcissism, resemblance and homeomorphism . . . and in its more flexible current usage, as found in the works of Slavoj Zizek . . . as the state of identification with the image in which we appear likeable to ourselves, with the image representing "what we would like to be"' (2007: 14). Mishra's idea of the *imaginary* makes it clear that like the Lacanian *Ideal-I,* which is the image of the self that the self can never materialise, the space of homeland is an image held by diasporic self that can never materialise. Just as the *Ideal-I,* that the self identifies itself with, is never in complete conformity with the subject's actual experience of itself, the space denoted by this *homeland* of the diasporic can never be mapped unto the contours of the real lived space.[2] However, one need not look at the notion of the 'imaginary' as a frustrating enterprise, but rather, read it as an enabling factor that allows for projections of the self and the directions for its endeavours. Thus, though the homeland may not correspond to any existent reality, it is nevertheless essential to any diaspora for the sake of its own projection even if it is, in a sense, 'fictional' and a construct. Its 'fictionality', therefore, is not to be seen as something opposed to the 'real', but rather, as an enabling force to move along and make sense of one's existential reality and in the formulation of identities by the self for itself. In its allied sense, the *imaginary* also entails that the image of the self is something that is worth striving for since the *image* represents what *the self would like to be*. This immediately brings about the division between what the self *is* and what it *ought* to be. Thus, though the space of 'homeland' may be descriptive in its appearance, it is, in fact, prescriptive in its nature given that it prescribes the self – *be like this* – rather than merely describe to it – *this is who you are*.

This enables us, at the least, to recognise the space denoted by the term 'homeland', but we must also be cautious here to clearly mark that the image that acts as the locus of the *diasporicness* of the diaspora is clearly distinct from any personal prescriptive image that I may construe for myself. For unlike these private subjective images that I may have for myself – both in terms of my actuality (who I think I am) and my projection (who I intend to be) – the diasporic image is, and must essentially be, *a-personal* and must necessarily transcend the individual.

Thus, though the image of this *homeland* neither needs to be *constructed* within the bounds of my subjectivity nor needs to be actually experienced by me, it demands that I existentially accept it as an imperative image that I *have* – though as a *given* in the social reality that I happen to exist in, and whose significance and appearance is itself historically shaped by this very construct. Thus, the diasporic image is not something that I construct and share, but is rather a shared image in which we all find locus *for who we are* and *what we must strive to be*, not just as an individual, but rather, as a collective that participates in the space constituted by this image. However, this transcendent nature of the image cannot be taken to entail an ascription of a higher reality to it. On the contrary, the image of the homeland, if left to itself without the commitment and participation of the diasporic selves, would lose all significance. The very being of the image of a homeland surges into existence through the conscious recognition of the selves that participate in the shared space of this image. Thus, in this sense, the notion of diaspora can begin its operation only through a reflexive idea of identifying the image as one's own and in the acceptance of the prescription that is entailed by the acceptance of this image. Through the lenses of diaspora, the consciousness of this diasporic image is a matter of knowing what is being offered by the image and then internalising it as one's own. It is, I would argue, this act of sharing the *image* that transforms the multitude of particular diasporic selves into a collective subject, thereby providing a collective identity.

Of course, treating this image of homeland as the *imaginary* is not to deny it the historical basis and the actual experiences carried by the individuals who were a part of that diasporic moment, but we should be careful not to equate the personal experiences of the individual and their memories with the collectively shared image of this space. One can also view this distinction as marking the difference between *nostalgia* from the idea of diasporic *longing*. To elucidate this marked difference, one could appropriate Jan Assmann's distinction between individual memory and collective memory in terms of 'the autobiographical memory of the individual looking back from certain vantage point over his own life, and the posthumous commemoration of him by posterity' (2011: 19). For Assmann, this distinction holds since, unlike in cases of individual memory, the posthumous commemoration of an individual by posterity is a collective effort of the group to retain the dead as a living being among them through the act of collective memory. Thus, Assmann's distinction between individual and collective memory is in resonance with our distinction between *nostalgia* and the idea of diasporic *longing* since this *longing* is not a subject's revisiting its own subjective past, but rather, the *upholding* of something shared and partaking in it. It is also in this sense that the diasporic image of the homeland provides the diasporic subject with the imperative to uphold and own a certain shared image with the prescriptive force *not to forget it,* thus lending it a shade of memory, though it, in fact, is not one.

In the light of the space of the 'homeland' as necessarily characterised as being distinct from a nostalgic personal memory for the very possibility of a Nepali diaspora, by and large, I am not sure if there is such a clear distinction between the nostalgic recollections of one's past and the notion of a collective *longing* for the homeland that is either in operation or even conceived, by those who are held to be belonging to the Nepali diaspora.[3] Barring a few, the idea of a common shared diasporic image with *a-personal* markers of space and time seems to be largely absent among them. For a large section of the members claiming the identity of a Nepali diaspora, the diasporic image largely seems to be constituted by and/or anchored upon spatial and temporal memory markers. But if we come to agree that the notion of a space is a formal condition of diaspora, then how does the Nepali diaspora define this space and what are the contours of defining this space? The legitimacy of the claim of the Nepali diaspora would have to first and foremost address this challenge in hand.

The first challenge in addressing this issue arises from the *conscious self-emphasis* on the cultural differences, and thus, from the existing emphatic force on the differences between the various ethnic groups in Nepal. This self-conscious emphasis translates itself into a daunting question of how those who are now outside Nepal, come up with a *uniform* shared image of the homeland without compromising their rootedness in their distinct cultural ethnicity. Or even more fundamental would be the question: can they ever discover such a uniform diasporic image for themselves or would this image be essentially heterogeneous, given the self-conscious emphasis on diversity? Of course, this task of discovering of the diasporic image must be done by the diasporic Nepalis themselves for it is, as already discussed, only in the encountering of the significant others that the self fragments, opening up the possibility of reflecting upon and forging its own identity and what *it must not forget*.[4]

In absence of such an articulate diasporic image, at best, we may call the Nepali diaspora an incipient one. Of course, one may argue that I stress far too much, and thereby privilege, the homogeneousness of this image of the *homeland* and ignore the possibility that this image of the homeland may itself have to accommodate such ethnic differences. I must emphasise that this charge tends to overlook the fact that it privileges the heterogeneousness over the possibility of homogeneousness of the image of the homeland. Thus, this charge misses the point that this privileging of the heterogeneousness of the image of the homeland also entails the privileging of the heterogeneousness of the experiences by the diasporic self that partakes in this heterogeneous image. It thereby negates the very possibility of a peculiar, yet a shared, space of *common experiences*, or at the least, makes it too vague to garnish the strength of capturing the imagination of the self to identify itself with this image. The primacy of the ethnic, and therefore of heterogeneousness, entails that my experiences would never be free from the ethnic colours that I am equipped with or share, and consequently, renders the possibility of any experiences that transcend such ethnic lenses as highly dubious – if not an outright impossibility. It might therefore lead, if the heterogeneousness prevails over the homogeneousness of the image of the homeland, to a construal of multiple Nepali diasporas.

However, even if undermining this fear of the impossibility of a shared image among the Nepali diaspora, we do assume that the Nepali diaspora already shares and upholds such a homogenous image it must yet fulfil, for the formation of a recognised diaspora, the second formal condition of being recognised as being diasporic. This second condition lies in the recognition of this diasporic image by the *significant other*, that is, by members of the host land who do not belong to this diaspora. This, I feel, is the inevitable challenge to be addressed for the very possibility of the Nepali diaspora. The looming challenge, therefore, is to negate any image presenting the Nepali self in the conception of the significant others within a diasporic space that might render the Nepali self as being encountered as non-diasporic. This challenge brings to the foreground the pivotal principle that individuals are experienced, encountered and made sense of by an 'other' and that this encountering of the self by the significant other is a fundamental aspect of any identity formation.[5] The importance of addressing this challenge is anchored not merely because of the demands of politics of recognition and the demands of meaningful discourse that were discussed earlier, but also because it is in this expressed sense of *how* and *what* others encounter me *as* that my identity emerges in my reflections as a problematic. It is through this encountering of the self as a self in the expressions of the significant others that the self ruptures and fragments, making room for reflective formations of self-identities, including the discovery and the realisation of the diasporic image. As Assmann underlines, though in a different context, 'experience of oneself is always mediated; (and that) only experience of the others is direct. Just as we are unable to see our face except in a mirror, we are unable to see our inner self other (than) by reflection, and it is the latter that creates awareness. Contact with others also entails contact with ourselves, and the self of personal identity is simply not available to us without communication and interaction . . . (it is) contact with others (that) lead to the formation of identity . . .' (2011: 116). Towards this end, for the Nepali diaspora, the challenge therefore lies in allowing oneself to be encountered as identical to being experienced as a *Gurkha*,[6] which is, by and large the case, not merely among many significant others, but also among the diasporic Nepalis themselves.

The primary reason for this confusion in identity is that a large section of the Nepalese who migrated in the early 19th century did so under the banner of the well-known Gurkha regiments, and hence, the Nepali diasporas have always been encountered within the bounded identity as mercenaries. The prevalence of encountering the Nepali self as a Gurkha, thus, confuses a professional identity of a self and superimposes this identity as the identity of the Nepali self *as such*. The issue here is not merely the occurrence of the logical fallacy of taking a part to represent the whole, but is rather the unwelcome effect that it brings about by barring all other aspects of the Nepali self and her experiences from the significant other, consequently rendering impossible the encountering of the Nepali self *as such* by the significant other. This image, thus, needs to be steadily negated as the chief marker of the experience in which the significant other encounters and identifies the Nepali diaspora, given the fact that not all of them are Gurkhas, which is a marker of a profession, paradigmatically entailing the predicates of the *brave* and the *loyal*.

These terms found transnational currency during the colonial period of the British Raj in India. Responding to the challenges that the British colonisation of India faced in terms of comprehending the colonised land, the British deployed the epistemic tools of working with neat categories, but they were not merely making an epistemic move in their categorisations; rather, they used these categories ideologically to justify their political ends. Take, for instance, the category of *barbarism*, which was, as is argued by Nicholas Dirks (2002), at first a missionary preoccupation, but was then 'progressively converted to other colonial uses when it failed to be a useful tool in its deployment in the hands of the missionaries, as an important justification for the military and the police on the one hand, and for the establishment of the new ideology of the Empire on the other' (2002: 176). The category of 'barbarism' was, as Dirks argues, selectively deployed, with a decreased degree of passion as compared to the missionaries and the category manifested itself even after the 1860s, which was a period marked by an enthused seeking of information about the Indian society to help the formulation of official colonial policies. As Meena Radhakrishna argues (2008), in the Indian context, the 'developing disciplines of anthropometry and anthropology . . . (that) addressed themselves to the study of particular sections of the Indian population, mostly indigenous "tribal communities" and itinerant groups . . . on bizarre or exotic ritual aspects of the social life of such communities, and at the same time also on their differential anthropometric measurements . . . (steadily created) the categories of the civilized and the barbaric individual' (2008: 3–4).

Similarly, it was post-1857 that the third category of the 'martial race' emerged forcefully. It is not surprising to find that the category of the 'martial race' shares its grounds with the category of the 'criminal' in so far as it dominantly echoes the voice of Eugenicism or that of something being hereditary to a section of the populace. The 1857 revolt episode led the British government to appoint a commission headed by Major General Peel, to examine the organisation of the Indian Army, as the army had a significant role to play in the revolt, and it was at this juncture that the colonial theories about the 'martial races' of India found their most forceful formulations. Though, as Dirks notes, Macaulay had long provided the impetus of the general observation of certain groups in India that were particularly well-suited for military endeavours, it was only post-1857 that the colonial recruitment policy became specifically tied to ethnographic classifications. By the 1880s, the effect of this constructed category was that, on the one hand, it led to a steady and progressive diminution of the Madras Army, whose members were, by this dominant category, 'inherently unwarlike'; and on the other hand, it led to the steady and progressive rise in the numbers of recruitments of the Sikhs, Pathans and the Gurkhas. The martial race theory was duly codified by the 1880s in a series of official 'recruiting handbooks' for different classes of the Indian Army and they continued to appear and guide the Empire's recruiting policy in India until the last days of their stay in India. Eden Vansittart's *Gurkha Handbook for the Indian Army* and MacMunn's *The Martial Races of India* can serve as representatives of these handbooks. MacMunn and many other commentators of the theory of martial races held most of the martial races to hail from the north, which included predominantly Punjabis, Sikhs, Dogras, Rajputs, Pathans and the Gurkhas. These handbooks, which served more as guides-for-dummies for recruitment purposes, bring to light the carefully crafted descriptions of the *martial races* such as the Sikhs, Gurkhas and the Pathans as 'having a natural respect for authority and a high military fidelity and loyalty' (Dirks 2002: 179). As seen from the very initial stages of the growing obsession of the theory of the martial races, the south of India did not manage to make it to this class due to 'their disloyalty and their stance towards authority'. Though these 'virtues' of the 'martial races' were probably based on the experiences of their loyalty during the 1857 revolt of the sepoys, it was implicitly based on the conviction that these martial races were hereditarily thick-headed, and hence, inferior and incapable of any anti-colonial ideologies (Dirks 2002: 179). The degree of seriousness with which the theory of martial races was taken can be gauged from the fact these handbooks of recruitment had several tips and trick questions to establish the recruit's ethnic roots through a mode of gauging his conformity with the qualities described and desired of a martial race (Dirks 2002: 179). In fact, so strong was the belief in the martial race theory, especially when it pertained to the Gurkhas, that they were selected to be a part of the British Army even after the Indian independence, and even in face of counterfactual evidence of non-loyalty to the crown.[7]

The lengthy discussion on the colonial category is undertaken here to highlight that these social categorisations, apart from being descriptive tools, implicitly prescribe an orientation in which an 'other' *ought* to encounter members belonging to a category. Thus, the category of the 'martial' or the 'criminal' too orients a mode for the significant other to encounter an individual belonging to a 'criminal' or a 'martial' race. However, the question here is not whether the Gurkhas were really martial or not. Rather, it is: who chose these identity markers and how did they gain worldwide acceptability? Thus, the question here is not of *truth* per se, but of the process through which the term systematically acquired its sense and provided a mode of encountering certain selves.

One of the many ways in which a category can acquire the desired meaning is through the modes of narratives that centre around the category that is sought to be circulated. Narratives can be designed to implant the vocabulary and the associated predicates implied by a category much in the same way inert symbols gather meaning and significance through circulation within a culture. Narratives often enable the association of certain predicates to be associated with a specific word. It is also through narratives that 'values' circulate and find currency within a form-of-life. The significations of ritualistic symbols within a specific culture can be seen as an instantiation of the point that I intend to drive home here. It must be stressed that, in itself, a narration is complete and independent of the 'truth-value' attached to it. A narrative, in itself, is neither true nor false; its truth-value demands validation procedures external to it. To hold the truth-value of a narrative as a necessary constituent of the narrative itself is a product of our obsession with the 'scientific truth'. This obsession overlooks the fact that narratives can have purposes other than the pursuit of truth and can also be seen as a meaning generating medium – as *myths*[8] that enable one to navigate the sphere of one's experiences. Myths are narratives too and a locus of meaning constructions. When viewed thus, a myth opens up the exploration of other functions of a narrative.

Here, I intend to bring to light the 'affective' function of the myth of the Gurkha in terms of the mode in which a Gurkha self encounters itself and is encountered by the significant other. This usage of the term *myth* must be brought to the foreground because it leaves aside the concerns of validation of the account found in these narratives or in the history of Nepal written by classical Western Gurkha scholars such as Brook Northey,[9] which describe the Gurkhas and their qualities, not because of the fact that history of the colonised was often confused with anthropology, and that by the late 19th century, knowledge 'was produced by or in terms of the logics of colonial rule, (and) the imperatives and institutions of the colonial state' (Dirks 2002: 194), but rather, because we simply do not intend to fall prey to the 'truth-trap' of the narrative. Questions of predications and their accuracy are not of pivotal concern here. Rather, we would like to force ourselves into questions of affections brought about by the widespread circulation of this dominant discourse of the Indian colonisers. It is of some importance that we pay close heed to this because it is this colonial myth that has crafted the contours that define the popular mode in which the Nepali diaspora is largely construed, and encountered, by the significant other.

Thus, though after independence, the Indian government did repeal the Criminal Tribe Act, 'the stigma attached to them persisted (since) the members of the public and the police continued (and continue) to look at them as criminals' (Devy et al. 2013: 5). The plight of the so-called 'Denotified tribes' in the 21st century strengthens our claim that a social categorisation, apart from being a descriptive tool, implicitly prescribes an orientation in which an 'other' *ought* to encounter members belonging to a category. Thus, the category of the 'martial' or the 'criminal' too orients a mode of encounter for the significant other while encountering those thus categorised. In the colonial constructs of categories, the *projected* descriptive predicates attributed to the Gurkhas, which were useful colonial constructs, transform into an *essence* of the entity that was being merely described. Thus, the Goojars or the Koravas were *essentially* criminal in nature while the Gurkhas were *essentially* brave, loyal and obedient. The blurring may simply seem to be a play of words, but it is not, for there is a marked difference in the claims that one *believes* that the Gurkhas are brave, loyal and obedient and that they *in fact are* brave, loyal and obedient, *essentially*. It is this blurring and the acceptance of this fused reality, either consciously or unconsciously, that has resulted in the transformation of what was a colonial construct – *a description* – into an essential *prescription* for a group membership. Thus, in a sense, within the ambit of the theory of martial races, 'Gurkhas' was not a mere denoter of a class, but a denoter of a specific class with a specific set of qualities predicated to the class. The term 'Gurkha', under the colonial category of the 'martial race', was a disguised evaluative term rather than being a mere descriptive denoter.

Thus, the name 'Gurkha' inevitably summons its ordained adjectives such as *courageous*, *brave* and *loyal*, and unlike ordinary names, these predications are unambiguous and render the name incomplete without them. In a sense, the term implicates these qualities in its very occurrence. Such adjectival bonds implicated by a noun, I hold, set up certain pressing boundaries for the self that is identified, or identifies itself with, as the bearer of such a denoter and that these confines are difficult to violate or absolve and transcend. In a sense, they entrap the self that identifies itself with, or is identified with, them. This is the reason I feel that the bigger challenge for the possibility of a Nepali diaspora, apart from the possibility of having a uniform image of the homeland among themselves, given their rootedness in conscious ethnic differences, is the challenge of erasing this historically constructed idea of the Gurkha, not merely because they are encountered thus by the significant others, but rather, and more importantly, because in the present day, the Nepali self too seems to encounter itself through this colonial orientation, thus bringing to the foreground the fact that we have somehow managed to lose our sense of self altogether.

Anti-colonial reformers such as Paulo Freire have constantly argued for the way in which the notion of the *native's* self-image changes postcolonial discourses. For Freire, a colonial discourse invariably touches the notion of the 'self' of the 'native' and makes an implicit attempt to alter it. Gandhi's *Hind Swaraj* too argues against the colonial rule on the grounds that the colonial rule systematically amounts to the loss of the *authentic* self. Both Freire and Gandhi argue that the colonial discourses alter the sociopolitical consciousness of individuals situated within those models. They argue that these discourses, centred as they are on categories, are themselves colonial constructs and are, thus, tools of securing the regime of the oppressed by indoctrinating the oppressed to structurally conform and uphold the structure of the oppressor. They argue that the colonial discourses enable colonialism for they enable the loss of the native's self. For them, the loss of the self is the most violent of the violence that colonialism inflicts upon the colonised. What I intend to emphasise here is that this loss of the self need not be necessarily brought about through explicit modes of oppression. Moreover, an explicit mode of oppression might lead to a strengthening of self-identity among the oppressed, and thereby, ignite the image of the oppressor as being distinct from the self (the oppressed, in this case). This danger can be foreclosed if it is introduced rather discreetly through a mode of narrative that is acceptable to both the dominant and the dominated, as it was done in the case of the Nepalis through the narrative of the martial Gurkha race. The erasure of the authentic self can be brought about through the construction of an image of the self that is acceptable to both the dominant and the dominated – an image of the self that the self willingly imposes upon itself. In this mode of self-erasure, a narrative is engaged in the genesis of an identity for the other that is acceptable to the other whose identity it is intended to be. Hence, such a narrative locates itself within an acceptable nexus of values or predicates attached to the construed and externally imposed identity. Such an attempt intends to fabricate a 'me' for an 'I' that the 'I' is willing to conform to. Such discourses do not dwell upon the notions of authenticity, but rather, upon the notion of conformity. The discourse of the Gurkhas and the theory of the martial races, as already seen, hinges upon the values of *bravery*, *honour* and the *obedience*, which have their history in the Empire, where courage has been closely upheld as a virtue, as is clearly manifested in the history of the institutionalisation of the Victoria Cross and other medals and honours for courage. Thus, these common predicates placed the 'me' of the colonised in complete conformity with the expectations of the colonial 'I'. The transposed virtues through the narratives provide a measure against which the colonised ought to measure their colonised 'selves'. This imposition loses its harsh shade of dominance since the world order, conceptually constructed, generates an identity not through the ploy of difference, but through the ploy of shared values in which both the dominant and the dominated partake.

Following Deschamps' work on social identity, one could argue that since both the dominant and dominated are defined through common values that are constructed and imposed through narratives by the dominant, it is systematically appropriated by the dominated over a period of time, leading to the distortion of the autonomy of the 'me' while giving it a sense of pseudo-autonomy through this superimposition (2010: 88). Thus, the membership to the group based on values so constructed by the dominant – though shared – nevertheless entails unequal membership, for while the image of the self as experienced by itself and the *construed image* are homogeneous for the dominant group, this is not essentially so for the dominated, and thus, the dominated group has the possibility of generating a pathological conflict due to this vague sense of identity that it might develop. The unequal membership to the group also emerges in the light of the fact that the dominated always has a set of complimentary characteristics that is absent from the dominant self. It is this complimentary set of marks that is essentially present in the dominated, that ensures the regality and the supremacy of the dominant self over the dominated self.

Here, we should also reflect upon the conceptual violence a word such as 'courage' does to the imagination of the 'space' by entrapping the experience of the self by the significant others in the 21st century. The important issue that must be underlined here is that the colonial theory of the martial race, in the case of the Gurkhas, blurred their ontological reality from the coloniser's constructed reality about them, which were propagated through the narrative that were constructed by them to strengthen the basis and the boundaries of the martial category. Thus, the attributes of brave, loyal and obedient cemented themselves as characteristic markers of the Gurkhas through the colonial narratives and it was, and to a large extent still is, the dominant mode in which we get encountered within any claimed diasporic space.

Thus, it would be, as has been argued by Hutt, an arduous task for the Nepali diasporic self to hold on to the claim of a legitimate diaspora since the historical baggage of the dispersion of the Nepalis would surely fall short of encompassing the entire space that is now populated by the Nepalis claiming diasporic status. The Nepali self would have to steadily overcome the encountering of herself within the confines of the colonial categorisation as a 'Gurkha' by both her own self and by the significant other within the diasporic space. The entrapment of the Nepali self within the confines of this colonial categorisation would not only burden the Nepali self with a certain orientation in terms of her aspirations, her reason for leaving the homeland, the projected image of herself and her imagined *homeland,* but would also entrap the significant other to view her thus – an image, as convincingly argued by both Hutt and Subba, is insufficient to legitimise a diasporic status.

Notes

1 As Tristan Bruslé suggests, the lone exception to this, perhaps, is Michael J. Hutt's indicative or suggestive essay titled 'Being Nepali without Nepal: Reflections on a South Asian Diaspora' (1997).
2 For instance, in cases of the homeland being a nation state, the experiences of the return-migration of the diasporic self to his/her homeland is not a welcome home returning, but a struggle to fit back into the real space of the homeland. See Takeyuki Tsuda's edited volume, *Diasporic Homecomings: Ethnic Return Migration in Comparative Perspective,* Stanford University Press, California, 2009.
3 Michael Hutt (1997: 102), has in fact argued highlighting the lack of this longing among the Nepali diaspora and thereby has difficulty in conceiving of a possibility of a Nepali diaspora altogether.
4 Further, given the recent conceptual debates between the categories of *Nepalese* (as citizens of Nepal) and *Nepalis* (Indian citizens who share historical roots and the language with the Nepalese), would the latter share the image of the Nepali diaspora or would they partake in the Indian diaspora or would they not constitute any diaspora at all? And if they share the image, then would it mean that the *Nepalis* would thus be a twice-displaced diaspora?
5 For an extensive argument see P. G. Jung (2009) 'Ethinic Identity, History and Cultural Anthropology: Some Reflections', in T. B. Subba, A. C. Sinha, G. S. Nepal and D. R. Nepal (eds), *Indian Nepalis: Issues and Perspectives,* Delhi: Concept Publishing House.
6 Officially spelt thus from 1891, but also alternatively spelt as *Gorkha,* especially within the Nepali-speaking community.
7 An instance of this 'non-loyalty' was the non-willingness to join the British on the way back home rather than remain in India as a part of the Indian Army. They in fact had to trick and cajole the Gurkhas to join them. See John Parker, *The Gurkhas: The Inside Story of the World's Most Feared Soldiers,* Bounty Books: London, 2005 (1999).
8 In today's parlance, the term 'myth' immediately tends to trap us up in the engagement with 'truth'. This relation of opposition to truth is what has rendered the term identical with something false or as a 'popular misconception'. This connotation of the term 'myth' has a long and illustrious history finding its classical exponents, notwithstanding their finer differences, in the likes of E. B. Taylor, G. J. Frazer, Lucien Levy-Bruhl, who viewed and pitted 'myth' against 'science'. This stance towards myths anchors itself upon the idea that the function of a myth is to *explain* as opposed to make-sense-of or *understand.* Such rendering of myth is already influenced by the notion of a 'positive science', where explanation is one of its primary functions.
9 He was the author of some early works on the Gurkhas, their customs and history. See his *Gurkhas: Their Manners, Customs and History,* Delhi: Asian Educational Services, 2001 (1928) and *The Land of the Gurkhas or the Kingdom of Nepal,* Delhi: Asian Educational Services, 1998 (1937).

References

Assmann, Jan. 2011. *Cultural Memory and Early Civilization: Writing Remembrance and Early Civilization*. New York: Cambridge University Press.

Bruslé, Tristan. 2012. *Nepalese Diasporic Websites, Signs and Conditions of a Diaspora in the Making?* http://www.e-diasporas.fr/wp/brusle.html.

Cohen, Robin. 1996. 'Diasporas and the Nation-State: From Victims to Challengers', *Royal Institute of International Affairs*, 72(3): 507–20.

Cohen, Robin. 2008. *Global Diasporas: An Introduction*. New York: Routledge.

Deschamps, Jean-Claude. 2010 [1982]. 'Social Identity and Relations of Power between Groups', in Henri Tajfel (ed.), *Social Identity and Intergroup Relations*, pp. 85–98. London: Cambridge University Press.

Devy, G. N., V. G. Davis, K. K. Chakravarty (eds). 2013. *Narrating Nomadism: Tales of Recovery and Resistance*. Delhi: Routledge.

Dirks, Nicholas B. 2004 [2001]. *Castes of Mind: Colonialism and the Making of Modern India*. Delhi: Permanent Black, 173–97.

Freire, Paulo. 2008. *Pedagogy of the Oppressed*. Trans. Myra Bergman Ramos with an Introduction by Donaldo Macedo (30th Anniversary Edition). New York: Continuum.

Gandhi, M. K. 2010. *Hind Swaraj: A Critical Edition*. Annotated, translated and edited by Suresh Sharma and Tridip Suhrud. New Delhi: Orient Blackswan.

Gopinath, Gayatri. 2005. *Impossible Desires: Queer Diasporas and South Asian Public Cultures*. Durham: Duke University Press.

Hutt, Michael. 1997. 'Being Nepali without Nepal: Reflections on a South Asian Diaspora', in D. N. Gellner, J. Pfaff-Czarnecka and J. Whelpton (eds), *Nationalism and Ethnicity in a Hindu Kingdom: The politics of culture in contemporary Nepal*, pp. 101–44. Amsterdam: Harwood Academic Publishers.

Mishra, Vijay. 2007. *The Literature of the Indian Diaspora: Theorizing the Diasporic Imaginary*. New York: Routledge.

Radhakrishna, Meena. 2008 (2001). *Dishonoured by History: 'Criminal Tribes' and the British Colonial Policy*. Hyderabad: Orient Longman.

Safran, William. 1991. 'Diasporas in Modern Societies: Myths of Homeland and Return', *Diaspora: A Journal of Transnational Studies*, 1(1): 83–99.

Safran, William. 1999. 'Comparing Diasporas: A Review Essay', *Diaspora: A Journal of Transnational Studies*, 8(3): 255–91.

Sheffer, Gabriel (ed.). 1986. *Modern Diasporas in International Politics*. Kent: Croom Helm ltd.

Subba, T. B. 2012. 'Do Indian Nepalis Constitute a Diasporic Society?' Paper presented at the workshop on Nepali Diaspora, Oxford University, 8–9 July.

Tölölyan, Khachig. 1996. 'Rethinking Diaspora(s): Stateless Power in the Transnational Moment', *Diaspora: A Journal of Transnational Studies*, 5(1): 3–36.

6

THE INDIAN GORKHAS

Changing orientation of a diasporic society

Rajendra P. Dhakal

The Indian Gorkhas, a conglomeration of culturally and linguistically heterogeneous, yet economically and politically rather homogeneous entity, are variously known as 'Gurkhas', 'Paharis' and 'Nepalis'. They were initially engaged in different parts of India as tea garden workers, sharecroppers, cattle graziers and labourers on roads, railways and forests. The internal homogeneity was necessitated by the need to survive in an alien environment.[1] They represented various ethnic groups belonging to the Tibeto-Burman language family, such as Rai, Limbu, Tamang, Gurung, Magar, Sunwar, Thami, and so on and other Indo-Aryan family speakers such as Bahun, Chhetri, Kami, Damai and Sarki. Among them, Limbu and Magar are regarded as indigenous to both Nepal and Sikkim.[2] Many of them settled in the region when Nepal overran and occupied Sikkim, which once included the present Darjeeling, in 1788[3] and ruled over it till the treaty of Segowli was signed in 1816, when Nepal had to return these territories to Sikkim. Others came as graziers or as labourers for tea gardens, development of agriculture, communication and transport in Darjeeling, Sikkim and north-east India besides those settling there after retiring from army or police services in India.

The above categories do not include the 'floating population', who reside temporarily in India under the provisions of the Indo-Nepal Treaty of 1950, which allows citizens of both the countries to migrate and earn livelihood in the other country on reciprocal basis.[4]

Early phase (1815–90)

The earliest people from Nepal to migrate to India in any large number were the 'Gurkhas' recruited to the British Army soon after the Anglo-Nepalese War of 1814–15. Some of them were recruited by King Ranjit

Singh of Punjab even prior to that, but we do not have a clear picture about the volume of their recruitment in his army. The other large category of immigrants from Nepal was the category of graziers, who were a sustainable source of revenue for the British administration, as each cattle was taxed. Ethnically, the former was mainly represented by Rai, Limbu, Magar and Gurung whereas the graziers were mostly high-caste Hindu Nepalis such as Bahuns and Chhetris.

The introduction of the tea industry and agricultural development during the second half of the 19th century drew a large number of heterogeneous groups to Darjeeling, swelling the working class of the region to its limits. As Tocqueville wrote, 'there are no surer guarantees of equality among men than poverty and misfortunes'.[5] Their migration did not trigger a 'sudden change from an average expectable environment to a strange and unpredictable one'[6] because ecologically or otherwise, Sikkim and Darjeeling hills were no different from the middle hills of Nepal, from where they migrated. Though the new place had a different political set-up, it was less hostile compared to the feudal system under monarchy or the Ranas back home in Nepal. The opening of roads and transport ushered in hopes of a better life without having to give up 'familiar food, music, social customs and even one's language', or face an 'unfamiliar landscape' and people.[7] The tea bushes evoked numerous poems, songs and prose. No wonder the two tender leaves and one stem of tea became the symbol of the All India Gorkha League, the first political party of the Gorkhas in India.

The Khas Kura or Nepali language became the lingua franca for all of them. Their settlements were both scattered and clustered. The place names were often derived from what was sown. Thus, where buckwheat was sown became Faparbote and where maize was grown was called Makaibari. Hundreds of such names narrate the stories of their settlements, gradually building the sense of belonging and identity, and stimulating their political, social and economic consciousness. The importance of the naming process has been well-noted by eminent scholars.[8]

Thus, a new identity was metamorphosed for the Gorkhas out of a common destiny, place, lingua franca and menial work. By the 1920s, the process of integration as a linguistically homogeneous identity as Nepali or Gorkha was almost complete, unlike the Rai, Magar or Gurung identities in the case of Nepal.[9] The word 'Nepali' continues to be a political term in Nepal, meaning Nepalese citizenship or nationality, whereas it took an ethnic meaning in India. The beauty and uniqueness of this development outside Nepal was rooted in their shared history, landscape and common life experience. They did not experience the trauma of leaving their homes, or a sense of displacement. Darjeeling, to those people, was a 'land where gold flowered on tea bushes'.

In the early phase of their history, it is not clear if they constituted a diasporic society in Darjeeling in the sense it was understood by William Safran, i.e. dispersal from homeland, collective memory of the homeland, lack of integration in the host country and a 'myth' of return and a persistent link with the homeland.[10] The same holds, perhaps, true of them in the sense Robin Cohen defined the word 'diaspora'.[11] Both Safran and Cohen assume that diasporic people have a close relation with the country of their origin, with friends, relatives and with tradition, culture and politics. A link between a particular group and a homeland or a host-land is preconceived. Many Gorkhas of Darjeeling claim that they came here 'with land' when the district of Darjeeling was ceded by Nepal to the East India Company. If this claim is true, it was a case of what Roger Brubaker calls 'migration of borders over people' and not migration of people over borders.[12]

For the Indian Gorkhas, it was an engagement with homeland and not 'a fixation to a home'.[13] The notion of 'home' is not so simple, as it is 'intrinsically linked with the way process of inclusion and exclusion operate and is subjectively experienced under given circumstances'.[13] As Peter Mandaville, writing about reimaging of Islam, points out, '... identity always needs to be situated and therefore also understood as product of particular sociopolitical circumstances'.[14]

The second phase (1890–1947)

This was a phase in which the social processes became more complex for the Gorkhas of Darjeeling with the coming of the print media and the introduction of Western education. Referring to Benedict Anderson, Appadorai observes: 'with "print capitalism", a new power was unleashed in the world, the power of mass literacy and its attendant large scale production of projects of ethnic affinity that were remarkably free of the need to face to face communication or even of indirect communication between persons and groups. The act of reading things together set the stage for movements based on paradox: the paradox of constructed primordialism'.[15]

With the setting up of the schools and the gradual spread of the print media, a foundation for social change was firmly laid in the Darjeeling hills. The first school for Europeans was established in 1846, but by 1898, a number of primary, middle and a few high schools were opened for the local people.[16] The rate of literacy increased rapidly in the following 50 years though there were no facilities yet for higher education. It is very interesting to note that in the initial years, Hindi was the medium of instruction in the schools. Kumar Pradhan, a noted historian, argues that if Nepali was not a popular lingua franca, the German priest would never have translated their preaching material into Nepali and prepared a Nepali dictionary by 1841.[17] With the circulation of *Gorkhay Khabar Kagat*, a Nepali newspaper published from 1901 to 1932, the establishment of Gorkha Library in 1913, Nepali Sahitya Sammelan in 1924 and Calcutta University's inclusion of Nepali as a subject,[18] the process of cultural change was accelerated.

A reference needs to be made to the controversy over colloquial Darjeeling Nepali used by Ganga Prashad Pradhan and a Sanskritised Nepali language used by educated Nepali writers such as Surya Bikram Gyawali and Dharanidhar Koirala, as it is closely connected with the contemporary discourse on Gorkha identity.[19] It is argued that the overwhelming influence of Gyawali and Koirala on the intellectual development of the region stunted the growth of the colloquial Nepali language spoken by the majority in Darjeeling.[20] The local poetic forms of *Lahari* and *Sawai* were disdained as *Pakhe*, an expression that connotes backwardness.[21] The history of modern Nepali literary narratives starts with the writings of Gyawali, Koirala and Paras Mani Pradhan. Delivering his first presidential speech at a meeting of the Nepali Sahitya Sammelan, Hari Prasad Pradhan, a close associate of the trio, argued: '. . . the association should be named Nepali Sahitya Sammelan because the word Nepali is inclusive term denoting Magar, Gurung, Kirati, Newar, Limbu . . . shows that they all have roots in Nepal'.[22] Paradoxically, it was from Darjeeling that the name 'Nepali' was given to the language hitherto known as Gorkha.[23] The Nepali Sahitya Sammelan was the first organisation to use the word 'Nepali'. It was only later on that Nepal renamed Gorkha Bhasa Pracharini Samiti as Nepali Bhasa Pracharini Samiti. All this indicated that Nepali nationalism first grew outside Nepal, in the tea bushes of the Darjeeling hills.

The Sammelan's main focus was to popularise Bhanu Bhakta's *Ramayana*, which became so popular among the Indian Gorkhas that *slokas* (rhymes) from it were chanted during the language movement for the inclusion of Nepali language in the eighth schedule of the Constitution in 1970s, virtually making Bhanu Bhakta the symbol of the movement. A number of his statues and busts were installed in different places and important roads were named after him in Darjeeling and Sikkim.

However, the sense of affinity with India in the writings of Bhanu Bhakta was more romantic than national. He wrote: '*Ati durlabh janos bharat bhumiko janma janale*' (Blessed is the man who is born in Bharat).[24] Similarly, Laxmi Prasad Deokota, Balkrishna Sama, Lekhnath Paudyal and other poets of Nepal eulogised Bharat as their own country. For instance, Deokota wrote:

> Dear to me are fond memories
> Of the ancient world,
> Of *our* Bharat, of her rise . . .
> Let us journey to the times past,
> Let us remember that Bharat . . . Sweet as Vrindavan to this poet.[25]
>   (emphasis mine)

The sense of cultural 'connect' with Nepal began to creep into the larger body of their society after the advent of the intellectual leadership in Darjeeling. The 1920s were crucial in the development of pan-Indian nationalism. According to Valentine Chirol, India had no sense of the nation before colonial rule,[26] but with severe internal fissures to contain, the Indian National Congress adopted a policy in 1920 of organising the provinces on linguistic basis once independence was achieved. This poignant juncture excludes the Gorkhas of Darjeeling and Duars. Their weak intellectual pedigree and their ambivalent national identity left them high and dry. Their own knowledge about themselves was based on the writings of British and Bengali intellectuals and officials. Such writings, barring a few, painted them all as 'immigrants' and 'foreigners' from Nepal, ignoring their complex history of migration, 'movement of borders' and relationship with India.

Subsequently, the idea of 'Prabasi', or a person living outside home, developed and has been used in Nepali literature rather freely. Though the few narrative fictions published in the 1930s reflected the inner contradictions of the Gorkha mind under the dual burden of being linked with Nepal as well as an intrinsically Indian ethos, an evaluation of these narratives shows that the Gorkhas did not suffer from divided national loyalties between Nepal and India during this period in history.

Rupnarayan Sinha in his novel, *Bhramar*, published in 1936, builds his characters against the middle-class family background – a rare feature of that time. His education in Calcutta and his exposure to Bengali literature are visible in his prototype characters akin to Bengali *bhadralok*, cultured with the taste for music, art, literature and philosophy. This, according to Schwarz Henry, is acknowledging their 'superiority', and entering 'into rivalry with it in an attempt to achieve parity'.[27] Sinha, however, also sympathises with the pathos of the immigrants from Nepal and the way they are treated in India.

Compared to Sinha's *Bhramar*, Indra Bahadur Rai's *Aaja Ramita Chha*, published in 1955, is more reflective and inclusive of the Darjeeling of that period. In the making of Darjeeling, Rai's characters engage in business relations with a 'Kainya' (a derogatory word for Marwari businessman) and politics, ranging from the urban milieu to tea garden trade unions. He makes a very strong claim of rootedness in Darjeeling. Janak, his central character, says, 'India and Nepal both love us', and at the same time, in his belongingness, he asserts, 'Darjeeling is ours' and 'it cannot belong to others', and declares, 'I belong to this soil on which I am standing'.[28] *Aaja Ramita Chha* is about building of economic, social and political space for Gorkhas in Darjeeling. This, incidentally, is the theme in most of Rai's writings.

On the contrary, Agam Singh Giri, a famous poet, expresses the trauma of leaving home in his short epic, *Yuddha ra Yoddha*.[29] But instead of lamenting, he 'wants his Yoddha to return to his own true self . . . and fight a metaphorical war against injustice, oppression and inequality'.[30]

The colonial administration in India put this region under the category of Backward Tract, Scheduled District and Partially Excluded Area and kept it outside the constitutional reform process in India. The politico-administrative demands made by certain sections of the hill people through memoranda submitted to Morley-Minto, Montague-Chelmsford and Simon commissions fell on deaf ears. The freedom movement did galvanise the hills of Darjeeling to some extent, but did not sufficiently insure the participation of the people, although there does exist a list of freedom martyrs from the Gorkha community such as Janga Bir Sapkota, who was nicknamed 'Hill Gandhi', Durga Malla and Sabitri Devi, not to exclude the numerous Gorkha soldiers in the Azad Hind Fauz.

The mythical image of the Gorkhas as brave, loyal and honest was a British construct, but it pervaded every aspect of their life.[31] The British attempted to encyst the Gorkhas as they did not want the freedom struggle to creep into the hill areas of Darjeeling and Dooars region. The Gorkha soldiers were told by the British that the freedom movement was not theirs and they were different.[32] The construction of the brave and the loyal Gorkhas by the British spawned other categories such as *darban*, *chowkidar* and *bahadur*. When India became independent, the role of these soldiers was projected negatively and even their positive contribution in containing communal riots on the eve of independence was greatly underplayed by nationalist historians of the country. However, their role in the massacre of Jallianwala Bagh is blown out of proportion by the same historians.

Nervous on the eve of independence and frustrated about their inability to extract any kind of concession in terms of separate administrative set-up or minority status from the British, the Gorkhas formed the All India Gorkha League to address their issues in India. Its objective was to preserve their 'shared culture as any of Hindustani and that they have their own history language and culture like Bengalis, Biharis and others . . . therefore, they have equal rights in Hindustan'.[33] Speaking at the Constituent Assembly debates in 1946, Dambar Singh Gurung, the leader of the All India Gorkha League, had demanded that Gorkhas be recognised as minority and that they must have adequate representation in the Advisory Committee to be formed for the purpose.[34]

The third phase [1947–]

The euphoria generated by Indian Independence created confidence in Gorkhas that their voice would be heard. The demands for autonomy of Darjeeling and Duars were made by various political parties participating in electoral politics of the country. The years up to the late 1970s could be considered as the period of normal political activities, with the expectation that electoral politics would fulfil the aspirations of the people.

The language movement in the 1970s demanding the inclusion of Nepali in the eighth schedule of the Indian Constitution can be considered as a period of rediscovering themselves. The perceived apathy of the Indian government was greatly exacerbated by a clumsy and insensitive statement made by Prime Minister Morarji Desai in 1979 that 'Nepali' was a foreign language and that the Gorkha Regiment could be thrown into the Bay of Bengal deeply wounded the sentiments of the Gorkhas. The gravity of such a statement made by the highest Indian authority during his official visit to Darjeeling was strongly condemned by one and all. A community that had sacrificed thousands of its men while securing the borders of the nation was shaken with disbelief.

A question that a Nepali speaker often encounters from a fellow Indian is 'Are you from Nepal?' Vijay Misra explains how the style of asking such questions in Fiji resulted in many Indians loosing Fijian citizenship. I like to bring here Misra's reference to V.S. Naipaul's essays in which he recounts being asked, 'Where do you come from?' The implication of this question in the Fijian situation, explains Mishra, is 'Where are you staying?'[35] After the 1987 coup, the indigenous Fijians shadowed this question with the idea of the 'Vulagi' or the foreigner, implying from which part of India one came from, whenever the addressee happened to be Indian.[41] The question 'Are you from Nepal?' thus implies 'you are not an Indian', which has politically dangerous implications, as is evident from the forced ouster of Nepali speakers from north-east India in the 1980s and the 1990s without identifying whether they are Indian or Nepalese. But, when the supposedly illegal migrants from Bangladesh were driven out from Mumbai, the state of West Bengal demanded that their citizenship be verified before ousting them.

To tag citizens as foreigners is to make these people citizenship-less and a right-less people.[36] The word 'foreigner' is used to reduce citizens to 'bare bodies', without any right.[37] This is not to suggest that Arnett's concept of bare bodies, which she develops in the context of the Jews in Germany, is applicable in the case of Gorkhas in India in the absolute sense of the term, but the basic premises in declaring a people of India as 'foreigners' without knowing the history of India or its borderlands is depriving them of citizenship, and thereby, rights that emanate from being a citizen.

With growing support for the Gorkhaland movement spearheaded by Subhas Ghising, the demand for abrogation of the Indo-Nepal Treaty intensified, as it began to be seen as a stumbling block in their desire to be recognised as full citizens of India. The movement tried to create an image of Gorkhas independent of and unconnected with Nepal. The GNLF discarded the term 'Nepali' and exhorted everyone to use the term 'Gorkha' and declared Agam Singh Giri, a Darjeeling-born poet as *jatiya kavi* in place of Bhanubhakta, who was born in Nepal. The logic may have been naive, but its poignancy made a deep and wide impact, leaving a few intellectuals divided on the issue. With the recognition of Nepali language by the Sahitya Academy in 1973, the process of their emotional disconnection with Nepal was almost complete. In their desire to be Indian, they even tried to exclude the writings of authors from Nepal from syllabi on Nepali literature. The lamentations for being called a 'foreigner' in India were 'enough to evoke a sense of captivity, exile, alienation and isolation'.[38] The 'foreigner tag' became the leitmotif, to borrow Robin Cohen's term, in the Gorkha political culture in Darjeeling.

This leitmotif perhaps explains why Prasant Tamang's shot at the title in the TV reality show called 'Indian Idol' took on the shape of a politico-cultural rally for the Indian Gorkhas. He became the embodiment of the Gorkha jati and a symbol of unity. His was the first chance to create a national space for the Gorkhas in the national media. The extent of support he got was historical as well as hysterical. Subhash Ghising's refusal to support Prasant cost him his political base. Already dissatisfied with his misrule and perceived betrayal about the Gorkhaland demand, his refusal to support Prasant was, to the masses, a refusal to support Gorkha jati. Bimal Guring's support to Prasant brought him to the centre stage, making him the undisputed Gorkha leader since then.

With the rise of the Gorkha Janamukti Morcha (GJM) under Bimal Gurung, the identity issue has come up again. The GJM believes that Gorkhaland is indispensable for preserving the Gorkha identity in India. It asserts that 'in spite of having been an integral part of Indian Union', they are 'constantly being viewed as alien'.[39] It reflects a Gorkha political psyche that the 'demand for identity means the Gorkhas want to be treated by the polity with the same level of political trust as it does for other communities'.[40] According to GJM, a separate state for the Gorkhas will be 'an emblematic home for all the Gorkhas of India . . .'.[41]

By bringing in the reference to Hall's two different ways of thinking about cultural identity in his analysis of Caribbean culture, I want to show how the Gorkha cohesiveness is gradually giving way to heterogeneity. The pan-Nepali cohesiveness based on shared culture and language fits into the first definition of Hall's cultural identity,

> defined in terms of shared culture, a sort of collective one true self, hiding inside the many other, more superficial or artificially imposed selves, which people with a shared history and ancestry hold in common. Within the terms of this definition, our cultural identities, historical experiences and shared cultural codes which provide us with the identity as 'one people' with stable, unchanging and continuous frames of references, and meaning, beneath the shifting division and vicissitudes of our actual history. This 'oneness' underlying all other more superficial differences, is the truth, the essence, of 'Carribbean-ness', of the black experience.[42]

Of late, the search for cultural roots is in focus in the wake of Limbus and Tamangs being granted tribal status in January 2003 by the Government of India. In view of the special facilities provided to the officially recognised tribes, there was a desire among many Nepali ethnic groups to be included in this category. This was also bolstered by the proposal to extend the provisions of the Sixth Schedule to Darjeeling. The search for lost traditional cultural codes, particularly folk music, dance, songs, food and dresses gradually got serious with the 'reservation status' in mind. Riding on this wave, the GJM imposed a dress code during the festival time of Dashain and Tihar, in which the people were asked to wear distinctive cultural attires belonging to each ethnic group. Similarly, a cultural parade was organised during the celebration of the Independence Day on tribal lines, with traditional dresses and musical instruments of each ethnic group. Paradoxically, in reviving almost obsolete cultural codes of this kind, either the representatives of these tribes entered Nepal to find out about authentic traditions or experts were brought in. On the more organised political front, the rhetoric of 'disconnect' with Nepal was established. Such rhetoric got more vigorous when forces such as Jana Jagaran Manch and Amra Bengali in Siliguri opposed Gorkhaland, alleging that Nepalis are foreigners who have migrated from Nepal. The GJM's response to such opposition was, 'we have not entered here by crossing barbed wire like thieves', referring to illegal Bangladeshi migrants. In a bid to broaden its base to gear support for the Gorkhaland demand, the GJM invited minority groups to extend support to them, which gave rise to the Gorkha Janamukti Minority Forum. The forum, representing the minority communities from the hills, participated in the relay hunger strikes, in a month-long 'dress code programme' during Dashain and Tihar, with their own traditional cultural attire and in the cultural parade in the Independence Day celebrations. It is perhaps too early to make any kind of statement on the recent compromise between GJM and the leaders of Adibasi Bikash Parishad from Dooars, but if it lasts for a decade or so, it will have significant impact on the political culture of the Gorkhas and the plains tribes. Indeed, as Peter Mandaville succinctly puts it, 'the construction of group identity is inherently a socio-political process, involving as it does dialogue, negotiation and debate as to "who we are" and, what it means to be "who we are"'.[43]

Cultural identity, in the light of Hall's second definition, is a matter of becoming as well as being.

> It belongs to the future as well as past. It is not something which already exists, transcending place, time, history and culture. But, like everything which is historical it undergoes constant transformation. Far from being grounded in a mere recovery of the past, which is waiting to be found, and which when found, will secure our sense of ourselves into eternity, identities are the names we give to the different ways we are positioned by, and position ourselves within the narratives of the past.[44]

Critics[45] of Indra Bahadur Rai and many other fiction writers who have openly expressed their love and affection for Nepal feel that such emotional and cultural linkages manifested in their fiction may cast a shadow of doubt on the national standing of the Nepalis in India. The main character of Rai in *Aaja Ramita Chha* declaring that India and Nepal love us equally is treated as creating ambiguity about being fully Indian. It appears that there is a misconception running through the Indian Nepali narratives that cultural roots and link with Nepal will undermine their status as Indian nationals. The historical evidence of some ethnic groups among Gorkhas being the indigenous people of this region does not necessarily mean that they have no cultural connection with Nepal. The historical connection of Nepali-speaking people with Nepal cannot be simply ignored or deleted like a computer file. Such linkages, developed through ages of social interactions in geographically contiguous areas, do not make the Indian Nepalis non-Indian, anti-Indian or less-Indian as the present borders of India and Nepal were drawn only in the end of the 19th century. The bitter experience of Indian Nepalis being treated as 'Nepalese', or the citizens of Nepal, by fellow Indians or sometimes by the officials too, have to be dealt with firmly by asserting citizenship rights that one gets from the Constitution, astute political dynamism and increased social, cultural and media interaction and activities by coming out of melancholic mindsets to more convivial ones. The Constitution of India provides full and equal rights to all its citizens, including Nepali-speaking Indians, whose language is recognised in the eighth schedule of the Constitution. However,

> . . . it is a serious misunderstanding . . . to suppose that the problems of social identity are resolved by formal (merely legal) definitions. For unevenly and at times precariously, but always through long experience substantially, an effective social identity depends on actual and sustained social relationships. To reduce social identity to formal legal definitions, at the level of the state, is to collide in the alienated superficialities of 'the nation' which are limited functional terms of the modern ruling class.[46]

A sustained effort has to be made to develop an 'actual and sustained social relationship' for which a beginning may be made by encompassing within contemporary Nepali narratives the life and sensibilities of a new generation of Gorkhas, who are contributing substantially to the diverse fields of science, technology, medicines, academics, films and photography, fine art, music, journalism, sports and the corporate sector in India.

This generation of Gorkhas, growing up as they are in an environment of information, technology and access to a whole lot of new experiences in a global world are far removed, both in time and space, from their urban and rural brethren of the Darjeeling region. Their collective memory and response to the sense of place or home is much broader as they interact with the wider society. In order to survive in a highly competitive globalised world, they have to contend with more interesting, but equally challenging issues. Thus, their self-image and perceptions resonate within these social milieus. It is this new emerging Gorkha identity that needs to be 'discovered, excavated and expressed through literary narratives'.[47] In the process, identity formation can be seen 'in terms of adaptation and construction – adaption to changes, dislocations and transformations and the construction of knowledge and ways of seeing the world'.[48] As James Proctor writes, 'diaspora can appear both as naming geographical phenomenon – the traversal of physical terrain by an individual or a group – as well as a theoretical concept, a way of thinking or of representing the world'.[49] According to John McLeod, '[I]t is this latter epistemological sense of the term which demands that the issue of diasporic imagination and representation are germane to everyone, rather than exclusively migrant descended or minority communities'.[50] Thus, Gorkha diaspora may be thought of 'not in substantial term as bounded entity, but rather as an idiom, stance, and a claim'.[51] Modern narratives of the Gorkhas are emerging in the writings of a new generation, for instance, of Manprasad Subba and Remika Thapa.

> I have been telling you for a long time –
> I am the hill, the mountain and *tarai*
> Telling you that I am the waterfall
> The stream and the river
> I am everything that you have seen.
> Alive, you can see all these things
> And not see me, your eyes
> Must be afflicted by some virus
> Or- if this is how they are programmed
> then the software must be outdated
> Seven generations old[52]

> I have spent many generations
> Wandering far and wide
> Building homes for all and sundry
> Leaving my own roofless and neglected [53]

> What? Would you that I could have a household?
> What? Would you that I could claim my ancestral properties?

What? Are we to sit at the same table for tea?
Oh, lovely![54]

Look into my slanted eyes
Therein lies my sky
Now listen to my sky's broadcast[55]

The quoted poems in footnotes 53, 54, 55, and 56 have been translated from Nepali by Anmole Prasad on my request.

Notes

1. Rajendra Prasad Dhakal, 2008, 'The Urge to Belong: An Identity in the Waiting', in T. B. Subba et al. (eds), *Indian Nepalis: Issues and Perspectives*, Concept Publishing House, New Delhi.
2. For details, see H. H. Risley, 1989, *Gazetteer of Sikhim*, Sikkim Nature Conservation Foundation, Gangtok, 1989 (1840); P. N. Chopra, 1985 (1979), *Sikkim*, S. Chand & Company Ltd, New Delhi; H. D. Hooker, 1854, *Himalayan Journals*, 2 vols, Murray, London; Kumar Pradhan, 1982, *Pahilo Pahar*, Shyam Prakasan, Darjeeling.
3. See Pradhan, ibid.
4. This category of population and the Treaty of 1950 have become a sensitive issue as the Indian Nepalis/Gorkhas feel that because of the treaty, their Indian citizenship and loyalty to the country are doubted by fellow countrymen and officials.
5. Alex de Tocqueville, *Democracy in America*, 2 vols, 2009, Waiheke Island, Rwating Press, p. 32.
6. Salman Akhtar, 1999, *Immigration and Identity, Turmoil, Treatment, and Transformation*, Jason Aronson Inc, Northvale, New Jersey, p. 1.
7. Ibid.
8. Ashcroft Bill, Griffin Graeth, Tiffin Helen, 1995 (eds), *The Post Colonial Studies Reader*, Routledge, London, Part XII, p. 391.
9. Ramakrishna Sharma, 1978, 'Nepali Sahitya Ko Pragati', *Nepali Gadya Sangraha*, Bhag 3, Sajha Prakasan, Kathmandu.
10. William Safran, 2009, 'Diaspora in Modern Societies, Myths of Homeland and Return Diaspora in Paola Tonintao', *The Making of Gypsies Diasporas, Translocation, Migration and Social Change: An Inter-Disciplinary Open Access E-Journal*.
11. Robin Cohen, 1996, 'Diaspora and the State-From Victims to Challengers', *International Affairs*, 72(3): 507–20.
12. Roger Brubaker, 2005, 'Diaspora', *Ethnic and Racial Studies*, 28(1): 1–19.
13. Ibid., p. 57.
14. Peter Mandaville, 2001, *Reimagining Islam Diaspora*, Sage, London.
15. Arjun Appadorai, 2003, cited in Braziel Evans Jana and Black Aninto Mannur, *Theorizing Diaspora: A Reader*, Blackwell Publishing, Berlin.
16. The schools were established from 1846. Loreto Convent in 1846, Darjeeling Government High School in1892, Scottish University Missionary Institution, Kalimpong in 1885, Middle Education School in 1887 in Kurseong which became Pusparani High School in 1942, St. Alphonse School, Kurseong in 1888, Girls'

Boarding School in 1890, Kalimpong Girls' School in 1891, Shantirani School, Sonada in 1898, etc.
17 Pradhan, 1982, *op. cit.* p. 23.
18 Ibid., pp. 2–50. It was only in 1918 that Nepali was 'included in the list of vernacular languages of the subject composition in the Matriculation, Intermediate and BA examinations of the University'. According to Kumar Pradhan, the Bengal government ordered to use Nepali instead of 'Nepali Paharia or khas kura' in the departmental examination by its notification dated 30 July 1926, and by notification of 8 January 1927, Nepali was recognised as one of the main languages. He also points out that it was only in 1932 that Calcutta University agreed to use Nepali instead of 'Nepali Parwatiya' on the basis of the letter dated 30 May 1932 by Hari Prasad Pradhan and Surya Vikram Gyawali. See also Nagendra Mani Pradhan, 1991, *Parasmani Jiwan Yatra,* Darjeeling, p. 74. A Notification of Calcutta University Vide Calcutta Gazette dated 24–7–18, November 1.
19 Ibid.
20 Ibid., p. 78.
21 Ibid., p. 88.
22 Ibid., p. 37.
23 Surya Vikram Gyawali, 'Nepali Sahitya Tatha Usko Awsyakta', in Kumar Pradhan, *op. cit.*
24 Translated by Indra Bahadur Rai and Gokul Sinha (eds), *Sri Indra Bahadur Rai Avinanadan Grantha,* Sri Shiva Kumar Smriti Academy, Kurseong, p. 30.
25 Ibid., pp. 27–34.
26 Valentine Chirol, 'Indian Unrest', in B. R. Nanda (ed.), *Essays in Modern Indian History,* Oxford University Press, New Delhi.
27 Henry Schwarz, 1997, *Writing Cultural History in Colonial and Post Colonial* India, University of Pennsylvania Press, Philadelphia, p. 21.
28 Indra Bahadur Rai, 1958, *Aaja Ramita Chha,* Sajha Prakasan, Kathmandu, p. 134.
29 Irshad Gulam Ahmed, 2005, 'Racial Pride and the Anguish of Identity', in George Thadathil, Jiwan Namdung, Terence Mukhia, Basanti Mukhia (eds), *Cultural Identity in Nepali Language and Literature,* Salesian College, Sonada.
30 Ibid.
31 See for details, Bidhan Golay, 2009, 'Rethinking Gorkha Identity: Outside the Imperium of Discourse, Hegemony, and History', in T. B. Subba, et al., *op. cit.*
32 Randhir Subba, 1955, *Gorkha,* 7th February, Darjeeling.
33 Ibid.
34 As mentioned in Gorkha Janamukti Morcha, 2008, *The Case for Gorkhaland-Creating a New State out of Darjeeling District and the Dooars,* documents presented in the Tripartite Talks between Government of India, West Bengal and Gorkha Jana Mukti Morcha on 8 September 2008.
35 Vijay Misra, 2007, *The Literature of Indian Diaspora-Theorising the Diasporic Imagination,* Routledge, Delhi, p. 4.
36 Ayten Glindodu, 2006, 'Rights to Have Rights'. Paper presented at the UN Political Theory Colloquium, 3 March 2006, www.polsci.umn.edu.
37 Ibid.
38 Cohen, *op. cit.*
39 Gorkha Janamukti Morcha, *op. cit.*
40 Ibid.
41 Ibid.

42 Stuart Hall, 1997, 'Cultural Identity and Diaspora', in Padmini Mongia (ed.), *Contemporary Post Colonial Theory: A Reader,* Oxford University Press, New Delhi, pp. 111–21.
43 Peter Mandaville, *op. cit.,* p. 170.
44 Hall Stuart, *op. cit.,* p. 225.
45 Man Prasad Subba, 2008, 'Kinaraka aawaajharuko Sandarvama', in Man Prasad Subba and Remika Thapa, *Kinaraka Awajharu,* Shyam Brothers, Darjeeling.
46 Raymond Williams, 1983, *Towards 2000,* Harmondsworth, Pelican.
47 Ibid.
48 Mark Shackleton makes this remark while commenting about diaspora as a theory. See his (ed.) *Diasporic Literature and Theory: Where and Now?* 2008, Cambridge Scholars Publishing, Cambridge.
49 James Procter, 2007, 'Diaspora', in John Mcleod (ed.), *The Routledge Companion to Post Colonial Studies,* London, New York.
50 Mcleod, ibid.
51 Brubaker, *op. cit.*
52 Subba and Thapa, *op. cit.,* p. 71.
53 Ibid., p. 65.
54 Ibid., p. 41.
55 Ibid., p. 69.

7

DIASPORIC IMAGINATIONS OF DARJEELING

Gorkhaland as an imaginative geography

Miriam Wenner

Euta ghar banau bhane
Ghaderi ni chhaina mero.[1]

Introduction

In February 2011, three members of the Gorkha Janamukti Morcha[2] (GJM) were shot dead by the West Bengal police while trying to enter Jalpaiguri district. This attempt to enter the district was part of a *padayatra*[3] initiated by Bimal Gurung, the leader of GJM, in order to fortify their claim on the district to be part of the demand for a state of Gorkhaland (*The Telegraph* 9 February, 2011). The GJM wants this state, comprising Darjeeling district and its adjoining areas, to be carved out of West Bengal. Its supporters engaged in day-long strikes, sitting sometimes for hours outside in the cold, while others attended demonstrations or hunger strikes in order to pressure the government to grant them Gorkhaland. But how has this vision of a separate state become so strong that people would be willing to subject themselves to injury or even death for it? There are many instances where people engage in violent struggles for 'ethnicity' or 'identity'. But can 'geography' be an equally effective rallying force?

Statehood movements can be understood as concerned with changing the existent set-up of state power over defined territories. Currently, there are about 30 demands of ethno-regional (Corbridge 1987) or subnational (Baruah 1997) groups in India aiming at an 'internal remapping' (Chadda 2002: 44) of the administrative state boundaries, officially in order to better accommodate their ethnic, identity-related or developmental aspirations.

However, as Agnew (2001: 103) noted, research on these movements often plays down the regional or territorial elements 'at the expense of the ethnic or cultural differences that movements supposedly rely on to mobilize local populations'. Also, research on the Gorkhaland movement has so far mainly focused on the 'why' and attempted to explain its emergence as resulting from a 'fear of losing [. . .] identity' (Subba 1992: 247) or a form of 'ethnic separatism' (Samanta 2000), thereby elaborating on the historical emergence of a shared sense of identity. Others explain the 'why' of the movement by pointing to economic reasons, such as economic deprivation and negligence, or see it as an expression of transferred anger, or exclusive administrative politics since the colonial times (Chakrabarty 1988; Chatterji 2007: 133 ff).[4]

But there is a lack of studies that focus on the ways in which statehood movements relate to the 'spaces' that they claim, *how* they contest and appropriate them. Edward Said stressed that this struggle over geography is 'not only about soldiers and cannons but also about ideas, about forms, about images and imaginings' (Said 1993: 6), or in short, about 'imaginative geographies'. In this chapter, I will argue that Gorkhaland is such an imaginative geography, which is strategically utilised to legitimise, invent and construct the space it envisions while, at the same time, providing a framework for mobilisation. Further, I argue that the specific form of the imaginative geography of Gorkhaland is mirroring what has been described as a 'de-territorialized subjectivity' of the Indian Nepalis (Golay 2009: 75) and their attempt to get full recognition as Indian citizens through the creation of a separate state.

The de-territorialised subjectivity of Gorkhas

A recurrent topic regarding Indian Nepalis is their 'identity crisis', which refers to their sense of feeling excluded from the Indian mainstream due to their stigmatisation as 'Nepalese' or citizens of Nepal (see Sinha and Subba 2003). These writings include reflections on the constitution of the Gorkha identity and subjectivity (see Golay, Thapa, Dhakal, Dhamala in Subba et al. 2009), and elaborate on the communities' shared experience of migration during the colonial times (Middleton 2010, chapter 2). In this context, Bidhan Golay writes:

> the problem of Gorkha subjectivity is not so much the problem of cultural displacement as it is a sense of being *deterritorialised*. There was a certain sense of lack that kept haunting him as he left his home and hearth. His subjectivity was bitterly *torn between*

the calling of the home and the hard reality of never returning to see it again.

(Golay 2009: 84, emphases added)

Middleton (2010) stresses the political aspects of belonging to a nation. He characterises the Gorkhas' experience in dwelling as 'precarious' and 'liminal' (ibid: 132), and their place in India as 'unstable' (ibid), all together adding to uncertainties over 'identity' and the 'anxieties of nonbelonging' (ibid.: 126) to the nation. This condition of diasporic societies entails a 'profound sense of a loss of territorial roots' (Tambiah 2000: 178). Such de-territorialisation is associated with the displacement of identities, persons and meanings (Kaplan 1987: 188). The relation between the diasporic society and territory is important in this context. Blunt has described this relation as the 'cultural geographies of diaspora'. These:

> encompass the material and imaginative connections between people and a 'territorial identity' [. . .]. The lived experiences and spatial imaginaries of people living in diaspora often revolve around ideas about home through, for example, 'the relationships between home and homeland, the existence of multiple homes, diverse home-making practices, and the intersections of home, memory, identity and belonging'.
> (Blunt and Dowling 2006: 199; Blunt 2007: 6)

What, however, distinguishes the Indian Nepali diaspora from this concept is their attempt at producing a 'territorial identity' related to Gorkhaland, which is yet to come into being. Yet, an analysis of the ways in which Gorkhaland is being constructed as an imaginative geography will reveal that connections with Nepal do indeed matter for the community.

Statehood movements and imaginative geographies

This section introduces the concept of regionalisation and the importance of imaginative geographies as strategies in this conflict-laden process.

Regionalisation and imaginative geographies

Since the 1980s, scholars have questioned the notion that space and spatial structures determine human agency, and instead, have stressed that categories such as space, scale (Marston 2000; Moore 2008), borders (Brunet-Jailly 2005; Van Houtum et al. 2005) or territory (Delaney 2005; Newman 2010) may not be regarded as pre-given entities, but as constructed and produced through human agency. In this understanding, the 'new regional geography' (Agnew 1999; Paasi 2002) stresses that also regions must be understood as social constructs and processes (Paasi 2002: 804). Such an approach focuses not only on the ways that regional boundaries come into being, but also on the practices of humans and the ways they produce regions through quotidian actions in historically grounded practices. Also, statehood movements are a form of regionalism as they attempt to construct new regions while challenging existing geographies of political control in order to establish different political-geographical orders – a process that Werlen has described as an 'oppositional form of geography-making' (1995: 358). Political regionalisations are the results of normative actions (Werlen 2005: 53) that assign meaning to space (Paasi 2002: 804). These historically determined processes are, however, not free of conflicts as different actors might have different imaginations about the 'proper' or most 'useful' political-geographical order, rendering regions expressions of 'a perpetual struggle over the meanings associated with space' (Paasi 2002: 805). At the same time, ideas about regions and regionalisations are constitutive elements of identity politics, and a possibility to gain access to resources (Paasi 2002: 805, 806).

Narratives of specific spatial units play an important role in the establishment of regions because they foster collective social classifications and identifications (Paasi 2002: 805). In this context, ethno-symbolic resources such as memories, myths, symbols and values form a repertoire, which elites may use to create a collective ethnic identity and to mobilise people for nationalist movements (Smith 1996b: 590). Anthony Smith has identified three foundations of nationalist movements: shared memories of a rich ethno-history and of a 'golden age', the belief in ethnic election and the belonging to an 'ancestral homeland' (ibid.). Such narratives make a specific space an indispensable part of shared memories so that the demanded space becomes an eternal home of ancestors and the 'own' (ibid.: 589). Also, imaginative geographies are endowed with such narratives, and thereby, not only contribute to the establishment of regions (Paasi 2002; Werlen 2005), but also to an ethno-regional consciousness. An analysis of such imaginative geographies, therefore, enhances the understanding of the regionalisation process in the context of ethno-regional movements.

Generally, imaginative geographies can be described as 'the descriptions and discursive constructions around place which are made and re-made within a particular cultural setting' (Radcliffe 1998: 275). They are grounded in specific sociocultural contexts and do not only reflect the imagining person's attitudes, socialisation and worldview (Travares and Brosseau 2006), but are also laden with his/her concerns, images, feelings and attitudes (Radcliffe 1998). Thereby, they transcend the subjective interpretation of physical territory (Morin 2011 [2004]: 339). While imaginative geographies can be the outcome of the unconscious and unreflective processes, they can also be consciously employed and invented in a strategic way as Edward Said's work (1978) demonstrates: Imaginative geographies are powerful constructs and expression of the power to define and interpret the world by imagining space as 'ours' and 'theirs'. As such, they attain the status of power-laden constructs, a form of the mental appropriation of space (Gregory 1995) that legitimises the physical appropriation of space (Gregory 1995: 463). Thus, imaginative geographies become a weapon in the struggle over geography (Said 1993: 6).

Reuber has termed such strategically designed imaginative geographies as 'strategic imaginative geographies' (Reuber 1999). These are selective descriptions of the claimed territory that are consciously invented by conflicting actors in a space-related conflict in order to legitimise and underline their claims on territory (Reuber 1999: 39, 2000). Strategic imaginative geographies are not distinct from imaginative geographies, but are a special form of these. The specific form of these strategic imaginations depends on the space-related objectives or spatial visions of actors. On the contrary, these imaginations reflect the socio-economic, political and historical contexts from which they emerge. Neither the space-related objectives nor the strategic imaginations are fixed; rather, they are adjusted to the course of the conflict and to the political context (Reuber 1999: 332).

Further, according to Reuber, 'strategic imaginative geographies' consist of four components: (i) selection of categories for the presentation of space-related data such as population and settlement structure, spatial linkages, physical terrain or history; (ii) single-sided interpretation of these data, (iii) raising the assertiveness and plausibility of the data, and (iv) deconstruction and discrediting of other actors' presentations and argumentations (ibid). The results of such selective presentations are strategically blurred presentations of 'reality' with the purpose to make the spatial visions become true. At the same time, strategic imaginative geographies serve as a source of information for decisive bodies and to support the mobilisation of population (ibid: 34). For the latter, ethno-regional-movements' attempt to foster a shared ethno-regional identity is important. This raises the question of how strategic imaginative geographies function for ethno-regional mobilisation and how such selective pre-sentations foster the aforementioned repertoires identified by Smith –, namely, shared memories, belief in ethnic election, and belonging to an ancestral homeland. Specifically the selective presentation of the contested area's history (Said 2000) is important here as this serves to legitimise territorial demands and to mobilise support (Agnew 2001: 106).

Through these selective presentations of data, strategic imaginative geographies do not only *carry* meaning, but also *produce* a certain view of the world and its geography (Snow and Benford 1988: 188). As such, they share elements with what social movements literature call 'frames', understood as 'conscious strategic efforts by groups [. . .] to fashion shared understandings of the world and of themselves that legitimate and motivate collective action' (McAdams et al. 1996: 6). Frames identify problems, propose a solution and motivate people to engage in order to fulfil the demand (Snow and Benford 1988). Viewing strategic imaginative geographies as frames enhances the understanding of their strategic character.

Based on these elaboration I will now focus on Gorkhaland as an imaginative geography. I concentrate on the ways the political parties demanding Gorkhaland strategically construct this imagination and utilise it not only to legitimise demands, but also as a collective action frame to mobilise support. Thereby, I will demonstrate that the specific form of this imaginative geography is not only endowed with ethno-symbolic resources, but also reflects the community's coming to terms with their own past and present as a 'de-territorialised' community.

Gorkhaland as an imaginative geography

In this section, I first make a brief review of the historical evolution of the demand for a separate state in Darjeeling. Next, I elaborate on the ways in which parties demanding Gorkhaland construct it as a strategic imaginative geography in order to legitimise their demand. Finally, I provide the account of different groups opposing the statehood demand by deconstructing the imagination of Gorkhaland. The findings are based on interviews that I conducted with representatives of different political parties demanding Gorkhaland in January/February, July 2011 and March 2012. The presentation of the Gorkha Janamukti Morcha (GJM) argumentation is further based on political speeches, interviews in newspapers and the party booklet, *Why Gorkhaland?* (GJM 2009). The presentation of Gorkhaland opponents includes the Communist Party of India (Marxist) or CPI(M), the Bangla O Bangla Bhasa Bachao Committee, Akhil Adivasi Vikash Parisad and Dooars Terai Nagarik Manch. The presentation of the

CPI(M) argumentation is based on an interview with the Member of Parliament, Suman Pathak, and Darjeeling's CPI-M president, K. B. Wattar, while for the other groups, their websites and blogs were consulted. The presentation of Trinamool Congress opinion builds on newspapers. An interview with Lyangsong Tamsang, President of the Indigenous Lepcha Tribal Association, conducted in March 2012 and an account in the Lepcha magazine, *Aachuley,* serves as the basis for Lepcha argumentation.

From Gorkhasthan to Gorkhaland

Darjeeling's eventful history and the shifting boundaries that made it part of Sikkim, Nepal, Bhutan and British India make it subject to controversial discussions about its affiliation, rendering it a 'contested space'. These demands are reflected in imaginative geographies. Some of these imagine Darjeeling as part of a 'Greater Nepal', or as 'Nye Mayel Lyang' (Lepchas), or as belonging to Sikkim, or as part of West Bengal. Among these different imaginations, the demand of Gorkhaland as a separate state is the most prominent. Among the parties making this demand most vociferously at present is the GJM, the currently leading party in Darjeeling. The Bharatiya Gorkha Parisangh (BGP), which defines itself as a national umbrella organisation of all Indian Gorkhas, also lobbies for Gorkhaland.

Although the aspiration for a separate administrative set-up had already evolved in 1907 with the establishment of the Hill Men's Association, which submitted a memorandum to the Government of Bengal in 1917, the term 'Gorkhaland' was only coined in the 1980s, first by Pranta Parisad, and then, more forcefully by the Gorkha National Liberation Front (GNLF). Of course, in the over 100-year-long history of demands for special administrative set-ups, their nature and the claimed territories changed. Demands ranged from 'Uttarkhand', including the areas of Darjeeling, Jalpaiguri, Cooch Behar and Sikkim, to 'Gorkhasthan', comprising the entire territory of Nepal, southern Sikkim and Darjeeling (Samanta 2000: 98). From 1986 to 1988, the peaceful struggle for autonomy turned violent when the GNLF launched a forceful agitation for Gorkhaland, mainly targeting members of the ruling CPI(M). The demand for Gorkhaland included, besides the three hill-subdivisions, Darjeeling, Kalimpong and Kurseong, the Dooars and Tarai areas of North Bengal too.

In 1988, the GNLF signed an agreement for the semi-autonomous Darjeeling Gorkha Hill Council (DGHC), which comprises the three hill-subdivisions and parts of Siliguri subdivision. The council, however,

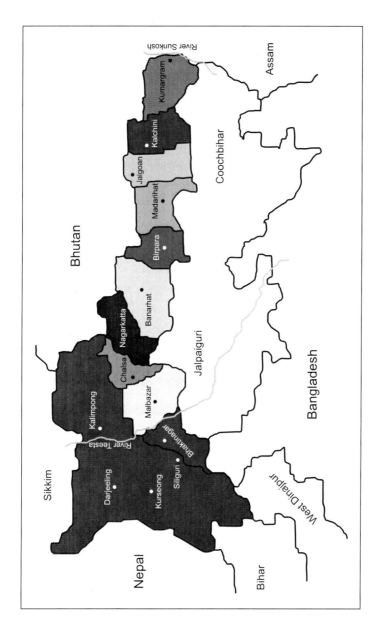

Figure 7.1 Map of proposed state of Gorkhaland as envisioned by the GJM

Source: GJM 2009.

did not fulfil the aspirations of people and was characterised by mismanagement and corruption (Benedikter 2009; Chakrabarty 2005). In 2008, when the public outrage had reached a critical point, the GNLF was ousted from power by GJM. Although having propagated and revived the demand for statehood, in July 2011, the GJM signed an agreement with the newly elected West Bengal Government under the Trinamool Congress (TMC) for the establishment of a Gorkhaland Territorial Administration (GTA), another semi-autonomous body to replace the DGHC, but with slightly more powers than the earlier dispensation. Nevertheless, the GJM stresses that the GTA is only a step towards statehood (speeches Bimal Gurung/Roshan Giri, GJM, 2011) – while the West Bengal Chief Minister Mamata Banerjee stressed that they would not allow 'another division of Bengal' (*Indian Express* 11 October 2011). This short account demonstrates the flexible nature of Darjeeling's imaginative geographies. Nevertheless, all demands share their aspirations for separation from West Bengal.[5]

In the following sections, I elaborate on the ways in which the demand for Gorkhaland is legitimised by the creation of strategic imaginative geographies. Second, I display how the strategic presentation of Gorkhaland functions simultaneously as a promise for a better life that contributes not only to the mobilisation of the population, but also renders the movement an issue of national importance.

Gorkhaland as a strategic imaginative geography

To legitimise the statehood demand, the Gorkha organisations apply a range of strategies such as the selective presentation of space and history-related data that culminate in the creation of Gorkhaland as a strategic imaginative geography, thereby endowing the claimed territory – Darjeeling, Dooars, Tarai – with meanings. At the same time, these imaginations reflect Smith's three foundations of nationalist movements: belief in ethnic election, shared memories of a 'golden age' and belonging to an ancestral homeland (Smith 1996b). Some of these imaginations and their contribution to the demand for Gorkhaland are discussed in detail below.

Darjeeling as a 'different place' and as a 'centre of all Indian Nepalis'

A group's belief in ethnic election is an element of a nationalist doctrine based on the assumption that every nation must possess an authentic identity to demonstrate its individuality and to reveal its unique contribution to the world (Smith 1996a: 453). The Gorkha organisations demonstrate their uniqueness and difference through two imaginative geographies: they draw a picture of Darjeeling as a different place, and present it as the centre of all Indian Nepalis. They do so by stressing their ethnic, historical, cultural and physical differences with Bengal (Chhetri 2011, GJM) including language, tradition, way of life and mindset which would make them a 'distinct race' (Thulung 23 July 2008, GJM). Further, Darjeeling is described as a 'topographical region with an entirely different climate'. As a result of this, there is 'a natural divide between the Gorkhas and the majority community in West Bengal' (Thulung 23 July 2008, GJM). An important reference point for proving Darjeeling's difference and the 'fact' that it had never been an integral part of Bengal is the district's special administrative status during the colonial times. Darjeeling had previously been classified as 'excluded district', 'scheduled district' or 'backward tract', so that rules and regulations of Bengal regarding land revenue and tax did not automatically apply to the area, but only after instructions from the governor of the province. This argumentation even reaches back to pre-British times because the parties stress that none of the proposed areas of Gorkhaland was ever possessed by any king of the 'plains of Bengal', but only by the kings of Sikkim and Bhutan, and had only been incorporated into India through various treaties (GJM 2009: 415). Thus, the parties disable their opponents' argument that the creation of Gorkhaland would lead to a 'second division' of Bengal after its first division from East Pakistan/Bangladesh in 1947.

This argumentation not only draws various boundaries between the Gorkhas and the Bengalis, and between Darjeeling and West Bengal, but also serves to legitimise the separation from West Bengal, as the following account of H. B. Chhetri, a spokesperson of GJM, shows: 'The government should recognise the fact that since the place is different you need to be treated differently. It needs a different kind of administration'. A second imaginative geography that evokes Darjeeling's uniqueness is its presentation as the centre of all Indian Gorkhas. Asked why Gorkhaland should explicitly be created in Darjeeling and not in another region of India, R. B. Rai, President, CPRM, stressed that Darjeeling was a 'social, political and symbolic centre' for all Indian Gorkhas. He describes it as the place of the freedom movement and as the centre of the language movement for the inclusion of the Nepali language in the Indian Constitution. Additionally, the GJM stresses that Gorkhas are the majority group in Darjeeling hills, whereas 'Lepchas, Bhutias and others' are in minority (GJM 2009: 16).

The reference to the Lepchas is particularly important as they are widely held as the indigenous population of Darjeeling. The pro-Gorkhaland parties stress that Nepali groups were long-term residents – besides Lepchas – of the region. However, H. B. Chhetri of GJM admits that Lepchas are 'right when they feel that initially this is their land' and describes them as 'the first people'.

Darjeeling as a 'place of previous wealth'

Shared memories are important as they contribute to the feeling of belonging of ethnic groups (Smith 1996b: 583). Particularly idealised memories of a 'golden age' foster the connection of an ethnic group with a certain geographical space (ibid.). The Gorkhas present Darjeeling as a place of wealth, which was lost resulting due to the neglect of the West Bengal government. Part of this neglect is also reflected in the imagination of Darjeeling as a place threatened by the alleged illegal immigrants from Bangladesh settling in Tarai and Dooars, thereby outnumbering the original Nepali population. This applies mainly to the contested city of Siliguri ('Siliguri was ours', H. B. Chhetri 2011, GJM). As a proof, H. B. Chhetri mentions place names such as 'Gurung Basti' and 'Pradhan Nagar', or names the 1952 municipality election winner, Jai Bahadur Subba.

Darjeeling as 'place of ancestors'

In order to make shared memories become 'national', they must be tied to a specific territory. Smith describes this process as the 'territorialisation of memory' (Smith 1996a: 453). Specific places are sites of key moments in the history of a group, or function as the locus of settlement. Narratives make the landscape an indispensable element of a community's history so that specific spaces become an 'ancestral homeland', thereby fostering territorial demands (Smith 1996a: 454, 1996b: 589). In this process, territories become 'ethno-scapes' (ibid.). Chhetri stresses: 'Everything that Darjeeling is today is the blood and sweat of our ancestors; it is not some Banerjee or Chatterjee who created Darjeeling'. By saying so, he draws a direct connection between body ('blood and sweat') and land.

Darjeeling, Dooars and Tarai as 'joined region'

The Dooars and the Tarai are especially contested as these areas consist of a mixed population, which includes Adivasis, Rajbanshis, Bengalis and others, some of who oppose their incorporation into the proposed Gorkhaland.

Yet, all Gorkha parties want to include the area although they acknowledge that it consists of a mixed population.[6] In order to support the togetherness of Tarai, Dooars and Darjeeling, they apply different argumentations.

First, they stress that till 1976, Mal, Mateli and Samsing areas in Dooars, Jalpaiguri district of West Bengal were part of the Darjeeling Parliamentary Constituency, which was split by the CPI(M), allegedly for electoral benefits. E. D. Pradhan describes this changing of boundaries of Darjeeling constituency by the CPI(M) as 'the greatest plunder on the fate of Gorkhas'. Second, while the Gorkha parties present Darjeeling as being distinct from the rest of West Bengal, they stress its commonness with the Tarai and Dooars in terms of cultural, social and linguistic affinities. Nepali is also described as the 'lingua franca' of the Dooars (GJM 2009: 6/7). Third, the Gorkha parties attempt to woo the Adivasis by reminding them of the 'tyranny of majority' (ibid: 10), poverty and domination as shared problems. The most forceful attempt at presenting Dooars and Darjeeling as one region was probably the short-lived re-naming of Gorkhaland as 'Gorkha Adivasi Pradesh' by GJM president, Bimal Gurung (*The Hindu* 01 June 2010).

Darjeeling as Ethnoscape

The various strategies legitimise the spatial vision of Gorkhaland by referring to history, population structure and ethnic boundaries. The form of this imaginative geography endows the demanded territory with a history of settlement, migration and appropriation. In these narratives, the imagined linkages between the colonial and migratory past, and the de-territorialised present become visible. Imagining Gorkhaland means to imagine it as a place of ancestors, a place of wealth that was lost due to governmental neglect. Through these purposefully established links between history, people and place in the hegemonic narrative of the Gorkhas, a 'regional identity' (Paasi 2001: 138) is created, an emotionally laden collective identification of people with their place. Through this connection of imaginative geographies with ethno-symbolic resources that tie shared memories of the community in the form of narratives to a specific place, the imaginative geographies unfold their mobilising potential and make people believe that the demand for Gorkhaland was their birth right, something worth dying for.

Gorkhaland as a promise

While the above section displayed the strategic utilisation of space-related data, it is also important to situate the demand of Gorkhaland in the socio-economic and cultural context from which it evolved. This includes the question of why Gorkhaland, and what the expected benefits are. Embedding the demand also discloses their problematic relationship with Nepal and their unstable status in India. All Gorkha spokespersons identify their 'identity-crisis' as the main reason for the demand. The 'identity-crisis' refers to the perceived lack of recognition as Indian and the stigmatisation as the citizens of Nepal. R. B. Rai and H. B. Chhetri identify as the main reason for this the similarities with the citizens of Nepal regarding height, dress, food, culture and language. As a second reason for this, they mention the open border between the two countries and the 1950 Treaty of Peace and Friendship between India and Nepal.

Based on this, the existence of Nepal is described as a major reason for the problem of Indian Gorkhas: 'If there was no Nepal, there would not be a problem for us. But because of the existence of Nepal we are in trouble' (E. D. Pradhan) or 'I believe, everywhere in the world where Nepalis are sad, the main reason is Nepal'[7] (R. B. Rai). Their feeling of being treated like foreigners also leads to concerns about their security in the event of ethnic violence and eviction, such as happened to the Indian Nepalis in Bhutan and different parts of north-east India in the 1980s and the 1990s.

This 'identity-crisis' is also linked to the perceived lack of development in the hills in terms of water, roads, medical and educational institutions, unemployment, and so on and the lack of scope for participation in decision-making processes. They blame the West Bengal government for a general neglect and for a policy of 'internal colonialism', exploiting the hills of their resources. A solution of the 'identity-crisis' would, therefore, also entail 'development': 'If we have an identity, then development automatically comes' (Nari Morcha, GJM, Darjeeling January 2011). H. B. Chhetri says:

> So once and for all if you want to resolve this crisis we will create a state. Create a state that will put it right. Then nobody will ask you: where are you from? And your developmental agendas are taken care of, you are there to rule yourself [. . .]. At least you enter the mainstream of Indian politics. Right now we don't have a direct link to the Indian government. We have to go via state, so automatically you become some kind of second class citizen.[8]

At the core of this logic stands the belief that a separation from West Bengal would solve their 'identity-crisis' 'because the boundary is that thing which creates identity' (H. B. Chhetri 2011). Or as E. D. Pradhan framed it: 'Give us Gorkhaland, within the Indian Union, and automatically there will be an address [for us]'.[9] At the same time, the separate state is seen as a way to 'de-link' from Nepal, reflecting their attempt of drawing a sharp line between themselves and Nepal.[10]

While opponents of the movement regularly accuse the Gorkhas of working towards the creation of a 'Greater Nepal', an idea of Nepal-based nationalists to 're-unite with the lost territories of Nepal' (Unified Nepal Nationalist Front 2011), including Darjeeling, all Gorkha parties stress that their demand was raised within the framework of the Indian Constitution by referring to Article 3, which provides for change of state boundaries.

As the decision about new states lies with the union government, the Gorkha leaders portray Gorkhaland as an issue of national importance. They apply a strategy of 'scaling' (see Jones and Fowler 2007; Moore 2008) by linking their statehood demand to a national security discourse, stressing that the geostrategically sensitive region of the 'chicken's neck'[11] could only be secured by the creation of Gorkhaland, thereby exploiting the Indian government's anxiety about foreign invasion (Unnithan 06 June 2011). 'Gorkhaland could be a "fortress" (H. B. Chhetri 2011) providing security against foreign infiltration and terrorism (*The Telegraph* 30 December 2008) and 'illegal immigrants and extremists (sic) from neighbouring countries' (GJM 2009: 12). It would be a buffer state of 'loyal Gorkhas . . . as the Gorkhas of India have always proved their unstinting loyalty to the nation' (GJM 2009: 12, 13). Here, they strategically present themselves as 'most loyal soldiers' (H.B. Chhetri) defending the country on its borders as brave Gorkha soldiers in the Indian Army. Also, their presentation as Indian independence fighters, or their role in the building of the Indian nation (Sinha 2008) adds to this picture. Thereby, imaginative geographies and geostrategic interests of the Indian government are actively utilised and connected to their demand.

Thus, Gorkhaland as a 'spatial vision' becomes more than a separate state or a physical territory in India; it is presented not only as a guarantor for development, justice, equality, participation, recognition, autonomy, democracy and national security, but also as the way to separate from West Bengal and Nepal. The vision of Gorkhaland is thereby presented as a solution to the outlined problems and takes the function of frames that identify the causes of problems and the suitable solution. Gorkhaland attains the form of a promise for a bright future. It becomes 'a dream worth living, a dream worth dying for' (Middleton 2010: 156).

From Gorkhaland to the Gorkhaland Territorial Administration

While the GJM, as the leading party in Darjeeling, has always stressed that nothing short of statehood would be accepted, after Mamata Banerjee became the new chief minister of the state, the party signed an agreement on GTA raising furious critiques of the other Gorkha parties, mainly the CPRM and ABGL, but also of the BGP, which accused the GJM of selling out the statehood demand. In order to defend their decision, Bimal Gurung, the president, and Roshan Giri, the general secretary, addressed the public in Darjeeling during the celebration of the new agreement in July 2012. While Roshan Giri stressed that the agreement had been signed 'without dropping the demand for Gorkhaland', Bimal Gurung legitimised the GTA by (i) portraying it as a solution to developmental problems, mainly underemployment and lack of big industries, and (ii) by portraying it as a carrier of identity, which came to many as a surprise as the GJM had previously stressed that only a *separate state* could solve these problems.

Deconstructing Gorkhaland

While the Gorkha parties attempt a construction of Darjeeling as 'Gorkhaland', there are many opponents of the statehood demand that employ a strategy of deconstruction. Among these groups are the CPI(M), the Bangla O Bangla Bhasa Bachao Samiti (BOBBBS), the Dooars Terai Nagarik Manch (DTNM), the Akil Bharatiya Adivasi Vikash Parisad (ABAVF) and the newly elected government headed by Mamata Banerjee.

Gorkhaland as threat to the state's power and class-consciousness

While the Gorkha organisations see the only way to solve their identity crisis in the creation of a separate state, the CPI(M) proposes the concept of 'state-within-the-state' to accommodate ethnic and autonomy aspirations. The overall aim is to retain strong states in order to balance the influence of the centre. The solution for Darjeeling is seen in the creation of an autonomous council under state rule (S. Pathak, CPI(M)). Any separation based on ethnic lines is rejected, as this would only obscure the division of society along classes (K. B. Wattar, CPI(M)). The CPI(M) starts by de-valuating the Gorkhas' 'identity-crisis', terming it as a political strategy to attain statehood. Accordingly, problems related to a feeling of discrimination should be solved through development and not through territorial boundaries. Also, the imagination of Darjeeling as 'homeland' for all Indian Nepalis is rejected (S. Pathak, CPI-M). Finally, S. Pathak sharply criticises the usage of the term 'Gorkhaland' in the new GTA set-up as it would dismiss all those things associated with the word 'Darjeeling' as a carrier of a history and identity. Instead of creating an identity, the identity which was there is lost (ibid).

Gorkhaland as national security threat

The BOBBS, DTNM and ABAVP, run by the Bengalis, share common elements regarding their argumentation against Gorkhaland and the Gorkhas in general. In order to make West Bengal state strong, 'assimilation' of other groups into Bengali culture and language is advocated. The BOBBBS portrays Darjeeling as an integral part of Bengal since 1865, but the district's previous special status as an excluded district is not mentioned. In order to support their demands and their opposition against Gorkhaland, two imaginative geographies are evoked: the first one of North Bengal overrun by illegal Nepali immigrants and the second portraying Gorkhaland as a threat to national integrity.

Darjeeling as part of Mâyel Lyâng

The Lepchas, or the Rong, are considered as the aborigines of Darjeeling district. This minority group with its concentration in the Kalimpong subdivision is mainly represented by the Indigenous Lepcha Tribal Association (ILTA), a non-political organisation that has as its aim, the preservation and revival of Lepcha culture, language and script, besides the upliftment of the community in developmental terms. A movement for these rights achieved the granting of a Lepcha Development Council (LDC) by the West Bengal Government in September 2011. Despite the Gorkhas' claim for statehood, the Lepchas view Darjeeling district as part of their ancient kingdom, 'Nye Mâyel Renjyong Lyâng', the 'holy hidden eternal land of the gentlemen' that can be regarded as representing a 'golden age' of the Lepchas. Lyangsong Tamsang, the President of ILTA, not only refers to old British sources, but also to many place names deriving from Lepcha language that were later changed by Tibetan, Nepali and British names. Also, the fact that huge portions of land were once owned by Lepchas supports his argument.

Discussion and conclusion

This chapter began with the question of how the vision of a separate state of Gorkhaland could become so powerful that people subjected themselves to injuries or even death for it. This question was assessed by focusing on the construction of imaginative geographies and their strategic employment in the struggle for Gorkhaland. I demonstrated that these mental appropriations of space are consciously created by Gorkha parties in order to legitimise and underline their demand for territory, as well as to mobilise supporters. Imaginative geographies powerfully connect narratives to places by ascribing a history of migration and appropriation to Darjeeling. Darjeeling becomes an ethno-scape mirroring the belief that each community needs its 'own' space to prosper.

The imaginative geography of Gorkhaland is presented as a solution to various problems of the Gorkha community in Darjeeling. The imaginative geography does not only explain the world as it is, but also as it *should* be. People's hopes, desires and aspirations for recognition as Indian citizens, for a secure place in India and development are projected on the physical spaces of Darjeeling, Dooars and Tarai. As such, the imaginative geography functions as a frame for collective action, according to the principle that 'people need feel both aggrieved about some aspect of their lives and optimistic that, acting collectively, they can redress the problem' (McAdams et al. 1996: 5). In this context, the spatial vision of Gorkhaland attains the status of a utopia, a 'placeless place' or a 'site[s] with no real place' (Foucault and Miskowiec 1986: 24). Utopias are imagined as 'fundamentally unreal spaces' (ibid.) still to become reality.

A closer look at the specific design and elements of the Gorkhaland imaginary reveals not only a colonial legacy of today's claim, but also their imagined relations to their ancestors' home country, Nepal. The entanglement of today's statehood demand with Darjeeling's colonial past becomes visible through the reference to the colonial administrative history of Darjeeling as an excluded/scheduled district or backward tract, or the observation that all wealth of the place was created by the British. The presentation of Gorkhaland as a 'fortress' for defence further links it with the perception of 'loyal and brave Gorkhas' and possibly reflects the 'martial race' (Caplan 1995) ascription of the British.

Second, Gorkhaland is described as an attempt of 'de-linking' from Nepal. Although their attempt at detaching themselves from Nepal is real, it is the migration history and the imagined cultural links with Nepal that form an important part of the construction of the imaginative geography of Gorkhaland and the way it is legitimised. In this respect, it underlines the assumption of Blunt (2007), who stressed that spatial imaginaries of diaspora societies are characterised by the 'relationships between home and homeland, [. . .], and the intersections of home, memory, identity, and belonging' (Blunt and Dowling 2006: 199). The demand for Gorkhaland reflects this 'standing in between' a lost home (Nepal) – to which the Gorkhas do not want to return – and their attempt to *re-territorialise* their present home, India. The Gorkha parties stress that only a separate state would guarantee an official recognition as Indian citizens and fulfil their project of delinking from Nepal. As such, the demand for Gorkhaland is founded on the sentiments of a de-territorialised community, which is made to believe that the creation of a separate state was the only way to re-territorialise themselves, and thereby, address its 'identity-crisis'. Yet, the agreement on the GTA and the allegedly violent marginalisation of other Gorkha parties by the GJM raises the question as to how far the vision of Gorkhaland is exploited by dominant political actors in order to legitimise their rule over Darjeeling.

Notes

1 If I want to build a house, I do not have a place for it (Source: Song: Ghar, from CD: Ghaderi).
2 This organisation overthrew the (till then) all powerful organisation called Gorkha National Liberation Front (GNLF), led by Subhas Ghising.
3 *Padayatra* means 'a journey on foot'. It also refers to a political strategy often employed by groups in order to further certain demands, or to mark a territory as their own.
4 Research on other statehood movements in India has so far mainly been concerned with their ethnic or identity-related aspects (e.g. Baruah 1997; Bhattacharyya 2001; Prakash 2001; Sarangi and Pai 2011). Others situated statehood movements with regard to the political and institutional structures in which these movements operate, including the ways the Indian government has attempted to accommodate their demands (Bhattacharyya 2005; Chadda 2002), the role of India's federal ideology (Adeney 2002; Mawdsley 2002), electoral politics that led to the emergence of these movements (Tillin 2011), the problematic appropriation of the European nation state concept in India (Baruah 1997), or the local effects of autonomy (Barbora 2009), including new states' administrative and economic effectiveness (Beck et al. 2010; Shah 2010), to name but a few.
5 The discussion below is only concerned with the current construction of Gorkhaland by the actual political parties and will not include any previous demands and accounts, although such a discussion would probably reveal much about the ways these geographic imaginaries were changed over time.
6 While GJM, ABGL and CPRM are only demanding those areas of Dooars and Tarai where the Gorkhas have a majority ('the Nepali belt', L. Pradhan, ABGL), therefore in line with the West Bengal government, the BGP stresses that the *entire*

Dooars and Tarai, referring to those areas that were once annexed to British India from Bhutan and Nepal, should be incorporated in Gorkhaland.
7 Thereby, R. B. Rai points to the problems of economic deprivation and hunger in Nepal, which caused Nepali citizens to migrate to India in search of employment.
8 Interview with Dr Harka Bahadur Chhetri, a prominent leader, on 7 February 2011 in Kalimpong, Darjeeling District.
9 This logic reflects the assumption that other Indian communities, such as Bengalis, Punjabis or Tamils, who are also spread over Bangladesh, Pakistan or Sri Lanka were not doubted to be Indian citizens because they have their own states in India, namely West Bengal, Punjab, Tamil Nadu, respectively.
10 This aspiration runs contrary to the fact that in order to present their distinctiveness, the GJM asks its followers to be dressed up in typical Nepali clothes, such as *topi, cholo* or *daura suruwal,* or play famous Nepali folk songs at its public meetings, again reflecting the problematic relationship with Nepal.
11 The geostrategic sensitivity and importance of the 'chicken-neck' for national security and integrity (Ramachandran 2011) derives from three factors. First, this small strip of land connects the Indian mainland with the insurgency-ridden north-east; second, it borders Nepal, Bangladesh and Bhutan; and third, there is a fear of Chinese invasion into the north-east of India (Unnithan 6 June 2011).

References

Adeney, K. 2002. 'Constitutional Centring: Nation Formation and Consociational Federalism in India and Pakistan', *Commonwealth & Comparative Politics*, 40(3): 8–33.

Agnew, J. 1999. 'Regions on the Mind Does Not Equal Regions of the Mind', *Progress in Human Geography*, 23(91): 91–96.

Agnew, J. 2001. 'Regions in Revolt', *Progress in Human Geography*, 25(1): 103–10.

Barbora, S. 2009. 'Natural Resources Contested in Autonomous Councils: Assessing the Causes of Ethnic Conflict in North-East India', in U. Geiser and S. Rist (eds), *Decentralisation Meets Local Complexity: Local Struggles, State Decentralisation and Access to Natural Resources in South Asia and Latin America*, pp. 191–215. Bern: NCCR North-South.

Baruah, S. 1997. 'Politics of Subnationalism: Society Versus State in Assam', in P. Chatterjee (ed.), *State and Politics in India*, pp. 496–520. New Delhi: Oxford University Press.

Beck, G., S. Destradi and D. Neff. 2010. Neue Bundesstaaten für Indien – eine Gefahr für die nationale Einheit? *GIGA Focus*, 9: 1–8.

Benedikter, T. 2009. 'Gorkhaland: Autonomy is No Longer the Issue', in T. Benedikter (ed.), *Solving Ethnic Conflict through Self-government: a Short Guide to Autonomy in South Asia and Europe*, Bozen: EURAC, 104–11.

Bhattacharyya, H. 2001. 'India Creates Three New States', *Federations*, 1(1), http://www.forumfed.org/libdocs/Federations/V1N3-in-Bhattacharyya.pdf. Accessed on 23 June 2012.

Bhattacharyya, H. 2005. 'Federalism and Regionalism in India: Institutional Strategies and Political Accommodation of Identity', *Heidelberg Papers in South Asian and Comparative Politics*. Working Paper No. 27, South Asia Institute, University of Heidelberg, Heidelberg.

Blunt, A. 2007. 'Cultural Geographies of Migration: Mobility, Transnationality and Diaspora', *Progress in Human Geography* online first, 1–11.

Blunt, A. and R. Dowling. 2006. *Home*. London: Routledge.

Brunet-Jailly, E. 2005. 'Theorizing Borders: an Interdisciplinary Perspective', *Geopolitics*, 10: 633–49.

Caplan, L. 1995. *Warrior Gentlemen: "Gurkhas" in the Western Imagination*. Oxord: Berghahn Books.

Chadda, M. 2002. 'Integration through Internal Reorganization: Containing Ethnic conflict in India', *The Global Review of Ethnopolitics*, 2(1): 44–61.

Chakrabarty, D. 1988. Gorkhaland: Evolution of the Politics of Segretation. Special Lecture X. Centre for Himalayan Studies, North Bengal University.

Chakrabarty, S. R. 2005. 'Silence under Freedom: The Strange Story of Democracy in the Darjeeling Hills', in R. Samaddar (ed.), *The politics of Autonomy: Indian Experiences*, pp. 173–95. New Delhi: Sage.

Chatterji, A. 2007. *Contested Landscapes: the Story of Darjeeling*. Kolkata: INTACH.

Corbridge, S. 1987. 'Perversity and Ethnoregionalism in Tribal India: The Politics of the Jharkhand', *Political Geography Quarterly*, 6(3): 225–40.

Delaney, D. 2005. *Territory: A Short Introduction*. Malden: Blackwell Publishing.

Foucault, M. and J. Miskowiec. 1986. 'Of Other Spaces', *Diacritics*, 16(1): 22–27.

Golay, B. 2009. 'Rethinking Gorkha Identity: Outside the Imperium of Discourse, Hegemony, and History', in T. B. Subba, A. C. Sinha, G. S. Nepal and D. R. Nepal (eds), *Indian Nepalis: Issues and Perspectives*, pp. 73–94. New Delhi: Concept Publishing.

Gorkha Janamukti Morcha. 2009. *Why Gorkhaland?* Darjeeling: Gorkha Janamukti Morcha, Central Committee.

Gregory, D. 1995. 'Imaginative Geographies', *Progress in Human Geography*, 19(4): 447–85.

Indian Express. 2011. 'Mamata Banerjee Rules Out Division of Bengal, Announces Projects', http://www.indianexpress.com/news/mamata-banerjee-rules-out-division-of-bengal-announces-projects/858536/. Accessed on 20 October 2011.

Jones, R. and C. Fowler. 2007. 'Placing and Scaling the Nation', *Environment and Planning D-Society & Space*, 25: 332–54.

Kaplan, C. 1987. 'Deterritorializations: The Rewriting of Home and Exile in Western Feminist Discourse', *Cultural Critique*, 6: 187–98.

Marston, S. A. 2000. 'The Social Construction of Scale', *Progress in Human Geography*, 24(2): 219–42.

McAdam, D., J. D. McCarthy and M. N. Zald. 1996. *Comparative Perspectives on Social Movements: Political Opportunities, Mobilizing Structures, and Cultural Framings*. Cambridge: Cambridge University Press.

Mawdsley, E. 2002. 'Redrawing the Body Politic: Federalism, Regionalism and the Creation of New States in India', *Commonwealth & Comparative Politics*, 40(3): 34–54.

Middleton, C. T. 2010. Beyond Recognition: Ethnology, Belonging, and the Refashioning of the Ethnic Subject in Darjeeling, India. Unpublished PhD thesis, Cornell University.

Moore, A. 2008. 'Rethinking Scale as a Geographical Category: From Analysis to Practice', *Progress in Human Geography*, 32(2): 203–25.

Morin, K. M. 2011 [2004]. 'Edward Said', in P. Hubbard and R. Kitchin (eds), *Key thinkers of space and place*, pp. 337–44. London: Sage.

Newman, D. 2010. 'Territory, Compartments and Borders: Avoiding the Trap of the Territorial Trap', *Geopolitics*, 15(4): 773–78.

Paasi, Anssi. 2001. Bounded Spaces in the Mobile World. Deconstructing Regional Identity, *Tijdschrift voor Economische en Sociale Geografie*, 93(2): 137–48.

Paasi, A. 2002. 'Place and Region: Regional Worlds and Words', *Progress in Human Geography*, 26(6): 802–11.

Prakash, A. 2001. *Jharkhand: Politics of Development and Identity*. Hyderabad: Orient Longman Limited.

Radcliffe, S. A. 1998. 'Frontiers and Popular Nationhood: Geographies of Identity in the 1995 Ecuador-Peru Border Dispute', *Political Geography*, 17(3): 273–93.

Ramachandran, Sudha. 2011. Gorkhas Divided over Autonomy Accord, http://www.atimes.com/atimes/South_Asia/MG21Df01.html. Accessed on 2 November 2011.

Reuber, P. 1999. *Raumbezogene politische Konflikte: Geographische Konfliktforschung am Beispiel von Gemeindegebietsreformen*. Reihe Erdkundliches Wissen 131. Stuttgart: Franz Steiner Verlag.

Reuber, P. 2000. 'Conflict Studies and Critical Geopolitics: Theoretical Concepts and Recent Research in Political Geography', *GeoJournal*, 50: 37–43.

Said, E. 1978. *Orientalism*. Harmondsworth: Penguin.

Said, E. 1993. *Culture and Imperialism*. London: Vintage.

Said, E. 2000. 'Invention, Memory, and Place', *Critical Inquiry*, 26(2): 175–92.

Samanta, A. K. 2000. *Gorkhaland Movement: A Study in Ethnic Separatism*. New Delhi: A. P. H. Publishing Corporation.

Sarangi, A. and S. Pai (eds). 2011. *Interrogating Reorganisation of States: Culture, Identity and Politics in India*. New Delhi: Taylor & Francis.

Shah, M. 2010. 'Governance, Identity and Statehood: India's Balkanization?', *Bericht aus aktuellem Anlass*, 22(10): 1–4.

Sinha, A. C. and T. B. Subba (eds). 2003. *The Nepalis in Northeast India: A Community in Search of Indian Identity*. Delhi: Indus Publishing Company.

Sinha, G. 2008. *The Role of Gorkhas in the Making of Modern India*. Delhi: Bharatiya Gorkha Parisangh.

Smith, A. D. 1996a. 'Culture, Community, and Territory: The Politics of Ethnicity and Nationalism', *International Affairs*, 72(3): 445–58.

Smith, A. D. 1996b. 'The Resurgence of Nationalism? Myth and Memory in the Renewal of Nations', *British Journal of Sociology*, 47(4): 575–98.

Snow, D. and R. Benford. 1988. 'Ideology, Frame Resonance, and Participant Mobilization', *International Social Movements Research*, 1: 197–217.

Subba, T. B. 1992. *Ethnicity, State and Development: a Case Study of the Gorkhaland Movement in Darjeeling*. New Delhi: Vikas Publishing House.

Subba, T. B., A. C. Sinha, G. S. Nepal and D. R. Nepal (eds). 2009. *Indian Nepalis: Issues and Perspectives*. New Delhi: Concept Publishing Company.

Tambiah, S. J. 2000. 'Transnational Movements, Diaspora, and Multiple Modernities', *Deadalus*, 129(1): 163–94.

The Hindu. 2010. 'GJM now for Gorkha-Adivasi Pradesh', http://www.thehindu.com/news/article442973.ece. Accessed on 2 October 2011.

The Statesman. 2011. 'Anti-Gorkhaland Bodies Oppose Area Inclusion', http://www.thestatesman.net/index.php?option=com_content&view=article&id=381738&catid=72. Accessed on 5 September 2011.

The Telegraph. 2011. 'Khukuri Slash Reopens Gash, Cop Shots Kill 2, Hills on Fire', http://www.telegraphindia.com/archives/archive.html. Accessed on 12 March 2011.

The Telegraph. 2011. 'Unity on Lips, CM Serenades Dar(jee)ling', http://www.telegraphindia.com/1111012/jsp/frontpage/story_14614119.jsp. Accessed on 14 October 2011.

The Telegraph. 2008. 'PC to Morcha: Go for More Talks – Hill Delegation Offers Chicken Neck Stability', http://www.telegraphindia.com/archives/archive.html. Accessed on 1 November 2011.

Thulung, A. 2008. 'Why Gorkhaland? Interview with Alok Thulung, GJM Youth Wing', http://www.darjeelingtimes.com/news/Interviews/Why-Gorkhaland.html.

Tillin, L. 2011. 'Questioning Borders: Social Movements, Political Parties and the Creation of New States in India', *Pacific Affairs*, 84(1): 67–87.

Travares, D. and M. Brosseau. 2006. 'The Representation of Mongolia in Contemporary Travel Writing: Imaginative Geographies of a Travellers "Frontier"', *Social & Cultural Geography*, 7(2): 299–317.

Unified Nepal Nationalist Front. 2011. 'Greater Nepal', http://www.greaternepal.org/. Accessed on 10 April 2011.

Unnithan, S. 2011. 'Gunrunners of North-East: Chinese Agents Smuggle Arms to Revive Militancy in North-Eastern India', http://indiatoday.intoday.in/story/chinese-agents-smuggle-arms-to-spread-militancy-in-north-east/1/139538.html. Accessed on 2 November 2011.

Van Houtum, Henk, Olivier Kramsch and Wolfgang Zierhofer (eds). 2005. *B/ordering Space*. Doris Wastl-Walter, Border Regions Series. Burlington: Ashgate.

Werlen, B. 1995. Sozialgeographie alltäglicher Regionalisierungen. Bd. 2: Globalisierung, Region und Regionalisierung. Reihe Erdkundliches Wissen 119. Stuttgart: Franz Steiner Verlag.

Werlen, B. 2005. Regions and Everyday Regionalizations: From a Space-centred towards an Action-Centred Human Geography', in H. Van Houtum, O. Kramsch and W. Zierhofer (eds), *B/ordering space*. Aldershot: Ashgate, 47–60.

List of interviews and speeches

Mr. Bimal Gurung, President of GJM; speech at celebration of the GTA agreement, Darjeeling, July 2011.

Dr. Enos Das Pradhan, BGP; interviewed in July 2011.

Dr. Harka Bahadur Chhetri, media spokesperson (now, MLA Kalimpong), GJM, interviewed in February 2011.
Mr. K. B. Wattar, President, CPI-M Darjeeling, interviewed in March 2012.
Mr. Laxman Pradhan, General Secretary, ABGL, interviewed in July 2011.
Ms. Pemu Chhetri, MLA Candidate Kurseong, GNLF, interviewed in July 2011.
Mr. R. B. Rai, President of CPRM, interviewed in July 2011.
Mr. Roshan Giri, General Secretary GJM, speech at celebration of GTA agreement, Darjeeling, July 2011.
Mr. Suman Pathak, Member of Parliament, CPI(M), interviewed in July 2011.
Mr. Lyangsong Tamsang, President of Indigenous Lepcha Tribal Association, interviewed in March 2012

List of websites and blogs

Akil Bharatiya Adivasi Vikash Parisad (ABAVP) http://adivasivikashparishad.blogspot.com/. Accessed on 29 September 2011.

Bangla O Bangla Bhasa Bachao Samitti (BOBBBS), http://banglabanchao.org/. Accessed on 28 September 2011.

Dooars Tarai Nagarik Manch, http://dtnm.blogspot.com/. Accessed on 29 September 2011.

8

WRITING FROM THE EDGES TO THE CENTRE

Theorising the fragmented identity of Indian Nepalis

Anastasia M. Turnbull

'This is an offering of who I am, where I come from and where I belong'.

Teresa Luciani

Introduction

The need is so intense and fundamental that we would lose humanity, we would cease to exist if we stopped telling stories of who we thought we were, and if we stopped wanting to listen to others' stories.

(Behar 1993: 19)

It had been a stressful few weeks. I was nearing the end of my first semester of graduate school when my maternal grandfather, Wing Kong, fell ill, and after a two-month period at a Mississauga hospital not too far from his home, my family and I were doing our best to celebrate our last day, his 80th birthday, with him. Our hearts have been heavy since. At the time, I did not foresee how my grandfather's passing would turn my life around, but it has become a moment in my history that changed the direction of my path, both professionally and personally, and to which I would return when settling into the beginnings of my PhD thesis (Cole and Knowles 2001: 120).

To cope with the profound feelings of the present, I found myself searching for the stories of his past. Unfortunately, much like the Rabbi

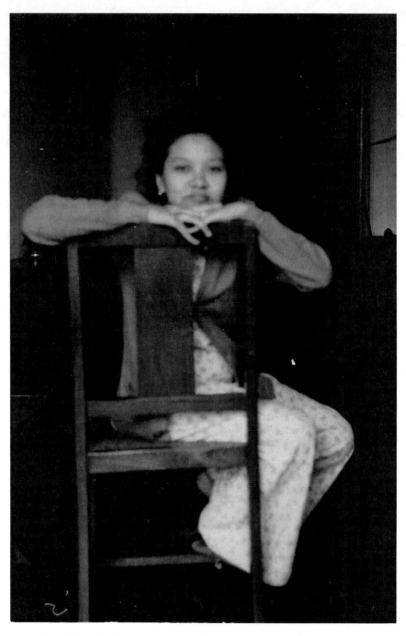

Figure 8.1 Kolkata, India (approximately 1961). My grandmother at her home
Copyright with the author.

from *A Book that was Lost*, each time I arrived at a question only he could have answered, the loss echoed in the silence. It simply broke my heart to think his death had come before we had enough stories of his life to carry forward his place in this world. Memories of his past might run deep enough to express and cushion these feelings, but the haunting reality is we can never return to the past or reclaim it now as it once was (Kuhn 2002: 1). The only thing left to dampen the echo for preceding generations is to resist the loss, to some extent, by documenting the stories around which our ancestors' identities were built (Behar 2008: 532), so that as the years pass by, they become part of someone else's story in a larger history (Ibid.: 532). After all, conceding to feelings of doubt and loss would, in effect, subordinate history to our single existence, and not writing a person's history is simply a great injustice (Kuhn 2002: vii).

Without committing a word to paper, my grandmother has been writing the story of her life from a very young age, when she called Darjeeling home. Impressed on her memory were the relationships with her family and peers and the places which housed these bonds. Yet, because it was not in her power to transform her memories to words, she has left me with this profound task (Behar 1993: 22). Together, we have restored the lives, places and relationships from another time, and hauled them into the present where they have been able to exist among us. Curbing the finality of death in this way has provided us with hope, a strategy to cope with feelings of guilt and loss, and a way to move forward, accompanied by the people and places that precede us. I attempt to retell the stories of her past from 'within' (Halifax 2008: 218) simply and honestly. This is especially important for people who have been left behind or forgotten in a society that stratifies people based on race, ethnicity, age, class and caste. I share this journey with my (and my grandmother's) readers vulnerably as a human being and researcher in the hope that it will move them as a reader to respond with the same vulnerability (Behar 2008: 185).

The objectives of writing this are two-fold: first, to restore the pieces of a fragmented identity through my ancestors and the people who would have, and still do, share in experiences of social isolation based on their ethnic heritage (both perceived and real). Though a quest for identity is an important task, it is also a difficult one, as Subba suggests, since finding one's roots can also bind them to a single place from which growth can be difficult to achieve (Thapa 2009: 104). It seems the obstacles are compounded even further by an identity which has roots in different parts of the world. Nonetheless, the alternative is simply not an option since I, like most people who are struggling with their identities, have a lot at stake. I have a young child who bears the features of my ancestors, and one day, she will find herself renegotiating her identity much like I have been. I hope the results of this write-up help her and others find their way.

Second, I hope to contribute to the academic discourse on identity in general, and the identity of Indian Nepalis, specifically. Indian Nepalis in Darjeeling, both past and present, are of particular importance to me because understanding my grandmother's and great-grandmother's lives in Darjeeling requires a sense of context – after all, a life lived cannot be understood in any other terms. And, though we may never know whether she was a Bhutia from Nepal or Tibet, unfortunately, we can say for certain that having spent part of her life in Darjeeling meant, at the very least, that she would have encountered Nepalis there in some capacity. It is for this reason that they are the focus of this chapter.

Making sense of a fragmented identity

'Identity', for all intents and purposes, is defined as being a component of an individual's overall self-concept (White and Parham1990: 41), including personal feelings, behaviours, attitudes and characteristics shared with familiar reference groups. However, it is also formed by a comparison to what the Other is and what one is not. As Bidhan Golay puts it, '. . . identities are as much self-constructed as it is constructed by the other' (Golay 2009: 76).

Part of my ethnic identity is rooted in a colonial past; the other, my maternal lineage, is what I have set out to better understand in this chapter. Put succinctly, I represent both the coloniser and the colonised, and through this tension, I have developed what Homi Bhaba calls a hybrid identity, which straddles between multiple worlds – in my case, a space of not quite either the coloniser or the colonised (Sunseri 2000: 2). To put it differently, I am neither here nor there; my sense of self exists somewhere in this in-between place, and as a result, these fragments amount to a sense of 'homelessness' for if the very soils upon which I was born do not welcome my participation and belongingness, what other option have I got to refer to as 'home'? This feeling of not belonging or not feeling grounded in a particular space marked the onset of my PhD research and a physical journey to Darjeeling on a quest for identity. Allow me to share a few excerpts from the interviews I conducted with my grandmother, which ultimately inspired my remarkable journey to Darjeeling in search of a presence from the past.

No one ever asked.
March 21, 2009

I drove along the QEW in Toronto towards my grandmother's house in Mississauga, Ontario, a route I had taken from a very early age in the back seat of my parents' car. But this time, the ride was different. I felt different. I was preparing for my first interview with my grandmother, and though the relationship had lasted my lifetime, these emotions were new. I set up my camcorder in the family room, and spread out an old family tree I had completed years ago as a school assignment. A lot of the information was given to me by my grandfather while he was alive, so it was like unravelling an old document that contained the secrets of the past. And, although she was unable to read a word, my grandmother leaned in with excitement because she understood what sort of information the document contained.

Nan, what was your life like in Darjeeling? I asked her.

Tacey, ten-year-old child here [in Canada] play with friends. I have no friends. I be work all my life. Just housework. I go to one house and cook, clean. I go to another house, cook, clean. My story nothing excited.

She recalls being sent to a roadside to sell *churpi* (a special Himalayan snack made from yak's milk), sugarcane and rice crispie balls. She would sit at a table alongside the pork and beef vendors, and sell what she could to help the family.

I go by self. Who gonna go with me? I know the Indian guy, right. I go there ask 50 lbs rice. Then I got a basket, carry on the back. Rice crispies you make, the white one. So, I bring, I don't know how many pound – 20lb or something. Like the red sugar – that also I buy 20lbs. Daddy melt that in the wok *(a sort of large Chinese cooking vessel). Then the rice crispie, put it, mix it up, make the rice crispie ball. Then I sit down there whole day. I don't know how much I sell. Sometime I sleep. Somebody take it too. The guy tease me say, 'Sara deen sota, koyee chorie karkay lay jaiga bhe nay janayga' meaning, 'You sleep the whole day. Somebody take also you don't know'. Everyday go. Nobody to talk. By self. I do all by self.*

> Nan, can you tell me about your parents?
> *What you want to know?*
> Can you tell me about your mum?
> *What to tell? My mum be Bhutia and she be live Darjeeling. When I come Kalimpong, mummy already pass away. Not much remember.*
> Do you have a photo of your mum?
> *Ek minute.*
> After several minutes, she returned with a small plastic wallet sleeve.
> *Here. This be my mummy.*

Figure 8.2 Darjeeling, West Bengal (approximately 1943). This photo was taken at a studio and in it (left to right) are: My grandmother's sister (only known as 'Kanchi' or the youngest daughter in Nepali), mother (Ingu Lamu), nephew (Kahing) and brother (Yeu Leung)

Copyright: Author.

Where was this picture taken?
In my room.
Nan, why didn't you ever tell anyone about this picture?
No one asked.
I knew then this project would be important for us both, but I was certain it would change me. I was glad I asked.
Nan, can you tell me what you remember about your mum?
Not much to remember. When I be young, she used to dance on the stairs with her friends. It be party something.
A festival?
Something like. When I come from Kalimpong, she be pass away.
This is all we know about my great-grandmother, Ingu Lamu.

Her memories were remarkably descriptive and full of rich detail, but I needed to go; I needed to be in the same places she once lived, and with any luck, meet the very people who graced our conversations, so that I could fill in the pieces of her life history . . . and also my own.

Darjeeling
January 2009
As we made our way up the winding mountain from the Bagdogra airport, the faces of the people working on their land, gathered with neighbours on their front steps and walking along the roadside became more and more familiar. I was able to see the resemblance to my grandmother and great-grandmother in their faces, although physical characteristics still today are not an accurate marker of the ethnic group to which one belongs. It was at this moment that I felt I had finally arrived. I was home.

This feeling of coming home may be a bizarre concept to some, considering the only place that has ever been home to me is Toronto, Ontario, Canada, where I was born and raised. However, I continue to feel out of place in this multicultural metropolis, which is said to be home to, and a place of opportunity for, people from various parts of the world, including people of Nepali origin. Notwithstanding the existence of racist ideology, practice and policy, it does fulfil this objective, but for most of my adult life, I have been asked, 'Where are you from?' as if to suggest I don't resemble Canadians, whatever that may be; 'But I don't see you as Chinese!' Well, this is because I am not *only* Chinese, but for those who are ignorant of the diversity among people from Asian communities in general and East Asian communities in particular, anyone and everyone with 'Asian' features is pegged as Chinese (people are still floored when they hear my mother speak fluent Hindi because they have preconceived notions of what constitutes an 'Indian' and she doesn't fit the template, not physically anyway). These are but a few comments which have stuck with me, that have reminded me of my difference and of the confusion and difficulty I present to a society that feels the need to compartmentalise me (along with the many others who are marked as 'different') in order to make sense of me, ultimately to make sense of themselves (Golay 2009: 58).

There is a need not only to understand or make sense of the people who are 'different' (Said's 'Orientalist'), but also a need to *contain* us/them in order to maintain a division between those with power and those with minimal or no power at all; for without these Marxist divisions, and more specifically, without one to dominate, one cannot come to know oneself as dominant. So, if the dominant group recognises that the Other is really not as different or as undesirable as the divide requires, then there is a risk that the (imaginary) borders which separate 'us' and 'them' will collapse, eliminating the lines along which people are stratified. The ideology which is at the core of questions such as, 'Where are you from?' or statements such as, 'But I don't see you as Chinese!' and which define categories of 'us' and 'them' are designed to keep certain people in, and simultaneously others out. As Thapa puts it, '. . . when we belong to a nation or an ethnic group, there is an automatic exclusion of others, as we introduce a principle of division' (Thapa 2009: 98). As a result, the dominant group has an interest in the workings of exclusion since it continuously carves out a path which reinforces dominant ideologies about the Other. It is a strategy to contain the subjugated positions of marginalised people.

Issues of identity facing Indian Nepalis

A timeline of events

The economic prospects of tea and cinchona plantations were used to entice the migration of the Nepalis to Darjeeling (Golay 2009: 82), while the colonial agenda was to recruit cheap labour to develop the infrastructure for its hill station and tea gardens and to enlist a large number of Gurkhas in the army (Dhakal 2009: 151). The Nepalis were considered suitable candidates to work in the plantations because they were casteless, docile and hardworking hill men, and since the Gurkha soldier was framed as simple and free of religious prejudices (Golay 2009: 82), he was best suited for the British Army. The colonial state, in effect, carved out a cultural identity of the Gurkha as a British import (Ibid.: 86), which has led other ethnic groups to understand their identities as tangential to the nation state, in spite of the fundamental roles they played in the building of the nation. A good example of its contemporary manifestations is the tea industry today: no Nepali, Lepcha and Bhutia owns a tea estate (Subba 1992: 46), making this lucrative industry, then, a reflection of the way the society is stratified ethnically.

Prior to the British, life was largely migratory in the Himalayas for many years (Subba 1992: 41), which meant ethnic identities and group memberships were fluid up until that point. Nepali society comprised, and still does, a diverse group of people with different historical, racial, cultural, spatial, class and occupational identities. (Subba 1989: 50; Subba 1992: 37; Subba 2003: 202). Yet, despite their differences and the soils upon which they were born, all Nepalis have been reduced to a singular and homogeneous category as a result of the *Janajāti* movement of the 1990s (Subba 2003: 204). It was said to be a project of unity and integration, but the Nepalis' will to both integrate into Indian nationalism *and* preserve their language and cultural roots were seen as a threat to the nationalistic fibres of India and the sociopolitical agenda of the political powers (Dhakal 2009: 171). A fear of nationalistic consciousness and its potential to subvert, and possibly dislodge, the existence of hegemonic powers, Noam Chomsky says, is connected to the ways in which 'dangerous others' are perceived and transformed into scapegoats in society. 'The building up of scapegoats and fear is standard . . . You don't want people to look at the actual source of power; that's much too dangerous, so, therefore, you need to have them blamed, or be frightened of, someone else' (Chomsky 1995: 134). Following this line of thinking, labels which push Indian Nepalis to the margins and relegate them to subjugated positions fulfil a strategy of containment designed to make divisive boundaries between those who belong and those who do not. Let us explore those labels here.

The foregrounding issue has less to do with Indian Nepalis' social and cultural identities as they are based on a 'shared history, common cultural roots and collective memory' (Dhakal 2009: 173). Instead, their request for segregation is an act of resistance against a double labelling: 1) racist labels of 'kancha' (household servant), 'daju' (porter) 'bahadur' and 'Gorkha', and more critically, 2) the misplaced labels of 'foreigner', 'alien' and 'immigrant', which eat away at their legitimate claim as Indian nationals (Subba 2003: 202; Subba et al. 2009: 385), and subsequently, create precarious living conditions. The fear of eviction is very real for Indian Nepalis whose past experiences of eviction from states such as Manipur, Mizoran, Nagaland, Assam, Meghalaya are vivid reminders of the impact the category 'foreigner' can have on one's political status. A glaring example is the All Assam Students' Union Movement (1979–85). This movement transformed the ethnic landscape into hostile grounds for Nepalis whose ancestors settled in India in the early 19th century (Subba 2003: 206) and who were integral to the history of India, and specifically, to the development of the region. Indian Nepalis were evicted in thousands and expected to return to what was perceived as their homeland, Nepal, when they were very much of Indian origin (Dhakal 2009: 172). The myth of a double homeland and a dual identity, which is located both locally and globally, complicates the notion of belonging, and a double consciousness, as W. E. B. Dubois refers to it, and forces them to represent two different identities without ever being whole in either one (Thapa 2009: 103). It seems natural here to ask: what constitutes 'enough' to gain citizenship into a multicultural landscape, such as India? In order to help paint the multicultural fabric, one must hold onto some part of their native language, art, customs and traditions and so on, yet relinquish enough to gain citizenship. So, how much is enough to gain access? This seems like a slippery proposition, and especially precarious when the tacit implication is some citizens will be given full rights and others not. If this is true, on what grounds does multiculturalism exist? And, if some are expected to give up more than others, then multiculturalism simply conceals the lines of stratification along which people and knowledge are hierarchically placed. An anti-oppression agenda seems to better address the realities of marginalised bodies.

My connection to Indian Nepalis

My mother was born and educated in Kolkata until the age of 16 when, along with her family, she immigrated to Canada so that my grandfather could pursue more stable employment prospects. It was here in Canada (specifically, Toronto) that she met my father, a young man from England who was himself in pursuit of similar opportunities. He often told the story of his mother's reassurance that he could create a life for himself anywhere in the world, which he did with great success.

From a very early age, I understood the notion of 'difference', that I was different, and how it was used to set me apart from my classmates. Children are said to discriminate differences in people from a very early age, and although I grew up in a robust and multicultural metropolis, I attended a school which predominantly comprised white children, none of whom bore the same features as I did, so even then, I was difficult to peg. Today, that same difficulty is presented in the form of questions such as, 'Where are you from?' which initially seem harmless and curious, but which effectively signify a *perceived* belonging and citizenship which, of course, also comes along with adjoining descriptions of those who do not belong or fit the template of a Canadian woman. It seems paradoxical, given the context, but the reality of multicultural spaces is that they are not devoid of or immune to racist ideology and practice. In fact, their impact has very real consequences in the daily lives of racialised bodies. Further to that, not unlike the stories of many people who, like me, renegotiate their identities all the time, the battle is often against others, in addition to oneself, from the same cultural and ethnic group which has internalised the status quo. Overcoming barriers is doubly difficult, then, when one is up against one's own ethnic group, as well as the wider society.

As a child, I was referred to as a 'chink' on a regular basis and although my features leaned slightly more to my matrilineal line, I inherited a few of my father's features, which made me both too Asian (broadly defined) for the white children in my school and just white enough to have my sense of belonging questioned by Asians and others who felt a category was necessary. This struggle was never one I felt I had to contend with within my home – I was encouraged to embrace and celebrate both heritages equally. The weight of societal demands, however, created insecurity and an incessant questioning of identity: Who am I? Where do I come from? Where do I belong? And, even as an adult, I still feel insecure and unsure of the answer I would provide if ever asked in greater depth. So, I embarked on a life history project, the focus of which was my maternal grandmother, in an attempt to locate myself concretely in and through the people who precede me and ultimately for the people who would come after. In effect, a project of this nature hints at my bloodlines quite matter-of-factly and its form is instrumental in reflecting the person I am and the subjects of importance to me.

My research led me to the stories of displaced Indian Nepalis, which immediately felt familiar to me. Although the sort of oppression they continue to face is far different from anything I have ever experienced, there is a common ground: I too feel isolated from the only home I know. And without any documentation to connect my bloodlines to theirs, my ancestors have left without a trace, leaving me only to speculate, given their presence in numbers during the early 1900s that one or more of my ancestors is an Indian Nepali. I may never know for certain, but they have an inherent story of perseverance amidst adversity, and to that end, a kindred spirit they will forever be.

Resistance movements in Darjeeling

Since the beginning of the 20th century, the Nepalis in Darjeeling have been demanding political autonomy. During the early 1900s in Darjeeling, almost all Nepalis were have-nots. It was only after the second half of the 19th century that there grew a middle class as a result of the educational institutions created by the British missionaries and administrators in the Darjeeling hills. From this newly formed middle class developed sociopolitical reforms and movements. But their struggle is distinct and unique from other regional movements for autonomy because although they share the common goal of combating marginalisation, their fight is not so much rooted in economic inequalities as it is in citizenship and the right to be recognised by the people of India as Indian citizens, which comes with the same economic and political rights as fellow Indian nationals. In the 1920s, a language movement began, which advocated for the introduction of Nepali as a mode of instruction in educational institutions. In 1961, this movement developed into a demand that the language be an official language in Darjeeling, and then, in the 1970s, into a movement for it to be included in the 8th Schedule of the Constitution (Dhakal 2009: 154). These socio political activities that formed the language movement illuminated the precariousness of their identities and created a sense of hope among the mass of supporters that it would transform into a separate state called 'Gorkhaland'.

Conclusion

Indians living with multiple identities seem to fly under the radar, but confusion continues to surround them because there are Nepalis in both Nepal and India, and even to an Indian Nepali scholar such as Subba, the discernible markers of difference are dialectical and emotional, neither of which are visible (Subba et al. 2009: 386).

This creates a disguise under which migrant Nepalis, who are said to have no vested interest in India, can cross back and forth between borders and allegedly commit crimes, leaving the Indian Nepalis who bear the same physical features and who share the same language to be blamed (Subba et al. 2009: 385). As a result, segregating the native Nepalis from the migrant ones is virtually impossible, and despite the 1950 Treaty of Peace and Friendship and a policing of the India-Nepal border, there will continue to be a migration of people between India and Nepal (Subba 2003: 199). Additionally, they will continue to be treated as outsiders even if the nomenclature crisis is rectified.

References

Behar, R. 1993. *Translated Woman: Crossing the Border with Esperanza's Story*. Boston: Beacon Press.

Behar, R. 2008. 'Anthropology: Ethnography and *The Book That Was Lost*', in A. L. Cole (ed.), *Handbook of the Arts in Qualitative Research: Perspectives, Methodologies, Examples, and Issues,* pp. 529–44. Thousand Oaks: Sage Publications.

Chomsky, Noam. 1995. 'A Dialogue with Noam Chomsky', *Harvard Educational Review*, 65(2): 127–44.

Cole, Ardra L. and J. Gary Knowles. 2001. *Lives in Context: The Art of Life History Research*. Walnut Creek, CA: AltaMira Press.

Halifax, Nancy Viva Davis. 2008. 'From the Corner of My Eye', in J. G. Knowles et al. (eds), *Creating Scholartistry: Imagining the Arts-Informed Thesis or Dissertation*. Halifax, NS: Backalong Books.

Kuhn, A. 2002. *Family Secrets: Acts of Memory and Imagination*. New York: Verso.

Dhakal, Rajendra P. 2009. 'The Urge to Belong: An Identity in Waiting', in T. B. Subba, A. C. Sinha, G. S. Nepal and D. R. Nepal (eds), *Indian Nepalis: Issues and Perspectives*. New Delhi: Concept Publishing Co.

Golay, Bidhan. 2009. 'Rethinking Gorkha Identity: Outside the Imperium of Discourse, Hegemony, and History', in T. B. Subba, A. C. Sinha, G. S. Nepal and D. R. Nepal (eds), *Indian Nepalis: Issues and Perspectives*. New Delhi: Concept Publishing Co.

Subba, T. B. 1989. *Dynamics of a Hill Society: The Nepalis in Darjeeling and Sikkim Himalayas*. Delhi: Mittal Publications.

Subba, T. B. 1992. *Ethnicity, State and Development: A Case Study of the Gorkhaland Movement in Darjeeling*. New Delhi: Vikas Publishing House.

Subba, T. B. 2003. 'Being a Nepali in Northeast India: Predicaments of a "Privileged Nation"', in A. C. Sinha and T. B. Subba (eds), *The Nepalis in Northeast India: A Community in Search of Indian Identity*. New Delhi: Indus Publishing Company.

Subba, T. B., A. C. Sinha, G. S. Nepal and D. R. Nepal (eds), 2009. *Indian Nepalis: Issues and Perspectives*. New Delhi: Concept Publishing Co.

Sunseri, Lina. 2000. 'Moving Beyond the Feminism versus the Nationalism Dichotomy: An Anti-Colonial Feminist Perspective on Aboriginal Liberation Struggles', *Canadian Woman Studies*, 20(2): 143–48.

Thapa, Tapasya. 2009. 'Being and Belonging: A Study of the Indian Nepalis', in T. B. Subba, A. C. Sinha, G. S. Nepal and D. R. Nepal (eds), *Indian Nepalis: Issues and Perspectives*. New Delhi: Concept Publishing Co.

White, J. and T. Parham. 1990. 'The Struggle for Identity Congruence in African-Americans', in J. White and T. Parham (eds), *The Psychology of Blacks: An African-American Perspective*. Englewood Cliffs, NJ: Prentice Hall.

9

THE INHERITANCE OF LOSS AND THE PORTRAYAL OF INDIAN NEPALIS

Geetika Ranjan

Forms of art often emerge from facts of life. So, similarities between the characters in fiction and those in actual life will always be there. The disclaimer at the beginning of *The Inheritance of Loss* is recourse to preventing any legal hassles. But it also appears that it is an attempt to gain the legitimacy of mixing fact, fiction and fantasy for art's sake. Any work of fiction involves storytelling. The plot, the characters and the events are all interwoven in such a way that they establish a link between the text and the reader. Reading and analysing fiction may, and at times does, result in contradictory reactions. What one reader finds uncalled for may appear just fine to another reader. Any form of art or creative writing is an expression of the creator, who has the sole privilege to choose the words for which novelists such as Salman Rushdie and Taslima Nasreen have suffered threats to life and social ostracism. Such violent reactions to an author's creations also enhance the readers' curiosity about the same, and hence, their market value. Amitav Ghosh writes, 'books by their very nature often give offence and create outrage, and this is bound to be especially so in circumstances where there are deep anxieties about how certain groups are perceived and represented' (Ghosh 2012: 5).

The Inheritance of Loss (2006), written by Kiran Desai, the focus of this chapter, grapples with diverse characters to represent multiple realities such as globalisation, multiculturalism, diaspora, racism and the like. This novel begins with Sai, a 16-year-old girl who lives with her grandfather, a Cambridge-educated retired judge settled in Kalimpong, a small town in the district of Darjeeling and bordering Bhutan. Obsessed with the panache and elegance that came with a judge's office in colonial India, her grandfather comes across as a complete misfit in the postcolonial era and derides anything and everything Indian. His dilapidated castle-like house personifies his life. He lives there with Sai and his cook, an old man whose son Biju had left for foreign shores to look for better avenues. Other main characters in the novel are neighbours of Sai — two anglophile sisters, Lola and Noni, Uncle Potty and Father Booty. In the environs of Kalimpong, Sai leads a lonely life till she finds a friend and a beloved in her Nepali tutor, Gyan, a 20-year-old youth. A sense of loss, despair and defeat forms the centre stage of the book. The novel ends with Biju, who after struggling and leading a hand-to-mouth existence in America, returns empty-handed in more than just material ways to his father. Sai loses Gyan, who leaves her to join the Gorkhas in their demand for a separate state.

The Gorkha uprising in the 1980s was, in a way, violent under the Gorkha National Liberation Front (GNLF), led by Subhas Ghisingh, an ex-corporal in the army who had tried his hands at writing novels himself. To quote Michel Hutt, 'As émigré workers, the Nepalis of north east India have suffered a high degree of exploitation. In the main industries of the Darjeeling district (tea, timber and tourism), Nepalis constitute the vast majority of the workforce, but are almost wholly absent from the ownership or management of any concern. Such positions are invariably occupied by plainspeople' (Hutt 2008: 119).

The Inheritance of Loss was awarded the prestigious Man Booker Prize. But the depiction of the Nepalis by the novelist invited words of outrage from several readers cutting across ethnic lines, such as D. B. Gurung (2011), Satis Shroff (2011), Paul Jay (2010), Randeep Ramesh (2006) and Arun Kumar Pokhrel (2008), to mention a few. Pokhrel (2008) wrote, 'what is more intriguing to me here is Ms Desai's use of negative stereotypes to describe Gyan and the Nepali community, thereby creating binaries between "we/us" and "they/them", "insiders/outsiders", and "mainstream Indians/subaltern Nepalis"'. Gurung (2011) accused her of misrepresenting Nepalis 'as crooks, dupes, cheats and lesser humans breathing amid a perpetually looming poverty'. On a slightly different vein, Shroff (2011) wrote, 'Instead of taking the trouble to learn Nepali and acquiring background knowledge about the tradition, religion, norms and values, culture and living style of the Gorkhalis in Darjeeling and the Nepalese in Nepal, and comparing it with her own Indian culture, and trying to seek what is common between the two cultures and moving towards peace, tolerance, reconciliation — she just remains adamant, like her protagonist Sai. She does not make an ethnic reflection, but goes on and on, with a jaundiced view, till the bitter end. . .'. He further wrote, 'Describing a country, landscape is one thing, but creeping into the skins of the characters is another. The Gorkha characters remain shallow, like caricatures in Bollywood films . . .' (Shroff 2007).

Some excerpts from the novel that seem to have agitated the readers from the hill station are reproduced below for a better assessment of one's reading of the novel:

> 'LOLA: What if these (Nepalis) hooligans come to Mon Ami? They're bound to come. But we have nothing. Not that that will deter them. They'll kill for fifty rupees.
> SAI: But you have a watchman . . .
> LOLA: Budhoo (name of the watchman, which also means 'idiot')? But he's Nepali. Who can trust him now? . . . Remember Mrs. Thondup? She used to have that Nepali fellow, returned from Calcutta one year to find the house wiped clean . . . Quick across the border, he'd disappeared back into Nepal'. (pp. 43–4)
>
> . . .
>
> 'LOLA: I tell you, these Neps can't be trusted. And they just don't rob. They think nothing of murdering, as well'. (p. 45)
>
> . . .
>
> 'It is strange the tutor is Nepali', the cook remarked to Sai when he had left. A bit later he said, 'I thought he would be Bengali'. (p. 73)
> 'Bengalis', said the cook, 'are very intelligent'. (p. 73)
> 'Everyone knows', said the cook, 'Coastal people eat fish and see how much cleverer they are, Bengalis, Malayalis, Tamils. Inland they eat too much grain, and it slows the digestion – especially millet – forms a big heavy ball. The blood goes to the stomach and not to the head. Nepalis make good soldiers, coolies, but they are not so bright at their studies. Not their fault, poor things'. (p. 73)
>
> . . .
>
> 'They (Gorkhas demanding Gorkhaland), have a point', said Noni, 'maybe not their whole point, but I'd say half to three quarters of their point'.
> 'Nonsense'. Lola waved her sister's opinion away. 'Those Neps will be after all . . . They've been plotting this a long while. All kinds of atrocities will go on – then they can skip merrily over the border to hide in Nepal. Very convenient'. (p. 127)
>
> . . .
>
> 'This state-making', Lola continued, 'biggest mistake that fool Nehru made. Under his rules any group of idiots can stand up demanding a new state and get it, too . . .' (p. 128)

'And here, if you ask me', she said, 'it all started with Sikkim. The Neps played such a dirty trick and began to get grand ideas – now they think they can do the same thing again . . .' (p. 128)

. . . .

LOLA: '. . . And then, baba, the way these Neps multiply'.
MRS. SEN: 'Like Muslims'.
LOLA: 'Not the Muslims *here*'.
MRS. SEN: 'No self control, those people. Disgusting'. (p. 129)
UNCLE POTTY AND FATHER BOOTY TEASED SAI: 'Goodness. Those Nepali boys, high cheek-bones, arm muscles, broad shoulders. Men who can do things, cut down trees, build fences, carry heavy boxes . . .' (p. 143)
MR. IYPE SAYS: 'Nepalis making trouble . . . very troublesome people . . .' (p. 228)
'They should kick the bastards back to Nepal', continued Mr. Iype. (p. 228)
LOLA SAYS: '. . . These people (Gorkhas) aren't good people. Gorkhas are mercenaries, that's what they are. Pay them and they are loyal to whatever. There's no principle involved, Noni . . . they are only Sherpas, coolies'. (p. 247)

These excerpts mirror the stereotypes attached with the Nepalis, who the media have often shown as servants, missionaries, idiots, *durban*s and coolies. Desai plays to the gallery and adds more colour and spice to such notions. Stereotyping the 'Other' is quite common; it goes on everywhere and it is even given some kind of 'scientific' credence at times. But they become an issue of concern and condemnation when they are blatantly negative and disabling for a community, ignoring all the good that is there in every people. After all, the good and the bad are our own constructions and are not an inherent part of the subjects we stereotype. Similar stereotypes are reported about the people of north-east India by many scholars (Baruah 2004; Plathottam 2008; Choudhury 2011).

Desai defended herself in an interview she gave to Anjali Rao of CNN (2007) in the following words:

ANJALI RAO: 'Not everyone was impressed though with your portrayal of the Nepali characters in the "Inheritance of Loss". Some people said that you painted them as crooks and thieves and beggars. So, you did receive a torrent of hate mail along with your Booker Prize. What did that correspondence say and how did you deal with it?'
KIRAN DESAI: 'I was very upset by it, of course, because I actually have a lot of sympathy for the cause. It did descend into violence and it was

sort of a very muddy time. And I did sort of portray the fact that there was a lot of police violence. And I tried to present it in a sort of, many-angled way, but from the viewpoint of an outsider because, of course, I am an outsider. It was from the viewpoint of a Westernized class on the mountain side, portraying people in a heroic side or not it's not really a writer's job to do that.

. . . But again, I do think that writers do have to stand up and say you are writing from the smallest perspective. . .it's from that private human space. As a writer, it's not your job to portray people in a particular way, a people, a nation, in a heroic light. So, you have to kind of fight for that little space, in a way'. (CNN International.com. 2007)

As I read the novel, several questions came to my mind. Does Desai have the right to insult other cultures even if she is writing from her little 'private human space', as she claims? Does she enjoy such freedom when she writes about real people and real places, like she was doing? In the novel, she weaves a situation where Lola Bannerjee, a Bengali lady from Kalimpong, approaches C. K. Pradhan, the leader of GNLF, Kalimpong Unit, to seek his help to stop the Nepali encroachment on her residential area. She quotes Pradhan as saying: 'I am the raja of Kalimpong. A raja must have many queens . . . I have four but would you', he looked Lola up and down, tipped his chair back, head at a comical angle, a coy naughty expression catching his face, 'dear Aunty, would you like to be the fifth?' (p. 244).

> 'And you know, you won't be bearing me any sons at your age so I will expect a big dowry. And you're not much to look at, nothing up' – he patted the front of his khakhi shirt 'nothing down' – he patted his behind . . .'
>
> (p. 244).

This presentation of real-life characters may be passé in the name of writing fiction, but it appears to me as a reader that Desai was poor on research and sensibilities, but rich in imagination. Further, Desai preferred to put her own words in the mouth of the real characters such as C. K. Pradhan. Her sheer lack of sensibilities can be evident from the following:

MRS. SEN: 'More Muslims in India than in Pakistan. They prefer to multiply over here. You know that Jinnah, he ate bacon and eggs for breakfast every morning and drank whiskey every evening. What sort of Muslim nation they have? And five times a day bums up to

God ... With that Kuran, who can be surprised? They have no option to be two – faced'. (p. 130)

. . .

'Buddha died of greed for pork'. (p. 196)

. . .

'At least our (Hindus) gods look like gods, no? Like Raja Rani. Not like this Buddha, Jesus – beggar types'. (p. 200)

I am not a Nepali. So, my reaction to the novel is not based on any ethnic belonging, but on account of my enculturation in anthropology, a discipline that draws home the reality of cultural pluralism and cultural relativism. My first reaction after reading the book was that the author clearly lacked sensibility and ethics of writing a novel. Are novelists not supposed to be sensitive to issues of cultural hegemony and cultural relativism? Can everything be justified in the name of writing fiction? I, for one, do not think so.

A field of aesthetics is a field of emotions. Any work of literature, when crafted with a hand expert in the art of expression, moves the reader. Whether a literary expression receives praise or condemnation depends on the manner in which the readers perceive the text. The perception of the text, in turn, is influenced by a reader's self-identification with a place, symbol, ideology, and so on. This explains why some readers from Kalimpong reacted against the novel the way they did even if all of them did not belong to the Nepali community. Novels have tremendous potential of communicating the author's mind and charging the heart, soul and mind of the reader. Wolfgang Iser (1980), while talking about his theory of aesthetic response, which he calls dialectic relationship between text, reader and their interaction, rightly draws our attention to the fact that readers have images in their minds as they read the text.

The Inheritance of Loss seems to me as a work of convenience; the convenience of telling a story on the comfortable pedestal of fiction while speaking about real places and people. This, I think, is like trying to adorn a grim history with the garb of a lustrous narrative. From the rich plethora of literature, many works of creative writing stand out as gems in literary field, which shine with the brilliance of a perfect balance between history and histrionics. Literary works such as *Mudrarakshasa* by Vishakhadutta and *A Tale of Two Cities* by Charles Dickens are widely separated in terms of the time period of their creation, but both stand out as engrossing pieces of saga built against the backdrop of their political history. *Mudrarakshasa*, a Sanskrit play dated variously from the late 4th century

(Varadpande 2005) to the 8th century (Singh 2008) depicts the rise of King Chandragupta Maurya to power and the era of the Mauryan empire in India. *A Tale of Two Cities* (Dickens 1859) unravels a heart wrenching story against the turbulent times of the French Revolution. Hence, many works of literature, cinema and theatre are successful expressions of the subtle relationship between historical events and storytelling. But Kiran Desai does not seem to care about this subtle relationship, and in her passion to tell her story her way, callously walks over the sentiments of a community and a place.

Desai defends herself by saying that she has written it from her small private space. Hemali Sodhi, Penguin Books' Head of Marketing for India, further defends Desai thus: 'We see the book as pure fiction and these views are not an issue for us or Ms Desai' (2006). The jury of the Booker Prize applauds her work and says that *The Inheritance of Loss* was selected for the prize because of its 'human breath and wisdom, comic tenderness and powerful political acuteness' (2006). It is comical, but it is far from being tender or politically acute.

Desai actually makes a feeble attempt to explain the causes, the feeling of alienation, of deprivation and despair of the Nepalis living in West Bengal. Yet, she wins the Booker for 'powerful political acuteness'. As a writer of fiction, she may use political information received from her relatives to help her story take a shape, but the novel certainly does not provide a powerful analysis of the Gorkhaland movement. A major flaw in this regard is what Ronit Frenkel, a scholar of English literature, University of Johannesburg, writes, 'The Gorkhaland movement distinguished Nepali speaking Indian citizens from Nepalese working in India on a temporary basis – distinction that Desai does not consider in "The Inheritance of Loss"' (Frenkel 2008: 82). It is obvious that her knowledge of the history and politics of the Darjeeling hills is very sketchy. Ignorance of facts or the tampering of the same in the name of writing fiction is certainly not passé. Further, in her depiction of the Nepalis, Desai seems to be giving vent to her own dislike for them. The description smacks of a personal grudge.

B. P. Giri (2007), Professor of English at Dartmouth College, raises certain interesting points regarding the depiction of Gorkhaland insurgency in Desai's novel. According to him, while emphasising the violent means adopted by the insurgents to meet their demands, the novel downplays the felt need of self-empowerment of a marginalised community. To quote him:

> humanistic education has ingrained in us a view of literature that tells us that literary works are above politics even when they delve

into a clearly political subject . . . and that the work of fiction as fiction is not relevant to the world of actual events, where politics presumably dwells. Despite these old fashioned pieties about literature's relation to politics, in India as elsewhere, non-professional readers do care deeply about literary fiction, and one of the reasons why they care is they find the fiction's account of the imagined world quite useful in the cultivation of their self-image as well as group identity, or, in short, in the business of living. To these readers, therefore, a novel's politics is as important as its aesthetics, as they are two parts of the same narrative coin. (2007: 76)

But when the jury of the Booker Prize credits the novel for its 'human breath', it is obvious that they have gone completely overboard and actually raised doubts about the credibility of the award itself. Ronit Frenkel argues that the Booker Prize 'is mediated by a politics of loss in terms of assessing post colonial fiction from India and South Africa, where texts must fulfill Western stereotypes of post colonial pathos in order to contend seriously for this award' (Frenkel 2008: 78).

The main reason for me in taking up this novel was to question the right of a fiction writer to meddle with facts, and do so selectively, with clear political intentions rather than the requirements of a fiction writer. A writer may have the exclusive right to express himself/herself from a 'private human space', but the same needs to be done with prudence and sensitivity. The liberty to create art may turn licentious without the necessary checks, and these checks are not to be sought anywhere else, but in the being of the writer himself/herself. I quite agree with Huntington Cairns when he writes: 'Despite the homage which we render to art we do not concede and perhaps in the whole history of mankind have never conceded that art should be irresponsible' (Cairns 1938: 76).

References

Baruah, Sanjib. 2004. *Durable Disorder: Understanding the Politics of North Eastern India*. New Delhi: Oxford University Press.

Cairns, Huntington. 1938. 'Freedom of Expression in Literature', *The Annals of the American Academy of Political and Social Science,* 200 (1): 76–94.

CBC Arts. 2006. 'Residents of town in Desai's Booker novel upset about portrayal', http://www.cbc.ca/news/arts/books/story/2006/11/02/desai-booker-nepalese.html. Accessed on 1 November 2011.

Chowdhury, Payel Dutta. 2011. 'Exploring the Relationship between Man and Nature in Dhruba Hazarika's *Luck*', *The Criterion: An International Journal in English,* 2(4): 1–6.

CNN International.com. 2007. Kiran Desai Talk Asia interview, 24 April 2007, http://edition.cnn.com/2007/WORLD/asiapcf/04/23/talkasia.desai/index.html. Accessed on 30 October 2011.

Desai, Kiran. 2006. *The Inheritance of Loss*. New Delhi: Penguin Books.

Frenkel, Ronit. 2008. 'The Politics of Loss: Post Colonial Pathos and Current Booker Prize Nominated Texts from India and South Africa', *Scrutiny: Issues in English Studies in Southern Africa,* 213(2): 77–88.

Ghosh, Amitav. 2012. 'Festivals and Freedom', *The Hindustan Times*, Lucknow, 6 February.

Giri, B. P. 2007. 'Review of *The Inheritance of Loss*', *Himalaya: The Journal of the Association of Nepal and Himalayan Studies*, 27 (1–2): 75–76.

Gurung, D. B. 2011. 'In Satis Shroff's Kathmandu Blues: *The Inheritance of Loss* and Intercultural Competence, http://www.boloji.com/index.cfm?md=Content&sd=Articles&ArticleID=4020. Accessed on 20 December 2010.

Hutt, Michael. 2008. 'Being Nepali without Nepal: Reflections on South Asian Diaspora', in David N. Gellner, Joanna Pfaff-Czarnecka and John Whelpton (eds), *Nationalism and Ethnicity in Nepal*. Kathmandu: Vajra Publications.

Iser, Wolfgang. 1980. *The Act of Reading: A Theory of Aesthetic Response*. London: John Hopkins University Press.

Jay, Paul. 2010. *Global Matters: The Transnational Turn in Literary Studies*. Ithaca: Cornell University Press.

Plathottam, George. 2008. 'Truth, Integrity and Social Responsibility of Media: Going Beyond Blood-dripping Stories on Northeast India'. Paper presented at the International Conference on Northeast India and its Transnational Neighbourhood, Indian Institute of Technology, Guwahati, 17–18 January.

Pokhrel, Arun Kumar. 2008. 'Respect the Indian Gorkhas', *The Statesman* (July), http://www.darjeelingtimes.com/news/Opinions/Respect-the-Indian-Gorkhas.html. Accessed on 5 November 2011.

Ramesh, Randeep. 2006. 'Book-Burning Threat over Town's Portrayal in Booker Winning Novel', *The Guardian*, 2 November.

Shroff, Satis. 2007. 'Kathmandu Blues: *The Inheritance of Loss* and Intercultural Competence', http://www.boloji.com/index.cfm?md=Content&sd=Articles&ArticleID=4020. Accessed on 20 December 2010.

Singh, Upinder. 2008. A History of Ancient and Early Medieval India: From the Stone Age to the 12th Century. Delhi: Pearson Education India.

Varadpande, Manohar Laxman. 2005. History of Indian Theatre. Delhi: Abhinav Publications.

10

THE MAKING OF GURUNG CULTURAL IDENTIFICATIONS IN SIKKIM

Melanie Vandenhelsken

This chapter explores the interactions between various factors that make up ethnicity, ethnic groups and ethnic boundaries in Sikkim, drawing on local, pan-ethnic and transnational references.[1] It is based on a field study carried out between 2010 and 2012 in Gangtok, and in Yangang village of south Sikkim, on the relations between Sikkimese Gurungs, the All Sikkim Gurung [Tamu] Buddhist Association[2] (SGA), the state of Sikkim and the Indian Union.[3] It shows how the interactions between these agencies contribute to the construction of various Gurung cultural 'identifications'.[4]

The interaction between categorisation, identification and belonging, and, as Brubaker (2004) phrases it, the distinction between socio-ethnic categories and ethnic groups are instrumental to my analysis. Here, I mainly use the notion of 'socio-ethnic categories' in the sense of state-built categories of population, which are politically and administratively active categories and hence could also be called 'categories from above' (Brubaker 2004: 13). This includes reserved categories such as the Scheduled Tribes (ST) and Scheduled Castes (SC). Drawing from the debate over the distinction between ethnic group and category,[5] I consider that though categories are less dynamic, flexible and porous than ethnic groups since they are institutionalised by the state categories and ethnic groups inform each other.

In brief, from the differentiation made by several authors between self-conscious group and category (Brubaker 2004; Gellner and Hausner 2012), I discuss the changes in the relationship between people and state institutions and categories, and how these changes are produced and what they mean and represent for various groups of people included within what is perceived as an 'ethnic group'.

The conflict within the SGA

The SGA was registered in Gangtok in February 1994.[6] Its objectives are to help the poor among the Gurungs, to educate their children and 'to study and research the history of origin, growth, tradition, culture, religion and language of Gurung community and collect them for future record'.[7] The association's members explain the need for such study in terms of the 'vanishing culture' of the Sikkimese Gurungs and to obtain ST status for themselves. The Limbus and Tamangs obtained such status in January 2003, but the Gurungs were declared only as Most Backward Classes (MBC) in 2003 in Sikkim. They are recognised as Other Backward Classes (OBC) in adjoining West Bengal.

With regard to Gurungs, in the aftermath of the announcement in 2001 by the Department of Cultural Affairs about funds allocated for construction of 'traditional houses',[8] the chief minister announced in 2003 a grant of INR 50,000 for the construction of a Rodhi House[9] in Gangtok (*Now!* 2009: 3). Additionally, since 2001, 30 December was declared as 'Tamu Lochar', i.e. Gurung New Year, in Sikkim. A member of the SGA explained, 'When we obtained this support from the state, we thought that we had achieved our main goal of achieving the ST status'. This indicates that the elements constituting 'distinct ethnic identity' are selected in negotiation with the state.

Soon after the foundation of SGA, its leaders got divided for several reasons. One of the reasons was religion. In the 1990s, most Gurungs of Sikkim considered themselves as Hindus. The SGA founders believed that Sikkimese Gurungs, like the Gurungs of Nepal since the 1990s,[10] should 'return' to Buddhism, which is believed to be their original religion, but had remained dormant for centuries under Hindu influence. This project was implemented by introducing Nyingmapa (Tib. *rnying ma pa*)[11] Buddhism in the Gurung community. But a group within the SGA disagreed with this project; it argued that Hinduism is interlocked with their social life and that they should adopt Buddhist practices without discarding Hinduism.[12]

Another reason for the division was the amendment to the constitution of the association brought by its former leader in order that no government employee could be a member of the association's board. Government employees who wanted to enter the board opposed this decision. In 2004, after an SGA founder lost the elections, another SGA board member who won sought the support of a politically influential member of the community and created another board for the same association.

This split within the association shortly followed the announcement by the chief minister of a grant for the construction of the Rodhi House mentioned above (*Now!* 2009: 3). This grant was eventually split into two halves in 2009, which was interpreted as an endorsement by the state of the division of the association. Moreover, the plot of land planned for the Rodhi House was registered under the name of the 'dissident' faction's president, which his followers saw as a 'full recognition' of the dissident group (ibid.).

In 2010, when the board's term was ending, young members of the community from Gangtok decided to put an end to the internal conflict. They gained support from B. B. Gooroong, who is known for his involvement in the first democratic movement in Sikkim, who was the chief minister of Sikkim in 1984, a founding member of the SGA and the political advisor to the chief minister from 1994 to 2009.[13] In May 2010, this new group organised a meeting for 'unit[ing] the two groups of the association and end[ing] the friction which was undermining the interests of the community at large' (*Now!* 31 May 2010: 3). Speakers on the occasion said that they would lose their identity if they did not unite. Gooroong pointed out that 'the demand for tribal status was still pending with the Central Government and stressed that this demand would not progress unless the Gurungs presented a united front' (ibid.: 4). The meeting further decided that both the SGA boards be dissolved, and an election committee be formed, which 'should include no member from either of the two factions' to organise new elections that would create a legitimate representation of the community. This election committee was soon formed and named Ekikaran Election Committee, but the 'dissident' faction did not take part in the movement, and, through the press, challenged several steps of the procedure followed for the unification. It even denounced the May 2010 meeting as illegal, and the mode of election as unconstitutional.

The Ekikaran Committee set detailed election rules and organised a tour of Sikkim to explain these rules to Sikkimese Gurungs. The election organised by the committee took place on 26 December 2010 and gathered several thousands of people. It was organised before the press, in a setting of strict democratic rules. People who attended the election declared the new board as representative of the entire community. Yet, the other faction informed through a newspaper a few days later that building of the Rodhi Ghar had started already.

The conflict within the SGA was partly due to the conflict between different sections of the Gurung elite.[14] The association gave its members a window to gain political favours; to be elected as president of the association would enhance the chance to contest the state legislative assembly or panchayat elections. The association's leadership could, thus, promote their position both within and outside the community.[15] However, the December 2010 elections not only highlighted persons 'draw[ing] upon the forms and practices of the state for their own ends',[16] but also criticised clientelism and its role in dividing ethnic elites.

Regarding the claim for ST status, both the SGA boards claimed being in charge of the procedures such as meeting central government officials, writing ethnographic report, and so on. Members of the SGA's main faction explained the demand for ST status with several arguments. Their ethnographic report[17] demonstrated the tribal character of Gurung culture, their members being described as pastoralists, hunter-gatherers, and so on and close to nature and forest. They also highlighted that they were a 'vanishing tribe'. A member of the association informed me that the population of Gurungs in Sikkim decreased from being the fourth biggest group, according to the Census of 1891 (2,921 Gurungs)[18] to the ninth biggest one (34,344 Gurungs) according to the 2006 Sikkim State Socio-economic Census.[19] Another argument they put forth was about the absence of high-ranking Gurung officers.

Among other reasons for claiming ST status, members of the association also mentioned the issue of a 'creamy layer' linked to MBC status, as with OBC status, but not with ST status. Thus, they also have economic reasons for demanding ST status. As Galanter explains,[20] SCs and STs receive a larger quantum of preference than OBC, to compensate for the disadvantages related to their social location at the bottom of the caste hierarchy for the SCs, and at the margin of the Indian social order for the STs. Subba also brings up this reason, and links it to the inter-ethnic competition triggered by the reservation system:

> The main reason why the seven ethnic groups demanding ST status (Rai, Gurung, Magar, Yakkha, Jogi, Bhujel and Sunuwar) do not want to be included in the list of OBCs is the 'creamy layer' clause dangling like Damocles' sword. They also avoid the OBC category because this is dominated, at least in Sikkim, by rather advanced castes like Bahun, Chhetri and Newar competing with whom is very difficult for other Nepali castes and ethnic groups living there.[21]

To conclude this section, the divide of SGA highlights competition for state resources and clientelism. It also highlights the role of the ethnic association in fighting for ST status as a means to access political and economic representation. Since 1975, only Bhutias and Lepchas were STs in Sikkim, but in 2003, Limbu and Tamang were also listed as STs, which made it plausible for the Gurungs to be declared as ST. The declaration of Limbu and Tamang as STs has also opened the debate over the sharing of seats in the legislative assembly for them. The Bhutia-Lepcha group is obviously opposed to sharing its seats, and according to experts, seats in the assembly were reserved for Bhutias and Lepchas as a special dispensation and not as STs.

The SGA leaders' endeavour to access 'citizenship' highlights a tight link between political representation and cultural identification. 'Tribal identity' and reinterpretation of the group's self-understanding in terms of tribalism have become a strategy for repositioning of the group in the political and social fields: the discourse of ethnic belonging and tribal rights allows for the organisation of political struggle.[22] This self-understanding of the Gurungs in term of tribalism and 'vanishing' culture reflects their self-displacement from the Nepali identity, since the former lost its political representation in Sikkim in 1979. It also highlights a new phase of competition with the Bhutias and Lepchas of Sikkim.

Return to Buddhism

Members of both factions of the association stress the fact that almost all Sikkimese Gurungs are now following Buddhism although they had previously been Hindus for generations. It is common to hear from Gurungs that Buddhism was their first religion, and that they became Hindus subsequently under the influence of Hinduism. They claim that their ancestors originally came from Tibet, hence they were Buddhists in the past.[23]

According to a member of the association, the Roy Burman report (2008) confirms that 'a group has to be Buddhist in order to obtain the ST status'. This report was commissioned by the Sikkim government to make recommendations, among others, about inclusion of certain ethnic group(s) in the central list of ST, SC or OBC.[24] It describes various aspects of Sikkimese ethnic groups – culture, history, socio-economic conditions, and so on – and includes reports sent by the group's representatives, including answers to a questionnaire. The questions highlight Roy Burman's criteria for identifying tribes, such as harmony with nature and harmony in human relations. But, it does not say that an ethnic group should be Buddhist to get ST status. Under the constitutional order of 1950, as amended in 1990, ST can be from any religion.[25] However Darjeeling Gurungs' 'initial application for ST status was denied on the grounds of too much Hindu assimilation'.[26]

At the beginning of the 20th century, when efforts to delineate tribes began, tribes were firstly identified and described as those groups that practised animism.[27] Even though criteria of primitivism and backwardness were added afterwards, religion remained the explicit element employed in delineating tribes: 'tribes were those groups that did not adhere to religions such as Hinduism, Islam, and Christianity. If a group were shown to be Hindu in its beliefs and religious practices, it was identified as a caste. If it were shown to be animist, it was treated as a tribe'.[28] Even though this has changed, the positioning of STs at the margin of the Hindu social order unofficially maintains the religious criterion.

In 'returning' to Buddhism, Sikkimese Gurungs join the movement of reintroduction of Buddhism among them. In the last decade of the 20th century, many Nepali ethnic groups have increasingly identified themselves as members of non-Hindu religions, and the population of Buddhists grew by 69.7 per cent in Nepal.[29] This 'religious transformation became loaded with oppositional meanings' against the Hindu rulers, and 'symbolically connected to the emergence of democracy'.[30] The story of Hindu domination was transposed to Sikkim as well.

The Mandal Commission's recommendations played a key role in the political rise of Pawan Chamling and the fall of Nar Bahadur Bhandari as the chief minister of Sikkim. Bhandari's opposition to the implementation of the recommendations in Sikkim was associated with a cultural and political domination of the Nepali high castes such as Bahun, Chhetri and Newar over other groups. The 'historiographic consciousness'[31] of Hindu domination in Nepal was spread in Sikkim during the 1993–94 political campaign, and Gopal Gurung's book, *Hidden Facts in Nepalese Politics* (1985), was instrumental in this campaign.[32]

The movement for reintroducing Buddhism among Gurungs in Nepal had considerable influence on the Sikkimese Gurungs as well. As early as 1992 and prior to the registration of the association, the would-be founders of the association went to Pokhara in Nepal to learn about Gurung culture. 'Gurungs are mainly Buddhists there', explained one of the founders of the Sikkim Gurung Association and 'In Nepal, Gurung culture has been preserved'. Since then, Sikkimese Gurungs went there numerous times. After the 1992 tour to Nepal, a Gurung Nyingmapa religious specialist named Shreeprasad Gurung settled in Sikkim in 1993. He was offered a house to settle with his family in Burtuk, a village in the northern suburb of Gangtok. In the following years, the Burtuk Gurung Tamu Gonpa Ugen Pema Choi-Ling Gonpa was built with financial help from the state government. The *gonpa* was registered in 2000 under the Sikkim Department of Ecclesiastical Affairs as a monastic school, and the teacher receives a salary from the government, like most of the monastic school teachers in Sikkim do. Since 2010, an annual subsidy is additionally granted to the gonpa by the Ecclesiastical Department.

The establishment of Buddhist teaching by the first master from Pokhara was welcomed with enthusiasm by the Gurung community, and eight more Gurung Buddhist masters from the same place in Nepal were invited by the association to settle in Sikkim. Those masters were sent to Gurung rural settlements in Sikkim. In Yangang, for example, a Gurung Lama from Pokhara named Chaya Bahadur Gurung came at the end of 1990s and stayed 4–5 years to teach local young boys, who are now studying in Nyingmapa monasteries in Mysore. Lasting relations were established with the Gurungs of Pokhara and Manang, and the exchange was reinforced before the visit to Kalimpong of the Indian Minister for Tribal Affairs, Faggan Singh Kulesti, in November 2002. At the time, the Gurungs submitted their memorandum to the minister regarding their demand for ST status.[33]

The 'shift' to Buddhism takes a particular meaning in Sikkim since it was also the state religion of Sikkim from 1642 to 1975. The state's support for Buddhist institutions is provided through the Ecclesiastical Department, which is commonly known as Gonpa Department. The department is responsible for building and maintenance of Buddhist temples and for funding teachers in monastic schools. Buddhism is also the religion of the Bhutias and Lepchas. All this gives more substance to the belief in the necessity to be Buddhist in order to get an ST status. It also gives ground to a connection between Buddhism, the access to political power, indigeneity and the rise in social status. For these reasons, the founding narrative of Yangang Gurung Gonpa largely borrows from Bhutia genealogies.

The movement for preservation and promotion of Gurung Tamu culture, of which the reintroduction of Buddhism is a part, goes far beyond Nepal and India, as can be seen from the website, www.tamusamaj.com. There are Tamu organisations in a wide range of countries including Korea, Kuwait, the Netherlands, Israel, the UK, USA, Malaysia, Bahrain and Qatar.[34] This international dimension helps us to see the 'multi-layered structures of people's citizenships that include, in intersectional ways, citizenships of sub, cross and supra-state political communities'.[35] Belonging to the Gurung community across the Indian border is a resource for the political struggle of the Sikkimese Gurung community: knowledge linked to the *janajati* movement and belonging to transnational networks provide ideational[36] resources for re-identification, which enables access to political recognition in Sikkim and provides a means to become more Sikkimese. The spread of janajati consciousness in Sikkim is, thus, not a mere imitation of the movement in Nepal, but it has been reinterpreted according to local political projects and strategies.

This part leads to a number of further questions: have the association's activities and views changed the practices and representations of the group members themselves? Has this influence led to standardisation of those practices and representations? How have the association leaders influenced the ethnic group as a whole? How do other Gurungs receive, internalise or reject these discourses and representations? These questions will be addressed by looking at Gurung practices and representations in the upper part of the Yangang village in the south district of Sikkim.

Rethinking Gurung village religious practices

In terms of administration, Yangang includes several hamlets or wards, each of which is multi-ethnic, though one ethnic group usually predominates.[37] I mainly carried out fieldwork in the hamlet of Pathing and in the

Table 10.1 Ethnic diversity in Yangang

Caste/ethnic groups	Number of persons	
	Pathing	Yangang Gonpa
1 Gurung	471	330
2 Chhetri	82	87
3 Bhutia	58	71
4 Rai	42	87
5 Lepcha	21	17
6 Bahun	21	8
7 Tamang	17	22
8 Sherpa	14	9
9 Sunwar/Mukhia	8	0
10 Bhujel	8	5
11 Limbu	4	34
12 Pradhan	0	5
13 Magar	0	4
14 Kami	0	8
15 Others	0	21

Source: Department of Economics and Statistics, Monitoring and Evaluation

upper part of Yangang Gonpa ward, which are mainly inhabited by Gurungs, and hence, commonly called Gurung *Gāũ* or Gurung village.

In Pathing and Gurung Gāũ, a wide range of religious specialists and practices coexist, as has been observed among Gurung communities in Nepal.[38] There are Gurung *jhākris* and any villager can commission their services. They cure many illnesses, and are more or less popular according to their success stories. The terms *jhākri* and *dhami* (shamans[39]) are used interchangeably for the same religious specialists. Hindu priests as well as Buddhist lamas officiate in Gurung houses. The community also uses the services of *ponjyo*, who specialises in the worship of ancestor spirits. In the past, Yangang Gurungs also had a *ghebring* religious specialist, but he is not to be found any more.

The ponjyo and the ghebring are two types of Gurung shamans well-known in Nepal. They are described as *pucu* and *klihbri* of the area north of Pokhara, as described by Pignède (1966) and *paju* and *ghyabre* of Gyas-umdo, as described by Mumford (1990).[40]

The Yangang ponjyo ritual specialists perform rituals, including naming of newborn babies (Nep. *nwāran*), weddings, funerals and the consecration of new houses. Many of these rituals are structured around the Hindu principles of purity and pollution and involve purification (Nep. *cokhyāunu*). The nwāran is also practised by other ethnic groups in the region, and sometimes perceived as a symbol of Hinduism.[41] Ponjyo ritual specialists chant what are considered as Buddhist texts and written in Tibetan script during rituals involving purification in the Hindu sense. In the past, they would also get into a trance during a death ceremony, where they had to 'kill' with an arrow the dead person's soul or the soul responsible for the death, depending on other interpretations. In the past, for death ceremonies, ponjyo ritual specialists wore a long white dress with red strips on the shoulders and around the waist, as well as a crow-like head-dress made of five painted paper images of Buddha called *rig nga* (Tib. *rigs lnga*).[42] For other rituals, they wore the normal monk's red garments.

Yangang ponjyo practice has changed since the 1980s, and informants recall that local ponjyo ritual specialists started wearing the red dress. This religious practice was introduced in the village in the beginning of the 1940s by a religious practitioner called Jas Bahadur Gurung, also called Migi Lama, who came from Nepal. He came in place of his brother-in-law, who could not stay in Sikkim. He was invited to Yangang by a prominent Gurung family of Pathing who needed a family priest. Migi Lama transmitted his practice to four men in the village, who later transmitted it to their own sons.

Nyingmapa Buddhism was introduced and institutionalised in the village from the 1980s onwards. The main ponjyo ritual specialist claims that Migi Lama and his disciples initiated the foundation of the village gonpa. The gonpa was christened as Yangang Chang Chu Nyingmapa Tamu Gonpa and registered in 1983 with the Sikkimese Ecclesiastical Department. Ritual specialists as well as villagers make a distinction between ponjyo religious practice and Nyingmapa Buddhism: the former is called *u-may* and the latter *u-chen*. These terms refer to two forms of the Tibetan script, i.e. the cursive letters (Tib. *dbu med*) and the printed Tibetan alphabet (Tib. *dbu chen*). The ponjyo's texts are indeed written with the u-may script, while the Nyingmapa printed texts are most often written in u-chen. Thus, these terms came to differentiate the two religious practices.

From the 1990s, Nyingmapa lamas replaced ponjyo ritual specialists in the Gurung gonpa, and the Gangtok SGA gradually increased its involvement in the gonpa's management. Gonpa committee members explained that Tibetan speakers could not understand the language used in ponjyo religious texts because the texts had too many grammatical and spelling mistakes. These are similar to arguments given by Buddhist lamas in Nepal to justify hegemony over Gurung shamans.[43] In Yangang, another argument used to justify the need to replace ponjyo religious practice by Nyingmapa Buddhism is the 'mixture' of the former – especially with Hinduism – as opposed to the 'purity' of Nyingmapa Buddhism. In 2008, the headship of the Yangang Gurung gonpa was given to a young Gurung lama trained in a Buddhist school of Gangtok, who had carried out the prestigious three years, three months and three days meditation retreat.

Yangang ponjyo priests have, thus, included in their religious practices elements of Nyingmapa Buddhism since 1980s. With the struggle for ST status that started in the 1990s, the adoption of Nyingmapa Buddhism by Sikkimese Gurungs has meant the removal of other religious elements, and finally, the differentiation of religious traditions that were earlier perceived as fluid.[44] The discourses counterposing Nyingmapa Buddhism with ponjyo practice strongly suggest an attempt to replace the latter with the former. The main Yangang ponjyo priest's son and Migi Lama's grandson were also trained as Nyingmapa lamas.

Conclusion

The Gurung elite's struggle for access to political representation provides the framework for the changes in self-identification of the group. The elite's view of Gurung identification is shaped, above all, by their understanding of state categories and their struggle for inclusion in the ST category, their relation to the state government, their competition for state power and their 'cosmopolitan project of belonging'.[45] Their conception of Gurung 'cultural identity' also draws on the political movement carried out by Gurungs in Nepal from the 1980s. Nepal is, therefore, perceived as a source of authenticity, but specific cultural elements are selected according to the needs of a particular political situation in India. In this context, members of the Gurung elite become their own ethnographers and 'vehicles of participant primordialism'[46]; in other words, the state's definition of ethnic categories allows for the reification of ethnic groups as bounded entities. This political struggle is better understood if viewed in relation to the long-term struggle of Sikkimese Nepalis for equal rights as older settlers in Sikkim and for a distinct Indian identity. It is also a struggle for emancipation from the Nepali category, dominated by Bahuns, Chhetris and Newars. Gurungs still accept 'Nepali' as a category of self-identity, but they are building an alternative self-identity, which they think would eventually enable them to access better social and political representation in Sikkim. Besides, the privileged place of Nyingmapa Buddhism in Sikkimese society gives a particular meaning to their 'return' to Buddhism.

At the village level, the confrontation between varying political projects led by local priests and supporters of the 'shift' to Nyingmapa Buddhism, has produced changes in local religious practices and hierarchy. It has led to a segregation of religious traditions that were formerly blended and caused local religious practices to end. Local priests have integrated their practice with Nyingmapa Buddhism, and, by doing so, sustained their religious authority in the locality.

Notes

1 Following a number of authors who have shown that ethnic identity and belonging were not pre-defined and 'natural', but continuously transforming themselves at the intersection of various political fields (see Barth 1969; Brubaker 2004; Wimmer 2008 and Comaroff and Comaroff 2009, etc.).
2 The term 'Tamu' is an ethnonym that politically active Gurungs have chosen to call themselves, instead of 'Gurung', which is the name by which outsiders know them. Tamu Kwyi is the name of their language (Macfarlane 1997).
3 According to the last census for ethnic groups in Sikkim conducted in 2006, their population was 34,344 (Department of Economics, Statistics, Monitoring and Evaluation 2006, p. 32.)
4 The theoretical background of this chapter leans mainly on Brubaker (2000 and 2004) and Wimmer (2008). I use the notion of identities 'making' as in Wimmer 2008, who argues that 'ethnic boundaries are the outcome of the classificatory struggles and negotiations between actors situated in a social field

[characterised by] the institutional order, distribution of power, and political networks' (p. 970). Additionally, the concept of identity is not used here as a category of analysis because it 'is too ambiguous, too torn between "hard" and "soft" meanings, essentialists connotations and constructivists qualifiers, to serve well the demands of social analysis' (Brubaker and Cooper 2000, p. 2). I use the term 'identification' in the sense of self-understanding (Brubaker 2004) because 'It invites us to specify the agents that do the identifying' (Brubaker and Cooper 2000, p. 14). 'Identity' is, however, used as a category of practice, and for this reason, it is put under quotation marks.

5 Jenkins's view (1994) is that an ethnic category may be entirely imposed by powerful outsiders and is associated with high degrees of discrimination and exclusion, in contrast to an 'ethnic group', which is based on self-identification and 'a shared sense of belonging' (as summarised by Wimmer 2008: 980). Jenkins also notices 'imposed categories may over time be accepted as a category of self-identification and thus transformed into a group' (ibid.). For Wimmer, this makes the dichotomous distinction lose its value (ibid.). To Barth, 'First, it is clear that boundaries persist despite a flow of personnel across them. In other words, categorical ethnic distinctions do not depend on an absence of mobility, contact and information, but do entail social processes of exclusion and incorporation whereby discrete categories are maintained despite changing participation and membership in the course of individual life histories' (1969, p. 10). In my understanding, this highlights two points of view on ethnic distinction. We find a similar idea in Weber (1964, p. 307 and 1968, p. 389), for whom 'ethnic commonality means more than mere category membership' (translated by Brubaker 2004: 206, fn10). Brubaker also proposes to make a distinction between ethnic groups and categories, drawing on Weber (see 2004, pp. 12–13). Taking inspiration from these writings, I consider ethnic categories as categories institutionalised by the state to which people may claim to belong, whereas the elements of belonging to an ethnic group will keep changing. On this distinction, see also McKay and Lewis (1978).

6 Registration number 623 of the official list of organisations in Sikkim currently under the authority of Law Department, Gangtok, Sikkim.

7 Memorandum of the All Sikkim Gurung (Tamu) Buddhist Association.

8 Sikkim Government Gazette No. 391 of 15.10.2001.

9 In the Pokhara region of Nepal, according to Macfarlane (1997: 188), *rodhi* is the communal Gurung dormitory, which is based on age groupings.

10 Adoption of Buddhism by the Gurungs of Nepal has been analysed by several authors (Macfarlane 1989 and 1997; Tamblyn 2002; Hangen 2005, 2007 and 2010; McHugh 2006; Letizia 2011).

11 Tibetan words are transliterated with the Wylie (1959) system at the first occurrence of the word, and transcribed in a simple form at other occurrences; they are preceded by 'Tib.' Nepali words by 'Nep.' are transcribed with diacritics, following the spelling provided by Turner's *A Comparative and Etymological Dictionary of the Nepali language* (1931).

12 I mainly worked with the group in favour of the 'shift' to Buddhism; the other group's leader was available only recently for a discussion, and I could meet him only once.

13 He was also a member of the committee commissioned in 2003 to examine the inclusion of Limbu and Tamang in the list of ST, and in 2004, to prepare an

GURUNG CULTURAL IDENTIFICATIONS

ethnological report to examine the claims of the Rai, Gurung, Mangar, Sunwar, Thami, Dewan, Jogi and Bhujel for inclusion in the ST list.
14 Regarding competition for power among ethnic elite, see Wimmer, Cederman and Min 2007.
15 Yuval-Davis 2011, p. 3.
16 Amster 2005, p. 38, quoted by Harris 2011, p. 4.
17 Man Bahadur Gurung, Kamal Gurung, Megraj Gurung, *undated*.
18 *Gazetteer of Sikhim* [1894] 1989, p. 27.
19 Department of Economics, Statistics, Monitoring and Evaluation 2006.
20 [1984] 1991, pp. xvii and 122.
21 2013, p. 4.
22 See Karlsson 2003, pp. 403–08.
23 According to Macfarlane 1997, the Tibetan origin of Gurungs is one of their possible origins. However, it is neither denied nor stated here, but examined only in relation to the current political project of the Sikkimese Gurungs.
24 See Roy Burman 2008; Vandenhelsken 2012; and Subba 2013.
25 A religious criterion is required only for SC, who can be only Hindus, Sikhs or Buddhists, according to the same order.
26 Middleton 2010, p. 104.
27 Xaxa 2008, p. 3.
28 Ibid.
29 Hangen 2007, p. 6.
30 Hangen 2010, pp. 132–33.
31 Middleton 2010, p. 103, fn51.
32 About Gopal Gurung's life, political activities and writings, see Hangen 2010 (esp. chap. 3).
33 *Now!* 2002, p. 8.
34 This is actually the case not only for Gurung organisations, but also for Nepali indigenous organisations more generally (see Hangen 2010, p. 43).
35 Yuval-Davis 2011, p. 6.
36 Defined by Godelier as 'the process of concept formation' (1978, p. 768).
37 I am aware of the problem with conveying such a 'groupist' description, using ethnic statistics which also participate in reifying a representation in terms of ethnic groups, while discussing the construction of ethnicity. This view is embedded in and institutionalised by administrative categories as well as representations in Sikkim, and my description conveys this situation.
38 Pettigrew 1995 and Tamblyn 2002.
39 I here use the term 'shaman' in the sense of a religious specialist resorting to trance and 'soul flight' in his practice (Reinhard 1976).
40 See also, Macfarlane 1976 and 1989; Messerschmidt 1976; Strickland 1982; Pettigrew 1995; Evans, Pettigrew, Kromchai Tamu and Turin 2009.
41 On the *nwaran* of the Thangmi in Kathmandu and Darjeeling, for instance, see Shneiderman 2009, pp. 452–58.
42 Each leaf depicts one of the 'Dhyani Buddhas' (Ramble 1982, p. 336).
43 Mumford 1990 and Macfarlane 1997, among others.
44 See Gellner 2005 and Hausner and Gellner 2012.
45 Yuval-Davis 2011, p. 7.
46 Brubaker 2004, p. 9.

Bibliography

Amster, M. H. 2005. 'The Rhetoric of the State: Dependency and Control in a Malaysian-Indonesian Borderland', *Identities: Global Studies in Culture and Power,* 12(1): 23–43.
Barth, F. 1969. 'Introduction', in Fredrik Barth (ed.), *Ethnic Groups and Boundaries: The Social Organisation of Culture Difference.* London: Allen &Unwin.
Bechert, H. 1990. 'The Original Buddha and the Recent Buddha: A Preliminary Report on Buddhism in a Gurung Community', *Ancient Nepal,* 119: 8–13.
Brubaker, R. 2004. *Ethnicity without Groups.* Cambridge, MA: Harvard University Press.
Brubaker, R. and Cooper, F. 2000. 'Beyond "identity"', *Theory and Society,* 29: 1–47.
Chalmers, R. 2003. 'The Quest for Ekrupata: Unity, Uniformity, and Delineation of the Nepali Community in Darjeeling', in A. C. Sinha and T. B. Subba (eds), *The Nepalis of Northeast India,* New Delhi: Indus Publishing Co.
Cohn, B. S. 1987. *An Anthropologist among the Historians and Other Essays.* Delhi: Oxford University Press.
Comaroff, J. and J. Comaroff. 2009. *Ethnicity, Inc.* Chicago, London: The University of Chicago Press.
Croucher, Sheila L. 2004. *Globalization and Belonging: The Politics of Identity in a Changing World.* Oxford: Rowman & Littlefield.
Department of Economics, Statistics, Monitoring and Evaluation. 2006. State Socio-Economic Census. Gangtok: Government of Sikkim.
Dirks, N. B. 2001. *Castes of Mind: Colonialism and the Making of Modern India.* Princeton, NJ: Princeton University Press.
Dominguez, V. R. 1986. *While by Definition: Social Classification in Creole Louisiana.* New Brunswick: Rutgers University Press.
Evans, C., J. Pettigrew, Tamu Y. Kromchai and M. Turin. 2009. *Grounding Knowledge/ walking Land: Archaeological Research and Ethno-historical Identity in Central Nepal.* University of Cambridge: McDonald Institute for Archaeological Research.
Gellner, D. N. 2005. 'The Emergence of Conversion in a Hindu-Buddhist Polytropy: The Kathmandu Valley, Nepal, c. 1600–1995', *Comparative Studies in Society and History,* 47(4): 755–80.
Gellner, D. N. and Hausner, S. L. 2012. 'Multiple versus Unitary Belonging: How Nepalis in Britain Deal with "Religion"'. Draft for Nepal Diasporas Workshop, 9–10 July 2012, Oxford.
Godelier, M. 1978. 'Infrastructures, Societies, and History', *Current Anthropology,* 19(4): 768.
Government of India. 1980. *Report of the Backward Classes Commission,* Second part (vol. III to VII).
Gurung, S. K. 2011. *Sikkim: Ethnicity and Political Dynamics: A Triadic Perspective.* New Delhi: Kunal Books.
Hangen, S. 2005. 'Boycotting Dasain: History, Memory and Ethnic Politics in Nepal', *Studies in Nepali History and Society,* 10(1): 105–33.
Hangen, S. 2007. 'Creating a "New Nepal": The Ethnic Dimension', *Policy Studies,* 34, http://ww2.ramapo.edu/ais/faculty/Hangen.aspx.

Hangen, S. 2010. *The Rise of Ethnic Politics in Nepal. Democracy in the Margins*. New York: Routledge.

Harris, T. 2011. 'Haunting the Border and Flooding the Market: Trade and the Indo-Tibetan Interface (Working Draft)'. Paper presented at the first ANHS Himalayan Studies Conference, St Paul, Minnesota, 28 October 2011.

Hausner, S. L. and Gellner, D. N. 2012. 'Category and Practice as Two Aspects of Religion: The Case of Nepalis in Britain', *Journal of the American Academy of Religion*, 80(4): 1–27.

Holmberg, D. 1989. *Order in Paradox: Myth, Ritual and Exchange among Nepal's Tamang*. Ithaca: Cornell University Press.

Hutt, M. 1997. 'Being Nepali without Nepal: Reflection on a South Asian Diaspora', in D. Gellner, J. Pfaff-Czarnecka and J. Whelpton (eds), *Nationalism and Ethnicity in a Hindu Kingdom: The Politics of Culture in Contemporary Nepal*, pp. 101–44. Amsterdam, Harwood Academic Publishers.

iSikkim.com. January 6, 2011. Better late than never (originally published by Sikkim Mail), http://isikkim.com/better-late-than-never/.

Jenkins, R. 1994. 'Rethinking Ethnicity: Identity, Categorization and Power', *Ethnic and Racial Studies*, 17: 197–223.

Karlsson, B. G. 2003. 'Anthropology and the "Indigenous Slot": Claims to and Debates about Indigenous Peoples' Status in India', *Critique of Anthropology*, 23(4): 403–23.

Letizia, C. 2011. 'Buddhist activism, new Sanghas and the politics of belonging among some Tharu and Magar communities of southern Nepal', in J. Pfaff-Czarnecka and G. Toffin (eds), *Facing Globalization in the Himalayas: Belonging and the Politics of the Self*, Delhi: Sage Publications.

Macfarlane, A. 1976. *Resources and Population: A study of the Gurungs of Nepal*. Cambridge: Cambridge University Press.

Macfarlane, A. 1989. 'Some Background Notes on Gurung Identity in a Period of Rapid Change', *Kailash: A Journal of Himalayan Studies*, 15(3–4): 179–90.

Macfarlane, A. 1997. 'Identity and Change among the Gurungs (Tamu-mai) of Central Nepal', in David N. Gellner, Joanna Pfaff-Czarnecka and John Whelpton (eds), *Nationalism and Ethnicity in a Hindu Kingdom: the Politics of Culture in Contemporary Nepal*, pp. 185–204. Amsterdam: Harwood Academic Publishers.

Macfarlane, A. and Indrabahadur Gurung. 1990. *Gurungs of Nepal (A Guide to the Gurungs)*. Kathmandu: Ratna Pustak Bhandar.

McHugh, E. 2002. 'Contingent Selves: Love and Death in a Buddhist Society in Nepal', *Cultural Anthropology*, 17(2): 210–45.

McHugh, E. 2006. 'From Margin to Center: "Tibet" as a Feature of Gurung Identity', in P. Kleiger (ed.), *Tibetan Borderlands: Proceedings of the 10th Seminar of the International Association for Tibetan Studies*, Leiden: Brill Publishers.

McKay, J. and F. Lewis. 1978. 'Ethnicity and Ethnic Group: A Conceptual Analysis and Reformulation', *Ethnic and Racial Studies*, 1: 412–27.

Messerschmidt, D. A. 1976. *The Gurungs of Nepal, Conflict and Change in a Village Society*. Warminster: Aris & Philips.

Middleton, C. T. 2010. Beyond Recognition: Ethnology, Belonging, and the Refashioning of the Ethnic Subject in Darjeeling, India. Unpublished PhD Thesis, Cornell University.

Ministry of Tribal Affairs. 2010–11. *Annual Report 2010–11*. Delhi: Ministry of Tribal Affairs, Government of India.

Mumford, S. R. 1990. *Himalayan Dialogue: Tibetan Lamas and Gurung Shamans in Nepal*. Madison: University of Wisconsin Press.

Pettigrew, J. 1995. Shamanic Dialogues: History, Representation, and Landscape in Nepal. Unpublished PhD dissertation, Department of Anthropology, Cambridge University.

Pignède, B. 1966. *Les Gurung: Une Population Himalayenne du Népal*. Paris, La Haye: Mouton.

Poutignat, P. and J. Streiff-Fenart. 1995. *Théories de l'ethnicité*. Paris: PUF.

Ramble, C. 1982 'Status and Death: Mortuary Rites and Attitudes to the Body in a Tibetan Village', *Kailash*, 9: 333–59.

Reinhard, J. 1976. 'Shamanism and Spirit Possession: the Definition Problem', in J. T. Hitchcock and R. L. Jones (eds), *Spirit Possession in the Nepal Himalayas*. Warminster: Aris and Phillips.

Roy Burman, B. K. 2008. *Report of the Commission for Review of Environmental and Social Sector Policies, Plans and Programmes (CRESP), Human Ecology and Statutory Status of ethnic entities in Sikkim*. Gangtok: Govt. of Sikkim.

Shneiderman, S. 2009. Rituals of Ethnicity: Migration, Mixture, and the Making of Thangmi Identity across Himalayan Borders. Unpublished PhD Dissertation, Cornell University.

Shneiderman, S. 2011. 'Synthesising Practice and Performance, Securing Recognition: Thangmi Cultural Heritage in Nepal and India', in C. Brosius and K. M. Polit (eds), *Ritual, Heritage and Identity: The Politics of Culture and Performance in a Globalised World*. London, New York, New Delhi: Routledge.

Shneiderman, S. and T. Middleton. 2008. 'Reservations, Federalism and the Politics of Recognition in Nepal', *Economic and Political Weekly*, 10 May: 39–45.

Sinha, A. C. 2006. 'Search for Kirat Identity: Trends of De-sankritization among Nepalmul Sikkimese', *Peace and Democracy in South Asia*, 2 (1 and 2), http://www.digitalhimalaya.com/collections/journals/pdsa/index.php?selection=3.

Strickland, S. S. 1982. Beliefs, Practices and Legends: A Study in the Narrative Poetry of the Gurungs of Nepal. Unpublished PhD Thesis, Cambridge University.

Subba, T. B. 1992. *Ethnicity, State, and Development: A Case Study of the Gorkhaland Movement in Darjeeling*. New Delhi: Vikas Publishing House.

Subba, T. B. 2013. 'Legitimacy through Procedures: Making Sikkim More Inclusive through Commissions/committees', in U. Skoda, K. B. Nielsen and M. Qvortrup Fibiger (eds), *Navigating Exclusion, Engineering Inclusion: Processes and Practices in Contemporary India and Beyond*. London: Anthem Press.

Tamblyn, B. 2002. 'Ancient Dialogue amidst a Modern Cacophony: Gurung Religious Pluralism and the founding of Tibetan Buddhist Monasteries in the Pokhara Valley', *European Bulletin of Himalayan Research*, 22: 81–100.

Turin, M. 2011. 'Mother Tongues and Multilingualism: Reflections on Linguistic Belonging in Sikkim'. Paper presented at the first ANHS Himalayan Studies Conference, St Paul, Minnesota, 28 October.

Vandenhelsken, M. 2011. 'The Enactment of Tribal Unity at the Periphery of India: The political Role of a new Form of the *Panglhabsol* Buddhist Ritual in Sikkim', *European Bulletin of Himalayan Studies,* 38: 81–118.

Vandenhelsken, M. 2012. *Reification of Ethnicity in Sikkim: 'Tribalism' in Progress.* Unpublished MSS.

Weber, Max. 1968 [1922]. *Economy and Society.* Berkeley: University of California Press.

Wimmer, A. 2008. 'The Making and Unmaking of Ethnic Boundaries', *American Journal for Sociology,* 113(4): 970–1022.

Wimmer, A., L. E. Cederman, B. Min. 2007. 'Ethnic Politics and Violent Conflicts, 1946–2005: A Configurational Approach'. Paper presented at the conference on Disaggregating the Study of Civil War and Transnational Violence. University of Essex, 24–25 November 2007.

Xaxa, V. 1999. 'Tribes as Indigenous People of India', *Economic and Political Weekly,* 34(51), 18–24 December: 3589–95.

Xaxa, V. 2008. *State, Society, and Tribes: Issues in Post-Colonial India.* Delhi: Dorling Kindersley.

Yuval-Davis, N. 2011. Power, Intersectionality and the Politics of Belonging. *FREIA Working Paper Series,* No. 75, http://www.freia.cgs.aau.dk/Publikationer+og+skriftserie/Skriftserie.

11

TIES TO NEPAL AND DIASPORIC CONSCIOUSNESS OF INDIANS OF NEPALI ORIGIN

Examples from Bokakhat, Assam

Tristan Brusle

Introduction

One of the first Indian Nepalis I ever met in Guwahati, the capital of Assam, knowing my background in Nepalese studies, told me he had nothing to do with Nepal: 'Nepal is totally foreign'. His grandfather came from Jumla district of Nepal and that was all he could say about the country of his forefathers. A few minutes later, I learnt that he had done all his studies in Kathmandu. He justified it, saying it was easier than in India. After having spent some more time in Assam, it appeared to me that the willingness of Indian Nepali activists to tie themselves to India and root themselves in ancient Indian history is strong, but needs to be interrogated regarding the fluidity of movements and of belonging in the region.

The context of Assam is a 'frontier land' (Baruah 1999), where historical migrations of people have led to ethnic politics, which climaxed with the Assamese movement (1979–85) or the Bodo movement (1993), both of which targeted 'foreigners' (Nath 2002). Even though Nepali-speaking people in Assam represented only 2.12 per cent of the total population in 2001,[1] almost 0.6 million, some of them, supported by the All Assam Gorkha Students' Union (AAGSU), demand an autonomous council. It is as if to be recognised as a full citizen of Assam and of India, a territorial base of belonging was needed. We will see that, as always, this kind of discourse is mainly spread by activists, whereas the grassroots population does not support or does not understand the stakes of such issues.

Given the crave of scientists worldwide to understand post-national forms of belonging – diasporas in particular – it sounded peculiar to me that the word 'diaspora' did not appear more (or at all) among Indian Nepalis, as it appears in the social life of Nepal itself. Quickly said, a diaspora can be defined by three main features (Ma Mung 2000): there should be a dispersion of a population of common 'national' or ethnic background in several 'poles' ('multipolarity'); there should be relations between these poles and not only between the home country and other communities ('interpolarity'); and last, there should be a diasporic consciousness. The last point is not just about dispersion, as Tölölyan (2007) emphasises. The question of 'what is home', the issue of return (Safran 1991), and more broadly, the question of links to Nepal will be raised. Actually, only a handful of articles about Indian Nepalis use the term 'diaspora': 'very little is known about this category of diasporic societies' (Subba 2008: 220). Moreover, the term is not much questioned or put in perspective with diaspora studies. As for Nepali activists in India, diaspora is not a catchphrase; it does not seem to be an idea they could rely on. It does not mean that the feeling that 'Nepalese are everywhere' is not present. But willingness to establish links with other communities of the same background, to display these links, is seldom observed. Why is the diaspora concept, which is de-territorialised and de-ethnicised (as Subba 2009 advocates), not popular? Is it because, in the framework of the Indian nation state, having a non-Indian diasporic identity is complicated? As already noticed by Hutt (1997), and emphasised by numerous publications in Sinha and Subba (2003) and in Subba et al. (2009), the divide between Indian Nepalis and Nepal Nepalis is perpetuated by the former, who are in 'search of an Indian identity' (Sinha and Subba 2003). However, whether Indian Nepalis like it or not, reference to Nepal always surge in discussions about their denomination, language or cultural traditions. The link to Nepal, although denied, exists in many cases.

Are the Nepalis in Bokakhat and elsewhere in Assam part of an imagined community that we may call a 'diaspora'? The tentative answer to the question revolves around the notion of diaspora as a group, which is socially constructed. The question also is: who builds it? To discuss the relationship between Indian Nepalis and the diaspora concept, we can divide our analysis between the 'etic' discourses or 'exo-nomination' (i.e. made by researchers) and 'emic' discourses or 'self-nomination' (i.e. made by members of the social group) (Tölölyan 2007) and see if it is heuristically fruitful. This debate involves Hovanessian (1998), Brubaker (2005) and Chivallon (2006) in particular. I will follow Hovanessian (1998: 11), who proposes to 'unravel the links between social reality and the [diaspora] concept',[2] in order to get a balanced view of a phenomenon we need to consider from the inside. First, we can ask ourselves the delicate question of categorisation made by researchers, which should have bottom-up perspectives and not impose their views on social groups. Contrary to the Nepal diaspora, which has been created by expatriate Nepalis in order to organise themselves as a political and economic lobby, forms of organisations of Indian Nepalis stay bounded within the Indian state. In the Indian Nepali case, the culture of diaspora is not yet considered as 'the pathway of a modern people and a modern culture' (Hall 1999). To assert how Indian Nepalis could belong to a diaspora and have, thus, a diasporic consciousness, we need to focus on representations and practices relating to Nepal.

Bokakhat as a place of investigation was chosen in accordance with a research programme about north-east India and mobility, in particular.[3] Situated in Golaghat district,[4] along the Brahmaputra river and the National Highway 37, Bokakhat is a small town (8,900 inhabitants in 2001). Its ethnic distribution is not known precisely, but Assamese are in majority, followed by Mishings, Biharis, Marwaris, Muslims, ex-tea workers and Nepalis. As far as Nepalis are concerned, they are said to represent approximately 15 per cent of the 174,000 voters of Bokakhat constituency. I spent 10 days in a village inhabited by Nepalis about 5 kilometres north of Bokakhat in November 2006 and three weeks in Bokakhat in January 2010. The family I was staying with belongs to the Brahmin (Bahun) caste and the household head is well-known and highly respected in Bokakhat. Most of the people I met were men aged between 20 and 80 years. In the following section, I discuss Indian Nepalis' diasporic consciousness according to vernacular and scientific discourses.

History of the Nepali settlement in Bokakhat

Arrival of the Nepalis in Bokakhat

I will not repeat the history of their migration to north-east India here as it has been done elsewhere in detail (Devi 2007; Nath 2002; Sinha and Subba 2003; Subba et al. 2009). The arrival of Nepalis in Assam, mainly as graziers on the Brahmaputra islands and as land clearers, was encouraged by the British colonial power in order to populate a region with low population densities, after its incorporation into the Raj (1826). I will not insist either on the 'cultural relationships between Nepal and Assam since ancient times' (Devi 2009: 249) although mythical links between the two countries are frequently stressed by the Nepalis in Assam.

Collecting the oral histories of Nepali migrants sometimes trips over the limits of memory. Histories of how their ascendants came to Assam are either vague or imprecise. Many old men told me that once established in Assam, their father or grandfather did not want to elaborate about the past. A few names of places of origin show that most of their ancestors in Bokakhat come from the eastern part of Nepal (Dhankuta, Ilam, Tehrathum, Okhaldhunga and Panchthar districts), Darjeeling and Sikkim. The partial history of their arrival in Bokakhat, however, enables us to add complexity to the linear history of Assam's peopling. Their settlement in Assam is more the result of the fixation of the population after decades of movement between Nepal and India. It is also the story of evacuation and flights from floods. When studying the genealogy of a Subedi family, one realises that coming and going was part of survival strategies, at least for the first or second generation. One Kasinath first arrived in Assam in 1839 from a now unknown place in Nepal. He had many children, among whom Kamalapati was born in Dhankuta, whose children were born in Assam and Nepal. His descendants are now in Bokakhat and in Hetauda, Nepal. It is apparent that coming and going between Bokakhat and Nepal were common earlier.[5] Contrary to songs mentioned by Subba (2008: 227) that explain the non-return to Nepal as a result of their failure to establish themselves in India, stories told by elders in Bokakhat emphasise the way they took hold of dozens of *bighas* and made progress. The reasons for them to stay were not setbacks, but success in leading a comfortable peasant life in a land described as empty of people and full of forest that had to be cleared. Anyway, when describing the move to Assam, both poverty in Nepal and plentiful land in Assam explain their migrations. Some remember an ancestor who belonged to the Gurkha army, but most of the Nepali population in Bokakhat belonged to the grazing community. As Nepalis specialised in cattle breeding and milk production, and were given grazing rights either on the banks of the Brahmaputra or on its islands (*sapori* in Assamese, *tapu* in Nepali), they have been highly subjected to flooding and erosion of their land. As all environmental refugees, their history is also one of displacement by natural events.

Thus, according to oral histories, most forefathers of Nepalis settled in Bokakhat arrived in Assam from the end of the 19th century to the 1920s. All interviewed people insist on the fact that their forefathers were graziers and cultivators living on the banks of the Brahmaputra, and particularly from a place called Moriahola, which does not exist anymore. In 1900, Chatrasingh Katuwal was the first settler in Bokakhat, which then was a small village along the road.[6] His descendants now occupy five houses in a hamlet called Manaspur and five in Nepaligaon, the other Nepali hamlet of Bokakhat.

Geographical and social composition of Nepalis in Bokakhat

On 16 January 2010, the Assam Gorkha Sammelan held its annual convention in Shantipur (Karbi Anglong district). The bus departing from Bokakhat started from Nepaligaon, picked up conference attendees in Manaspur and took the last stop in front of Gajanan Hotel to wait for latecomers. In a few minutes, it went through the two main Nepali hamlets and the only hotel run by a Nepali.[7] Jyotinagar, also known as Kholakowa, officially became Nepaligaon a few years ago.[8] It is the 'main Nepali hamlet where 124 Nepali households are situated, out of 330 houses (mostly Assamese and to a lesser extent Marwari, Bengali and Bihari)'.[9] There live only high-caste Bahuns (26% of Nepali households) and Chhetri (74%).[10] Such a high concentration of Nepalis in a hamlet is due to the fact that there was a time when almost all the lands of this hamlet belonged to one Nepali man, who progressively sold parts of it to his fellowmen. First comers arrived in 1950s, while more recent newcomers too chose to live among their fellowmen. The inheritance rule, according to which land is divided in equal parts among brothers, is another factor explaining the concentration of kin in this part of Bokakhat. The only distinctive Nepali features in Nepaligaon are the presence of *bar-pipal* trees and a Lakshmi Narayan temple.[11]

The second hamlet was officially named Manaspur in 2000 because of the presence of a Shiva temple and the belief that Manas is the abode of Shiva. The first Nepali, who owned all the land in Manaspur and Jyotinagar, settled in the former in the 1920s. There are now 34 Nepali houses (73% Chhetri, 23% Bahun and 3% Rai). The Shiva temple was inaugurated in 1970 by Bishnu Lal Upadhyaya, a prominent Nepali Indian freedom fighter and a two-time member of the Assam State Assembly. The bar-pipal trees were planted next to the temple at the same period. In both hamlets, kinship relations are very dense and not a single lower-caste family lives in either of these two hamlets. Contrary to many other Nepali settlements, there is no active or ex-Gurkha either.[12]

Without economic data concerning the Nepalis in Bokakhat, it is difficult to conclude that they belong to a marginalised or socio-economically depressed community, as it is usually told by authors about them in Assam. There is no impression of wealth, nor of dire poverty, in the two Nepali neighbourhoods, but the standards of construction of most houses are well above many bamboo houses in the outskirts of Bokakhat. Many Nepalis are or have been teachers at the primary level, a job that was easy to get a generation ago. Others have small jobs in shops or in the local administration. But in 2010, there were only two shops owned by them – a cycle repair shop[13] and a tea shop.

'Emic' discourses and rejected diaspora

When Indian Nepalis get hassled by common Indian people or at the border, 'they tend to over-emphasise their Indian identity and ignore the long historical, linguistic, religious, and cultural linkages with the Nepal Nepalis' (Subba 2008: 229). This statement is straightforward and could settle the question I raise here. However, the study of Nepali discourses in Bokakhat in more common situations shows that diasporic feelings are not easily displayed. When we get interested in 'emic' discourses, it is striking to notice that diaspora is not a 'category of practice' (Brubaker 2005) recognised as such. It is even lesser a stance or a claim. Moreover, the term 'diaspora' never surfaced when I met the Nepalis in Bokakhat and Nepali activists in Guwahati.[14] The former always asserted their belonging to the Nepali *jati* in general, situated in the Indian framework of caste and ethnic system.

Distinction and identity

Every encounter with Nepalis in Bokakhat, and particularly with grassroots activists, either belonging to AAGSU or to a literary society, proved that 'an Indian Nepali identity is not an easy goal' (Subba 2008: 229). Has this to do with hidden diasporic feelings?

The necessary distinction between Indian Nepalis and Nepal Nepalis is well-documented (See Sinha and Subba 2003; Subba 2002; Subba et al. 2009). In Bokakhat too, there is a desire to distinguish themselves from both other Assamese and Nepal Nepalis: 'there is no new Nepali here, only old Nepalis'. The date of arrival is reminded to create distinctiveness among Nepalis and to assert the rights of those who arrived generations ago. These local distinctions echo the one made by Upreti (2009: 348) about the necessary revision of the 1950 Treaty between India and Nepal: Nepali migrants 'may be broadly divided into two categories: one, descendants of those who settled in India during the British era and are *bona fide* citizens of India and, two, the recently migrated Nepalis who are scattered all over the country' (my emphasis). Later, he asserts that 1947 should be the dividing line, whereas in Assam, 25 March 1971 has been chosen as the cut-off year to be recognised as a citizen. Even though there did not seem to exist any Bangladeshi issue around Bokakhat, when it comes to population movements, the comparison with Bangladeshis is classic.[15] When Nepalis stress their ability to assimilate, it is to differentiate themselves from the Bangladeshis: 'a Bangladeshi is obviously a citizen of Bangladesh; the term does not admit any other interpretation. But a Nepali may not always be a citizen of Nepal' (Chettry 2009: 351).

Nepalis in Bokakhat are willing to stress their migration, and at the same time, show that their cultural features have almost not changed since their forefathers came. The longing for 'pure' traditions is made evident even though the few rites I have seen seem different from what they may be in Nepal.[16] But the feeling of not having altered their culture and of forming a homogeneous group with a strong distinct identity is widespread. As Tika Ram Upadhyaya says, 'Nepalis have left their country but not their culture'. These diasporic 'ideologies of purity' (Clifford 1994: 307) make some of them believe that they have a role in preserving Nepali culture. The tendency to reify it is portrayed while people describe the main festivals celebrated by them. Their culture is seen as something fixed, little influenced by surrounding communities. It is also essentialised. Their customs, thus, are seen to be much more conservative than the ones in Nepal.

Apart from religious traditions, the language itself is something shared and seen as defining them. Nepali is fought for, and demands are made to make it a teaching medium in schools. The feeling of being different, when asserted, does not translate into a claim for belonging to the diaspora. It is also clear from the debate around their name (Nepali or Gorkha) that every Nepali in Bokakhat had something to tell about. At the grassroots level, both names compete whereas other appellations such as Bharatiya Nepali and Bharateli Nepali were never heard. Surprisingly, the distinction between Nepali and Gorkha often revolves around the opposition of Aryan against Mongoloid Nepalis. The identification of Mongoloid people such as Rai, Limbu, Magar and Gurung with those employed in Gurkha regiments – when most of high castes in Bokakhat are from grazing communities – is a way for higher-caste people to differentiate themselves from others. 'We are not the sons of Gorkha but descendants of Nepalis. We do not speak Gorkha but Nepali. Our culture is Nepali, not Gorkha', says one Bahun. But, at the same time, in common conversations, phrases such as 'hamro gorkhaliharu . . .' (our Gorkhas) appear. In Bokakhat, the dividing line seems to be between caste and tribal Nepali groups, high castes putting the blame on tribals for creating divisions, with the name issue in particular. Allegiance to the history of their forefathers and also, perhaps, a transmitted history of deeper integration of high castes in Nepal may explain these appreciations. If most people prefer Nepali as a name, local activists (from the AAGSU) claim a name which puts them at a distance with Nepal, 'Nepali' being considered as detrimental to their identification with the Indian nation. But the history of both terms definitely links them to Nepal. To show a distance from Nepal Nepalis is a central issue and reflects the difficulty of any transnational or diasporic belonging. The proposition of Subba (2009: 390) for the word 'sakhaa', which aims at erasing all colonial, caste, tribal or hierarchic overtones in the name of the Indian Nepali communities, is unknown to the Nepalis of Bokakhat.

Assimilation and political demands

The desire to identify themselves as Indian has, of course, political dimensions, but in Bokakhat, except for a handful of activists, the issue of Gorkhaland or of Gorkha autonomous council remains unknown to the common people. Their narrative of belonging to Assam is embedded in the expression, 'Hami Asssambasi' (We are Assamese.). Apart from their rootedness, justified by settlement generations ago, Nepalis in Bokakhat insist on their speaking Assamese, on their participation in local festivals such as *Bihu,* in particular, where Nepalis are said to have won dance contests, and in the political life of the municipality.[17] The rhetoric of integration and assimilation 'with the great Indian nationhood' (Subba 2009: 391) is enhanced by the freedom movement the Indian Nepalis took part in.[18] I was reminded very often of the history of local Nepali freedom fighters: their names are known by Nepalis who consider them martyrs of the Indian liberation movement. The 'sons of the soil' movement in Assam (1979–85) at first targeted both Bangladeshis and Nepalis, but then focused on the latter (Baruah 1999; Dasgupta 2003). If most Nepalis testify that they were never threatened during this period, some admit that they went to Nepal to buy land in case the situation got more complicated. A few of them, and notably, Chandra Kharel, the nephew of the historic local Indian Congress leader, joined the Assam Andolan. Kharel's ideas of their commitment to Assam lie on the permanence of their presence in Assam, contrary to Bangladeshis, who are 'newcomers'. According to him, there were eight Nepali martyrs in the Assam Andolan. He is still a member of the Asom Gana Parishad (AGP) and participated in the creation of the Asom Nepali Parishad, a sub-branch of the AGP. According to him, 50 per cent of the Bokakhat Nepalis vote for AGP. It is noticeable that the vocabulary of rootedness in Assam is now used by Nepalis, who say 'we are sons of the soil' or 'we are *thaluwa*' or local.[19]

In total, we see that Bokakhat Nepalis reflect the way Indian Nepalis see themselves as a *jati* united by their culture and strong ties with India. This pan-Indian perspective of belonging is seen in major Nepali associations such as Nepali Sahitya Parishad, Bharatiya Gorkha Parisangh and Assam Gorkha Sammelan.[20] Student activists are the only ones focusing on Gorkha Autonomous Council issues and there seems to exist a 'necessity to carve out a political space for [Nepali] cultural identity in India' (Golay 2006: 43).

A rejected diaspora

The double wish to be assimilated to the Assamese and Indian community while keeping their identity intact, in fact, seems to be granted. It also corresponds to a will to get out of the discourses of duality – indigenous vs migrants – introduced by the British (see Baruah 1999). By participating and emphasising their participation in the struggle for independence and in the struggle of the AGP's 'sons of the soil' movement, the desire to make demonstration of their belonging here is strong. When Golay (2006: 45) proposes to 'think of the Gorkha identity as a post-national identity or a South Asian identity', he does not talk about a diasporic identity, but that is what he may have in mind. However, the question is that this kind of transnational or de-territorialised identity is not put forward by the concerned people, to say the least. Diasporic people express a strong sense of difference, 'a sense of being a "people" with historical roots and destinies outside the time/space of the host nation' (Clifford 1994: 310–11). Although this is the case for Indian Nepalis, the fact of being from elsewhere is hidden and diasporic feelings are rejected. So, do we have to follow Brubaker (2005: 11) for whom 'ancestry is surely a poor proxy for membership in a diaspora'? Dispersion does not equal diaspora. Even though sentences such as 'there isn't a country without Nepalese' or 'Nepalese are everywhere' are heard from time to time, does it really mean that a consciousness of diaspora exists?[21] Listening to Indians of Nepali origin in Bokakhat, diaspora is not a claim, nor does it really exist. They are not even considered as Non-Resident Nepalis.[22, 23]

Affective and imaginative links to Nepal: Nepal as a layer of belonging

While talking about identity, Nepal is never very far. Despite a long presence in India, the call of the ancestors' country is still important. The idea of Nepal has not vanished yet. Affective references to Nepal are common, especially among the older generation. There is no doubt about where home is for activists and people of the third generation born in Assam, but some older people, whose father or grandfather came from Nepal, have ambiguous feeling towards that country. Nepal has not vanished from the memories of all Nepali families, even though it can be tough to make people talk about their links to Nepal. For older people, aged more than 70 years in 2010, the 'original wound of exile as a founding act' (Bordes-Benayoun 2006: 192) remains vivid, as these examples taken from my conversations with some of them show. An old lady, born in Assam, whose parents had come from Dhankuta in Nepal and whose husband was born in Nepal, described about the two trips to Nepal she undertook thus: 'I went to Dhankuta, Kagbari, Kathmandu. I travelled everywhere. It's a hilly area. Over there, there are a lot of fruits and peanuts too. Here, in other land, there isn't any peanut. But in "our" Nepal, it grows'. I asked her if Nepal was not a foreign country for her. She answered, smiling: 'no, it [Nepal] is my country, India is another country. I do not feel like India is our country. For my children, it is their country, but not for me'. These statements seem awkward, given that this woman raised all her family in Assam. When I asked Chandra Bahadur Chhetri, born in Manaspur, what was his age, he told me he was born in 1988 Vikram Sambat, which means 1931 in the Gregorian calendar. He then explained to me that his parents were born in Nepal. The same answer was given to me by the wife of Tika Ram Chhetri, 70 years old: 'my parents were born in *our country*'.

Calling Nepal *desh* is far from being a neutral thing as, from a legal point of view, Nepal should be in the *bidesh* realm. Asserting one's belonging to Nepal is more troubling for people who have lived all their life, sometimes successfully, in India. As Subba (2008) noticed, the memory of the places of origin fades away: knowledge of ancestors' places is often vague. Most people do not know the name of the village they came from; they simply say, 'my grandfather came when he was young, from Nepal'. However, of all the houses I went to, I only encountered once a common Nepali poster called 'Top of the World', which is a panoramic view of the Nepal Himalayas.

Affective links to Nepal still exist, especially among the elders. The imagination, the words used to speak about the country of origin depict some kind of diasporic feeling, in that a part of these people's mind is homeland-oriented. Practices of circulation to and from Nepal support this hypothesis.

Practices related to Nepal

According to Safran (1991), orientation to homeland is a major feature of diasporic population. In our case, it is clear by now that it is difficult to speak about Nepal as homeland. Anyhow, relations with Nepal can be interpreted as links of a diasporic nature. Links with Nepal are not only based on memories or imagination: circulation of people between India and Nepal is common, facilitated by the open border enabled by the 1950 Indo-Nepal Treaty of Peace and Friendship between India and Nepal. Nepalis from Bokakhat also participate in these trans-border movements, and it is difficult to get a clear view of these dynamics to be able to tell if such movements are diminishing or increasing.[24] Moreover, it is often difficult for people to admit that they actually have links with Nepal, be they direct or indirect. One has to spend time with people to understand how Nepal, as a place of practices, is integrated in their world. Arun Chhetri, a staunch believer in Gorkhaland, develops an official discourse about Indian Nepalis having nothing to do with Nepal. But, as the conversation goes on, I realise that his maternal uncle, born in Assam, now lives in the eastern district (Jhapa) of Nepal and has Nepalese citizenship. Thus, Nepal is not far from his family, even if Arun himself has never been that far.

Pilgrimage to places of origin is not so much in the habit.[25] Some have made it, often to see a parent, to meet a son or a brother settled in Nepal or to see the ancestral land of the family.[26] Most of them say they are not interested and invoke a lack of financial capital to be able to visit places. Tika Ram Upadhyaya, 72 years old, born in Assam, has two brothers who live in Biratnagar, Nepal. The first time he went to Nepal was to meet his younger brother, who had married a girl from Nepal. That is how he describes his entering Nepal: 'at this time, a long time ago, there was a lot of devotion for Nepal. At the border, in the morning, when I entered Nepal, I bent to the ground saluting Nepal. The soil of Nepal is the place of our ancestors: it is our land, our main ground'. As he entered Nepal, he realised, for the first time in his life, differences between Indian Nepalis and Nepal Nepalis. The language of the latter was sweeter (*mitho boli*) than that of the former: 'when I asked for tea in a teashop, the hotel owner immediately asked me where I was from. I was surprised: "Do you ask everyone where they're from?" "No", answered the hotel owner, "it is because you are from India". "How do you know?" I asked him. "You said *chai* and not *chia*"'. Experiences of the difference also related to the way he was dressed. Wearing a *dhoti* in Assam, he did not think it would assimilate him with an Indian in Nepal: 'You are not a Nepali, as you do not wear a *topi*', he heard many times. Ambivalent feelings, thus, appeared for someone who considered himself Nepali at heart. Apart from this testimony, others insist on the gap between Nepal Nepalis and Indian Nepalis, on the poverty of their uncles or cousins. None of those I met ever considered settling in Nepal.

In almost every family, it is possible to locate a kin in Nepal, even though sometimes, the links are completely cut off. Dhan Bahadur Chhetri, who was a civil servant in the Indian Administrative Service, was born in Assam of a father who arrived in 1896 in India. His father never talked about Nepal to his children, never told his children to go to Nepal. His father's brother finally settled in Nepal, where his cousins were brought up. Nowadays, Dhan Bahadur Chhetri still calls his kin over when someone dies or gets married. But he is doubtful if his sons will keep the relations with their family members in Nepal. Death is a social event that also enables the crossing of borders and the re-assertion of weak bonds. After the death of his father, who was born in Nepal, Hom Bahadur Basnet took back his father's ashes to immerse them in the Kosi river. But his own ashes, when he died in 2008, were not taken to Nepal. The mourning period is also an occasion for reverse movements, from Nepal to India or vice versa. A man from Katmandu, who was born in Assam but returned to Nepal at a young age, came to Bokakhat to observe the death of his uncle. Seeing the poverty of his kin, he wanted to take back some children with him to give them a better future.

In a booklet written by local historians, in the part about Nepalis in Bokakhat, the Nepali author underlines that the first Nepali woman who graduated from Bokakhat has taken Nepalese citizenship. Two more young Nepalis from Bokakhat have graduated from Nepal and established there. Actually, Nepal represents an opportunity for young educated people. Even if the cases are few, the phenomenon is meaningful about links with Nepal. As one has to have contacts to find work in Nepal, broader family relations are needed to fulfil such projects. Amitabh Upadhyaya, after completing his diploma from a local college, went to Hetauda, Central Nepal, to work in his paternal uncle's primary school. Another son of a Brahmin went to Kathmandu to pursue higher studies and finally got married and settled there. But the son of my landlord, who studied at the premier Indian Institute of Technology, is now working in Mumbai. I heard a lot of young people say that it is easier to go abroad with a Nepalese passport than with an Indian one. From Nepal, international migration is well-organised, and demands for Nepalis in the Gulf and in Malaysia are still high.[27] Through these examples, we see that links with Nepal can be reactivated in case of need. Nepal as a destination is not randomly chosen. Language and cultural affinities explain such diasporic moves.

At last, people agree that flows from Nepal have dried up. No Nepali comes to breed cattle on the Brahmaputra islands anymore. In 2006, there were numerous Nepali Madheshi boys working in the only

Nepali-owned Bokakhat teashop. In 2010, there was none. The reorientation of labour migration towards the Gulf or Malaysia has diverted migrants from Bokakhat.[28]

Nepal as a possibility: 'The dormant diaspora' and the Nepalese *aliyah*

For many Bokakhat Nepalis, and perhaps for many Indian Nepalis, Nepal is a possibility, in both common circumstances and in extraordinary situations. It is a place for potential refuge, a place where they know, or imagine, that they could take refuge in case of dire need. If we consider those connections can be reactivated, that return can be possible, it means that the ancestors' original homeland is meaningful. Despite claims that Nepal is just another foreign country, it has a special room in the minds of Indian Nepalis.

Safran (1991) describes the possible return to the ancestor's land as a feature of the diaspora: a 'continuing orientation to a homeland and to a narrative and ethno-symbols related to it' (*Ibid*.: 39). 'To many, going to Nepal is unthinkable; leaving Assam even more unimaginable. To them, Nepal is a foreign land. Some visit Nepal occasionally . . . As such their connections with their homeland are very tenuous and fragile. Nor is there any desire to resume links with the land, wherefrom their forefathers migrated' (Nath 2002: 86). This is true for Bokakhat Nepalis, but if there is no 'return issue' in the current political situation, this has not always been the case. First, a few decades ago, some Nepalis born in Assam decided to go back to Nepal, to find a job, or to get married. Second, when the Assam Andolan caught momentum, some people in Bokakhat, although they were not directly threatened, took land in Nepal, or renewed contacts with their relatives in Nepal (see Nath 2005). Bhupati Upadhyay's brother bought land in Jhapa district in order to secure his family: his son nowadays lives in Nepal. Testimonies of return to Nepal after major floods and loss of all land also exist.

Nepal as a refuge space was also used in case of threat. Chandra Kharel, the leader of the Bokakhat AGP branch, took refuge in Nepal because he was wanted by the police for being the district chief of the All Assam Students' Union. In Nepal too, he got involved in politics. This example, unique to Bokakhat to my knowledge, reflects quite a paradox. The one who was involved in the defence of the indigeneity of Nepalis in Assam takes refuge in Nepal and finds himself involved in politics there. Thus, the twin effects on the Nepalis of the 'sons of the soil' politics in Assam were a reassertion of the demands for Gorkha Autonomous Council, and, at the same time, the reactivation of links with Nepal.

Thus, it appears that Nepal can be a resource for people in a dispersion situation. Temporary migration to Nepal can also turn into a more permanent one, or at least, to dual residency. Although both India and Nepal forbid dual citizenship, those who have it may be numerous. Many Indian Nepalis took Nepalese citizenship in the 1980s, when large-scale evictions occurred in many parts of India's north-east.[29] In some cases, the grandfather was born in Nepal, the father never went there and the son makes his living as a teacher in Nepal's tarai.

Sheffer (2003), in a somehow objectionable linear view of the evolution of diasporas, distinguishes 'core, marginal and dormant' members of diaspora. There are phases when 'diasporas may become dormant. That is, during such periods they may integrate into host societies, show less interest in their homelands, experience hybridization processes, reduce the activities of their diaspora organizations' (Sheffer 2003: 142).[30] What concerns us here is that changing circumstances in the homeland or host land can make 'their commitment to the diaspora [...] renewed' (ibid.). Indian Nepalis seem to behave the way Sheffer sees social groups with roots in another country. The call for Nepal is not permanent; there is no ideology of return, but Nepal can be considered by people in times of distress. There is a kind of right to return, although not formal, but applicable in numerous cases. To make one's *aliyah* (ascent) (see, for example, Sheffer 2005), that is one's return or 'go up', is not an obligation as in the Jewish case. Few actually do it, but many know that it is a possibility. For insecure Nepali communities in India's north-east, Nepal has been a horizon of hope.

'Etic' discourse of the Nepalis in Bokakhat and people's practices bring a different perspective on the possible diasporic feelings of Indian Nepalis. I consider the diaspora as a hidden, but real, layer of Indian Nepalis' belonging.

Conclusion: Diaspora as a hidden layer of belonging

In the case of Bokakhat Nepalis, inheritance of language, culture, and so on and roots in Nepal are not sufficient for the diasporic Nepalis to make a legitimate claim. The path towards hybridity, de-territorialisation and diasporic forms of belonging is not the one adopted by Indian Nepalis. In the context of Assam, where identity needs to be grounded in definite Indian places, claims and assertiveness of relations with Nepal are not easily proclaimed. However, the study of the Bokakhat community shows that these links exist. In my view, they should not be considered as detrimental to their Indian identity. After all, identity is multi-layered, contextual and in perpetual evolution. The fact that the Nepali identity is perhaps too cast in one piece prevents the public affirmation of different belongings. However, practices show that the Nepali identity is a little more complex than people are willing to display. The question of the possible inclusion of Indian Nepalis in a Nepali diaspora, transnational in essence, can be raised. But, for its political affirmation, the Indian Nepalis need a spatial form of belonging, based on a territory rather than a de-territorialised idea of diasporic space, based on imagination and on irregular connections. The Indian Nepalis are, perhaps more and more, attached to fixity within its nation state. On a pragmatic point of view, the Indian identity is much more functional, effective and integrative than a diasporic or transnational one, which only stands in the realms of imagination, whatever power it may have to unite and give a sense of belonging.

The time spent by the Nepali community in Assam could be an argument for diasporic consciousness. They are not just recent migrants, but in most families, there are fourth-generation Indian Nepalis. For Tölölyan (2007), two to three generations are necessary for migrants to become part of a diaspora. But the fresh memories of the Assam Andolan, the impression of being second-grade citizens and the political quest for a place of their own in India hamper diasporic consciousness. The question is not to belong to an abstract social form, but to belong to a state that guarantees and respects their rights. The willingness to preserve cultural differences could have made them look to Nepal for support, but discourses never give way for enhanced international links. Activists of their rights deny the transnational dimension of their society. On the contrary, to many diasporas whose 'core' members (Sheffer 2003) are the only active ones and the masses cannot see any interest in diaspora, the elite is the one denying links to the country of origin. It even seems that the process of rising consciousness about diasporic dimensions of their belonging has not started yet. Even though it is rejected as a form of belonging, the diaspora is a category of practice and a resource. Links to Nepal need not be advertised, but they are real. Multipolarity, on the contrary, is weak and exists mainly within India, Gorkhaland demand being the focus point. But in an individual and family life course, the question of Nepal as a place is bound to emerge. It is not just a 'foreign country', but a place to find a job or find refuge in case of crisis.

The Indian Nepalis show that at a time when scientists are obsessed with mobility, other forms of belonging based on networks, fixity, sedentarity, boundaries and limits are also looked for, even by population with a history of dispersion.

Notes

1. After Sikkim (63%), Arunachal Pradesh (8.7%) and Meghalaya (2.25 %), Assam is the fourth Indian state in terms of concentration of Nepalis.
2. « démêler les liens entre la réalité sociale et la notion » (French quote).
3. The 'Languages, Cultures and Territories in Northeast India' project was funded by the French National Research Agency.
4. Nepalis represent about 2.5 per cent of Golaghat district population (Devi 2007).
5. Tika Ram Upadhyaya.
6. The 'official' Nepali historian of Bokakhat told me the first Nepali arrived in Bokakhat in 1828.
7. I only met three families living in Bokakhat outside the two hamlets. They were from Sherpa and Damai backgrounds.
8. A few kilometres from Bokakhat is a village called Subbagaon, inhabited by Rais and Limbus.
9. I did a survey of all Nepali houses situated in Bokakhat Ward no. 2 with a student aged 21 in 2010. He could tell almost all Nepali household heads' names and their kinship relations.
10. The feeling (and desire) to live with one's own group is very much present.
11. It was built by Nepalis in 2000 on land given by the municipality. A second temple, dedicated to Gayatri, is being built.
12. I mean here a soldier belonging to the Gorkha regiment.
13. The cycle shop was owned by a man living a few kilometres from Bokakhat, in Palasguri.
14. On the contrary, it is widely used among Nepal Nepalis abroad, in particular by social organisation leaders.
15. Bangladeshis are commonly called Pakistanis.
16. This point should, of course, be analysed in depth by anthropologists. The question of the hybridity of the diasporic religious practices should also be made clearer.
17. On the 2010 celebration of the Republic Day in Bokakhat, there was only one Nepali sitting on the dais.
18. For a broader approach, see Bhandari (1996).
19. As one Tika Ram Upadhyay says: 'Our ancestors had their brothers, their sons come to Assam and we all became *thaluwa*'.
20. The branches of all these associations in Bokakhat are led by Bahun-Chhetris, especially by a particular family.
21. Ma Mung (2000) considers it to be a major feature of diasporas.
22. All Nepali-origin people residing in South Asia are *de facto* excluded from the main diaspora organisation.
23. Sheffer (2003).
24. Subba (2008) asserts that orientation to Kathmandu is much less now than it was in the 1970s.
25. Some devotees have been to Kathmandu's holy places, as part of a Himalayan sacred places tour.
26. In any case, paternal places of origin only are looked for.
27. When I was in Qatar in September 2011, I met the man responsible for the Syangja District Association, a mid-western Nepal district. He was very keen on stressing

all what he did for his home-district and his fellow countrymen. But after talking for a while with him, he told me he originated from Assam, where he was born and where his parents were still living. The first time he came to Nepal was in 1994 to get a Nepalese passport and to be able to fly to Qatar. He now only puts forward his Nepal Nepali identity. In Qatar, I met other Assamese Nepalis who had taken the Nepalese citizenship to be able to work in Qatar.

28 In other parts of north-east India, seasonal migration from Nepal still continues.
29 Despite quite strict citizenship laws on paper, it seems easy to acquire the Nepalese citizenship.
30 Brubaker (2005: 11) is critical of this view and raises the question of the integration of 'dormant members' in diaspora as problematic.

References

Baruah, S. 1999. *India against Itself: Assam and the Politics of Nationality*. Philadelphia: University of Pennsylvania Press.

Bhandari, P. 1996. *Freedom Movement and Role of Indian Nepalese 1800–1950*. Guwahati: Mrs. Rama Bhandari.

Bordes-Benayoun, C. 2006. 'L'exil, Figure Littéraire, Figure Sociologique', in W. Berthomière and C. Chivallon (eds), *Les Diasporas dans le Monde Contemporain*, pp. 189–93. Paris: Karthala, MSHA.

Brubaker, R. 2005. 'The "Diaspora" Diaspora', *Ethnic and Racial Studies*, 28(1): 1–19.

Chettry, D. B. 2009. 'Nepalis and Bangladeshis: A Comparative Study', in T. B. Subba, A. C. Sinha, G. S. Nepal and D. R. Nepal (eds), *Indian Nepalis: Issues and Perspectives*. New Delhi: Concept Publishing Company.

Chivallon, C. 2006. 'Diaspora: Ferveur Académique autour d'un Mot', in W. Berthomière et C. Chivallon (eds), *Les diasporas dans le Monde Contemporain*, pp. 15–27. Paris: Karthala-MSHA.

Clifford, J. 1994. 'Diasporas', *Cultural Anthropology*, 9(3): 302–38.

Dasgupta, A. 2003. 'Othering of the "Not-So-Other": A Study of the Nepalis in Assam', in A. C. Sinha and T. B. Subba (eds), *The Nepalis in Northeast India: A Community in Search in Indian Identity*, pp. 230–49. New Delhi: Indus Publishing Company.

Devi, M. 2007. 'Economic History of Nepali Migration and Settlement in Assam', *Economic and Political Weekly*, 21 July, 3005–7.

Devi, N. 2009. 'History of Nepali Settlement in Assam', in T. B. Subba, A. C. Sinha, G. S. Nepal and D. R. Nepal (eds), *Indian Nepalis: Issues and Perspectives*, pp. 249–58. New Delhi: Concept Publishing Company.

Golay, B. 2006. 'Rethinking Gorkha Identity: Outside the Imperium of Discourse, Hegemony, and History', *Peace and Democracy in South Asia*, 2(1&2): 23–49.

Hall, S. 1999. 'Thinking the Diaspora: Home-Thoughts from Abroad', *Small Axe*, 6: 1–18.

Hovanessian, M. 1998. 'La Notion de Diaspora. Usages et Champ Sémantique', *Journal des anthropologues*, 72–73: 11–30.

Hutt, M. 1997. 'Being Nepali without Nepal: Reflections on a South Asian Diaspora', in David N. Gellner, J. Pfaff-Czarnecka and J. Whelpton (eds), *Nationalism and*

Ethnicity in a Hindu Kingdom: The Politics of Culture in Contemporary Nepal, pp. 101–44. Amsterdam: Harwood Academic Publishers.

Ma Mung, E. 2000. *La Diaspora Chinoise, Géographie d'une Migration*. Gap: Ophrys.

Nath, L. 2002. *Ethnicity and Cross border Movements in the North-East: A Study of the Nepalis in Assam*. Kolkata: Maulana Abul Kalam Azad Institute of Asian Studies.

Nath, L. 2005. 'Migrants in Flight: Conflict-inducted Internal Displacement of Nepalis in Northeast India', *Peace and Democracy in South Asia*, 1(1): 57–72.

Safran, W. 1991. 'Diasporas in Modern Societies: Myths of Homeland and Return', *Diaspora*, 1(1): 83–99.

Sheffer, G. 2003. *Diaspora Politics: At Home Abroad*. Cambridge: Cambridge University Press.

Sheffer, G. 2005. 'Is the Jewish Diaspora Unique? Reflections on the Diaspora's Current Situation', *Israel Studies*, 10(1): 1–35.

Sinha, A. C. 2003. 'The Indians of Nepali Origin and Security of Northeast India', in A. C. Sinha and T. B. Subba (eds), *The Nepalis in Northeast India: A community in Search of Indian Identity*, pp. 360–77. New Delhi: Indus.

Sinha, A. C. and T. B. Subba (eds). 2003. *The Nepalis in Northeast India: A Community in Search of Indian Identity*. New Delhi: Indus Publishing Company.

Subba, T. B. 2002. 'Nepal and the Indian Nepalis', in Kanak Mani Dixit and Shastri Ramachandran (eds), *State of Nepal*, pp. 119–36. Kathmandu: Himal Books.

Subba, T. B. 2008. 'Living the Nepali Diaspora in India: An Autobiographical Essay', *Zeitschrift für Ethnologie*, 133: 213–32.

Subba, T. B. 2009. 'The Last Word so Far . . .', in T. B. Subba, A. C. Sinha, G. S. Nepal and D. R. Nepal (eds), *Indian Nepalis. Issues and Perspectives*, pp. 383–93. New Delhi: Concept Publishing Company.

Subba, T. B., A. C. Sinha, G. S. Nepal and D. R. Nepal (eds). 2009. *Indian Nepalis: Issues and Perspectives*. Delhi: Concept Publishing Company.

Tölölyan, K. 2007. 'The Contemporary Discourse of Diaspora Studies', *Comparative Studies of South Asia, Africa and the Middle East*, 27(3): 647–55.

Upreti, B. C. 2009. 'India-Nepal Treaty of Peace and Friendship: Nature, Problems and the Question of Identity of Indian Nepalis', in T. B. Subba, A. C. Sinha, G. S. Nepal and D. R. Nepal (eds), *Indian Nepalis: Issues and Perspectives*, pp. 339–50. New Delhi: Concept Publishing Company.

12

BETWEEN TWO WORLDS
A re-reading of *Brahmaputraka Cheuchau*

Utpala Ghaley Sewa

Two important factors have led to the almost natural movement of people from Nepal to India, especially Assam and the north-east of India: the 1,900-km-long international 'open' border and the British induction of the 'Gurkhas' into the army, post-1815–16 Treaty of Segowli. The added impetuses were the push factors of economic hardship and illiteracy of the large and economically vulnerable population of Nepal. The physical contiguity, in unison with the commonality of socio-religious aspects of the society, further combined with the comparatively lower population density, specifically of north-east India, created the magnetic pull factor into undivided Assam from the beginning of the 19th century itself.

An interesting aspect of Nepali migration to these regions is that it is largely the rural, unskilled and mostly unlettered Nepali who migrated to these parts of India (Bhattarai 2003). The areas of challenges, especially for the first-generation migrants, have revolved around their self-image, as they attempted to root themselves in the host land while negotiating with their separateness in terms of ethnicity and customs, religion and rituals.

It is against such a backdrop of history of migration and diasporic social reality that Lil Bahadur Chhetri's celebrated novel, *Brahmaputraka Cheuchau,* may be read. Published in 1986, its merit was acknowledged by the Sahitya Akademi with its prestigious award in 1987.

The novel presents a mix of the historical and the fictional, with a strong autobiographical undercurrent of felt experience. In fact, in the preface, the author not just declares, but most unapologetically draws attention to this unusual presence of history in the fiction. There, he mentions the period of about 24 years (1943 to 1967) as forming the background of the narrative, and the Nepali–Assamese relationship as its foreground. The writing of this novel, using the most recognisable icon of Assam, the river Brahmaputra, in its title, unequivocally locates and contextualises the narrative. The river is a living entity, but extends to encompass in metonymic relation the sense of not just geographical space, but the complex of the culture, people and the history of Assam. The title does more than geographically locate the narrative. The phrase 'cheuchau' denotes 'alongside' or 'by the side of' – a sense that characterises a marginalised diasporic society. As the narrative progresses, this meaning becomes increasingly significant with the protagonist, Gumane, making several attempts along with his fellow migrants, with various degrees of success and failure, to join or be recognised as part of the mainstream Assamese world, without compromising the notion of being a Nepali.

Brahmaputraka Cheuchau is written by the same author who was able to graphically portray the unmitigated misery and gut-wrenching want of rural Nepal in *Basai* (1989). Broken by the exploitation of the moneylender and an unyielding earth, as well as heartless arrogance of the Nepali landlords, Dhane, in Chhetri's earlier novel *Basai*, is compelled to leave his village in search of a job and financial security. This novel grew out of the author's intense interest in understanding the reasons behind the huge and steady volume of Nepali migration into Assam, mostly from the far-flung villages of Nepal. As he says in his preface to the novel, this interest had led to innumerable interactions with the new migrants as they landed in the railway stations (much like Khalal in *Brahmaputraka Cheuchau* waiting for new arrivals to take home to Kachugaon as graziers) and also to investigative talks with earlier migrants, which opened his eyes to the problems of a world and a lifestyle that he was unacquainted with and definitely could not have imagined. What he discovered from their narratives was a world of such want and desperation that to those who migrated, facing the most dire risk in going out of the village and the country appeared a better option than the certainty of a future of drudgery and increasing impoverishment at home in Nepal. As the novelist, an Indian Nepali of Assam, grew curious to know what dreams or desperations brought them to the point of opting for a blind gamble of moving into unknown lands, he began the many-years-long interactions with the new migrants. On the basis of these researches, he arrived at certain conclusions that finally went to form the bedrock of the novel and to shape it into a narrative of pathos and realism. The novel, *Basai* thus is born out of his basic interest in the causes behind the unceasing stream of people from Nepal to Assam.

In his earlier novel, the protagonist, Dhane (ironically, the word 'dhane' in Nepali means 'wealthy') is portrayed as a well-meaning young man of

25 years, whose plans for the future are star-crossed as he is constantly confronted with bad luck. His is a small household of wife Maina, sister Jhumavati, aged about 15 years, and a small son. He is poor, but owns a small patch of agricultural land, more in the nature of a biggish kitchen garden, a modest hut and an equally modest but completely plausible dream of financial betterment. He dreams of success, or at least, material upliftment, and sets about turning his dreams into reality. His dreams are not actually improbable and it would have been well within the realms of possibility for their realisation, was he not so persistently dogged by ill luck. As Dhane is unable to repay the small loan he had taken (actually, not even the interest), his run of misfortune begins. Had he perhaps been given a longer period of grace, the loan could have been repaid. But the creditor shows no mercy or understanding and brings the village headman and other stalwarts into the fracas so that they are able to publicly permit him to take away the only bull that Dhane owns. Dhane had been using the bull for agricultural work, and without the bull, the field would not be ploughed. So, he hires himself out to the village elder as a hired help, now that he is without his bull.

In a piece of knavery employed by the village landlord's son, the water that should have been directed that particular night, as per the rules followed by farmers in the village, to the field that Dhane is now working on, where new seedlings are wilting without water, the big flow of water is surreptitiously directed to the fields of the rich landlord. Dhane, in his youthful zest and bitter disillusionment at this underhand behaviour, beats the servant of the landlord whom he catches in the act of sabotage. A village level enquiry and judgement blames Dhane and puts him under warning. His run of bad luck is not over yet, however. A pregnant buffalo is let loose into the field with the seedlings, probably by the same miscreants. Dhane chases the animal all over the field, and in her pregnant state, she is unable to move fast enough to escape Dhane's angry blows on her body with the 'kodali' (spade). She falls into an inert heap. Dhane continues to rain blows on her still form. By the time he realises the inhumanity of his action, the animal is almost dead and the field totally trampled over. Dhane weeps tears of regret, but the damage is done already. The pregnant buffalo dies. Dhane is charged for the repayment of the price of the dead buffalo and her unborn calf. Meanwhile, Dhane's cup of misery truly runs over when his young sister, Jhumavati is made pregnant by a visiting 'Rikkute' (a corruption of the English word 'recruit') who works in the plains of India ('Muglan'). Unable to bear the shame, she tries to commit suicide, but is saved by the decision of Motay Karkee, the man who has always loved her, to marry her. Her condition forces her to gratefully accept the marriage offer of a man much older than her and physically unattractive, whom she has known all her life, but never been impressed by. Hers, one cannot help but feel, is going to be a life of compromise. One can only hope that the betrayal of her love and the unlikely conjugal companion will not embitter her in the future once the crisis in her personal life is over.

It is equally possible that the knowledge of the 'sacrifice' Karkee has made in 'saving' her will compensate for the lack of love on her side, the one whom she loved having shown her the actual irrelevance of romantic love in life by his desertion of her. They leave the village surreptitiously, without meeting Dhane or Maina, either due to shame or a desire not to add to the sum of misfortunes that Dhane is already grappling with. They just leave a letter explaining the circumstances. Motay Karkee and Jhuma leave for an unknown destination just as Dhane leaves the village of his birth and of his ancestors soon after he is evicted from it and forced to sell his meagre property to the owner of the dead buffalo in order to compensate for his loss. The novel concludes in a very open-ended manner. Chhetri comments that the small family wends its sad way out of the village and it is uncertain as to what nature of destiny they head towards. They could be moving towards a better future or the struggles ahead could be indeed very daunting.

As a person who has lived the migrant's destiny, perhaps through family narratives, Chhetri was best placed to not give the ending a hopeful and optimistic tone. The author has uncovered the sad truth behind most Nepali migrations. There are three reasons for the villagers of Nepal moving out of their land and they are: the unbearable load of financial burden, a desire to better oneself economically and emotional/societal reasons such as that of Jhuma and Karkee. The next phase of the lives of the migrants is unclear. The author, himself born of parents who migrated to India, was too aware of the uncertain nature of the fortunes of migrants in India, specifically in north-east India, to express much hope in the future of his characters once they leave hearth and home. In fact, there is deep pathos at the picture of the three sad figures moving out of their home and their village at the crack of dawn, carrying a small bundle of meagre possessions, clueless as to where their next stop may be.

Thus, his earlier narrative, born out of his curiosity, performs the role of a social scientist in answering the questions regarding the push factors leading to the migration of Nepalis.

In what appears almost like a sequel to Dhane's leaving the village of his ancestors, in *Brahmaputraka Cheuchau*, Manbir leaves home and hearth and the reasons are the same as Dhane's: he is unable to make ends meet in his village in Nepal. Selling his meagre possessions back to his creditor to square off his debts, Manbir leaves with his small family comprising wife Jureli and infant son Gumane in search of a sustainable earning. The narrative, *Brahmaputraka Cheuchau*, thus appears to begin at the point where *Basai* had left off.

The unlettered villager leaves home and the reader assumes a happier future for him, but does he really live happily ever after? The attempt to answer that question becomes the core of *Brahmaputraka Cheuchau*. It portrays in this personalised narration of the fictional protagonist, Gumane, the issues and challenges a diasporic people negotiate in the host land. In epic fashion, this narrative begins with a hauntingly beautiful description of the overlapping hills in the background behind the small hut towards which a few people are making their way in the morning. Manbir has breathed his last and arrangements for his funeral are underway. His wife Jureli, a companion and emotional support in his journey to the unknown, had predeceased him by three years. Gumane is thus orphaned at 12 years with no kin for him to claim as his own. He is all alone in a land which is not his birthplace, but which he thinks is his home, in being the only one he knows. His story of survival and emergence of a sense of self that is neither Assamese nor Nepali in its entirety, but 'Assameli – Nepali', is the trajectory this narrative traces.

That Gumane was born to parents who had nothing left back in Nepal to call their own is significant as it confirms his emotional rootlessness and the ambiguity of his political status. Nepal can never be home for him; it will forever stand symbolically for his ethnic roots, but mean very little else. Like Gumane, Chhetri too has indicated a similar personal position of ambiguity when he speaks in the preface both to *Basai* and *Brahmaputraka Cheuchau*, of his being unacquainted with the ways of the world of a villager in Nepal. He tenders his apology in advance should his portrayal be inadequate or off the mark, as he says in his defence, he has never lived the life in Nepal that he writes about, nor was he acquainted with the language spoken in the villages of Nepal. Thus, Gumane's situation is almost a reflection of that of Chhetri himself. Gumane's lack of memories of his past makes room for another important reality. It implies that his first memories and consciousness, as the novel opens, were created in a land that he has lived for twelve years. But the attendant problem to this is that though he may think of the land he is now in, Assam, as his own, he may not naturally claim it as his own, as the author has denied him the legitimacy of a natural-born Indian by deliberately creating ambiguity in rightful citizenship by making his birth in a land that is alien to him. Gumane has no roots to go back to: his is the true dilemma of a diasporic, for him, home is Assam, although he is not ethnically Assamese. To legitimise his claim to be recognised as a Nepali who is Assamese in loyalty and emotion, and that of others like him, then becomes his continual struggle throughout the narrative.

His first struggle is to throw off the yoke of Kesar Khalal, the Dairy Mahajan who had yoked his parents to years of drudgery and penury, like the landlords back in Nepal. Picked up at the railway station when Manbir, just landed from Nepal with his wife and infant son, was totally clueless about what or where he should go, following only the vague direction of a Nepali soldier visiting his distant relatives whom he had got talking to in the train. Khalal lies waiting for new migrants such as Manbir and taking advantage of their vulnerability, he promises them a home and a world of security and relative prosperity. What follows is a plight almost paralleling their drudgery back in Nepal. Exploitation is shamelessly carried on in his 'Chapari' on cowhands and graziers; cowhands Bom Bahadur Subba and Nandlal have not been paid wages in years nor has Bom Bahadur been given leave to go home back to Nepal.

The diverse strands in the community, namely, the various individuals within the Nepali community, are slowly examined by Chhetri as other characters and their interpersonal equations begin to occupy the narrative space. Khalal, having successfully turned Manbir and Jureli into unpaid slaves, had – in the true feudal mindset of the landlords in Nepal – expected Gumane to continue the servitude. He expected this also because Gumane as an orphan, a status often used for denigrating Gumane by the community members several times in the narrative, would have to find his legitimate place within his community even if the community be represented by a man as devoid of any redeeming quality as Kesar Khalal. But the young boy, sensing the Assamese freedom fighter, Keshav Kakati's support, refuses to stay under Khalal's protection. In this brave decision, the youngster echoes his father's rejection of the life of servitude and exploitation, first in Nepal, and then, under Khalal. Manbir had not hidden from his son his distrust and disappointment with his employer. He had instead spoken, with an intuitive recognition of the good, of Keshav Kakati, the Assamese freedom fighter, and had, in fact, already requested Kakati to take care of his son, Gumane, in the event of his death. This rejection of the Nepali stalwart of the community is a crucial milestone in this narrative that narrates the growing vision of the identity and the emerging sense of self of the Assameli-Nepalis, a term the Nepalis in Assam have coined to reflect the twin realities of their self. It reflects Chhetri's desire to show that Gumane, like his father, is totally without any communal bias. The feudal arrogance and spiritual bankruptcy of Khalal is measured against the idealism and genuine goodness of Kakati and found wanting. This rejection becomes the cause of the personal antagonism Khalal nurtures against Gumane till the very end, using money, position, power, even demeaning himself to floating rumours to balk at Gumane's attempt at happiness, growth in stature and influence. Does it represent Gumane's rejection of Nepal as his homeland? Perhaps it does, and Khalal's continued and unyielding desire to own Gumane might symbolically represent the mother country's undeniable, yet in certain instances, untenable and confusing presence in the evolution of the self-image and identity of the Assameli-Nepali.

The rejection of Khalal by Gumane is a replay of Manbir's rejection of his homeland and his consequent move towards Assam. His move from the world of his birth, where all he has known are poverty and indignity in the hands of the Nepali landlords and moneylenders, to what might have actually have been a better life in Assam, were he not haunted by a replica of the same tormentors, is the central irony that Gumane has to negotiate. Gumane's first decisive step is to reject one who would perpetuate his misery and choose Kakati.

But 'mother' Assam (*Ai-Asom*) and 'young' Assam, may not accept the outsider, this 'other', quite so easily. It is Mrs Kakati who refuses to accept or welcome the young Gumane into her home. Her son, Haren, studying in nearby Tezpur, is then not at home. But he poses a greater threat to Gumane when he returns; Gumane is the 'outsider', the 'other' who challenges him by seeking space in his hearth, having already appropriated the father's affection. A very interesting parallel is quietly introduced: while Haren is the son of a renowned freedom fighter and a true idealist, he bears no trace of his legacy, while Gumane, the son of an unlettered cowherd from Nepal, has all the virtues and values that Kakati wishes in a son. As Iago tells Othello in Shakespeare's *Othello*, it is the 'daily goodness' of Cassio that enrages him to acts of heinous devilry, this human weakness that Shakespeare so insightfully stated as an important reason for evil, may also be the motive force behind Haren's enmity. There is this same 'daily goodness' in Gumane that challenges and antagonises Haren. Haren's antagonism towards Gumane becomes physical and reckless, and remains so till the end.

The symbolic significance of this is obvious. The mother-son duo, apparently symbolising new Assam, proceeds to make Gumane's life unbearable. Although it may appear that Gumane has just traded one type of servitude and misery for another, the important difference between his father's fate under Khalal and his own under Kakati is that he begins the process of being empowered through education. Whereas the buffalos eventually given to his parents, Manbir and Jureli, as settlement for the years of unpaid service to the Khalals become further source of their financial and physical ruin, the education in the village school that Kakati and Headmaster Surya Prasad ensure for Gumane finally grooms and empowers him. The parents' servitude and suffering remained endless and static, but there is growth and evolution in Gumane despite his period of servitude to the Kakati family. His story of empowerment continues with small, but significant milestones – like his being made capable of taking care of himself, of being regarded as an individual who counts through the help of Kakati. He helps him secure the post of a chowkidar in the school where he studies along with Malati, Kakati's daughter. Khalal uses his power and influence as a board member of the school to question, and then, finally embarrass the headmaster into revoking this appointment. But this event is not to be seen as a reversal of fortune for Gumane; rather, it is one further step towards realisation of his selfhood. He now moves into a family that he might well think of as his own, almost as if the process of real rooting in the alien soil has begun. Gumane is taken into the headmaster's home. The headmaster has no son, the daughters and mother are affectionate towards Gumane, and at one level, apparently, Gumane too does accept them as his own. On return from the army, he gives his dearly won and the only possessions to the two: the medals to Malati and the bag of money to the headmaster's wife.

The national freedom movement and the contributions of two Assameli-Nepalis in times of the nationalistic political ferment in Assam, Chhabi Lal Upadhyaya and Dal Bir Lohar, who subsequently won the 1952 elections from Dibrugarh on Congress ticket, are mentioned. These actual events and names are meshed seamlessly with the fictional narrative. Thus, a reader may confuse this as a historical representation, but the purpose of their inclusion is clear: apart from chronicling the Nepali history in Assam, the community's contribution is reiterated by inscribing these significant names and milestones in the state's political evolution. The moral and political right that the Assameli-Nepalis feel they have to call Assam their homeland are underscored by the reviving of these major contributions from the very early days of Assam under independent India. That the Assameli-Nepalis have been with the state from the beginning so that today, Assam's post-independence history cannot be retold without mentioning some of their crucial contributions seems to be the message that these historical details actually intend to convey.

As a character who can be taken as representative of the Assameli-Nepalis, constituting about 550,000 as per the Census of 2011, Gumane's stance towards the stalwarts of the community makes interesting reading. While his knowledge of his ethnic roots is never questioned by him, his struggles and vision of his future and those of others like him are associated with Assam. He never once thinks of leaving his village, Kachugaon, to return to Nepal. In a very telling statement, Gumane expresses this when he is questioned in Guwahati as to the village he hails from – a question all Nepalis are invariably asked and expected to reply with the name of a village in Nepal. Home for him will always be Kachugaon and he may not even know or remember the name of the one his parents came from. Thus, Gumane has to learn to negotiate his relationship with the keepers of the community in Assam in his attempt to accept and be accepted as a significant member of Assameli-Nepali community. Hence, the evolution of his relationship with Khalal becomes the yardstick of his empowerment and acceptance by the host society.

Gumane faces hurdles stoically, but when it comes to a direct dealing with the Dairy Mahajan Khalal or his family, he remains respectfully acquiescent or leaves to avoid confrontation. When he is asked by Khalal's brother to return to Kachugaon for a short visit with him after a chance meeting during a Nepali ritual at the Parshuram Kund in Makar Sakranti, Gumane is unable to refuse. He leaves Kharel Baje's group of pilgrims with the promise of a quick return, only to find himself unable to refuse the offer of a job at Khalal's creamery in Tinsukia. But when he is offered their daughter, Muna in marriage, he leaves. He shies away from any real ties with this prime Nepali family of the region, and it may not only be because of the tragedy of his parents' fate under the Khalal yoke, but because he is wary of being in their total control. Instinctively, he realises he would be then another pawn to this unscrupulous family and the right to chart his own course would be taken away from him. But later, after his army stint, with supporters such as the headmaster, Kakati and Tope Master behind him, Gumane is able to pursue a confrontational path with Khalal in his pursuit of recognition of the plight of the graziers at Mainapada and his demand for recognition of the Nepali desire for inclusion in the mainstream.

But it is not just within the Nepali community and with power centres such as Khalal that Gumane negotiates for space and voice. Haren's escalating violence towards him, though met by Gumane with stoic endurance each time, gradually becomes the cause of Haren's own downfall. He goes missing from the village after his last bout of violence towards Gumane, which lands Gumane in the hospital. Nemesis seems to finally catch up with Haren as he is not heard of again in the village. Gumane has, at the end, evolved into a person who finds his space and acceptance within both the communities, the Assamese and Nepalis.

Earlier in the narrative, Gumane's flight to Guwahati leads him into contact with other types of the Nepali migrants, those who represent the text-book definition of a diaspora in being people whose sense of home is ambiguous at best. Even before he meets them, he hears of them. As he makes his enquiries about the presence of Nepalis in the city from the owner of the hotel in Paltanbazar, Guwahati, where he enters for his first meal, he hears about how the Gorkha platoon brought in by the British had camped in that part of Guwahati that began to be called Paltanbazar. They had constructed the rudiments of the Nepali temple that stands even today, declaring the past association of the place with this community. But as the city developed and the locality emerged as an important commercial centre, the few Nepali settlers who had settled there began to shift to neighbouring suburbs with their cows and buffalos. They were graziers and milk vendors and they were most comfortable outside the city margins. They laid no claim on the area though they were the first to arrive there, nor did they wish to move into trades such as shop-keeping or other similar business such as Khalal Mahajan's creamery in Tinsukia town. As the hotel owner says very graphically, and very disparagingly, these early settlers vacated this prime area of settlement holding 'the tails of their cattle'.

The settlers at Aath Mile area that Gumane comes in contact with represent the most disturbing variation of this category of migrants. He is looking for a job and the hotel owner introduces him to a member of that group who had actually come to pick up grains and cattle fodder, and at the same time, was also looking as usual for fresh migrants from Nepal to employ as cowhands and graziers. When he learns of Gumane's education and his aim to study further, he offers him a job as the teacher in a makeshift school in their locality. Gumane discovers that at Aath Mile, the Nepalis have several cattlesheds or *khutti*s. They do good business supplying and meeting nearly all the milk demand of the city, but live in shabby and makeshift houses. In fact, the returns are good, but most of the profit goes into the pockets of the middlemen, who buy their milk at the roadside and sell it in Guwahati at a handsome profit. Kharel Baje has a family of a first wife and grown-up sons and grandsons at Bhairava, in Nepal, but also a young wife and two very young children at this home in Aath Mile – a situation often seen in the diaspora: main home and family in Nepal, and a second, much later one at their job sites. Hence, the home at Aath Mile is so flimsy that it appears like a temporary settlement, though they have been there for a long time. Kharel Baje speaks for far too many like him when he explains that they keep the settlement temporary since their main interest is in earning money and then going back to Nepal. Gumane observes that none of them is like him in Kachugaon for no one desires to settle permanently. The daily earnings are all that concern them and 'home' is always Nepal. On enquiring further, Gumane finds that none of the lands is in their names; they have not even tried to avail of temporary land deed. When Gumane advises Kharel Baje on the wisdom of getting the land deed, the defeatist attitude of the uninterested surfaces: he asks who would give them these. The question appears more rhetorical than real, even to Gumane. Hence, they expect to be chased out any time as they have not sought nor been given permanent *pattas* for the land. They will have to eventually return to Nepal, he says. Kharel Baje sends 'home' (Nepal) money; he has an enormous building at Bhairava, but lives in total shabbiness in Aath Mile. They earn and leave without a fuss when the time comes. Gumane sets about trying to make them understand the need to buy land, avail the title deeds in order to become a part of the land. Every evening, the inhabitants of the locality gather in Kharel Baje's house to listen to Gumane. The first light of understanding is only just beginning to dawn when Gumane leaves, never to return. The reader is, thus, left with the impression that lack of wise leadership, proper insight and guidance are behind the plight of some of the Nepali settlers in Assam, who make themselves vulnerable to acts of injustice and violence time and again. Many of the graziers in Gumane's area too have this attitude: when chased, they either go deeper into the jungles or migrate to the coalfields far away. They cannot think of Assam as home, and so, will not assert their rights, who balk at Gumane's attempt to establish an identity within the Assamese society. This ambiguity is what defines the Nepali diaspora in Assam.

The author addresses the question of loyalty and patriotism in this narrative, an issue that plagues discussions on identity. The word 'Nepali' immediately associates one with Nepal (Nath 2003). After a close account of Gumane's heroic surmounting of odds in his single-minded pursuit of education as the one certain way of personal empowerment and of leading his people out of helplessness and ignorance, he mysteriously disappears for a few years. He resurfaces, battered, disfigured, but honourably discharged from the army. The transformation in him is physical as well as psychological: he speaks with the mannerism of a well-travelled, seasoned soldier, and with Malati, now married; he sublimates his pain with a zeal to work for his village and his people, transforming himself now to the archetypical social reformer. The next step is politics. He cannot follow it to its logical conclusion because of Haren's and Khalal's interferences. Gumane returns after fighting for his country, the only one he knows, India. His disfigurement and maiming is a device Chhetri uses to show that his involvement, sincerity and loyalty are no longer in doubt.

Examined from the perspective of literary and psychological credibility, the transformation of Gumane, post-army, may appear as far-fetched as Hamlet morphing into Othello. But the author has used the intervention as an expedient mode to address the issue of the migrant's loyalty. A look into Chhetri's motive forces in writing this saga of his community's woes and challenges may be also indicative of the delicate balance between the two worlds that the Assameli-Nepali traverses. In his preface, Chhetri mentions as his inspiration the constant request of old friends to document the trials and hurdles of his people in this narrative, 18 long years in the making. This clarifies the core purpose of the narrative in so far as it elucidates, brings to life and also presents the community as basically not too different from that of the Assamese, each with a Khalal and a Haren.

Gumane's relationship with Malati is carefully handled by the author. The very idea of a Nepali boy being chosen above all others, and wooed by an Assamese girl, with the only other Assamese boy in the village, Haren, being shown as an unmitigated scoundrel, and the educated and refined doctor from Guwahati, who marries Malati, as infertile, was a potentially volatile scenario. But Chhetri handles this with consummate finesse. He has structured it so that it is Malati who first expresses her love for Gumane. His actual words reciprocating are in the passive voice. The other's voice is unvoiced by the author. In doing so, he has successfully conveyed the sense of Gumane's deep and reciprocal love, but as the actual words are not recorded, he has skilfully diffused the potentially disturbing situation. Later, after her marriage, when Malati continues to meet him and help him in his political campaigns, Gumane shifts the relationship to one of spiritual bonding, answering her maturely and calmly, always aware and respectful of her marital status. If Gumane of the later part of the narrative appears much too ideal and moralistic, a role model rather than a real feeling-thinking person, an automaton rather than human, one has to keep in mind that the author has a mission to fulfil: he is duty-bound by his commitment to the purpose of the novel to delineate the archetypical Nepali migrant of Assam, whose idealism and genuine goodness can only add to the sum quality of the host population.

The other major character of the narrative that requires some attention is the Dairy Mahajan Khalal. Kesar Khalal is a power-monger and devoid of moral values. Yet, he is important in this narrative as, often, his is the only representative presence and voice of the Nepali community that is recognised by the authorities, if for no other reason than the money he has to buy their help and loyalty. This landlord is able, even in his land of migration, to wield the same influence and power as do those like him in Nepal. In the Mainapada incident, a large number of Nepalis were evicted and they were, including women and children, treated in the most inhuman manner by the officials and Gumane plays an important role in ending the misery of the poor Nepalis. But Gumane's good intentions and valour are no match to Khalal's money power. Khalal has cleverly identified the areas of importance in the village that he must associate himself with. Thus, he is the member of the governing body of the village school, although his own educational achievements remain unmentioned. Khalal knows that having an educated son-in-law would increase not only his prestige among the group of powerful men he associates with, but also his sphere of influence, hence his desire to trap Gumane into marrying his mentally challenged daughter, Muna.

His identification of education as an important agency of empowerment is also demonstrated by the fact that he has given all his children, even Muna, the chance to pursue education. He realises the importance of education, unlike his counterparts at Aath Mile, where the only education for their children is a totally non-serious endeavour where the children have to be cajoled and called out of their homes to attend school in the makeshift bamboo structure that has no furniture, except a desk and chair for the teacher whose salary fluctuates as per the number of student attendees. The children there attend school with books and a sack folded neatly under their arms. This is what they spread and sit on in the class. Temporary is the adjective that comes to mind with everything associated with the school, and the residents, at Aath Mile. But Khalal's farsightedness, despite his total lack of scruples, is impressive. So that Khalal's sphere of influence on the nascent or future power figures be assured, his association with the headmaster Surjya Prasad and Kesav Kakati keep him abreast of the evolving centres of power. Like a typical village villain, he has in his employ many powerful, or just plain notorious, characters to do his bidding. He represents the maxim that money has no caste or religion. When the Congress politicians are brought in through the efforts of Gumane and Tope Master to help resolve the Mainapada crisis, to meet the Nepali graziers who are threatened by the officials of the government with the destruction of their houses with elephants, Khalal turns this to his advantage and emerges even more powerful in the eyes of the villagers and the officials when the invited politicians stay at his place, hold a meeting there and in enjoying his hospitality, actually forget to address the issue or even make time for a visit to Mainapada. He has at no point in the narrative ever mentioned or thought of the land of his origin, Nepal, as 'home', unlike Kharel Baje and his group in Aath Mile. Like Kharel Baje, he too has more than one wife: he has three of them, in fact. But they all live at various locations of his business or near his 'chaparis'. His daughters and sons are all married to spouses from Assam. It stands as a clear statement to all that unlike the Nepali migrants in Guwahati, the Assameli-Nepalis of Upper Assam are not always going to be content to stay at the back of beyond with buffaloes and cows. Democratic rights and laws given by the nation are known to them and they will demand their share of them.

At the end, when Gumane meets Khalal again in the village, he finds that Khalal has shut down some of his 'chaparis', and has, instead, bought more agricultural land. One last sees him mulling over the idea of giving up the milk business totally and moving over to agriculture, full-time. This is the move that unites his vision with that of Gumane. They are a part of Assam and they want to be acknowledged as such.

But to be widely accepted, it may take some time, Chhetri indicates in the novel. Hence, although Kakati had initially had no objection to the marriage of Malati with Gumane, it is the consideration of communal and familial responses that later dampen his acceptance. Perhaps just such considerations also were in Chhetri's mind when dealing with this relationship. Malati marries the Assamese doctor, much liked by Haren and Mrs Kakati, but one who can have no offspring. Does Chhetri intend to indicate that Assam's future is doomed without integration of other ethnic groups? The family is witness to the gradual wasting of Malati and her final suicide. Mrs Kakati dies and Kakati leaves on a pilgrimage and hands over his house to Gumane to turn it into a library for the village youngsters. Haren is untraceable. Malati's family disappears, as if overtaken by nemesis. The library gradually falls to disuse and dust. Kakati's handing over of his house to Gumane when he, sadly, is its sole master, is a crucial detail. The 'other' is finally accepted, and perhaps would have been much earlier if Kakati could have brought about the marriage of Malati with Gumane. However, the world that Gumane inherits at the end, the world of acceptance and responsibility, is different from the world that he struggled through childhood and young adulthood for the elders are either no longer alive or without their erstwhile power to change destinies by their decisions. It is a sad, gloomy world that accepts Gumane in the end. Gumane himself seems spent by his struggle. The future appears equally bleak. Hence, Chhetri's final vision of the world of the Assameli-Nepali is ambiguous, to say the least.

References

Bhattarai, P. L. 2003. 'Evolution and Growth of the Nepali Community in North-East India', in A. C. Sinha and T. B. Subba (eds), *The Nepalis in Northeast India: A Community in Search of Indian Identity,* pp. 106–23. Delhi: Indus Publishing Company.

Chhetri, L. B. 1989. *Basai.* Kathmandu: Sajha Prakashan.

Chhetri, L. B. 2002. *Brahmaputraka Cheuchau.* Kathmandu: Sajha Prakashan.

Nath, L. 2009. 'Conflict-Afflicted Nepalis of Assam: The Reality', in A. C. Sinha and T. B. Subba (eds), *The Nepalis in Northeast India: A Community in Search of Indian Identity,* pp. 208–09. Delhi: Indus Publishing Company.

Sinha, A. C. and T. B. Subba (eds). 2009. *The Nepalis in Northeast India: A Community in Search of Indian Identity.* Delhi: Indus Publishing Company.

13

GURKHA DISPLACEMENT FROM BURMA IN 1942

A historical narrative

Tejimala Gurung

The Nepali diaspora in South-East Asia was an outcome of the imperatives of British colonialism and was facilitated by the geopolitical and economic compulsions of the monarchical state of Nepal. From the 19th century onwards, the Gurkhas as military soldiers were the vanguards of British expansion in and outside India. As part of the British colonial force, they participated in the First (1824–26), Second (1852–1853) and Third Anglo-Burmese (1885–1886) wars leading to the annexation of Burma (Myanmar), and subsequently, they were recruited from eastern Nepal[1] to serve in the military police battalions in Burma. As a consequence, there were Gurkha settlements in Myitkyina and other headquarters of the Burma Military Police (BMP) in which Gurkha officers and men were encouraged to settle down with their families on being discharged from active service.[2] The British occupation of Burma, which formally became a province of British India in February 1887 and the opportunity for military service, the exploitation of its resources for commercial purposes such as plantation, mining and construction of railways created favourable conditions for the migration of people from British India, including Nepal, to Burma. The census of 1931 enumerated 1,017,825 Indians in Burma; of these, 617,521 had been born in India.[3] It was reported in 1942 that there were some 200,000 Gurkhas domiciled in Burma.[4]

In the early part of 1942, there were reports of Gurkhas fleeing from Burma in the wake of the Japanese invasion during World War II. Hundreds of refugees, consisting mainly of women and children and dependents of Gurkha soldiers belonging to the Burma Frontier Force (BFF), Burma Military Police (BMP) and Burma Army (BA) besides Gurkha civilians, arrived at various Gurkha recruiting depots on the Indo-Nepal border in a destitute condition. The British authorities were particularly concerned about the condition of the destitute population and the impact stories of their hardships would have on new Gurkha recruitment in general, vital for the Allied war effort. The Maharaja of Nepal, on the contrary, wanted to prohibit the entry of Gurkhas who were of mixed parentage and who were Burmese born and bred. The question of the rehabilitation of the displaced Gurkhas from Burma, hence, became a subject of common 'concern' for the governments of India, Nepal and Burma. It was decided to establish such a rehabilitation camp at Motihari, located in the Champaran District of North Bihar. This chapter is a brief historical narrative of this event gleaned from the archival records and secondary sources available in the form of published books and articles relating to the issue of Gurkha displacement and rehabilitation in 1942.[5] Through this chapter, the author seeks to provide some historical narratives to fill in and contribute to the larger narrative of the Nepali diaspora.

Recruitment of Gurkhas in Burma

After the annexation of Upper Burma in 1886, a number of units were raised specifically for service in the newly annexed areas that came under British administration. Among the first to be raised in March 1886 was the Mogaung Levy[6] of about 500 men, which is recorded as being a Gurkha unit.[7] Their strength on 1 January 1919 was 262. The Putao Battalion in North Burma was raised in 1914 and consisted almost entirely of Gurkhas whose number was 700 in 1919. The battalion was disbanded in 1920.[8] The Military Police Force was raised in 1886, and during 1894, it numbered 16,000 men.[9] The Military Police owed its existence to the extensive operations necessitated by the 'pacification' of Upper Burma. The intention was to recruit half the force from among the people of Burma.[10] When this was not possible, the British officers from India recruited from the Punjabis, Gurkhas, Sikhs, Garhwalis and Hindustanis. The Gurkhas recruited were either those domiciled in Assam or Burma or those from the Kirata tribes of eastern Nepal. In 1891, five of the battalions were converted into Native Infantry Regiments of the Madras Army (29th to 33rd Madras Infantry, known also as Burma Battalions). During World War I, 4 battalions of Burma Rifles were formed for general service. The battalions were constituted on the 'class company basis',[11] with the Karens representing the largest section. Burmese Arakanese, Kachins, Chins, Shans and Gurkhas were also enlisted.[12] During World War I, 13 battalions were raised, but after the war, they were reduced to 10 battalions and the personnel were drawn from Gurkhas, Burmese, Karens, Kachins and Shans.[13]

In 1937, Burma ceased to be administered as a part of the province of British India and a new Burma Army was to be raised. Till then, a force of the BMP was responsible for guarding the frontier. In 1932, the strength of the BMP was nine battalions – two located in Rangoon and one each in Mandalay, Chin Hills, Lashio (Northern Shan State), Taunggyi (Southern Shan State), Bhamo, Myitkyina and one was a Reserve Battalion. The forces comprised mainly Punjabis and Kumaonis, Gurkhas and Karens serving under the British command. Subsequently, around 1939, the BMP was reduced to three battalions – two in Rangoon (Lower Burma) and one in Mandalay answerable to the Inspector-General of Police, Burma. The remaining six mustered as the BFF with battalions in the northern and southern Shan states, the Chin Hills, Bhamo and Myitkyina. The Burma Frontier Force drawn from the units of the BMP was manned largely by Gurkhas and administered by the Defence Department of the Government of Burma and came under the command of the General Officer in Command (GOC), Burma Army. The function of this force was to guard and police the eastern borders of Burma bordering China, Malaya and Thailand. Non-commissioned ranks of the BFF were recruited particularly from the Gurkhas and the hill tribes of Burma, especially Karen, Kachin, Chin and Lahu. In 1939, the defence forces consisted of some 12,000 men in the Frontier Force and the Military Police had 5,000 regular troops.[14] With the outbreak of World War II in 1939, the BFF was used to guard the airfields and supply dumps. As the name suggested, the force was not meant to serve as regular troops in a war. In April 1942, as reported by Major Chappell, belonging to the 2nd Rangoon Battalion, BMP, the total strength of the combined BMP, which had retreated to Myitkyina was 3 British officers and 728 men. Of these, 184 were Punjabi Muslims, 194 Kumaonis, 198 Gurkhas, 139 Karens, 12 Burmans and 1 Sikh. On 1 May 1942, the BMP at Myitkyina was transferred to the Myitkyina Battalion of the Burma Frontier Force. By April 1942, the units of the Burma Frontier Force had disintegrated, first through desertion and casualties, and later, as a result of the decision to allow the men to return to their homes if they so wished. The majority of the Gurkha soldiers continued the retreat into India, where it was decided to form them into the Burma Regiment in September 1942.

After Japan's entry into the war in South-East Asia in December 1941, the Japanese attacked Rangoon and soon overran Burma. After the fall of Rangoon, the Allies attempted to fight back the Japanese in Upper

Burma, which was unsuccessful. With the forces cut off from all sources of supply, it was decided by the Allied commanders to evacuate and retreat from Burma to India. The retreat was conducted in very difficult circumstances. There was mass exodus of Indian refugees, which began in February 1942 and continued till July 1942. Only a small percentage of the refugees were evacuated by sea and air, most of the exoduses taking place either via Arakan to Chittagong or via the Chindwin Valley to Manipur or in the later stages via the northern passes to Ledo rail station and other termini in Upper Assam,[15] from where subsequently, the refugees continued on their onward journey to their homes or camps. Major General E. Wood[16] reported that between Burma and India, there were no organisations and no camps were established by the Burmese government to provide relief to the refugees.[17] With the arrival of the battle-weary Burma Army from Upper Burma, General Wood had, by early May, directed that the camp staff at Tamu, near the Manipur border, be reduced to a minimum, which led to inadequate relief measures for the civilian refugees. At the end of May 1942, there were 25,000 Indians on the road between Kalewa in Burma and Palel in Manipur. The Japanese air raids over Imphal on 10 and 16 May led to large-scale desertion by the refugee staff stationed there. All these added to the plight of the civilian refugees of whom '70 to 80% were described to be definitely ill, 30% desperately so; many were received ill clad and even naked and practically all were suffering from lack of suitable or sufficient food...a mob without discipline of any sort, with a complete absence of morale'.[18] The breakout of the monsoon compounded their difficulties and sufferings.

Gurkhas of Burma and their displacement

The Gurkhas of Burma were part of a larger process of Nepali migration during the colonial period. The positive factors encouraging Nepali migration to the geographically contiguous Eastern 'frontier' were not only an ecology suitable to their economic subsistence, but also the scope for employment in the colonial army, as well as the conscious patronage extended by the colonial state to their migration and settlements.[19] Small peasants in particular, who migrated from the hills of Nepal during the 19th century, did so because of their inability to subsist there. In the hill regions of Nepal, agricultural production failed to keep pace with population growth, subsistence was difficult and emigration soon became the only alternative to declining yields and deteriorating living standards.[20] The repression of the autocratic Rana regime, increasing taxation and rising rents, indebtedness to local money lenders and absence of employment in non-agricultural sectors pushed the people to migrate to neighbouring British India, where prospects of living appeared brighter. Following the Anglo-Nepal War (1814–16), during which the 'magnificent' fighting qualities of the Gurkhas were quickly recognised by the British, and with the signing of the Treaty of Segowli (1815–16) between Nepal and India, the practice of recruitment of Gurkhas into the British colonial force began. The excellent record of the Gurkha sepoys in suppressing the Revolt of 1857–58 (which attempted to overthrow British rule in India), and in particular, their relative immunity to 'subversive propaganda' enhanced the desirability of Gurkha recruits for the British. Subsequently, the number of Gurkha Infantry units in the Indian Army increased from 5 in 1862 to 13 in 1885, and to 20 in 1914, and a corresponding reduction in the recruitment of other groups such as Mahar, Bengali, Ahir, Gujar and Hindusthani Muslim.[21]

After the First Anglo-Burmese war (1824–26), the British occupied Pegu, Tennasserim and Assam, which subsequently were annexed to British India. The 1st Assam Light Infantry in Guwahati (renamed in 1903 as 6th Gurkha Rifles), the 2nd Assam Light Infantry at Sadiya (renamed afterwards as 2/8 Gurkha Rifles) and the Sylhet Light Infantry (which became the 1/8 Gurkha Rifles in 1907) served entirely in Assam and Burma until 1899, taking part in every border expedition.[22] After their retirement, Gurkha soldiers were allowed to settle near the military headquarters and outposts, which tended, in course of time, to create pockets of Gurkha settlements. As noted earlier, the British annexation of Upper Burma after 1886 created a favourable opportunity for the people of Nepal for military and other services under the British colonial state. Gurkhas were not only serving in the eight battalions of the Burma Frontier Force and Burma Military Police, but were also settled and domiciled in Burma, where they were dairymen and vegetable growers on a large scale besides being employed in mines.[23] They were found to be employed in the Bawdin mines (for silver, lead and zinc) near Lashio and the Mawchi mine in Karenni (the greatest Tungsten mine in the world), which happened to be the most important industrial enterprise in Burma.[24] Military and civilian Gurkhas, thus, came to reside in Burma, many of whom were domiciled in Myitkyina and the Shan states. On account of their long stay in Burma, they could be considered as the Nepali diaspora of Burma and many of them had reportedly become lax as regards their customs and religion.[25] There were others who had intermarried with Burmese women. By 1941, there were nearly 200,000 Gurkhas settled in Burma. In 1936, Burma became semi-independent; it had its own flag and its own prime minister, though it had no proper army. What passed for Burmese defence forces comprised recruits from the minority peoples along with the Anglo-Burmese and Gurkhas.[26]

In the early part of 1942, there were reports of Gurkhas fleeing from Burma in the wake of the Japanese invasion. Soon, recruiting officers for Gurkhas were reporting that hundreds of refugees in a destitute condition, consisting mainly of women and children and dependents of Gurkha soldiers belonging to the BFF, BMP, Burma Army and Gurkha civilians were arriving at various Gurkha recruiting depots on the Nepal border in British India.[27] All had suffered incredible hardships. Many of them were born and bred in Burma, and in many cases, the husbands of the destitute women were either killed or were taken as prisoners of war or considered missing in action. In some cases, the Gurkhas had Burmese or Chinese wives. In some cases, they did not even know where their homes were in Nepal.

The Gurkha displacement from Burma was part of a larger exodus of population – British, Indians, Burmese, Gurkhas and Chinese retreating from the Japanese occupation of Burma in 1942. With the fall of Rangoon and the closure of the sea routes, there took place a mass exodus from Burma by land and on foot of an unnumbered multitude of people. The great majority were Indians, some 400,000[28] seeking escape to India by means of little-known land routes into Assam, many of whom died on the way. The probable estimate of the dead ranged from 10,000 to 50,000 though official figures gave a low total.[29] The focal points towards which they advanced in a swelling stream were the towns of Mandalay, Kalewa on the Chindwin River, Bhamo and Myitkyina in upper Burma, all of which, by May 1942, fell into Japanese hands. It is estimated that between 25,000 and 30,000 refugees crossed into India via Manipur alone. The bombing of Myitkyina aerodrome in upper Burma on 6 May put an end to any possibility of air evacuation of the thousands of hapless refugees. There remained now only the bleak prospect of a dangerous and difficult trek through the unknown northern passes of the Indo-Burmese border to upper Assam. The big concentration of refugees at Myitkyina and other places broke up into small parties for the journey. The great majority of them set out for Shinbiwyang, a frontier political outpost consisting of a barely half a dozen thatched bamboo huts with half a dozen armed policemen, then under a young political officer for administering the local Kachin and Naga tribes. By mid May, 'this extremely primitive village, devoid of food supplies, sanitation or the most elementary communal amenities became the main junction of the flood of the evacuation that had set in by the northeastern route to India'.[30] It became the focal point from which the refugees from Myitkyina, Sumprambum, Mogaung and other places in upper Burma converged. During a period of five months, some 45,000 refugees came to Shinbiwyang.[31] Viscount Wavell, who later became the Viceroy of India, described the escape of refugees from upper Burma in 1942 as 'a tale of human suffering, human endeavour and human endurance'.[32]

As early as on 25 February 1942, the Government of Assam had been notified by the Government of India that a mass movement of refugees towards the Assam border had begun and that the main surge would be towards Tamu, just inside the Burma border,[33] adjacent to the princely state of Manipur. Yet, when it happened, the Government of Assam was caught unprepared to handle the situation. In this context, one must note the contribution made by the Indian Tea Association (ITA) towards assisting the authorities in the relief efforts on the frontiers of eastern India. The three main routes[34] on which the ITA operated were

1. Tamu–Imphal–Dimapur and the Brahmaputra Valley.
2. Imphal–Bishenpur–Jhirighat–Silchar and the Surma Valley in Assam. This route was brought into operation by the end of April 1942.
3. The routes in the extreme north-east, via the Hukwang Valley in Burma and the Patkai mountains to Ledo in Upper Assam, from there by train or steamer down the Brahmaputra Valley. This was the least hospitable of the three evacuation routes.

Ultimately, there arrived, via Imphal, capital of Manipur, and through the Dimapur camp in the foothills of the Naga Hills District about 150,000 refugees, 35,000 through the Silchar camp and 22,000 through the Ledo camp in Upper Assam.[35]

Process of rehabilitation of the displaced Gurkhas

Till the beginning of June 1942, the number of Gurkha evacuees from Burma was manageable for the recruiting officers. Early in May, the Assistant Recruiting Officer for Ghoom (in Darjeeling) reported that a dozen Gurkha families had arrived at Ghoom from Burma, having been evacuated by air to Chittagong, and from there, they had reached Darjeeling by train. The families were accommodated in the bazaars close to Ghoom. The women were paid advance money according to the ranks of their husbands and the number of children with them – the amount being debited to the units concerned. From the beginning of June, a large number of Gurkha families of the BFF, BMP, Burma Rifles and other Burma Army units, together with a few pensioners and families of deceased pensioners were reported to have arrived at Ghoom,[36] after experiencing great hardship. Many women and children had died en route.[37] They had come on foot overland from various places in Burma to Manipur, and thence, to Dimapur rail station and had been sent on from there by train. Most of the women were penniless, travelling without their husbands, of whose whereabouts they knew nothing. A large number of them, being Burma-born and-bred, had nowhere to go. Most of them were without any warm clothing for themselves and their children, and Ghoom was up in the mountains at an altitude of about 7,000 ft above sea level. Most of the women had malaria and several were admitted to the Victoria Hospital in Darjeeling. All the families were temporarily accommodated in the Gorkha Dharamsala, which had been built in memory of the Gurkhas killed in World War I and maintained from the Gurkha War Memorial Fund. Families who had homes were sent as soon as they were fit to travel. Some 160 families were accommodated in the tea gardens by the Darjeeling Planters' Association.

In June the same year, many Gurkha families of serving, captured, missing or killed soldiers began to arrive at Nautanwa, a subsidiary depot near the Indo-Nepal border, in destitute condition. They included pensioners and civilians with their families, who were originally from Nepal, but who had long settled in Burma. Arrangements were made by the Extra Assistant Recruiting Officer, Nautanwa, to dispatch those who had homes in Nepal. Problem arose with those who had no home either in British India or Nepal, i.e. the Burma-born and-bred families. In this category were included children whose parents were dead. In Kunraghat, the recruiting officer was able to accommodate them in the rest house in the depot lines, as recruiting season had not begun. But recruitment was due to begin by 15 September. As the displaced Gurkhas had gone to the recruiting centres, the recruiting officers took the responsibility of providing relief such as shelter, food and so on at the centre itself. This led to increased and additional pressure on their resources. In July, the recruiting officer for Gurkhas at Kunraghat wrote the following to Geoffrey Bentham, the Minister of the British Legation, Nepal:

> it is only those of us who are personally confronted daily with this crowd, every single one of whose cases had to be enquired into in detail and decided on its merits, who can possibly realize just what it means. . . . The crying need is for the Government of India and Government of Burma to get together and realize this destitute population wants collecting, sorting and apportioning.[38]

The report of the Gurkha Recruiting Officer at Kunraghat in July 1942 stressed the necessity of 'the disposal of the Gurkha refugees from Burma'. The heavy damage to railway property to the track east of Gorakhpur during the 1942 Quit India Movement added to the difficulty of the recruiting officer, who was unable to shift hundreds of the Burma evacuees residing in the depot at Kunraghat to the proposed refugee camp at Motihari.[39] He reported

> There is no possibility, I am told, of early communications being restored to these parts and the refuges meanwhile remain on my hands and I am compelled to accommodate them for a variety of reasons in recruits' reception camp area. If this expedient has to continue longer than mid-September at the latest, then this will constitute a serious handicap to the efficient and expeditious handling of the many thousands of recruits which are expected daily as soon as the recruiting season begins . . .

The recruiting officers were keen to shift the problem of rehabilitation to some other responsible body before the start of the recruiting season. From 1 October, a big recruitment drive for some 26,000 to 30,000 was expected from Gorakhpur alone. The nature of the issue of the displaced Gurkhas was such that it involved the governments of India, Nepal and Burma. The Defense Department, Government of India, subject to such arrangements to be made later with the Government of Burma, took the responsibility of the reception and maintenance of families of the BFF, BMP and other military units from Burma. The External Affairs Department also, subject to the same condition, accepted the financial responsibility in respect of the above families.

The Motihari camp

A permanent relief camp for the Gurkha refugees was set up to relieve the recruiting centres of the pressure of handling them. In consultation with the War Department and the Burma Government, such a refugee reception camp was set up at Motihari, located in Champaran District in north Bihar under the control of Geoffrey Bentham, who was His Majesty's Envoy Extraordinary and Minister Plenipotentiary at the Court of Nepal. Motihari was selected because of its suitable climate, its lakes and open spaces, a hospital and adequate police force, besides its proximity to Raxual, and therefore, its accessibility to the Nepalese government and the British Legation and for its proximity to the bottleneck railway junction at Muzaffarpur. The object of the Motihari camp was to accommodate, feed, clothe and provide medical care to the Gurkha refugees from Burma before they were sorted out, to be sent either to Nepal or passed on to various camps set up in India for the military and civilian refugees. For this purpose, a sum of INR 5,000 was donated by the Maharaja of Nepal for construction of the camp and to also provide free from his forests all timber and building materials. The Government of Burma accepted in principle to meet the expenses of the camp not met from the 'generous donations of the Maharaja of Nepal' so long as the refugees accommodated in the camps were primarily Burmese refugees.

On arrival, the Legation Staff led by Geoffrey Bentham was shown a rest house nearing completion by W. N. R. Kemp of the Bihar Light Horse, Circle Officer, Motihari and it was taken on a rent of INR 250 per month for three months. The rest house, which belonged to the Bettiah Raj estate, consisted of an enclosed three masonry buildings with 40 cubicles, each having a window and a door. Six of the cubicles were reserved for the staff, a grocery shop and a dispensary. After construction of seven more huts, there was accommodation for nearly 400 persons. Two wells suitable for washing and bathing purposes and a tube well for drinking water were also inside the enclosure. On 30 July, two Gurkha Subedars of the 18th Gurkha Garrison Company, a clerk and six Gurkha orderlies reported at the camp, having been detailed for duty by the Defence Department. On behalf of the Nepal government, Deputy Collector Upendra Bahadur Basnet also reported for duty in the same afternoon. The concerned officer was to personally look into the case of each evacuee and give advice regarding the disposal of each individual case. Four Brahmin cooks at INR 8/- each per month with food; two sweepers at INR 12/- each per month without food and one *bhisti* (traditional water carrier belonging to Muslim community) at INR 8/- per month with food were employed. The camp at Motihari was opened with effect from 23 August 1942. As on 11 August 1942, an amount of INR 10,000 had been given for the camp by the Maharaja of Nepal and the Government of India. The average cost of food per evacuee per month was expected to be under INR 10. On 18 September 1942, the charge of the Motihari rest house, which now functioned as a reception-cum-transit camp, was handed over by Lieutenant Colonel J. D. Ogilvy, who had earlier served as commandant of 1st Gurkha Rifles of the Legation Staff to W. N. R. Kemp. The Burmese government agreed to pay Kemp INR 200 per month for his services. The Gurkha refugees who had earlier been temporarily accommodated at the Gurkha recruiting centres at Ghoom and Gorakhpur were transferred to Motihari. All new arrivals went to Motihari, where they were 'screened' by the agents of the Nepal government as to their eligibility or otherwise to proceed to Nepal. The Maharaja of Nepal was anxious that only those who were bona fide Nepalese refugees were to be sent to Nepal. It is interesting to note that the Maharaja did not want the Nepalese domiciled in Burma who were possibly lax about Nepali customs and religion to go to Nepal. He 'particularly desired to prohibit the entry into Nepal of those Gurkhas who through inter marriage with Burmans and others had ceased to be of pure Gurkha blood, methods of living and religion'. Many of them, however, were Burmese-born-and-bred.

On urgent requisition from the Government of Burma and the Government of India, work on a second camp started in September 1942 at Motihari Polo Ground, with supplies of building materials given by the Maharaja, who also donated an additional amount of INR 5000. The Polo Ground, which was given free of rent by the planters of the Bettiah Raj, was roughly 500 by 150 yards. The civil, military and medical staff of the Burma government arrived in Motihari at the end of September that year. Lieutenant Colonel Tudor Craig of BFF took over as military commandant of the Gurkha Evacuee Camp, Polo Ground and Mr. Bazett of the Burma Frontier Service as Civil Assistant Commandant in subordinate charge of the camp. By November, the camp was completed to hold 600 persons, including the camp staff.[40] This camp was primarily meant for civilian Gurkha refugees who had nowhere to go and who were to be looked after until such time as they could return to Burma. As on 29 September, the number of evacuees in the Motihari camp was recorded as 298. On 19 October, the total number of evacuees was recorded at 385 with the arrival of more evacuees from Kunraghat (24), Dibrugarh (30), Darjeeling (10), Margherita (7), Ghoom (14), British Legation, Nepal (1) and a child born in the camp (1) and 85 departures. A monthly sum of INR 10,000 each was made available for running the two camps.

In July 1942, Major Chappell, belonging to the BFF, arrived at Ghoom Recruiting Depot in connection with refugee work. He was to report on the situation regarding Gurkha evacuees from Burma. His report dated 22 August 1942 relating to the Gurkha evacuees from Burma was submitted to the Government of Burma, Defence Department, Shimla.[41] As suggested by him, a conducting party of the Gurkhas from the BFF was posted at Margherita in Upper Assam (1942) by the Defence Department, Government of Burma, to meet evacuees and to conduct them to the camp at Motihari (vide letter dated 10 October 1942).[42] From a telegram dated 16 September 1942 from the Defence Department of the Government of Burma, about 600 Gurkha evacuees were expected to arrive in Assam. Those without homes were to be 'dispatched' to Motihari. It was also suggested that a relief officer from the BFF with a small staff be stationed at Ghoom to deal with any needs of the Gurkha refugees, pensioners or members of the Burma Forces arriving there.

Some of the refugees went back to Nepal, Darjeeling and Sikkim after their arrival at the railheads or railway stations of Darjeeling, Jogbani, Bhaptiahi, Jainagar, Raxual, Nautanwa, Jarwa and Nepalgung. The evacuees listed in Table 13.1[43] were recorded to have gone to their homes or found accommodation elsewhere.

However, as Major Chappell noted, the authorities agreed that the earlier figures in Table 13.1 represented only a small number of the evacuees that had arrived in India. The following were the figures for evacuees in the Gurkha Recruiting Depots in Kunraghat and Ghoom and in the camp at Hoshiarpur (Punjab) and Motihari.

Table 13.1 Places and categories of evacuees

Place	Categories of evacuees	Men	Women	Children	Total
Kunraghat	Serving men	45	106	138	289
	Pensioners and civilians	14	13	9	36
Ghoom	Serving men	225	281	259	765
	Pensioners and civilians	89	64	155	308
Motihari	Civilians	2	1	–	3
Total		375	465	561	1,401

Table 13.2 Details of serving personnel as evacuees

Place	Categories of personnel	Men	Women	Children	Total
Kunraghat	BFF and BMP	22	23	24	69
	BA	–	1	–	1
Ghoom	BFF and BMP	10	27	37	74
	BA	5	5	5	15
Hoshiarpur	BFF and BMP	1	23	13	37
	BA	–	1	2	3
Total		38	80	78	196

Note: BFF=Burma Frontier Force, BMP= Burma Military Police, and BA= Burmese Army

Table 13.3 Details of pensioners as evacuees

Place	Categories of personnel	Men	Women	Children	Total
Kunraghat	BFF, BMP and BA	12	14	36	62
	Special police and civilians	1	–	2	3
Ghoom	BFF and BMP	8	7	24	39
Hoshiarpur	BFF	16	16	16	48
Total		37	37	78	152

Note: BFF=Burma Frontier Force, BMP= Burma Military Police, and BA= Burmese Army

Table 13.4 Details of civilian evacuees

Place	Men	Women	Children	Total
Kunraghat	40	34	77	151
Ghoom	9	26	25	60
Motihari	2	3	1	6
Hoshiarpur	–	–	–	–
Total	51	63	103	217

Table 13.5 Evacuees who had no home either in India or in Nepal

Categories of evacuees	Men	Women	Children	Total
BFF and BMP	16	40	29	85
BA	–	2	2	4
Pensioners	33	32	60	125
Civilians	50	42	90	182
Total	99	116	181	396

Note: BFF=Burma Frontier Force, BMP= Burma Military Police, and BA= Burmese Army

Table 13.6 Statement showing arrival of Gurkha evacuees in Motihari Camp up to 29 September 1942.

Arrived from Kunraghat on 23.9.42	Men	Women	Children	Total
Serving men	2	16	28	46
Pensioners	13	17	46	76
Civilians	45	33	72	150
Received at Motihari on 4.8.42				
Civilians	1	2	–	3
Received at Raxaul on 4.8.42	1	1	–	2
Civilians	1	1	–	2
Received at Birganj on 3.9.42				
Pensioners	1	–	–	1
Received at Motihari on 28.9.42	2	–	–	2
Received at Motihari on 29.9.42				
Civilians	5	2	11	18
Total	70	71	157	298

Some of the displaced Gurkhas were noted to have halted at various places, such as Shillong, Darjeeling, Kurseong, Tezpur, Amingaon Ghat, Pandu Ghat and Guwahati, where some were reported to have found employment and accommodation.[44,45] While some of them were stated to be waiting for favourable weather to leave for their homes in Nepal, others were destitute. The authorities wanted those who had found employment and accommodation in India to be left where they were.

In his letter dated 9 August 1942, the assistant recruiting officer for Ghoom estimated the number of Gurkha evacuees from Burma who arrived in Darjeeling at 1,000 approximately. Those having their homes in eastern Nepal, Darjeeling District and Sikkim had proceeded home. But 'those born and bred in Burma do not wish to proceed to Nepal where they have no connections, and may now be considered as having been absorbed into Darjeeling District'.[46] He noted that 'no power on earth will be able to move the Gurkha evacuees who have found homes and employment in Darjeeling district, which contains the largest settlement of Gurkhas in British India nor is it desirable that those who have settled in British India, should be uprooted again'.[47] As a matter of fact, for more than four decades, eastern Nepal had provided the recruits for Burma. As such, many Burma pensioners, including Gurkha officers, had settled in Darjeeling District. There was, thus, a connection of long standing between eastern Nepal, Darjeeling District and Burma.

It was noted by Major Chappell in his report that many displaced Gurkhas, due to sickness or lack of physical strength to proceed further, had halted at camps and villages in Burma. Some of them were at the Shinbwiyang camp in the Hukong Valley. Information recorded by the authorities referred to deaths due to diseases and exhaustion en route of half of the original groups. It was reported by Major Chappell[48] that many Gurkha settlers living in Gurkha colonies in Burma, who had not been evacuated earlier, either due to their inability to dispose off their cattle and crops, encumbered by many children or lack of money, might do so after the monsoon. If such an exodus from Burma was to take place, it was estimated by him that any number up to 30,000 or more could be expected. He suggested that those Gurkhas who were still in Burma may be discouraged to do so by dropping pamphlets from the air or by sending agents to them, so they may not impede the movement of the Allied troops through the north-east frontier of the Assam-Burma border. It was further noted[49] that approximately 708 Nepali refugees from Burma had arrived in Assam since the end of November 1942. The Indian Overseas Department was also informed by Justice Braund of the Rangoon High Court that he had received intimation of the movement of some 400 evacuees via Aijawl in Lushai Hills and that there might be some evacuation from the Chin Hills. But it was not certain how many would actually come or the number of Gurkhas in the exodus.[50]

The Serai Camp at Motihari was eventually closed down on 15 January 1943, and the evacuees were shifted to the Polo camp at Motihari, which was under Lieutenant Colonel Tudor Craig. The Polo camp was to be maintained as long as the Gurkhas who were 'unsuitable' for domicile in Nepal, and who could not find suitable employment in India, were unable to return to Burma. The half yearly report submitted by the commandant of the Motihari camp covering the period 1 January 1943 to 30 June 1943 provided the following details:

1. Total number of evacuees received =743
2. Those sent to their homes (a) in Nepal = 60, (b) in British India=394
3. Number for whom employment was found during the period =101
4. Total strength of the camp on 30.6.43=665

It was noted in the report that an elementary school for camp children had also been started a few months ago and the 200-odd students were being taught by the evacuees themselves.

Conclusion

The Gurkha displacement and exodus from Burma, when looked at from a historical perspective was ephemeral. Historically, the Gurkhas have been displaced from different places. Their displacement from Burma and rehabilitation in India in the mid-20th century has found detailed official mention and record primarily due to the perceived political and military ramifications in the context of the then Allied war efforts. Since it involved non-civilian Gurkhas with the possibility of military recruitment being hindered and because of the multi-national composition of the Gurkha evacuees, who belonged to Nepal, India and Burma, the matter became an issue of official concern for the governments of India, Nepal and Burma. The British authorities in India were particularly concerned that the large influx of family refugees of Gurkha soldiers might interfere with their recruitment drive, leading to a delay in their deployment to respective units, which was vital for the Allied war effort. Thus, the Defence Department of British India was keen to shift the problem of rehabilitation to some other responsible body before the start of the recruiting season. As mentioned earlier, the Maharaja of Nepal wanted to prevent the entry into Nepal of those Gurkhas who were of 'mixed parentage' and who had become 'lax' about Gurkha customs and religion. The External Affairs Department felt it would be 'extremely unwise to upset' the Maharaja of Nepal during that stage of the war. The Motihari rehabilitation camp for Gurkha evacuees was, therefore, set up for a specific purpose, i.e. to relieve recruiting depots and sort out the refugees. The Serai Camp in Motihari was to function as a reception and transit camp before the evacuees were 'sorted' to be sent either to Nepal or to their homes in India. In the second camp at Polo ground, mainly those Gurkhas who were born and bred in Burma were rehabilitated temporarily till such time as they could return to Burma. The rehabilitation camps for them were created to facilitate the interests of the British in the war effort and not by any primary humanitarian concern of an imperial power.

Acknowledgement

The author would like to acknowledge the UGC SAP-DRS programme of the Department of History, NEHU, Shillong, for financial assistance received for archival collection.

Notes

1. The Eastern Nepal Recruiting Area consisted of eastern Nepal, Darjeeling District and Sikkim. The Ghoom Depot in Darjeeling from its inception in the early 20th century provided recruits from eastern Nepal for Burma.
2. Gurkha Settlements in Burma, Letter from the Deputy Secretary to the Government of India in the Foreign and Political Department, to the Chief Secretary to the Government of Burma, dated Shimla, the 27th April, 1928.
3. Hugh Tinker, 'A Forgotten Long March: The Indian Exodus from Burma, 1942', *Journal of Southeast Asian Studies*, 6(1), March 1975, p. 2.
4. Geoffrey Bentham, Minister, British Legation, Nepal, 29 June 1942 in his letter to the Secretary to the Government of India in the External Affairs Department, New Delhi.
5. The archival material for the paper has been procured from the *Proceedings of the External Affairs Department, 1942* and *Proceedings of the Ministry of Home Affairs (Pol. 1 Section 1942)* National Archives, New Delhi; Hugh Tinker, 'A Forgotten Long March: The Indian Exodus from Burma, 1942', *Journal of Southeast Asian Studies*, 6(1), March 1975, pp. 1–15 presents a general description of the exodus without any particular reference to the Gurkha refugees; Geoffrey W. Tyson's *The Forgotten Frontier* provides an invaluable account of the event through the relief measures undertaken by the Indian Tea Association in Assam.
6. www.britishempire.co.uk/forces/armyunits/burma/bmp.htm.
7. It was later amalgamated into the Bhamo Military Police Battalion, which survived till 1942.
8. www.britishempire. *op. cit.*

9. Extracts from a lecture delivered by Lt. Col. F. C. Carter D.A.Q.M.G and D.A.A.G. Bengal Army, cited in H. S. Bhatia, *Military History of British India* (1607–1947), Deep Publications, New Delhi, 1977, p. 80.
10. Sir C. Crosthwaite, *The Pacification of Burma*, London, 1912, p. 16.
11. Class company regiments had a different class in each of its three companies; the companies were themselves always 'pure'; see Stephen P. Cohen, *The Indian Army: Its Contribution to the Development of a Nation*, Oxford University Press, New Delhi, Third Impression, 2004, p. 42.
12. Hugh Tinker, *A Study of the First Years of Independence*, Oxford University Press, London, 4th Edition, 1967, p. 313.
13. *Ibid.*
14. *Ibid.*, p. 316.
15. Hugh Tinker, 'A Forgotten Long March', *op. cit.*, p. 2.
16. An engineer–officer was appointed Administrator-General of Eastern Frontier communications, with overall control of the Manipur Road, to speed up evacuation. He arrived only in March 1942.
17. *Ibid.*, p. 8.
18. Cited by Tinker, ibid., p. 12.
19. Tejimala Gurung, 'Human Movement and Colonial State: A Study of the Nepalis in North-East India under the British Empire', in A. C. Sinha and T. B. Subba (eds), *The Nepalis in India: A Community in Search of Indian Identity*, pp. 172–83, Indus Publishing Company, New Delhi, 2003.
20. M. C. Regmi, *A Study of Nepali Economic History, 1768–1847*, Manjushri Publishing House, New Delhi, 1971.
21. Stephen P. Cohen, *op. cit.*, p. 44.
22. L. W. Shakespear, *History of the Assam Rifles*, Firma K.L.M, Calcutta, 1977, p. 7.
23. Colonel Geoffrey Bentham, 'Notes on Eastern Nepal and Nepalis (or Gurkhas) in Darjeeling, Kalimpong, Kurseong, Sikkim and Burma', File No.87-x/42 (secret), External Affairs Department, X Branch.
24. Hugh Tinker, *op. cit*, p. 283.
25. Geoffrey Bentham in his note, 'Gurkha Evacuee Camp, Motihari'.
26. Christopher Bayly and Timothy Harper, *The Forgotten Armies: British Asian Empire and the War with Japan*, Penguin Books, London, p. 34.
27. Geoffrey Bentham, 'The British Legation, Nepal', 29 June 1942. D.O. No .20 (42)/90 File D. 5832-X/42.
28. John F. Cady, *A History of Modern Burma*, Cornell University Press, London, Fourth Printing 1969, p. 439.
29. Hugh Tinker, 'The Long Forgotten March', *op. cit.*, pp. 2–3.
30. Geoffrey W. Tyson, *The Forgotten Frontier*, W. H. Targett & Co. Ltd., Calcutta, 1945, pp. 56–7.
31. *Ibid.*
32. Preface, *ibid.*
33. *Ibid.*, p. 25.
34. *Ibid.*
35. *Ibid.*, pp. 25–26.
36. Geoffrey Bentham, *op. cit.*
37. *Ibid.*
38. Extract from copy of the letter from Recruiting Officer, Gorakhpur, cited by G. Bentham, 11 July 1942, ibid.

39 Col. G.C. Strahan, Recruiting Officer for Gurkhas, Kunraghat, to the Adjutant General in India, General Headquarters, New Delhi, Gurkha Recruiting Depot and Record Office, Kunraghat (Gorakhpur) dated 25 August, 1942.
40 Letter from the Commandant, Gurkha Evacuee Camp, Polo Ground, Motihari to the Representative of the Government of Burma, New Delhi, dated 21 November 1942.
41 From Deputy Secretary to the Government of Burma, Defense Department, Shimla to the Deputy Secretary to the Government of India, External Affairs Department, New Delhi, dated 10 October 1942 (No. ID (FF) 42. Government of Burma, Defence Department, Shimla).
42 Ibid.
43 Major Chappell's Report on the Situation Regarding Gurkha Evacuees from Burma, dated 22 August 1942, pp. 1–2.
44 Office of the Gurkha Evacuee Camp, Motihari, dated the 29 September 1942.
45 Chappell's Report, *op. cit.*
46 Assistant Recruiting Officer for Gurkhas, Ghoom, Letter no 15/29/167, Gurkha Recruiting Depot and Record Office, Ghoom, Darjeeling, dated 9 July 1942.
47 Ibid.
48 Chappell's Report, *op. cit.*
49 External Affairs Department U.O. Note No 10819-X/42, dated 10 December 1942.
50 External Affairs Department U.O. Note No 11967-/42, dated 12 December 1942.

14
NEPALIS OF MANIPUR FROM THE PERSPECTIVE OF 'CULTURAL COLLECTIVE'

Vijaylakshmi Brara

Introduction

Manipur is a land of monographs. There are monographs on almost every tribe of Manipur such as the Chothe, Tangkhul, Zomi, Paite, Kuki, Hmar and, of course, the dominant Meiteis.[1] There are also numerous historical and sociological books on the state, such as my own.[2] But, interestingly, there is virtually nothing published in English on the Nepalis of Manipur. For some strange reason, they have never attracted any serious sociological research in this state, just as there are no studies on Bengalis, Punjabis, Marwaris, Biharis, Muslims, and so on who settled in this state since colonial times. I would myself have perhaps never thought of writing on the Nepalis if I was not invited to the seminar on Nepali diaspora, which led to the publication of this book. One of the reasons why there is virtually no published literature in English on the communities mentioned above is the clear divide between the local/indigenous and the migrant populations. This has somehow tended to make the history of the migrant populations trivial and their contributions to the making of modern Manipur of no significance whatsoever. The local academicians are guilty of keeping the migrant communities out of the ambit of the academic discourse.[3] So, there is a need to make the academic discourses in Manipur free from the indigenous paradigm.

One of the reasons for the academic negligence has to do with how Nepalis in Manipur are perceived. They are perceived to be a peace-loving and hardworking people who can survive on a small patch of maize cultivation. They were strategically settled by the British so that the colonial rulers could have a control over the raids by the hill tribes on the valley people and arrest the rebellious behaviour of the hill tribes. Most of them had retired from the British Indian army or police personnel who were deployed for securing the vast, revenue-rich areas in the Imphal Valley, which were often raided by hill tribes living in the hills that surround it. Over generations, they settled down permanently in the state and turned into bonafide citizens of Manipur with proper domicile records. They do not trace their origin from Nepal and Nepal is as foreign to them as any other country except that they speak the same language, just as a Bengali from Kolkata has no language problem when he goes to Bangladesh. It is widely believed that they taught the hill tribes how to do terrace cultivation and introduced the consumption of cow's milk. They were also engaged to clear the forests, construct the roads and other development activities in Manipur.

A short history

According to a Nepali school teacher in Imphal, the capital of Manipur, the Gorkhas, as they would like to call themselves in Manipur, are protectors of cows by profession (*Go Rakshak* = *gorakha*, cow protectors), Hindu by religion and Indian by nationality.[4] It is claimed that the first Gorkha came to Manipur at the beginning of the 10th century and married a Meitei girl called Kumbi, who was a member of the clan called Mayang Heikhong.[5] Others trace their migration to the beginning of the 16th century.[6] The available documents, however, reveal that the first batch of Gorkhas came to Manipur during the time of King Gambhir Singh[7] in the year 1824. Many Gorkhas were enlisted in the army by a British captain for supporting the Manipur king in 1825 to defeat the aggressive Burmese forces. The Burmese at that time had devastated Manipur and reigned for seven years, which is marked in Manipur historical records as *Chahi Taret Khuthakpa* (seven years of devastation). The Burmese forces were pushed back successfully, but it also led to the end of the independent monarchical rule of Manipuri kings because this alliance was converted into the Treaty of Yandaboo, signed by the king and the British, which allowed the British political agent to be stationed in Manipur. The British were accompanied by Gorkha soldiers, Gorkha families as cooks, milkmen, traders and agriculturalists. Around 1880, another batch of Gorkhas was brought by the Chief Commissioner Quinton. Eighty per cent of the personnel of the Assam Rifles comprised the Gurkhas when it came into existence in 1917. Another source of advent of Gorkhas in Manipur was their recruitment in the Indian National Army of Subhas Chandra Bose. During World War II, many Gorkha soldiers were captured in Singapore, along with other Indian soldiers. It was there that some Gorkha soldiers deserted the British Army and joined Subhas Chandra Bose's Indian National Army (INA). Some of those Gorkha INA soldiers settled in Manipur. Their families, even today, proudly narrate the stories of their valour and loyalty to India. Yet another wave of Gorkhas came when the last king of Manipur, King Bodhchandra, married Ishwori Devi, the eldest daughter of Prince Rama Raja of Ram Nagar to the south-east of Kathmandu. She was the cousin of the king of Nepal. She was accompanied by 44 Gorkha soldiers with whom the Manipur Rifles was established and which is a prominent Manipur Police Force even in the present times. Other retinues were allowed to settle in and around the palace, which holds a prominent Nepali presence even today. They are famous for their valour, strong military sense, honesty and loyalty. This is the reason why even the insurgent groups want to recruit them in their armed wings.

One important aspect of the Gorkha settlements in Manipur is that although they were established by the British themselves, they collected foreigners' tax from the Nepalis, while the Manipur State Council granted them domicile status in 1947. Today, most of them have land documents officially given to them by the British through the orders of the State Durbar. But these rights are being challenged by the hill tribes, who want to place these lands under the Hill Areas Act, which does not allow the non-tribals such as Nepalis to buy lands in the hills. On the contrary, the Nepalis want the government to extend the Manipur Land Record Act to the hill areas so that their land rights can be guaranteed.

Some of the educated Nepalis have kept records of the original settlements in Manipur, along with the names of the first families who had settled there. Places such as Maram, a predominantly Naga-inhabited area in Senapati district, have had people from the Nepali community since 1894. A poet named Tulachand Ale wrote a book of poems called *Manipurko Sawai* from there. His book is among the first printed books in the history of Manipur literature. The Gorkhas were systematically settled in Manipur since 1933 by C. Gimson, the then political agent, on behalf of the Manipur Durbar. In Senapati district, they were settled in Irang on the Imphal Tamenglong Road. It was there that the Gorkha Panchayat was first formed and recognised as one of the 40 panchayats of Manipur as early as 1930.[8] This system of governance gave them a distinct identity vis-à-vis the surrounding hill communities. The Gorkha Panchayat Hall of those times still exists at Kangpokpi area of Senapati district. The head of this panchayat contributed a lot in terms of money as well as labour to build a bridle road connecting Imphal with Tamenglong, another district of Manipur, through Senapati, famously known as the IT road.[9] Recently, the hill communities surrounding these areas have been pressurising the government to scrap the panchayats and bring them under the Autonomous District Council Act, since topographically, these are hilly areas of Manipur. The issue of indigenous versus the diasporic community was brought into sharp focus when the Nepalis of Manipur were not allowed to cast votes in the last panchayat elections. Since they have been told to resign, the elected representatives are afraid to go to their villages and are stationed in Imphal in a place called Mantripokhari, which is dominated by Nepalis. In 1978, they even filed a petition in the High Court, which listed 17 gram panchayats to be listed under the Manipur Panchayati Raj Act, 1975. This meant that the governance system of the Nepalis was recognised by the state of Manipur, which gave them the feeling of being included. In recent times, one can see some Gorkha representatives in the Autonomous District Councils in the hill areas. Padam Acharya, a Nepali intellectual, was the first member of the Legislative Assembly in Manipur, who was ousted by one Kishore Thapa in 1972–74. Later, Padam Acharya went to Nepal and retired as Home Secretary, Government of Nepal. Today, there are no members from the Nepali community in the Manipur Legislative Assembly.

The issues of land and the panchayat system of governance have created a lot of rift among the hill tribes and the Nepalis. About 10 years ago, some Nepali youths wanted to establish their own armed wing to counter the attacks by the armed wings of various tribes, but were deterred by their elders. Apart from the money involved, they would soon be overpowered by the bigger insurgent groups. Nevertheless, during the ethnic conflicts between Nagas and Kukis in the 1980s, they emerged as a buffer community, whereby the warring tribals camouflaged themselves as Nepalis to pass safely en route to other villages. However, some Nepalis have also been a target of the insurgent groups on charges of siding with one tribe or the other.

In 1919, the Gorkha graziers who were scattered in different places were allotted the Kanglatombi-Kangkpokpi Grazing Reserve, KK Reserve in short, with an area of approximately 140 sq. miles. But in 1946, this area was de-reserved for grazing and a move was initiated to convert it into cultivable area. The Gorkhas who wanted to do settled agriculture bought regular *pattas*, but they were not given more than half an acre of land for each Gurkha family for cultivation. The settlements in 1950s at Pukhao and Serou have been mainly due to the great floods at Sadiya district, popularly known as 'Sadiya Dubao'.

Socio-economic scenario

The Nepalis of Manipur are almost synonymous with soldiers, but many members of this community are also pastoralists and agriculturalists. In Senapati District alone, 60 per cent of the total Rabi and Kharif crops are produced by them. They have also formed a panchayat-level multipurpose cooperative society encompassing four areas. However, there are very few of them in government jobs. There are just two professors at Manipur University, one IAS officer, five government college lecturers and a few other government servants in the whole state.

One of the reasons for their insignificant position in government service is their dismal literacy rate and their poor economic condition. As a matter of fact, keeping this in mind, the Manipur State Assembly passed resolutions twice in 1954 and 1980 to put the Gorkhas in the category of backward and minority community. However, when the Other Backward Community list of the state was prepared, most of the Gorkha community was left out. The expert committee constituted for the identification of Other Backward Classes in the state only recommended five castes, which constituted only 5 per cent of the total population of the state. Majority of the Gorkhas live below the poverty line and do not feel secure about their land on which they grow crops, as the Manipur Land Records Act is yet to be extended to the hill areas, which they inhabit.

The orthodox traditions of the Nepalis are receiving further encouragement from within in an atmosphere where they feel threatened about their culture, language and identity. One of the strategies of ensuring their survival in matters like this has been to go back to their roots, or to their religion, customs and traditions and encyst themselves from their cultural environment. Raising the voices for reform is not appreciated and is even considered as against the interest of the Nepali community. Given this scenario, the real issues of food, livelihood, health, gender and vulnerability get deflected under oppressive structures of their own traditions, which are strengthened in the name of protecting their culture and identity.

There are some inter-marriages between Nepalis and other communities today, but such couples have to face a lot of social resistance. Despite their emphasis on their identity, they rarely wear their traditional dresses and ornaments to camouflage themselves in an ethnically hostile atmosphere; they wear the tribal or the Meitei *phanek* (a lower wrap around). Yet, the Aryan-looking Nepalis stand out in the Mongoloid-looking milieu. It is also the Aryan-looking Nepalis who are called *mayang*s (a term used to connote outsiders) whereas the Mongoloid-looking Nepalis blend with their surroundings. During the anti-foreigners' agitation in Assam (1979–85), many Nepalis with Aryan features were even targeted by the valley insurgents in Manipur.

Established in 1967 and registered in 1979, the All Manipur Gorkha Students' Union conducted a survey of the Gorkha population of the state in 1990. The survey revealed that the total population of the Gorkhas hardly crossed 45,000. Following this revelation, the Gorkhas started asserting that their population is decreasing whereas the local people claimed that the Gorkha population was increasing in the state, which is actually a pointer to the precarious state of affairs between the indigenous and the diasporic.

Conclusion: Idea of 'cultural collectives'

Historians and political scientists working on the issue of governance in north-east India have often focused on military engagements and defining and re-defining territorial boundaries, but have ignored age-old cultural interactions between communities. Hence, there is a need to pick up the threads from such interactions to see if the existing conflict and tension between the local and the diasporic people could be mitigated.

Cultural interaction should actually form the basis of understanding the ethos of any society. Myths, legends, folklores, belief systems, notions of collectives, systems of hierarchies, value systems, systems of social order and consensus as well as society's own law of progression need to be studied to understand the functioning of the state structure. If one takes Hocart's perception, traditional structures/polity is not a system of governance, but an organisation to promote life, fertility and prosperity. Gradually, its scope was enlarged and its functions modified to become a centralised means of organising the activities of society (1970: 27–8).[10] Denouncing theories based purely on economic factors, Hocart says that these are a very small fragment of life, and the pursuit of wealth is not one that inspires much zeal for common good. One cannot build a state on the narrow basis of prices and wages; it can only be premised on the widest cooperation for life. The reason why we have failed nations and ever-increasing demands for homelands in our region is because we have not been able to understand the evolution of the state and appreciate the issues of governance from the cultural point of view. Instead, our understanding of the state structure has been based on authority and a jural system. This notion has debarred us from encompassing the traditions of widest cooperation in life.

Some African scholars have reported that there were traditional forms of democracy, autocracy, monarchy and oligarchy in state-organised societies as well as stateless societies in their pre-colonial history. They assert that African traditional political systems functioned, not because of their forms, but because they fulfilled the felt needs of their societies. I am of the view that if the cultural notions of India's north-east could be studied and incorporated in our policy frameworks, the issues of separation, marginalisation and self-assertions would have been relegated to the realm of non-issues. As Uya has rightly said, we need to build on the 'traditional structures of inclusion' rather than on the 'progressive democracies of exclusion' (Uya 1987: 39).[11] If that happens, the so-called outsiders, migrants, and others also have a chance of living with some dignity as humans, if not as equal citizens of the country.

Let me briefly touch upon the Iroquois confederacy to consolidate my argument here. The Iroquois confederacy had the longest oral constitution. It was given the written form only in 1917. The thrust of the constitution is on public opinion and public consensus and the clearly defined role of the leaders. One of the major criteria is that the leader cannot earn more than the modest earnings. Thomas Jefferson said that Iroquois is the best government since it is the least government. President Franklin's writings also indicate that as he became more deeply involved with the Iroquois and other 'Indian' peoples, he picked up ideas from them concerning not only federalism, but also concepts of natural rights, the nature of society and man's place in it, the role of property in society, and other intellectual constructs, which were eventually incorporated as he and other American revolutionaries shaped the official ideology for the soon-to-be-founded United States of America. The way the Constitution of Iroquois League was adopted by the Americans was called the 'Americanization of the White people'. In an equally bold statement, Francis Jennings, in his *The Invasion of America: Indians, Colonialism and the Cant of Conquest* (1975) states, 'What White (American) society owes to Indian society, as much as to any other source, is the mere fact of its existence.'

Even Marx and Engels drew on Iroquois models to support their theories and designs. Engels, like the American revolutionaries a century earlier, was, for instance, impressed with the Iroquois' ability to achieve economic equality without coercion and to maintain social consensus without a large state apparatus. It is interesting to note that the roots of American democratic government and communism came from similar ideologies, one emphasising individualism, and the other, communal holdings. Both the key elements are held in balance by the Iroquois.

Concluding remarks

The Nepalis in Manipur, like the Parsis in Mumbai and Gujarat, have generally maintained cordial relations with the general public and are usually categorised as a 'peace loving people'. Like the Parsis again, the Nepalis have kept their traditions alive. It also appears that the two communities, like most other minority communities in the country, are undergoing a similar stress being pulled towards opposite directions by primordial and modernist forces.

Notes

1. All these are various tribes of Manipur.
2. Vijaylakshmi Brara, 1998, *Politics, Society and Cosmology in India's North East*, Oxford University Press, Delhi.
3. Recently, there has been an upsurge in reviving the Inner Line Permit by different groups so as to protect the indigenous peoples.
4. Ghanshyam Acharya, 1999, *The Gorkhas of Manipur*, published by the Organising Committee, 44th Annual Gorkha Conference of Manipur Gorkha Welfare Union, Manipur.
5. Indira Kumar and B. Sharma, 1994, *Meitei Bamon Haurakpham Amasung Sageigi Gotra* (in Manipuri). Imphal: Authors.
6. G. K. N. Chettry, 1994, *Brief History of Gorkhas and their Settlement in Manipur*, published by the author on behalf of the Nepali Research Society, Manipur.
7. One of the 19th-century Manipuri kings.
8. Interestingly, democracy ushered in Manipur much before the elections were announced in independent India. It was the women's war against the British, famously called the *nupi-lan* of 1939, which generated political awareness in the masses and established the foundation for the aspiration for a just and egalitarian society. The ultimate victory of the women's struggle was to bring down the feudal regime and initiate the move to have democratic elections. The elections took place in 1948, four years before the first democratic elections in India. By November of that year, the Maharaja was replaced by an elected government. The tenure of this government was short-lived, as Manipur was soon merged with India.
9. IT = Imphal-Tamenglong Road.
10. A. M. Hocart, 1970, *Kings and Councilors: An Essay in Comparative Anatomy of Human Society*, The University of Chicago Press, Chicago, pp. 27–28.
11. O. E. Uya, 1987, *African Diaspora*, Enugu: Fourth Dimension Publishers, p. 39.

References

Acharya, Ghanshyam. 1999. *The Gorkhas of Manipur*. Imphal: Organising Committee, 44th Annual Gorkha Conference of Manipur Gorkha Welfare Union.

Brara, Vijaylakshmi. 1998. *Politics, Society and Cosmology in India's North East*. Delhi: Oxford University Press.

Chettry, G. K. N. 1994. *Brief History of Gorkhas and their Settlement in Manipur*. Imphal: Nepali Research Society.

Daly, Janet L. 1997. 'The Effect of the Iroquois Constitution on the United States Constitution', E-magazine of the Indigenous People of Africa and America, www.ipoaa.com/iroquois_constitution_united_states.htm. Accessed on 5 July 2012.

Kumar, Indira and B. Sharma. 1994. *Meitei Bamon Haurakpham Amasung Sageigi Gotra* (in Manipuri). Imphal: Authors.

Lloyd, Peter C. 1970. 'Traditional Rulers', in James S. Coleman and Carl G. Rosberg Jr. (eds), *Political Parties and National Integration in Tropical Africa, Nigeria: Background to Nationalism*. Berkeley: University of California Press.

Owusu, Maxwell. 1991. 'Democracy and Africa: A View from the Village', *The Journal of Modern African Studies*, 30(3): 369–96.

Uya, O. E. 1987. *African Diaspora*. Enugu: Fourth Dimension Publishers.

15

EVICTED FROM HOME, NOWHERE TO GO

The case of Lhotshampas from Bhutan

A. C. Sinha

The Lhotshampas, or the Nepalis of the southern Bhutan, are predominantly Hindus. The community has been in turmoil for the past 25 years, subsequent to their forceful eviction by the Royal Government of Bhutan (RGB) and their settlement in the refugee camps in eastern Nepal and elsewhere. In 1991, more than 75,000 Lhotshampa refugees were sheltered in UNHCR-run camps in Nepal. The UNHCR tried its best to repatriate them, but failed. Meanwhile, it found it increasingly difficult to manage the funds for the maintenance of the refugee camps. The Royal Government of Nepal (RGN) and the RGB were goaded to hold 15 rounds of talks with a view to solve the refugee problem, but nothing came out of those deliberations. This is the background in which the USA proposed to take the refugees from the camps to the USA and inspired other Western countries to follow suit. This move led to acrimonious debate among the refugees in the camps and outside, as their first priority was their repatriation to Bhutan. However, in spite of opposition from a section of the refugees, about 40,000 of them have been relocated in Western countries. After the initial euphoria for going to the West withered away, the refugees realised that it had raised new questions such as: What will happen to their culture? How will they communicate with others in the new situations? What will happen to their language? What about their religious performances? How will they cremate/bury their dead bodies and where will they go for worship? These questions continue to haunt the Lhotshampas and there is no clear answer yet.

Constructing the Lhotshampa culture

The Lhotshampas represent an underdog migrant population in Druk-yul (Bhutan), where modern education itself was introduced in 1962. They had to struggle all the time to survive in the administratively and politically hostile environment. They were themselves divided among castes and communities and many of them had their own languages. However, *daura-suruwal, dhaka topi, khukuri* and Nepali as the lingua franca were the items in their cultural kitbag, which gave them a common identity against the dominant Drukpas, who were the rulers of the land. In the lawless feudal Bhutan, the oral orders of the local feudal, priestly or administrative functionaries were the laws of the land, which were invariably used against the Lhotshampa migrants. Formal education was unheard of and the only literates were priestly Brahmins, who informally, invariably and illegally ran the Sanskrit schools or *pathsalas* at home or in the make-shift temples and trained Brahmin boys in priestly vocation. Dress, inter-dining, food taboo, recitation of *Bhanubhaktako Ramayan*, singing and reciting Hindu mythologies from *The Mahabharata, Puranas* and the *Upanishads* among the unlettered masses and visiting holy places such as Varanasi by a select few were what gave them a distinct sociocultural identity. Even the communities known as Kiratis, who were not directly part of the classical Hindu great tradition, found it convenient to join caste Hindu Nepalis in such congregations as a mark of migrant Nepali solidarity. It was a loosely hierarchical society, in which caste status and social disabilities were moderated by a common struggle to make a living. As the rulers were hostile to any form of organised activities among the Lhotshampas, there was no question of producing a written literature by them. Hence, it is not surprising how the community, which at one time claimed to represent 64 per cent of Bhutanese population, did not produce any significant literature (Gurung 1960).

Michael Hutt notes that the Lhotshampas were regarded as 'more conservative, more submissive to the figure of authority, more "old-fashioned" than their "Nepali" or "Gorkha" counterparts across the border in India and Nepal' (Hutt 2003: 102–3). The reason is historical, and not sociological or lack of creativity. In general, migrant communities zealously stick to their cultural baggage in alien social contexts. In the relative absence of contact with the mother country, their language, cultural items and even religious practices get fossilised in course of time. The unlettered indentured labour or manual agricultural labour are invariably engaged in daily drudgery of negotiating mere survival, which hardly leaves them with any time or leisure for literary creativity. That is why Australia did not produce any great literary giant in the 18th century in English, and the same is true of Mauritius or West Indies Indians about any classic in Hindi in the 19th century. The Lhotshampas too had no opportunities for engaging in any literary activity in the first 100 years of their habitation in Bhutan, as they did not have any access to the reading, writing and publishing world. Even the dominant Drukpas could not develop Dzongkha as the national language. Incidentally, the national lingua franca of Bhutan was Nepali. In fact, the Lhotshampas used to take pride in their language. Their contact with Nepal was less, as they did not want to be seen as hobnobbing with their Nepalese counterparts. Even their meetings with Indian Nepalis were watched by the Drukpas. Many Lhotshampas were educated in India like the Drukpas themselves, and they had plenty of friends and relatives across the border.

In the changed situation of temporary refugee camps in eastern Nepal, a different type of experiment is being made, which may have far-reaching consequences in the future. Rosalind Evans informs how the refugee children are being ideologically oriented through games and play. The Bhutanese Refugee Children Forum (BRCF) engaged itself in cultural expressions and tried to address how various actors use cultural expressions to transform individual consciousness and create collective identities (Evans 2010: 306). With a view to developing *chetana* or 'awakening' or 'consciousness' among the youth, the Communist Party of Bhutan (BCP) utilised the BRCF as a means of raising people's consciousness about the structures that oppressed them. Though the BRCF tried to cultivate normative ideals of proper childhood and increased the children's confidence in persuasion and expression, the forum seems to be hijacked by the BCP with its revolutionary ideology and anti-American agenda expressed through poems, dramas and articles.

Bhutanese response to Lhotshampa aspirations

Certain historical events must be kept in mind before tracing the roots of Nepali migration to Bhutan. After the Anglo-Nepalese War of 1814–15, the British discovered a reliable fighting force in the Gurkhas. Darjeeling was secured from Sikkim and 18 Duars from Bhutan and they were instituted into districts of Darjeeling and Jalpaiguri under Bengal Presidency. The two districts were soon turned into thriving tea plantations in no time with the help of migrant Nepali labourers. The Anglo-Bhutan War of 1863–64 led to peace between the British and Bhutan. Hard-pressed by cruel administration, chronic drought and pestilence and diminishing cultivable land, the Nepalis migrated first to Darjeeling, and then, to Duars and Sikkim. By then, Ugyen Dorji, the king of Bhutan, emerged as a reliable ally of the British, who desired to interpose Nepalis as a buffer community between the Drukpa highlanders and the Bengali plainsmen. Sinha writes

> Ugyen Dorji's father, the Kazi of Jungta, was an influential figure in the western Bhutan and Bhutan court in 1860's. It appears that his services were frequently commissioned by the British to settle the matters of importance related to the south-western Bhutan borders . . . (He) settled down at the emerging trading mart of Kalimpong in Darjeeling district with his estates in the British territory as well as western Bhutan . . . In 1898, he was appointed Haa Thrugpa, chief administrator of Haa, with rights over the whole of southern Bhutan and the rights vested in him to settle immigrant Nepalese in his territory. He was also made Bhutanese Agent in Kalimpong besides being interpreter of the Deputy Commissioner, Darjeeling. Sir Charles A. Bell, ICS, the Sub-Divisional Officer, Kalimpong, cultivated the Agent of Bhutan and used him to carry the Viceroy's Letter to the Dalai Lama in 1903. He provided valuable services to the British during the Younghusband Expedition to Lhasa, 1903–04. As a recognition of his services rendered to the British, the title of 'Raja' was conferred upon him.
>
> (Sinha 1991: 36–37)

From malarial jungle to thriving settlements

Prior to introduction of the Wangchuk dynasty in December 1907, Bhutan was ruled by a faction-ridden oligarchy of clergy and gentry. Social structure and economy were based on theocratic feudalism. Technologically, it was a simple society. The people were afflicted with goiter, syphilis, bronchial, malarial and other chronic diseases.[1] The Drukpas ruled over the serfs, slaves and bonded peasantry with primitive harshness. In 1867, a British surveyor noted 'the absence of inhabitants and want of footpaths or roads' in western Bhutan. The Nepali settlers came to the south-western part in 1870s to quarry lime. They visited the south-eastern district of Chirang for a few months during hot weather in order to tap rubber trees for natural rubber till the trees died out of over-tapping. Charles Bell noted in 1903 that the British subjects used to 'go in to the

(Bhutanese side of the) land for grazing and other purposes during the part of the year'.[2] The following year, he wrote about the forests in Bhutanese Duars thus:

> The area over 7,000 feet elevation is and will no doubt remain under dense forests. It contains many kinds of trees suitable for timber, fuel, mat-making and other purposes, among them rhododendron, maple, magnolia, oak and walnut. The forests have also a certain value as grazing grounds. The number of graziers is comparatively small at present owing to the scanty population in low lands. But they are capable of . . . cattle farms to a large number of all races . . . many of the graziers, who supply Darjeeling town with milk, send their cattle, when off milk to the forests at the head of (river) Dikchu.[3]

Bell noted further: 'raiyats (tenants) in Bhutan can cultivate any unoccupied bits of land, and burn the jungle as they please for the purpose. This is much appreciated in the backward state of cultivation there, as good land and forest are still abundant, and the waste entailed by such a system is not yet brought home to them . . . They can cut wood wherever they like, since there is no reserve forests. The burning of the jungle and promiscuous felling of timber will, however, before long leave them worse off than if they had been subjected to restrictions imposed by our administration in these respects'.[4] This wanton destruction of the forests attracted the attention of the British within a couple of years, as noticed in the following words:

> A great deal of friction between ourselves (British) and Bhutan has originated in the Bhutanese dread of fever in the lower hills, of which they know nothing whatever, nor do the officials ever go there . . . The authorities have allowed the Paharias (the Nepalese) of doubtful character to settle on the frontier taking quite nominal rent and have thus deprived themselves and the Government of all the profits which have been made of timber and charcoal etc. Besides this, in some parts near the tea districts (in Indian district of Jalpaiguri), all the valuable timber has been cut and probably sold as firewood. The cutting is quite indiscriminate, the contractors even go so far as to fell a tree and cut only the branches for firewood, as they are too lazy to cut the trunk.[5]

After signing the Anglo-Bhutan Treaty, 1910, Captain Robert E. Kennedy, accompanying Political Officer Charles A. Bell on their return journey, noted in his diary about Menchu, a site on southern Duars at the height of 1,550 feet from the sea level as a 'Nepalese settlement on the hill side . . . (where) only a small portion is cultivated. Jhumming is extensively indulged in; it consists of burning a patch of jungle, roughly cultivating it for a few years and then repeating the process with another patch'.[6] Ascending a height of 3,950 feet from the sea level at Miritsen on 30 December 1909, he had 'passed by a few patches of cultivation, but practically all the country was under dense forests, though there were many promising looking "flats" on the sides of the hills'.[7] After signing the Treaty, Bell recorded in his report: 'we can now safely accept Bhutan's offers to exploit the forests and mines of her lower hills with the British capital and the Indian (Nepalese?) labour'. Incidentally, the Bhutan agent, Raja S. T. Dorji, controlled the entire southern Bhutan through his two allies, Nandlal Chhetri and Garajman Gurung, who were contracted to settle southern Bhutan with Nepali immigrants and pay house tax to the cash-starved Bhutanese *durbar*.

Negotiating with the settlers

Within no time, the Nepali peasants organised themselves into village settlements such as the ones they had in Nepal. Their settlements were rarely characterised by compact villages, as they required extensive land for grazing and transhumance. The internal administration was left in the hands of their traditional headmen or *mandal*s, who were held responsible for collecting and depositing the revenue to the 'contractors', who handed it over either to the Bhutan agent or Paro Dzongpen, as the order might be. The villagers also developed agricultural *haat*s at nodal points on various days of the week. Similarly, they evolved a system of weight and measure in terms of *pathy* for measuring the land and grains. There was no police and no agency to enforce law and order. It was the contractors or the Bhutan agent, who were the ultimate laws of the land for the settlers. Socially, the Nepalis followed their own rules based on *Muluki Ain* promulgated in Nepal and vaguely claimed to be the subjects of Panch Sarkar, the king of Nepal in the absence of the Bhutanese king among them. In fact, most of the Lhotshampas had never seen Bhutanese kings in the first half of the 20th century.

While Bhutan apprehended trouble from the increasing number of Nepalis on the southern frontiers, whose loyalty they were not sure of, the British were more concerned with using them as soldiers' farm. In this regard, Peter Collister writes that the first approach was made by the officiating Political Officer W. L. Campbell in 1917–18 to permit recruitment of the Bhutanese Nepalis to the Indian Army, which was turned down (Collister 1987: 174). This request was renewed more than once in 1920s, but it was denied. However, two Bhutanese returned after training in the Indian Army as Jamadars and another 14 were recruited in Shillong with 2/10th Gurkha Rifles in 1930. Captain C. J. Morris came to south-central Bhutan to assess the possibility of recruitment to Gurkha regiments and surveyed the area extensively for the purpose. He found that the Nepalis constituted about 20 per cent of the total Bhutanese population of 300,000 in 1932 (Sinha 2003: 139–61). Even this survey did not convince the Bhutanese to let the Nepalis join the Indian armed forces. But a small number of trained soldiers from the Indian Army ultimately provided the nucleus to the palace guards, when such a unit was raised in Bhutan. The British noted in the early 1930s that both Zhabsdrung and Nepalis were sympathetic to the cause of the Indian freedom movement. Naturally, by the 1940s, seeds of political cogitation began to be felt among the well-settled Nepali peasants in Bhutan, who used to travel south in the Indian plains for a variety of purposes. They could not be kept immune to the influence of Indian National Congress, Sikkim State Congress and Nepal's Nepali Congress. Politically conscious and otherwise dissatisfied elements from among them got together to organise the Bhutan State Congress, with populist demands, which was ruthlessly suppressed by Bhutanese militias.

Ethnic assimilation of Lhotshampas

By the early 1950s, the second Druk-rGyalpo and his main ally and Bhutan agent, Raja S. T. Dorji died and they were succeeded by their sons, Jigmi Wangchuk and Jigmie Palden Dorji, respectively. Two young functionaries were trained in public administration at Dehradun in India and had travelled abroad, and thus, were exposed to the fast-changing political contours of the developing countries. They possibly realised soon that their old Bhutanese policy of isolation may lead them to serious trouble, as it happened in the case of Tibet. So, they decided to go for social and economic development of their country. In this context, Indian Prime Minister Jawaharlal Nehru made an arduous journey across Himalayan heights to reach Bhutan as the first international dignitary. India agreed to finance the socio-economic development of Bhutan and provide technical expertise as well. But development required not only financial support and technical expertise, but also inexpensive and sufficient labour force. Here came the Bhutanese Nepalis handy. The king was foresighted enough to grant citizenship to long resident, landowning Nepalis of southern Bhutan and the latter came forward to work for all types of constructions such as roads, office buildings, power houses, airport, township, repairs and construction of the monasteries, and so on.

The Lhotshampas acted wisely for themselves by not taking sides in factions in the royal court in 1964 and 1972, when the ruling oligarchy was divided into two conflicting blocks. These national crises followed the murder of Jigmie Dorji, the first prime minister of the country, at Phuntsholing in 1964 and death of the third Druk-rGyalpo led to dispute between two of his sons in 1972–74 over succession to the throne. An obliged Drukpa regime took two important decisions pertaining to the Nepalis as reward. One, they decided to assimilate them by officially encouraging inter-ethnic marriages and providing incentives to such unions in cash rewards of INR 5,000 to begin with, teaching of Nepali language in schools in the southern districts and opening Sanskrit schools for the Brahmin priests. Two, the regime sent a number of deserving Nepali students on scholarships to study abroad in technical and other subjects, who manned important positions in the administration on their return. One may identify a third significant favour of the Druk-rGyalpo to the Nepalis in constitutionally providing a nomenclature for them in 1975, namely 'Lhotshampas' or the southerners. It appears that the fourth king, Jigmi Singhe Wangchuk, in his enthusiasm for the national language Dzongkha, desired that the Lhotshampas be given a territorial nomenclature, as they were permitted to settle only in designated southern foothills. They were also represented in the National Assembly of Bhutan along with the Drukpas, though it was more of a token representation. It is another matter that the term got currency only after the flight of thousands of Nepalis from their villages in southern Bhutan to the refugee camps in Nepal in 1991.

Ethnic catharsis and expulsion of Lhotshampas

Alarmed by the Gorkha National Liberation Front (GNLF) movement in Duars and Darjeeling district of West Bengal, the Royal Government of Bhutan (RGB) initiated a motivated census operation to identify the alleged illegal Lhotshampas of Bhutan in 1985. In many cases, even old settlers with citizenship certificates were declared illegal migrants and pushed out of Bhutan. Next, the RGB introduced its notorious policy of 'Driglam Namza', the code of conduct for the southerners. All efforts by the Lhotshampa bureaucrats and *Chimis* (members of the National Assembly or *Tshongdu*) to reach the king to acquaint him with their problems were frustrated by the determined Drukpa courtiers. T. N. Rizal, one of the senior members of the Royal Advisory Council and a member of the National Assembly of Bhutan representing the Lhotshampas, tried to petition the king on the grievances of the community, but he was punished instead. As a result, the organisationally inexperienced Lhotshampas began to demonstrate at various points on southern border towns to ventilate their frustration.

D. N. S. Dhakal, one such leader and contributor to this volume, records two waves of Lhotshampa demonstrations: one, throughout southern Bhutan on 19–25 September 1990 and the other on 4 October 1990 (Dhakal and Strawn 1994: 214). It is reported that about 15,000 Lhotshampas resorted to demonstration at Chamurchi in Samchi district on 25 October 1990 and the royal militia opened fire, leading to the death of many demonstrators. That event proved to be the turning point in the history of Lhotshampas. The RGB began an operation to flush them out of Bhutan in an organised way. Within months, about 100,000 Lhotshampas left Bhutan, either for the refugee camps set up by the UNHCR in Nepal or got dispersed among their kinsmen/friends in Darjeeling and Sikkim.

The RGB also mounted an effective publicity campaign against the Lhotshampas by alleging that they had planned to usurp southern Bhutan as a part of their design for 'Greater Nepal'. They appeared to be not only successful in selling this theory to the Indians, but also tried to convince them that Darjeeling and Sikkim would be the next target of the Greater Nepal zealots. The Bhutanese also convinced the leaders of the Indian National Congress and took special care to court the rightist Rastriya Swayamsewak Sangh (RSS) allegedly with mini gold bricks for the Ram temple in Ayodhya and the leftist Communist Party of India (Marxist) by inviting the chief minister of West Bengal as a state guest. After securing the support of the border state of West Bengal, they mounted publicity blitz to convince the western world, which is ever awed with anything Buddhist, that the very existence of the Shangri-la was at stake. The Bhutanese establishment successfully managed to do this. On the contrary, the beleaguered Lhotshampas had no spokesmen and their miserable plight did not attract any attention of the international community. The Indian establishment stood steadfast by the Bhutanese official stand and declared the issue as a bilateral one between the RGB and the RGN. The two Himalayan governments were forced to hold 15 rounds of talks over the issue of repatriating the refugees, but not a single refugee was repatriated to Bhutan. Meanwhile, the UNHCR began reporting donor fatigue and pressed for quicker solution to the problem. About 100,000 Lhotshampa refugees continued to reside in the seven camps in eastern Nepal for longer than two decades. Their unequivocal desire to go back to their country, Bhutan, remained unheard by the international community and remains so even today.

At this juncture, the United States came forward to take as many as 60,000 refugees and it persuaded its other Western allies such as Australia, Great Britain, Canada, Denmark, the Netherlands, New Zealand, Norway and others to share refugees from the camps. This move created total confusion among the refugees, who were initially unwilling to consider such a proposal. Slowly, a section of youths came forward to accept the proposal, but left-oriented youths were against it. There was violence on the issue, but the UNHRC welcomed the move and reasoned with them that the camps could not be run indefinitely without Western support. The RGB welcomed the move and the RGN had a sense of relief that, at long last, the camps on their soil would be closed, while the Government of India remained unconcerned. After a considerable period of conflict in the camps, the refugees began to enrol themselves as potential migrants to various Western countries, and, in 2009, many of them actually left for their new destinations.

By the 1990s, Bhutan had changed significantly. A rudiment of the middle class, representing the Drukpas as well as Lhotshampas, had evolved. While the Lhotshampa elite was not content to settle for crumbs, the Drukpa rulers saw themselves as vulnerable because of a sizeable Lhotshampa population in a compact area away from Thimpu, the capital of Bhutan, but close to Nepal and Darjeeling. Bhutan's two South Asian neighbours, India and Nepal, had their own priorities. While India, as the emerging regional power, did not appreciate another trouble spot in its backyard, Nepal, enthused with the dawn of the second wave of democracy in 1990, gleefully welcomed the refugees without realising the consequences. The Bhutanese leaders did not waste time in whispering to their benefactors – the Indian policymakers, in particular – that the Lhotshampa trouble was a part of the 'Greater Nepal' strategy. The Lhotshampas finally saw a design in the

Bhutanese policy to assimilate them within the Drukpa fold, but then, it was rather too late.

Demography: politics of statistics

Population figures in Sikkim, Bhutan and Nepal have always been suspect, as the three Himalayan kingdoms identified certain communities for special treatment at the cost of a real or putative migrant community. Thus, the Namgyals in Sikkim inflated the Bhutia-Lepcha population against the Nepalis, the Wangchuks in Bhutan conceded a mere 14 to 25 per cent to the Lhotshampa population against the pastoralist Drukpas, and the Shahs in Nepal deliberately displayed a linguistically fragmented and small Madheshi population. In case of Bhutan, it was actually quite comical. In 1960, the National Assembly decided that the population figures to be presented to the foreign dignitaries would be 700,000, of which 25 per cent were Nepali speakers. The accuracy and source of data at the time remained unstated. It claimed in 1971 to have a population of a million in its application for the membership of the United Nations Organisation. It was revised to 1,200,000 in 1979, which naturally rose to 1,375,000 in 1988. At the end of 1991, Bhutan declared its population to be 600,000 only. Even a naive reader can detect the politics of statistics as all the figures given above have three zeros at the end, which means all these statistics are based on estimates without enumeration on the ground and for administrative convenience only (Sinha 2003: 177–78). Same is true of the Lhotshampas. Their population is invariably declared as 14 to 25 per cent, but their claim goes as much as 64 per cent. However, scholars agree that Lhotshampa population should be anything between 25 and 33 per cent.

Estimate of Lhotsampa population

The Lhotshampa population at present exists not only in Bhutan and in the refugee camps of Nepal, but also in India and the West. Hence, a region-wise estimation of their population is in order here.

Inside Bhutan

Keeping in mind the voters' list of 2008 and making allowance for the transfer of Drukpa population from north and eastern Bhutan to southern districts in recent times, anything from 80,000 to 100,000 will be a reasonable guess as the population of the Lhotshampas in Bhutan. Even today, the RGB informs that Lhotshampas constitute 25 per cent of their national population.

In the refugee camps in Nepal

As of 30 November 2010, the record of the Government of Nepal provides the following figures of the Lhotshampa refugees:

In India

There is no compact settlement of the Lhotshampas in India. As per the national obligation between the two countries, the Bhutanese may stay and work in India. So, their scattered population in India is estimated anything between 30,000 and 50,000.

The West

The Government of Nepal maintains such a list, as embarkation of the Lhotshampas from the refugee camps is carried through it. The records as on 30 November 2010 display the following figures of the Lhotshampa refugees, who left Nepal for their Western destinations:

Table 15.1 Number of families, huts and population of Lhotshampa refugees

Camps	No. of families	No. of huts	Population
Beldangi-I	2,263	3,086	13,305
Beldangi-II	2,914	3,916	15,288
Beldangi-Ext	1,264	1,582	8,893
Goldhap	772	722	5,028
Khudunabari	1,746	1,853	10,773
Sanischare	2,518	2,568	14,244
Timai	1,019	1,264	759
Out of camp register	34	46	72
Total	**12,530**	**15,087**	**74,861**

Table 15.2 Destinations of male and female Lhotshampa refugees

Destination	Male	Female	Total
USA	16,834	16,509	33,143
Canada	1,125	1,131	2,256
Australia	995	1,057	2,152
New Zealand	248	250	498
Norway	154	219	373
Denmark	155	171	326
The Netherlands	112	117	229
Great Britain	53	58	111
Total	**19,770**	**19,309**	**39,079**

The above figures come to a grand total of 245,931, which may be conveniently put to anything between two and a half to three hundred thousand. The purely domestic problem of the Lhotshampas became a bilateral one between Bhutan and Nepal after 1990. India did not mediate the problem between its two neighbours. With their dispersal in a number of Western countries, the Lhotshampas have become a global community with new challenges and opportunities. With their largely monolingual and rural agricultural background, they are worried about the future of their Lhotshampa identity in the new environments.

Future of Lhotshampa identity

The Lhotshampas are quite different from the Drukpas. They are naturally closer to their ethnic cousins in Darjeeling, Sikkim and Nepal than the Drukpas of Bhutan, but a century and a half long history of living in the same physical environment as the Drukpas has made them different from their ethnic cousins as well. Their social structure, cultural practices, shared memory, religious performances, literary output, worldview and a vision of the future make them a distinct community. Their worries for the future are uniquely theirs, for which their ethnic cousins from Nepal and India can sympathise, but do precious little to help them, as was the case during the past two decades. They have gone to their new destinations in the West with a lot of anxieties. The elderly among them are particularly anxious about the disposal of the dead and subsequent death rituals. The younger generation is worried about jobs, education and employment while a small intelligentsia among them seeks an 'honourable solution' to their problem.

Despite the currently depressing situation, what happens to the leftover Lhotshampas in Bhutan may hold the key to the future of all the dispersed Lhotshampas. Will they be absorbed by the dominant Drukpas or will they continue to maintain a distinct identity of their own? Will they be forced to leave Bhutan or will they be allowed to stay on, and if so, on what terms and conditions? Partially, Lhotshampa destiny may also be influenced by events unfolding in Nepal and the Western countries where they have settled. Equally significant to watch will be the ongoing demand in Darjeeling district for a separate state called Gorkhaland. If they achieve Gorkhaland, which is difficult, but not impossible, will they like to lend their support to the Lhotshampas? Will the Lhotshampas ever have the wherewithal to influence the national politics of Bhutan, Nepal or India?

Apprehension of the Lhotshampas in Bhutan

Of late, some concessions have been given to the Lhotshampas, such as 'No Objection Certificates' (NOC) and use of dress on certain occasions. One has to wait and see whether these concessions are temporary to appease the international community or they would revert to the post-1990 situation once the glare of the international community is shifted to some other country. They fear that they would be slowly pushed out of the country, as the international community is working in tandem with the Bhutanese establishment. Bhutan's objective is to create a Buddhist country. It believes that its long-term security depends on a mono-cultural landscape. It has the tacit support of India, some Western countries and the People's Republic of China. Thus, it appears that the fate of the Lhotshampas is, at least for now, sealed.

How Lhotshampas respond to the evolving situation will be interesting to observe. The Indian Nepalis are ideologically divided into many groups to give them any united support. Nepal is submerged in political catharsis and there is hardly any chance of a concrete support from that country in the near future. Indian policymakers know that economic integration of Bhutan would serve their long-term purpose, but there is no immediate reason for supporting the democratic movement of Lhotshampas. Keeping these possibilities in mind, the best they can do is to keep them united. The dawn of democracy in Nepal has given a voice to the Madhesi population in Nepal. The Lhotshampas may expect the same to happen in Bhutan someday.

Cultural space for Lhotshampas in India

Recently, an important former Indian diplomat wrote the following, which deserves to be quoted here at length for its cogent enunciation of the formal Indian assessment of the Lhotshampa refugee problem:

> a solution was possible (in 1996) . . . I believe Bhutan had identified 12,000 such refugees at a time when the total figure quoted was 80,000. The number now exceeds one lakh, with an uncertain influx. The next step would be to identify the numbers which Nepal would accept, and leave the remaining for India to negotiate, with a scheme to resettle a substantial number within India, and persuade Bhutan to increase acceptable figures within a reasonable limit . . . In fact, these refugees were instigated to cross into Bhutan, and India had to prevent such an influx. There was also reason to believe that such refugees were approached by the Indian insurgents from Assam, known as ULFA to join hands in creating problems both for Bhutan and India. Our M(inistry) of E(xternal) A(ffairs) was aware of these developments. Keeping the larger view of Bhutan's stability and ethnic balance in mind, India could not support the demand of the refugees, or of Nepal. It has been a very wise decision, Bhutan being most vulnerable on its southern boundaries, which are dominated by people of Nepalese origin. The late King Jigme Dorji (Wangchuk) often talked to me of his apprehensions that Nepal would visualise a 'Maha Nepal' constituting Nepal, Bhutan, and Sikkim, and some Nepalese dominated regions of West Bengal, like Darjeeling. The Southern population of Bhutan, consisting over 90% Nepalese origin, would be used as a launching pad in Bhutan, apart from the 75% of the entire Sikkim population which is Nepalese. One prime reason for his policy of closeness to India was to ensure protection of Bhutanese culture, and independence from the Nepalese political intrusion.
>
> (Das 2010: 97–8)

About a 150-years-old Lhotshampa community has a history of suffering, survival and quest for identity in Bhutan. In spite of all odds, the community mounted a heroic effort for its survival and their struggle has proved that they have the tenacity to protect their rich cultural legacy against all odds. Their dispersed existence may force them to go for the use of modern means of communication technology to maintain their cultural ties and unity intact. Their cultural cousins from Nepal and

India, and, of course, their kith and kin in Bhutan may provide moral support, but ultimately, it is they who have to help themselves.

Of late, there has emerged a new possibility in the form of Facebook (Scrutton 2011). The journalist who reported from Bhutan writes: 'face book has opened the flood gate for open criticism of the government. People feel the need to be vocal. Only two years ago, criticism – constructive or not was quite anonymous'. The Lhotshampas may rise to the occasion to see that their culture survives, no matter where they have been resettled and how much against their own will.

Notes

1 India Office Library & Records, London (IOLR): MSS/EUR//L/Pes/2224: Collection 8: Bhutan, Letter from Political Officer in Sikkim to the Government of India, No. 16 (1), P/30, dated 2 April 1931.
2 IOLR/MSS/EUR/F/80/15c, p. 32, C.A. Bells, 'Confidential Report to the Deputy Commissioner, Darjeeling', dated 23 September 1903.
3 IOLR/MSS/EUR/F/80/5c; Confidential Report to the Chief Secretary, Government of Bengal, dated 21 July 1904.
4 IOR&R/MSS/EUR/F/80/15c, p. 32; Charles A. Bell, 'Confidential Report to the Deputy Commissioner, Darjeeling', dated 23 September 1903.
5 Report on the Relation between the British and Bhutan during 1905–07 as an enclosure of a letter to the His Majesty's Secretary to the State of India, No. 25; dated 21 February 1907.
6 F.153-c/224(b); Captain Robert E. Kennedy's Bhutan Diary, 1909–10.
7 Ibid.

References

Collister, P. 1987. *Bhutan and the British*. London: Serindian Publications.
Das, B. S. 2010. *Memoirs of an Indian Diplomat*. New Delhi: Tata McGraw Hill Education Private Limited.
Dhakal, D. N. S. and S. Strawn. 1994. *Bhutan: A Movement in Exile*. New Delhi: Nirala.
Evans, Rosalind. 2010. 'Cultural Expression as Political Rhetoric: Young Bhutanese Refugees' Collective Action for Social Change', *Contemporary South Asia*, 18(3): 305–17.
Gurung, D. B. 1960. 'Bhutan's Woes', *Mankind*, 4(7): 33–45.
Hutt, M. 2003. *Unbecoming Citizens: Culture, Nationalism, and the Flight of Refugees from Bhutan*. New Delhi: Oxford University Press.
Scrutton, A. 2011. 'Facebook May Soon Herald Deeper Changes in Bhutan', *The Asian Age*, New Delhi, p. 11.
Sinha, A. C. 1991. *Bhutan: Ethnic Identity, and National Dilemma*. New Delhi: Reliance Publishing House.
Sinha, A. C. 2003. *Himalayan Kingdom Bhutan: Tradition, Transition and Transformation*. New Delhi: Indus Publishing Company.

16

LHOTSHAMPA REFUGEES AND NEPALI DIASPORA

D. N. S. Dhakal and Gopal Subedi

The word 'Lhotsampa' refers to the Nepalis of southern Bhutan, which includes all castes and ethnic groups found in the middle hills and mountain regions of Nepal. If a person were to visit southern Bhutan before 1990, he could have mistaken the place for one of the middle hills of Nepal. They built houses in Nepali style, spoke in Nepali and celebrated Nepali festivals such as *Dasai* and *Tihar*. They came to Bhutan in groups of individuals and families, and in some cases, entire villages, bringing with them animals and household items. They were encouraged to settle in southern Bhutan by the ruling elites of Bhutan to convert the malaria-infested virgin forests into fertile agricultural farmlands.

Legends have it that the first migration of Nepalis to Bhutan happened along with the entourage of Guru Rimpoche, who came to Bhutan to preach Buddhism in the 8th century. Ramesh Dungel mentions an official agreement between the founding father of Bhutan, Shabdrung Rimpoche, and the Shah rulers of Gorkha about the resettlement of Nepalis in Bhutan. Michael Aris, one of the most authoritative historians of Bhutan, records the footprints of Nepali artisans in the construction of *dzongs* (forts) and *lakhangs* (receptacles of worship) in Thimphu during the reign of the Dharma Rajas in the 17th century (Aris 1994).

No Lhotshampa had ever imagined that their fertile lands would someday be confiscated by the Bhutanese government and they would be forcefully evicted from the land. They had cleared the forests and turned them into agricultural lands and villages. They had contributed significantly to the socio-economic development of the country. They had served in the army, police, royal bodyguards and bureaucracy; they had participated in conscripted labour forces for construction of roads, bridges, hospitals, schools and administrative headquarters. They were proud subjects of Bhutan. Their intercourse with the greater Nepali diaspora was limited. If at all, they were in touch with the people in the hills of Darjeeling and Kalimpong from where they had received education between the 1960s and the 1980s. Bhutan was their country and an overwhelming majority of them had never visited Nepal before becoming refugees.

What went wrong in the late 1980s that turned them into hapless refugees overnight was a great surprise to them and to the outside world. Bhutan was a little-known kingdom to most countries of the world. The presence of a large Nepali population in southern Bhutan was reported by some British administrators in the late 19th or early 20th centuries, but such reports were known to only a few researchers on Bhutan. The ruling elites in Kathmandu had little time to think about the Nepalis living outside Nepal; they were busy containing the voices of ethnic and class discontentment within Nepal, and, of course, fighting for democracy. Those who had power and resources had no interest in Lhotshampas and those who did not have resources were struggling for daily survival. That was when the Bhutan government began its Bhutanisation of the Lhotshampas. The community itself was ill-prepared to face such contingency and its inexperienced leadership collapsed under the military operations to flush them out of what they considered to be their homeland.

Making of Lhotshampa refugees

The refugee exodus in 1990 was triggered by the fear of the Bhutanese army, about whose brutality everyone in Bhutan was aware of. The Royal Government of Bhutan first denied the Nepalis the right to practise the Hindu religion, speak in Nepali, follow Nepali culture, and in some cases, even the citizenship rights. To this, the Nepalis of southern Bhutan demonstrated spontaneously in all the Nepali-dominated six southern districts, demanding redressal of their grievances.

The demonstrations took everyone by surprise, including the ruling elites. The rulers soon had their grip over the demonstrators by resorting to arbitrary arrests, perpetrating rapes and extortions and evicting the ordinary villagers with the help of the Bhutanese army. Over a period of three years, some 84,000 Bhutanese of Nepali ethnicity were compelled to flee the country, leaving behind what they had earned and inherited for more than a century. All this happened between September 1990 and the first half of 1993.

India did not provide shelter to the fleeing Bhutanese. Though there was initial support to them from local politicians of the border districts of Jalpaiguri, Darjeeling and Sikkim, it was neither strong nor sustained for long. The Bhutanese army, with the support of the local Indian authorities, intensified the eviction with more brutality. Eventually, the fleeing Bhutanese were compelled to knock at the gate of the Kankarvita outpost in Nepal for safety and security, to which Nepal responded positively.

Being unable to cope with the flow of Bhutanese refugees in Jhapa district, Nepal invited the United Nations High Commission of Refugees (UNHCR) to provide the much-needed humanitarian assistance (*Human Rights Watch* 2007). Initially, Nepal tried to engage Bhutan in 'quiet diplomacy' with the hope of finding a quick solution to the Bhutanese problem. After having failed to make any headway with Bhutan, the Government of Nepal sought assistance of the Indian government in persuading Bhutan to take back its citizens. India simply suggested that the solution to the Bhutanese refugee problem should be found by Nepal and Bhutan only. Bhutan and Nepal began to engage in bilateral discussions from April 1993.

The bilateral discussions dragged on for about a decade, which was full of turmoil, confusion and violence in Nepal. In 2000, the UNHCR chief, Madame Sadoka Ogata visited Bhutan and Nepal and announced in Goldhap Camp in Jhapa that Bhutan would take back its citizens (Dhakal 2007). From the very beginning, Bhutan had asserted that 'not all the people in the camps were Bhutanese citizens' (Dhakal and Strawn 1994). On one occasion, Dawa Tshering, the then foreign minister of Bhutan, stated that 'some 35,000 of the total population in the camps were Bhutanese citizen, but not everyone as registered by the UNHCR' (Dhakal and Strawn 1994). He instead alleged that 'Nepal was providing shelter to the poor Nepalis from northeast India to garner political support for the creation of Greater Nepal annexing the contiguous areas of Darjeeling, Sikkim, Bhutan and the Indian states of Arunachal Pradesh in the east and Uttarakhand and Himachal Pradesh in the west' (Dhakal and Strawn 1994).

Such statements were well-received by many countries even though there was no evidence of such claims. Unfortunately, Nepal agreed to Bhutan's proposal for categorisation of the refugees to: (a) Bhutanese who were evicted, (b) Bhutanese who emigrated, (c) Bhutanese with criminal records, and (d) non-Bhutanese people. This clearly was a tactical move on the part of Bhutan's government to de-franchise the citizenship rights of the Lhotshampas. Bhutan even coerced the innocent villagers to sign the 'voluntary migration form', which proved that they had left Bhutan out of their own choice (Chandrasekharan 2003).

Confused with contradictory versions of the refugee community and the Government of Bhutan on the reasons for fleeing Bhutan, the international community could not do anything. On the contrary, Bhutan's government hired noted writers from India such as Pramananda, Bhawanisen Das Gupta and Sunanda K. Datta-Ray to write in its favour and discredit the claim of Bhutanese refugees. Bhutan also engaged its embassy in Delhi to liaise with key opinion-makers in India to silence the voice of those who were in support of the refugee community. This handicapped the refugee leaders from moving forward with their democratic movement. Some scholars such as Michael Aris, A. C. Sinha, Michael Hutt, Tang Lay Lee and some human rights reporters did write about the legitimate claim of the Bhutanese refugees and the need for finding an honourable solution. However, their expert knowledge on Bhutan was no match for the meticulous propaganda the Bhutanese authorities carried out with the help of their sympathisers in India.

Initially, the international community was hesitant to intervene in the refugee issue for the fear of annoying India, which still controls Bhutan's foreign and defence policy. India decided to side with the regime in Thimphu in exchange for its exclusive rights to tap hydropower potential in Bhutan. Seeing no interest of other regional powers for the cause of Bhutanese refugees and realising India's intention to advance economic integration of Bhutan by taking advantage of the political situation, the international community decided to make the first diplomatic debut in the tiny Himalayan county, which was considered, until then, a backwater of India.

Thus, a high-level delegation from the United States of America and the European Union visited Bhutan soon after the visit of Madame Sagato Ogata. The international community managed to convince Bhutan to form a Joint Verification Team (JVT) with Nepal and establish the identification of refugees, including categorisation and harmonisation of position on each of the four agreed categories. As planned, the JVT was formed in 2001, and the verification of Khudunabari Camp was completed by 2003 (Table 16.1).

The JVT declared that over 75 per cent of the 12,181 refugees at Khudunabari camp were Bhutanese citizens (Hutt 2005). This percentage could have been much higher had the Royal Government of Bhutan not confiscated the documentary evidences from the refugees at the time of eviction or if documents were not lost during the escape to Nepal. In addition, this camp was established towards the end of the refugee flow to provide shelter to Bhutanese refugees who had spent some years in the

Table 16.1 Verification results of the Bhutanese refugees in Khudunabari Camp by the JVT (as of 31 December 2002)

	Families	Individuals	%
Bonafide Bhutanese	74	293	2.5
Emigrants	2,182	8,595	70.5
Non-Bhutanese	817	2,948	24.2
Criminals	85	347	2.8
Total	**3,158**	**12,183**	**100**

Source: Hutt, 2005

bordering state of Assam, Bengal and Sikkim before entering Nepal. If the verification exercise had continued in other camps, the percentage of refugees eligible to return to Bhutan would have increased over 90 per cent even with strict adherence to the documentary evidences as a proof of residence in Bhutan (Dhakal 2006).

Despite many flaws in establishing the verification and categorisation process, there was a hope in the refugee community that they would be able to return to Bhutan. Unfortunately, this hope was dashed to the ground when the Bhutanese JVT members returned to Bhutan on protest against an inappropriate behaviour of the refugees when the delegation visited Khudunabari camp to announce the terms and conditions of repatriation. The Nepal government permitted the Bhutanese team to enter Khudunabari camp without proper security arrangement, and this gave an opportunity to the refugees to express their dissatisfaction, which eventually ended up in a scuffle. It was reported that the terms and conditions for repatriation were very annoying for the refugees, leading to their discontentment.

Bhutan demanded from Nepal an investigation report on the incident. Making an excuse of this incident, Bhutan refused to resume the bilateral talks for repatriation. Several hundred acres of land and other property in six districts of southern Bhutan belonging to over 100,000 southern Bhutanese refugees were distributed to eastern and northern Bhutanese families under the resettlement scheme of the Royal Government of Bhutan (Basu 2009). Bhutan also renamed the villages and districts of southern Bhutan, eliminating any evidence of Nepali culture, tradition and history from the land.

The international community worked hard to put together the JVT and the verification exercise, but was soon frustrated with the evolving situation. The rise of Maoists in Nepal, end of the institution of monarchy in Nepal and the growing frustration of the refugee community flashed a danger signal to the international community. In the meantime, Bhutan began to project itself as potential victim of Nepali insurgency and design of 'Greater Nepal'. This led the international community to come up with the concept of 'burden-sharing mechanism', in which the USA, Australia, Canada, New Zealand, the Netherlands, Denmark and Norway would absorb as many as 80,000 Bhutanese refugees in Nepal, and other members of OECD, namely, Switzerland, Germany and Japan would share the financial burden of the third-country resettlement. The international community then believed that Nepal could be enticed later to absorb the remaining refugees if Bhutan could be convinced to repatriate a token number of refugees as a face-saving measure. Evidently, this was the assumption of the international community when it approached the Government of Nepal for the third-country resettlement option.

Seeing no hope of getting India and the international community involved in the resolution of Bhutanese refugee problem, Nepal could not turn down the offer. In addition, there was interest in a section of Bhutanese refugees to press for third-country resettlement option though this idea was not accepted by all the refugees, particularly the leaders. Nepal agreed to permit the international community to set up the International Office of Migration (IOM) in Kathmandu and Jhapa and to provide one-way travel documents to refugees seeking third-country resettlement.

India took no interest in responding to this new development about the Bhutanese refugees though it was taking place at its door. There was hardly any support to the call of refugee leaders for a careful examination of the third-country resettlement plan, taking into consideration religious and cultural background of the refugees, including its long-term implications for the region.

All this unfolded at a time when Nepal was going through a major political crisis. Nepal could not stand against the international pressure for third-country resettlement, especially when the international assistance for the upkeep of Bhutanese refugees was drying up. Given the indifferent attitude of the neighbouring countries, the Government of Nepal decided to open the door for third-country resettlement option while assuring the refugee community that the country would keep the bilateral talks on board and continue trying to engage Bhutan for the repatriation of remaining refugees who wish to return to their place in Bhutan. The third-country resettlement programme began in 2008.

Table 16.2 Bhutanese refugee population in overseas countries (as of 31 August 2011)

Country	Male	Female	Total
Australia	1,475	1,428	2,903
Canada	1,699	1,737	3,436
Denmark	230	258	488
The Netherlands	114	119	233
New Zealand	281	295	576
Norway	154	219	373
Great Britain	53	58	111
USA	22,303	21,686	43,989
Total	26,309	25,800	52,109

Sources: Refugee Coordination Office, Government of Nepal, Chandragadi, Jhapa, Nepal, 2011

Thus far, some 52,000 refugees have left Nepal for third-country resettlement (Table 16.2).

Table 16.2 clearly shows that the USA is the prime destination for Bhutanese refugees. Table 16.3 below shows the details of their settlement in the country.

In Canada, the refuges have settled in English- as well as French-speaking areas. In Australia, they are resettled from the southernmost island of Tasmania to the Western desert of Perth. In Denmark, Norway and the Netherlands, they are struggling hard to learn the local languages in order to be comfortable with day-to-day activities.

The people who lived as a close-knit society in southern Bhutan are experiencing cultural shock and identity crisis. Those who have passed the age of 50 are finding it difficult to adjust to the new environments. Their religious beliefs, cultural practices and value systems are facing the threat of extinction.

There are also some positive aspects of the third-country resettlement programme. The able-bodied members in refugee families are employed, senior members are in social benefits payroll and the children are attending better schools. For brighter students, opportunities are open to dream about education at Harvard, Yale or Princeton. They are in the land of opportunities, where hard work pays. Some of the refugee families have begun buying homes, almost all the resettled families own cars and they have begun to pool resources to establish businesses or save for the future. A new generation of community leaders, scholars

Table 16.3 Resettlement of Bhutanese refugees in the USA (as on 12 October 2012)

Destination	2008	2009	2010	2011	2012	Total
Arizona	293	918	547	234	671	2,663
California	259	443	217	152	180	1,251
Colorado	252	588	565	310	840	2,555
Connecticut	0	5	78	45	108	236
Florida	109	207	126	59	136	637
Georgia	558	1,004	715	425	1,525	4,227
Idaho	174	312	335	78	283	1,182
Illinois	145	404	477	210	745	1,981
Indiana	0	0	21	12	53	86
Iowa	35	210	71	38	140	494
Kansas	55	89	107	49	186	486
Kentucky	94	383	314	159	612	1562
Louisiana	0	0	13	0	20	33
Maryland	172	197	269	203	757	1,598
Massachusetts	112	389	402	197	848	1,948
Michigan	100	342	295	123	482	1,342
Minnesota	61	105	204	64	276	710
Missouri	80	168	179	59	404	890
Nebraska	0	54	90	90	381	615
Nevada	26	85	65	5	66	247
New Hampshire	275	470	385	147	538	1,815
New Jersey	31	186	64	50	21	352
New Mexico	15	20	27	14	42	118
New York	404	1,116	1,006	566	1,926	5,018
North Carolina	142	404	484	229	1,003	2,262
North Dakota	121	202	217	129	584	1,253
Ohio	264	509	632	274	1,829	3,508
Oregon	83	131	127	59	228	628
Pennsylvania	230	781	1,190	937	3,524	6,662
Rhode Island	0	29	73	28	95	225
South Carolina	0	4	1	2	38	45
South Dakota	40	105	118	81	456	800
Tennessee	63	330	211	96	454	1,154
Texas	430	1,646	1,249	628	1,952	5,905
Utah	140	286	251	136	317	1,130
Vermont	132	158	189	127	474	1,080
Virginia	122	516	433	305	870	2,246
Washington	303	596	510	232	654	2,295
Wisconsin	0	10	60	66	116	252
Total	5,320	13,452	12,363	6,625	23,834	61,617

Sources: US State Department, Government of USA, Washington, DC, 2012

Table 16.4 Bhutanese refugee population in Nepal (as of 31 August 2011)

Camps	Male	Female	Total
Beldangi	16,946	17,911	34,857
Khudunabari	4,512	4,480	8,992
Sanischare	5,545	5,756	11,301
Timai	2,884	3,001	5,885
Outcamps	20	36	56
Total	29,907	31,184	61,091

Sources: Refugee Coordination Office, Government of Nepal, Chandragadi, Jhapa, Nepal, 2011

and journalists is in the making. They have the potential to play vital roles for their country in future.

What is important is for the refugee leadership to think about the 63,000 people still in the camps although the UNHCR is claiming that more than 80 per cent of the population has filled the third-country resettlement form (Table 16.4).

The Goldhap camp has been closed and the UNHCR is in the process of closing down Khudunabari and Timai camps. The remaining population will be housed either in Beldangi or Sanischare camps until a permanent solution is found for them.

The best option for Bhutanese refugees was to return to Bhutan, where their forefathers had lived and died. They would have been at home with the environment, the spirits and the cultural milieu. Not allowing them to return to southern Bhutan is a clear violation of their fundamental human rights. The eviction of one-seventh of the country's population belonging to the ethnic Nepalis is comparable to genocide. Human rights specialists have described the exodus of Bhutanese refugees as the 'Bhutan brand' of ethnic cleansing. Bhutan achieved this by humouring the international community with royal hospitality, expensive gifts, the concept of gross national happiness and its carefully crafted foreign policy of pleasing the giant neighbours. The ethnic cleansing in Bhutan has not stopped, yet the world is quiet about it. Even after eviction of 84,000 Lhotshampas, they constitute about 30 per cent of the total population of Bhutan. The future of this population remains uncertain unless their leaders come up with an appropriate strategy to secure their future in Bhutan.

During the last two decades, Bhutan has not only beaten Nepal in diplomacy, but also humiliated it and successfully kept itself protected from any pressure from the international community. Nepal could do nothing even after 15 rounds of bilateral talks with Bhutan and after pilot verification that proved over 75 per cent of the population in Khudunabari camp to be Bhutanese citizens, and after absorbing all kinds of allegations about harbouring the ambition of 'Greater Nepal'. This was largely possible because of the political instability in Nepal and inconsistency in the positions taken by different political parties of Nepal on the issue of Bhutanese refugees. The Nepali Congress agreed to categorisation of Bhutanese refugees, the United Marxist-Leninist (UML) and Rastriya Prajatantra Party (RPP) tried to correct the wrongs in the categorisation agreements, the Moaists did not make any serious attempt to engage Bhutan on the issue of Bhutanese refugees. There is no national policy of Nepal towards its diasporic people and no wherewithal to take any action on their behalf.

On the contrary, the Bhutanese refugee leadership failed to muster the required support of Nepalis in India and Nepal to take forward their democratic movement. The leaders in Nepal and Nepali leaders in India knew less about the Lhotshampas and cared even lesser about them. Taking advantage of this scenario, the Government of Bhutan invited some important Nepali leaders and scholars of India to Bhutan, accorded them the status of state guests, gave them royal audience and made them permanently obliged to the kingdom with their unique hospitality.

The plea of Nepal was defeatist; it believed that nothing could be done about the refugees unless India took a stand in favour of them. J. N. Dixit, India's foreign secretary, had surprised the diplomatic corps in Kathmandu when he announced in 1995 that 'Mother India would ultimately take care of the Bhutanese refugee problem'. This statement gave a lot of confidence to Nepal and the refugee community at large. They interpreted his statement to mean that India would eventually resolve the problem of Bhutanese refugees. India could perhaps have done so, but Bhutan pre-empted this by engaging quietly the People's Republic of China in signing the 1998 bilateral treaty, giving an indirect signal to India that Bhutan is no longer bound by the treaty of 1949, and it could exercise its right to seek China's assistance for socio-economic development and defence.

History of denial

The remittance-dependent Rana regime had compelled the out-migration of Nepalis as soldiers, milk suppliers, coolies on roads and tea gardens during the British era. The self-indulging Ranas took little interest in the long-term welfare of their subjects, either within or outside the country. The panchayat regime continued with the legacy of the Rana regime and did not make any serious effort to put together a 'think tank' who could provide policy prescriptions on cultural or religious interests of the diasporic Nepalis. On hindsight, the Bhutanese refugee problem would never have surfaced in the late 1980s had Nepal taken cognizance of the presence of a large ethnic Nepali population in southern Bhutan and engaged Bhutan diplomatically. The Nepali community has always and everywhere been found ill-equipped with resources and ideas to handle unexpected situations. It was, therefore, a combination of circumstances that forced the Lhotsampas to settle in four continents, which is seen as a curse for the elderly, and a blessing for the youth.

Conclusion

The refugee leadership has realised that bringing justice to Bhutanese refugees is an uphill task. Third-country resettlement has added a new dimension to the already complex problem. One could draw parallels between the issues of Lhotshampas with some of the still unresolved political problems, such as in Armenia and Cyprus Island. The Armenian people were forced to flee their country by the Ottoman rulers in 1915, because of which, there are more Armenians living outside the country today than inside. Their struggle has been to get recognition of the 1915 genocide in Armenia by the Ottoman Army, to which there has been little governmental support either from the US or the European Union. More recently, the situation seems changing in their favour, as the European Human Rights Commission questioned the application of the Turkish Government for the European Union on the basis of its human rights violation to the Armenian people. Their strategy has been to meticulously keep chronological records of their genocide in museums and memorials while occasionally organising social events to remind the international community about the injustice meted out to them. There is a similar ongoing campaign by the Turkish Cypriots to highlight their case for compensation. The Cyprus Island was partitioned between the Turkish and Greek Cyprus after the ethnic clash of 1974. One could see ghost towns in both sides of the island, and the Cypriots have been negotiating for compensation for lost lives and properties.

Political issues seldom die, and the Bhutanese refugee issue is also likely to last for a long time. The Lhotshampas had contributed a lot to the building of modern Bhutan; they cleared the forests to convert them into productive agricultural farms; they built roads, hospitals, schools and forts. If they still have no right to live there as equal citizens of the country, they do not deserve to be driven out of the country overnight like wild animals either.

The Lhotshampa refugee community wants an 'honourable solution', which includes, among others, an apology by the Government of Bhutan for the atrocities perpetrated to them and their recognition as Non-Resident Bhutanese (NRB), including compensation to them for the loss of life and properties. The 'honourable solution' also includes repatriation to their own homesteads in Bhutan with restoration of their citizenship rights. How and when that will happen are, however, difficult questions given the fact that they have no one to turn to except themselves, and if the recent developments are anything to go by, the 'honourable solution' may take decades to come their way.

One of their biggest failures has been lack of unity and an effective and experienced leadership. The petty factional politics that overshadowed the democratic movement in Bhutan has resurfaced among the resettled refugees in overseas countries. In the US, for instance, the refugees have two national-level organisations: Association of Bhutanese in America (ABA) and Organization of Bhutanese Community in America (OBCA). The objective of ABA is to work as an NGO to promote integration of the resettled refugees in America, while that of OBCA is to promote Lhotshampa culture and tradition among the resettled population. Neither of the two organisations is willing to undertake advocacy for an 'honourable solution' of Bhutanese refugees. They are busy saving resources, adding household assets and making themselves employable in the corporate job markets.

Similar organisations have been formed in Norway, Denmark, the Netherlands, England, Canada, Australia and New Zealand. At present, their stated objectives are organising activities for meeting the cultural and religious needs of the resettled people. It is too early to say how these organisations would work to establish links with Bhutanese organisations that are operating in exile, or, those formed inside the country with a commitment to restoration of human rights and inclusive democracy in Bhutan. Their future trajectory also depends on their present status as people who now need a visa to meet their relatives in both Nepal and India. They also need a visa to visit their own villages in Bhutan from where they were evicted overnight.

References

Aris, Michael. 1994. *The Raven Crown: The Origins of Buddhist Monarchy in Bhutan*. London: Serindia.
Basu, Pratim Sibaji. 2009. *The Fleeing People in South Asia: Selections from Refugee Watch*. London: Anthem Press.

Chandrasekharan, S. 2003. 'Bhutan: Forward Movement in the "Refugee Problem"?' South Asia Analysis Group, February 13.

Dhakal, D. N. S. 2006. *Genesis of the Bhutanese Crisis, Creation of Refugee Problem, and Possible Solution*. Jhapa: Bhutan National Democratic Party.

Dhakal, D. N. S. 2007. 'Bhutan: Democratization amidst Protracted Refugee Crisis'. Brussels, Pamphlet, 8 November.

Dhakal, D. N. S. and S. Strawn. 1994. *Movement in Exile*. New Delhi: Nirala Publication.

Human Rights Watch. 2007. 'Last Hope: The Need for Durable Solutions for Bhutanese Refugees in Nepal and India'. Vol. 19, No. 7, May.

Hutt, Michael. 2005. 'The Bhutanese Refugees: Between Verification, Repatriation and Royal Realpolitik', *Peace and Democracy in South Asia*, 1(1), January.

17

RIOTS, 'RESIDENCE' AND REPATRIATION

The Singapore Gurkhas

Hema Kiruppalini

Introduction

The Singapore Gurkha Contingent (SGC) located beside the Mount Vernon crematorium grimly mirrors the nature of their service and memories of Singapore. Notwithstanding superficial understanding about the role of the Gurkhas as legendary warriors, very little is known about the community even among Singaporeans. This is a result of the elusive nature of their service and residence in Singapore, and the fact that any data about the community are shrouded in mystery. This chapter aims to unearth the hitherto understudied experiences of Gurkha families, and in doing so, to demonstrate how the SGC figures in Singapore government's wider initiative to sustain a multiracial and harmonious society.

The SGC was officially formed on 9 April 1949. However, the origins of the Gurkhas in Singapore pre-date their official inception and need to be postulated against British Malaya's early interactions with the Gurkhas. In short, Britain's strategic involvement in the Far East witnessed the recruitment of Gurkhas to Malaya during World War II (1939–45) and the Japanese Occupation (1942–45), and thereafter, in the immediate post-war period, when the Gurkhas became a part of Britain's Cold War strategy as they were deployed to fight communist insurgents during the Malayan Emergency (1948–60). The historical trajectory of the Gurkhas in Singapore and the early origins of the community here are to be understood within the broader context of Britain's involvement in post-war Malaya and how they were a means by which the British Commonwealth influence was sustained.

One of the critical factors contributing to the formal recruitment of Gurkhas in Singapore in the late 1940s was the need for an alternative special force to replace the Sikh Contingent that formed an integral part of the armed police force. According to Scott Leathart, who commanded the Gurkha Contingent in Singapore for 10 years, the pre-war Sikh Contingent had disintegrated in dishonour under the impact of foreign invasion, and in 1948, the Nepal government sanctioned the recruitment of its nationals. Leathart explains that the Gurkha Contingent, as it was to be called, was to have a British Officer (subsequently increased to two) and 149 Gurkhas were employed.[1]

Over the years, the recruitment of Gurkhas has increased significantly. At present, it is estimated that there are about 2,000 Gurkhas serving under the Singapore Police Force under the Ministry of Home Affairs. Together with their families, there are approximately 5,000 to 6,000 of them residing in Mount Vernon Camp, which is an approximation based on data collated from informants and some secondary sources.

Colonial imagination about the martial races and the representation of Gurkhas as warriors endowed with innate attributes par excellence is a discourse that has fed into the construction of the Gurkha Contingent as a neutral force in Singapore. This perception has, for decades, predicated its function as a special force suitable for the policing of a multiracial Singapore. The notion that the Gurkhas will exercise impartiality in an event of a racial riot has underpinned the need for their families to reside as a gated community within the boundaries of the Mount Vernon Camp, and thereafter, to be repatriated to Nepal subsequently, as they are not allowed to take Singaporean citizenship.

Methodology

Broadly speaking, there is a lack of data directly relevant to the Singapore Gurkhas and this was further compounded by the inaccessibility to the information concerning the Gurkha Contingent. Given their predominant role in Singapore's national security, acquiring data on the Gurkhas has been an uphill task. The issue of confidentiality was constantly raised by ministry officials and potential Gurkha informants. My attempt to go through the formal channel of acquiring data from the Singapore government bodies was largely unsuccessful. I had initially sent out emails to the Ministry of Foreign Affairs, Ministry of Home Affairs, Singapore Police Force, Immigration and Checkpoints Authority and Ministry of Manpower. Emails boomeranged with replies that stated 'we will not be able to accede to your request for an interview with Gurkha officers',[2] 'we have carefully considered your request but regret that we are unable to assist you in the matter'[3] and 'we are unable to provide you the data and statistics on the Nepalese community in Singapore'.[4] Only the Ministry of Home Affairs replied to my query in a short paragraph that shed light on the neutral role of the Gurkha Contingent. Research on Singapore Gurkhas, therefore, necessitated grounded fieldwork in both Singapore and Nepal. I initially tried to interview the serving Gurkhas in Singapore. Unfortunately, most of them were afraid of breaching the rules and regulations defining the Gurkha Contingent. One possibility that emerged was to turn towards the repatriated Gurkhas in Nepal.

In the beginning stages of my fieldwork in Nepal, it was important to develop a sense of trust among Gurkha families due to their unfamiliarity with me. One of them frankly said, 'I will meet you but I will not tell you everything that you may need'.[5] Another informant said, 'Actually, our pension might get affected if we defame the Singapore government in any way. Sharing our grievances outside of the Gorkhāli community is discouraged.'[6] However, these were minor setbacks, as all the other Gurkhas who I interviewed warmly welcomed me to their homes, and were more than happy to share their experiences in Singapore. I often received special treatment simply because, as most of them would nostalgically tell me, 'You are from Singapore, and we were all there once . . .' Furthermore, there was an element of curiosity among Gurkha families as to why a Singaporean, and that too a non-Nepali, would be interested in their migration history and experiences. To a considerable extent, conversing with them in basic Nepali aided in bridging the gap and developing a sense of trust within the community. My fieldwork in Nepal in 2009 spanned approximately two months, with most of my time spent in Kathmandu, and a fortnight in Pokhara. I returned to Nepal again in 2011 to visit the Gurkhas I interviewed previously and to meet other retirees as well. In all, I interviewed about 25 repatriated Gurkhas, with their families included in some cases, and this chapter largely draws from that experience in Nepal.

Gurkha contingent as a neutral force

According to the Ministry of Home Affairs in Singapore, the Gurkha Contingent was formed as part of the Singapore Police Force on 9 April 1949. From the onset, they played a crucial role in safeguarding and policing Singapore. During the 1950s and 1960s, the Gurkha Contingent was deployed for containing some of Singapore's biggest riots, such as the Maria Hertogh riot (1950), the Hock Lee Bus riots (1955), the Chinese Middle School riots (1956) and the 1964 racial riots.[7] Over the years, as Singapore transformed into a global city-state, the Contingent also evolved. In 1978, Changi Prison and Moon Crescent Centre were guarded by an elite Gurkha unit known as the Prison Guard Unit, and this was the first time that any country had enlisted Gurkhas as prison wardens.[8] The Gurkhas' principal roles in contemporary Singapore are to act as a specialist guard force at key installations and to serve as a force supporting police operations. They have also provided security for major events such as the International Monetary Fund and World Bank meetings in 2006 and the 13th ASEAN Summit in 2007.[9] Increasingly so, the Gurkhas assist the police in guarding Singapore against terrorism.

Newspaper articles published in Singapore between the 1940s and 1950s aver the early function of the Gurkha Contingent as an anti-riot squad. A *Straits Times* article published in 1949 states, 'Gurkhas were built into a single contingent to be used exclusively for anti-riot purposes, and one hundred and fifty Gurkhas were undergoing training as Singapore's future police anti-riot squad'.[10] Two years later, another press release served to emphasise that the training that the Gurkhas undergo is designed to enable them to assist in the maintenance of internal security and restore order in the event of riots.[11] Reinforcing the apolitical function of the Gurkha Contingent in Singapore, the Ministry of Home Affairs informed that the presence of the Gurkha Contingent as a 'neutral force during the early years after Singapore's independence was crucial as local police officers were often perceived to be biased towards their own ethnic groups when handling racial disturbances'.[12]

For reasons of neutrality, coupled with their role in guarding key facilities and working as guards for prominent political persons in Singapore, the Contingent has been residing as a gated community for over 60 years. When asked how they regard their role within the Singapore Police Force, many Gurkha informants replied, 'we are here (Singapore) as an impartial force', and in the light of this perceived function, majority of them consciously seek to maintain a distance from the Singapore citizenry. In principle, they have the freedom to interact with the locals and develop friendships. However, they are institutionally disallowed to integrate into Singaporean society and take up citizenship.

A product of a colonial immigration heritage, independent Singapore continued to pride on the Gurkhas as an elite militia. Colonial discourse on martial races and the characterisation of Gurkhas as supra-talented soldiers contributed to shaping the rationale behind the construction of the

Gurkha Contingent as a neutral force in Singapore. The 'martial race' theory expounds that war-like individuals inherit martiality through blood from their ancestors, and they are found in hilly regions with a tough terrain. This describes the physical environment in hilly regions of Nepal, from where they originate.[13] In short, these factors have contributed to the idolisation of the Gurkhas as a 'martial race'.

The branding of Gurkhas as brave, loyal and legendary warriors gained currency when they became an ubiquitous part of British Malaya during World War II and the immediate post-war period. In particular, Gurkhas made an indelible impact on Singapore's first prime minister, Mr. Lee Kuan Yew, a prominent political figure often associated with the recruitment of Gurkhas in Singapore. He wrote in his memoir that 'There were some soldiers who won my respect and admiration . . . The Gurkhas were like the Highlanders. They, too, marched erect, unbroken and doughty in defeat. I secretly cheered them. They left a life-long impression on me. As a result, the Singapore government has employed a Gurkha company for its anti-riot police squad from the 1960s to this day'.[14] They are popularly known to work as guards for Mr. Lee Kuan Yew and for other key ministers in Singapore, and they continue to do so even today. Their impartial identity is further highlighted by him thus: 'When I returned to Oxley Road, Gurkha policemen (recruited by the British from Nepal) were posted as sentries. To have either Chinese policeman shooting Malays or Malay policemen shooting Chinese would have caused widespread repercussions. The Gurkhas on the other hand were *neutral*, besides having the reputation for total discipline and loyalty' (emphasis added).[15]

The Gurkhas are valourised for their martial qualities, and undying loyalty towards Singapore. As part of the neutrality rhetoric developed by the state, these legendary warriors are trophy Gurkhas as only a select few hundred from a pool of thousands are qualified to render their services to Singapore after a gruelling six-month-long recruitment procedure that is conducted under the aegis of Britain. Furthermore, in contemporary Singapore, the Gurkha Contingent continues to be commanded by a British officer and this is a tradition that has remained unchanged since its inception. The impact of British colonial representations of the Gurkhas on Singapore has indeed been very significant.

Residence at Mount Vernon Camp

Since its humble beginnings, the Mount Vernon Camp in Singapore has functioned as a self-sufficient compound to make Gurkha families feel at home. Over the years, the Singapore government has been magnanimous in its efforts to expand the Camp and to provide modern facilities, and yet, project a distinctly Nepali outlook. Much of Joo Seng and neighbouring areas were relinquished to expand the parameters of the now 19-hectare camp.[16] The sprawling premise of the Camp is located in the vicinity of a residential estate and is surrounded by public housing, schools, and so on. However, the high fencing with barbed wires that encircles the Camp and the various signboards alerting 'No Photography, Entry for Gurkha Personnel Only, Protected Place, etc.' lucidly draws attention to the gated nature of the community's residence in Singapore. However, Gurkha families are not confined within the camp and it is common to see them in shopping areas along Little India and also at the East Coast Beach, enjoying a picnic outing with their families.

Interviews with informants and the pictorial repository they shared reflected the changes that have taken place within the boundaries of the Camp and the renovations that have occurred. From short four-storey blocks during the early years of Singapore to high-rise flats; from a modest Hindu temple to a majestic and traditionally architectured Nepali Hindu temple; and, from basic facilities during the founding years of the Gurkha Contingent to fully furnished house units, the entire landscape of the Mount Vernon Camp has witnessed manifold changes. The respective high-rise flats with Nepali architectural roofing are each named after popular towns, districts, rivers, and places in Nepal (e.g. Pokhara Garden, Everest Heights, Babai, Makala, etc.). Interestingly, Everest Heights and Pokhara Garden have been structured to form 'G' and 'C' respectively. From an aerial viewpoint they form the initials GC – Gurkha Contingent.

Apart from the Gurkha headquarters, the camp also includes an officers' mess, a family welfare centre, a clinic and a mini mart. Furthermore, it has a large range of sporting amenities that include a large swimming pool, gymnasium, basketball court, tennis court, soccer field, track and field stadium and some playgrounds. In an effort to cater to Gurkha children, the Camp has a Gurkha Children School (popularly termed as *bhitra* school, which translates to 'inside' school), and a GC Boys' Club and Girls' Club, where *bhānjās* and *bhānjīs*[17] can interact and organise dance, games and cultural shows. Assistant Superintendent of Police Kumar succinctly conveyed that 'At Mount Vernon, it feels like mini Nepal but only we are living in an advanced Nepal with all the modern facilities. It is a different type of Nepal since we are in a different geographical town'.[18]

The Singapore government has made concerted efforts to foster a Gurkha-family-oriented policy. A conducive environment for Gurkha families is created right from the early beginnings of their service and regardless of their rank. However, this is not the case in other countries.[19] To make them feel at home, they celebrate various festivals such as Dasaĩ, Tihār and Maghe Sankranti inside the camp so that they will always remember Nepal. Assistant Superintendent of Police Gurung said, 'We never forgot home (Nepal) while we served in Singapore . . . we celebrated festivals to remember our homeland'.[20] During the festive occasion of Vijayā Dashami, special arrangements are made so that rituals such as the sacrificial slaughtering of the goat can be observed within the premise of the Camp. There is also a Brahmin from Nepal who works as a priest in the temple of the Camp.

On the one hand, the Camp alludes to the magnanimous nature of the Singapore government while, on the other, the state-sponsored initiative to give the Camp a distinctly Nepali outlook shows a strategy adopted to ensure the preservation of Gurkha identity. One of the retirees said: 'At the Camp, you are within your Gorkhāli community and ironically, most of the time you will not even realise that you are in Singapore. You are looking at the same people who are speaking the same language . . . It is only when you go out of the Camp that you will realise that you are in Singapore . . .'.[21]

Singaporeans are strictly disallowed from entering the Camp unless they have an invitation. In one incident, I was accompanying a couple from Nepal who was visiting their relative inside the Camp. Unfortunately, upon finding out that I was a Singaporean, I was politely told by a Gurkha at the gate: 'Sorry, but you are Singaporean, and foreigners are not allowed'. The Gurkha Contingent in the Camp acts like an independent territory with defined rules and regulations that demarcate the 'insider' and 'outsider' parameters between Gurkhas and Singaporeans. This ethnic enclave is a result of state policies geared towards avoiding the interactions between Gurkhas and Singaporeans. The boundary of the Camp not only serves to barricade their residence, but also psychologically defines the 'outsider' position of Gurkhas.

Furthermore, state policies pertaining to them are aimed at ensuring that they remain sojourners, and thus, ironically treating them as an exquisite and yet dispensable and renewable source of labour. They are immediately repatriated upon completion of their long service in Singapore, and, as part of the overall policy, their men are strictly disallowed to marry Singaporean women. Though formed under the Singapore Police Force, it is evident that the Gurkhas are themselves 'policed' in various ways by the Singapore state as there are special rules and regulations governing the Gurkha Contingent and Gurkha families.

Repatriation to Nepal

Coping with challenges

The differential impact of service in Singapore on Gurkhas is striking. There are various activities that they engage in upon repatriation, from embarking on a second career to doing *samāj sewa* (social service). For them, one main priority upon return is to invest in property in Nepal with the Central Provident Fund (CPF) savings that they earned while serving in Singapore. Usually, the arrangements for purchasing land to build a home are made during the periodic visits that they make to Nepal during their service. After every three years of their term in Singapore, they return to Nepal for a six-month-long leave. Generally, the Singapore Gurkhas are about 45 years old when they are repatriated to Nepal – a considerably young age and it is no surprise that many of them seek re-employment in other countries. Since the wives are disallowed to work in Singapore during the period of their husband's service, the husbands inevitably become sole breadwinners of their families. The continued need to support their family after retirement and to fund their children's studies overseas propels many of them to undertake risky security-related jobs abroad.

Informants contend that there is a mismatch between the training they have received in Singapore and what they can do in Nepal. There are retired Singapore Gurkhas who, together with their British officers, have set up private recruitment agencies that hire and facilitate the re-employment of many retired Gurkhas in countries such as Brunei, Afghanistan, Iraq and Hong Kong for security-related services. Re-employment in these countries allows them to undertake a job that is familiar to them. One informant jovially remarked 'When we retire from Singapore, our family also retires, since our children cannot continue to study in Singapore. When our children have to go overseas to study, we also have to go overseas for a second career'.[22]

Resigned to the unique terms and conditions of their contract in Singapore, most Gurkha families have conformed to rules and regulations implemented by the Singapore state by seeking ingenious ways to cope with the challenges confronting them upon repatriation. However, the Singapore Gurkha Pensioners' Association (SGPA) in Nepal, a welfare organisation that addresses the concerns of retired Gurkhas from Singapore, has time and again raised their grievances to Singapore authorities. Some of the requests raised by the SGPA include: a review of pension revisions to Gurkhas, provision of widows' pension, re-employment in Singapore for repatriated Gurkhas, increment in inflation allowance, citizenship or permanent residency to Singapore-born Gurkha children, and extension of student visas to Gurkha children after their fathers' service ends.

The appeals made by the SGPA needle the very rubric of Singapore's national immigration policy concerning the Gurkha Contingent. Responding positively to the grievances raised by the SGPA would, however, amount to affecting the operational effectiveness of the Gurkha Contingent and imply a radical change in the state's national immigration policy pertaining to Gurkha families.

Sustaining Singaporean identity in Nepal

The migration trajectory of the Gurkhas to Singapore represents an anomaly in terms of trying to tease out ideas of home, belonging and identity as they live in Singapore for a substantial period of time before experiencing repatriation. From the commencement of their service there, special conditions are laid on them as the citizens of Nepal. The Gurkhas know that they will eventually return to Nepal and the elaborate initiatives adopted by the Singapore government vis-à-vis the Mount Vernon Camp also act to undermine the development of a Singaporean identity. Yet, for having served in Singapore for a substantial period of time, there is a pervasive sense of loyalty, attachment and an element of 'Singaporean-ness' among many retired Gurkhas and their families. This feeling is particularly accentuated among Gurkha children who are born and bred there.

The linguistic orientations of the Singapore Gurkhas and their families also provide an evidence of their sense of connection to a country where they lived for a long period of time. Apart from some Nepali, conversations with them were peppered in *Singlish* (Singapore English) and a smattering of other local languages spoken in Singapore. Among the older generation of Gurkhas who served during the early years in Singapore, they were able to converse in Malay, a language they learnt during the early years of Singapore. Conversing in Malay, Inspector Dhanpathi and Sergeant Tulsi spoke about their changing linguistic orientations during their years of employment in Singapore from learning Malay to English and how they picked up the languages in an effort to adapt to the requirements of their service. In spite of the number of years that have passed since their repatriation to Nepal, many old retirees are still able to speak a language that they had picked up in Singapore, thus nurturing their intrinsic ties with the country.

Thus, the Gurkhas have a strong sense of attachment to Singapore. Corporal Dhoj is not able to forget Singapore because he went there at a very young age and he continues to be connected to the country by reading online newspapers.[23] Assistant Superintendent of Police Kumar asserts that he loves Singapore more than Nepal because he was a former Singapore *bhānjā* (nephew) turned Singapore Gurkha.[24] Corporal Tek, an earlier retiree, said that he felt very sad upon repatriation and since he continued to receive his pension from Singapore, he felt like a Singaporean.[25] In the course of settling down in Nepal after retirement, many of them long to return to Singapore.

The affective bond that the Gurkhas have with Singapore is evident in the environmental landscape of Nepal. In Pokhara, for instance, an entire locality is named after Singapore. Singapure Tole is an area that is home to numerous repatriated Singapore Gurkhas. There is no 'Britain Tole', 'Brunei Tole' or 'Hong Kong Tole' there although there are Gurkhas who served in those countries too. The existence of 'Singapure Tole' demonstrates the topophilic bond that the retired Gurkhas have with Singapore. It was further observed that their homes often contained framed pictures depicting Singapore-style studio photos of their family hung on the wall, including various displays of memorabilia such as the Merlion, Singapore-inspired wall runners and other mementos. Upon repatriation, many Gurkha families have created an enclave for themselves by vicariously living in Singapore through the objects of decorations in their houses. Paradoxically, just as how locals in Singapore regard the Mount Vernon Camp as mini-Nepal, local Nepalese stepping foot into the houses of the repatriated Gurkhas enter a space that is defined by memories of Singapore.

Furthermore, inspired by the Singapore model of integrated community living, various ex-Gurkhas in their effort to engage in *samāj sewa* have initiated the development of community halls in Kathmandu and Pokhara that resemble Singapore-style local community centres. Various ex-Gurkhas raise money and build them at their respective localities to provide facilities such as a badminton court, large stage and rooms to accommodate their relatives who come from far-off villages. Such centres also serve as a venue to settle intra-community disputes, educate children and host weddings, funerals, games and sports.

The interior decorations of their houses in Nepal, the Singapure Tole in Pokhara and their linguistic orientations serve to sustain a Singapore an identity among Gurkha families. Most importantly, the anecdotal stories about Singapore narrated miles away in Nepal elucidate the forgotten voices of the Gurkhas who are themselves a reflection of the history that has shaped a multi-racial and modern Singapore.

A Gurkha diaspora in Singapore?

The Singapore Gurkhas and their families bring to the fore a lacuna apparent in the existing conceptual framework of diaspora studies. The elusive nature of their 'residence' in Singapore marks them out as an atypical immigrant community. Notwithstanding the reasons for repatriation, for over 60 years the Gurkha Contingent as a unit has been an indomitable part of Singapore. In other words, as individuals, the Gurkhas are sojourners, but in terms of a Gurkha community as a whole, they remain a permanent entity in Singapore, and this problematises the issue of how to conceptualise them as a diasporic community.

William Safran, in his essay on 'Diasporas in Modern Societies: Myths of Homeland and Return', has discussed a variety of collective experiences. He defines 'diaspora' as follows: a historical trajectory of dispersal, conjuring up memories of the homeland, feelings of exclusion in the host country, a longing for eventual return and a strong myth of return, rendering support to the homeland and a collective identity importantly defined by this relationship.[26] While the Gurkhas in Singapore exhibit some of the above features, they do not neatly figure in the diasporic discourse because the very notion of 'myth of return' to the place of origin is a misnomer among a community that experiences compulsory repatriation.

The critical role played by the Singapore government in determining the migration trajectory of Gurkha families is another element contributing to the anomaly of their identity formations. Arguably, the Gurkha Contingent is a contemporary version of the contract labour structure that defined some labour diasporas during the colonial period. The notion of 'contract labour' and 'labour camp' exudes the image of slavery, forced labour and imprisonment. The Mount Vernon Camp, on the contrary, is a sophisticated residential facility with various modern amenities catering to the comforts of Gurkha families. Further, unlike most diasporic community formations where typically the migrants themselves initiate the growth and development of their community, in Singapore, the role of the state in creating, developing and sustaining a Gurkha identity is significant.

The feelings of exclusion and dislocation experienced in the host country and the identity quandaries of a migrant community are salient features of a diasporic community. The double de-politicisation of the Gurkhas, being historically under-represented in the political sphere of

Nepal and at the same time, disenfranchised in Singapore, is a poignant element to substantiate the sense of loss and displacement experienced by them. The feeling of dislocation is more apparent among Gurkha children who are born in Singapore and undergo the public schooling system in the country. Such children are usually asked where they would like to go after their fathers retire from Singapore, to which they would often reply, 'I'd like to go to a foreign country'. They are startled when told 'Well, you are in a foreign country. Singapore is not your home'.[27] The reality of their temporary residence in Singapore sinks in after their repatriation to Nepal. In the process of attempting to renegotiate their Singapore identity, and accentuate a Nepali identity, Gurkha children are once again perceived as foreigners in Nepal. The locals regard them as foreigners since they were raised in Singapore for almost 20 years. They speak and behave differently from the local children. Despite Singapore's initiatives to emphasise Nepal as their country of origin while living in the Camp, these children feel twice-displaced, like their parents themselves.

From the perspective of many Gurkhas, Nepal is a country of their birth and Singapore is a country they feel attached to. This attachment does not simply refer to their over two decade-long service in Singapore; it is a deeper sense of attachment binding the families that have long served in the city-state where their grandfathers, fathers and sons vividly recollect their service and memories of Singapore. Their collective memories precede the city-state's independence in 1965, indicating the historical depth of their nostalgia about Singapore.

The ambivalent sense of belonging to Singapore and Nepal necessitates a redefinition of the 'host country – homeland' praxis that conventionally places emphasis on the former as a means to understand the struggles faced by diasporic communities. The Gurkhas in Singapore understand the significance of their original homeland (Nepal) in playing out the oscillating sentiments that they harbour towards their 'host country' and 'homeland'. Here, notions of 'host-country' and 'homeland' undergo complex negotiations shaping a dual sense of belonging.

Conclusion

In the process of historicising the Gurkha Contingent, their impartial positionality is poignant as it defines the gated nature of their residence in Singapore, which ends after their contracted service for a period of approximately two decades. The Gurkha Contingent's role in Singapore's national security as a neutral force, the elusive nature of their residence in the Mount Vernon Camp, their limited interactions with the local populace and their experience of repatriation have, for years, shaped the identity of the community in both Singapore and Nepal.

The representation of the Gurkha Contingent as a neutral force impinges on British colonial discourses that have portrayed the Gurkhas as an exotic 'Other'. Mary Des Chene writes that Gurkhas are regarded as 'the Orient': loyalty, honesty, cheerfulness and pluck; and as an alien, even exotic being. She argues that their Mongolian appearance, their enigmatic homeland and their seemingly superhuman abilities in battlefields marked them out as the quintessential 'other'.[28] The Gurkha Contingent's anomalistic position within the context of Singapore stems from this essentialisation of their identity, and highlights the racial determinism that underlies policies preventing them from integrating with the larger Singaporean society.

The Gurkha Contingent acts as a trope to illustrate the Singapore state's anxieties about the fragility of national cohesion despite four and a half decades of cordial ethnic relations. Social harmony coexists with an ominous prospect of a racial tension. As Goh succinctly highlights, '. . . political leaders themselves remain uneasy about the strength of national cohesion . . . and continue to remind Singaporeans of the fragility of the nation and the spectre of racial riots'.[29] Among other functions, the Contingent's key role as an anti-riot squad exhibits the possibility of Singapore's national cohesion coming under threat. In an effort to ensure the operational effectiveness of this Contingent, the state considers it necessary to insularise it from the public domain and Gurkha families are repatriated to Nepal after they retire from their service in Singapore.

Although the Gurkhas have been instrumental in the shaping of Singapore's history from the colonial period to the present, they continue to remain apart from the rest of the country and they live with their memories of Singapore for the rest of their life in Nepal. The challenges they face upon repatriation and the struggles they go through in negotiating a dual identity are a product of the long period of their residence in Singapore. The Gurkhas in Singapore render it difficult for social scientists to neatly categorise them as a diasporic community in view of the incompatibility of notions such as sojourn, return and repatriation within the existing parameters that define a diasporic people. Here, the 'host-country-homeland' praxis undergoes complex interactions as they return to Nepal periodically during their service in Singapore before their final repatriation, and as a result, the 'homeland' itself becomes the site where negotiations of home, identity and belonging are teased out. The exceptional dynamics evident in the emigration of Gurkhas to

Singapore necessitates a reconfiguration in the conceptual understanding of diasporic communities.

Notes

1. Scott Leathart, 1998, *With the Gurkhas: India, Burma, Singapore, Malaya, Indonesia, 1940–1959,* Edinburgh: Pentland Press, p. 186.
2. Assistant Superintendent of Police, e-mail correspondence, Public Affairs Department, Singapore Police Force, 13 April 2009.
3. Senior Customer Relations Executive, Customer Relations Branch, Immigration and Checkpoints Authority of Singapore, 26 August 2008.
4. Customer Service Associate Executive, Ministry of Manpower, Singapore, 27 August 2008.
5. Anonymous, Gurkha 1, interviewed in Pokhara, Nepal, 24 May 2009.
6. Anonymous, Gurkha SGT, interviewed in Pokhara, Nepal, 22 May 2009.
7. Charlotte Loh, email correspondence, Senior Public Communications Executive, Ministry of Home Affairs, Singapore, 16 October 2008.
8. Peter H. L. Lim (ed.) 2009, *Chronicle of Singapore 1959–2009: Fifty Years of Headline News,* Singapore: Editions Didier Millet, p. 154.
9. Charlotte Loh, email correspondence, Senior Public Communications Executive, Ministry of Home Affairs, Singapore, 16 October 2008. In addition, Ravi Vellor has highlighted that apart from their role in security, the Gurkhas also have a strong presence in sports and are often winners in events such as The New Paper Big Walk, and reported that two of Singapore's representatives in the 2007 World Open Karate Championships in Tokyo were from the local Gurkha Contingent. For further information, see, Ravi Velloor, 2008, 'Legend of the Gurkha Warrior', *The Sunday Times,* 27 April.
10. 1949. 'Anti-Riot Squad Being Formed', *The Straits Times,* 6 December.
11. 1951. 'Model Life of Gurkhas', *The Singapore Free Press,* 21 August.
12. Charlotte Loh, email correspondence, Senior Public Communications Executive, Ministry of Home Affairs, Singapore, 16 October 2008.
13. For more information, see Lionel Caplan, 1995, *Warrior Gentlemen: "Gurkhas" in the Western Imagination.* Oxford: Berghahn; Cynthia Enloe, 1980. *Ethnic Soldiers: State Security in Divided Societies,* Athens: University of Georgia Press.
14. Lee Kuan Yew, 1998, *The Singapore Story: Memoirs of Lee Kuan Yew,* Singapore: Federal Publications, p. 20.
15. Lee Kuan Yew, 2000, *From Third World to First: The Singapore Story, 1965–2000,* New York: Harper Collins Publishers, pp. 21–22.
16. http://www.cpgcorp.com.sg/portfolio/viewdetails.asp?Lang=EN&PCID=3&PDID=25. Accessed on 18 August 2010. It is also reported that S$68 million was spent to expand the camp.
17. These are common terms used to describe the children of Gurkhas with the former referring to nephews and the latter to nieces.
18. Assistant Superintendent of Police Kumar, interviewed in Pokhara, Nepal, 29 May 2009.
19. For more information, see Manisha Aryal, 1991, 'To Marry a *Lahuray*', *HIMAL,* July/August Issue.

20 ASP Gurung, interviewed in Pokhara, Nepal, 25 May 2009.
21 Raj Gurung, interviewed in Kathmandu, Nepal, 14 June 2009.
22 ASP Gurung, interviewed in Pokhara, Nepal, 25 May 2009.
23 Corporal Dhoj, interviewed at Pokhara, Nepal, on 24 May 2009.
24 Assistant Superintendent of Police Kumar, interviewed in Pokhara, Nepal, 29 May 2009.
25 Corporal Tek and wife, interviewed in Pokhara, Nepal, 23 May 2009.
26 William Safran, 1999, 'Diasporas in Modern Societies: Myths of Homeland and Return', in S. Vertovec and Robin Cohen (eds), *Migration, Diasporas, and Transnationalism,* Northampton, MA: Edward Elgar, pp. 364–65.
27 Anonymous *Bhānjā*, interviewed in Singapore, 17 April 2009.
28 Mary Des Chene, 1991, *Relics of Empire: A Cultural History of the Gurkhas, 1815–1987.* PhD Dissertation, Stanford University, Ann Arbor, University of Michigan, p. 1.
29 Daniel P.S. Goh, 2010, 'Multiculturalism and the Problem of Solidarity', in Terrence Chong (ed.), *Management of Success: Singapore Revisited,* Singapore: Institute of Southeast Asian Studies, p. 562.

18

DREAMS OF SACRIFICE

Changing ritual practices among
ex-Gurkha immigrants in the UK

Mitra Pariyar

Following the recent ban on the full *burqa* in France, and other European nations considering the same, the issue has been passionately debated in the UK as well. A Yougov poll, published in July 2010, shows that 67 per cent of British adults want a total ban on the face cover, while 42 per cent strongly feel that this should be the case. A Tory Member of Parliament has presented a private member's bill in Parliament calling for the ban, prompting the Immigration Minister, Damian Greene, to label the proposed move as 'un-British'. There are questions being raised about why Muslim women should be allowed to appear in public with their faces covered, while others are not permitted to do so. The opponents see the cover as an overt means of suppressing women, under Islamic laws, which should no longer be tolerated in a country such as Britain. However, those who disapprove of the call argue that the UK is a free society; therefore, it would be wrong to outlaw religious practices of minority groups.

Another published case will also be relevant here. A man of Indian origin in Newcastle demanded that his dead body be cremated in an open pyre, according to the traditional Hindu practice. Despite his long campaign, the local Council was adamant in its stance that the cremation should take place only in a closed-door venue with a traditional, Anglo-Saxon design. The struggle culminated in a court case, where the judge presented an 'ingenious compromise', which allowed the cremation to be conducted inside the four walls with no roof, so that the sunlight could fall on the corpse (*Guardian*, 11/02/2010). This verdict has encouraged, as the media reported, other Hindus in the UK to design new crematoriums that suit their traditional practices better. What this shows, among other things, is that there are many Hindu rituals that cannot be practised strictly according to the original customs in the UK, due to legal and other barriers.

My argument here is that publicly-known cases, such as the veil and the open pyre, are just the tip of the iceberg. Beneath the popular notion of a tolerant and multicultural Britain, there are numerous problems that migrants face while conducting their religious or cultural functions, such as rituals. Sociologist Frank van Tubergen observes, 'Within the sociology of religion and the sociology of immigration, surprisingly little large-scale empirical research has been done on immigrants' (2006: 167). Armed with their unique methodological approach, not least the long-term observation of small-scale societies, anthropologists are in a unique position to explore these hidden problems. I. M. Lewis laments, 'Dismayed by the facile emotional theories of the origins of religion . . . British social anthropologists have studiously avoided paying much attention to anything that could be called spirituality' (1989: 1). Katy Gardner and Ralph Grillo note, 'There is an absence of discussion of transnational religious practices (rituals) at the level of households and families' (2002: 180).

Using the case of the funeral of a Caribbean migrant in a British town, Karen Fog Olwig suggests: 'If research takes a point of departure in specific situations such as life-cycle rituals, where contexts are generated, it may be possible to question and explore unexpected connections and disconnections in the lives of migrants and their descendants' (2009: 534). She shows in a *JRAI* article that rituals play a crucial part in forging connections between immigrants, and generating a sense of community among those who share common place of origin, descent, kinship, and so forth. What I have tried to do here is to unpack certain 'disconnections' that the Gurkha immigrants have experienced in their new homes, as a result of not being able to perform their rituals properly, i.e. strictly according to their customs. My exploration goes beyond Olwig's, in the sense that I attempt to problematise not only the connections and disconnections between people, but also between people and their gods.

Peggy Levitt observes, 'Migrants participate in religious pilgrimages, worship particular saints or deities, or engage in informal, popular religious practices that affirm their continued attachments to a particular sending-country group or place' (2003: 851). The experience of the Gurkhas in Oxford validates this argument. I show this by exploring some of their rituals that are difficult to perform in the host country due to several constraints. Identifying 'giving to the god' as the fourth form of 'total prestation' – on top of the three, i.e. the obligation to give, the obligation to receive, and the obligation to reciprocate – Marcel Mauss (1990[1922]) has argued that ritual is a form of interaction between humans and deities. Using this concept, I will demonstrate here that the Gurkhas' inability to perform their rituals properly has disrupted their 'interaction' with their deities, and hence, created a sense of isolation from their spiritual realms.

The chapter aims to unveil multiple challenges – legal, societal, economic and others – that the Gurkha families face, in their new homes in the UK, which disable them to perform their rituals properly. This has, *inter alia*, reduced their sense of belonging to the host society or country. Although they arrived fairly recently, the Oxford Gurkhas do not appear to be poorly incorporated into British society, if we studied only their level of income, class, English language proficiency, employment, and so forth. And yet, they do not quite feel at home in Britain.

Methodology

I lived in Rose Hill, a Gurkha settlement in an eastern suburb of Oxford, for over a year, since April 2009. I shared a house with two Gurkha families belonging to the Limbu community. Although a few Nepalis from other ethnic backgrounds also live in different parts of Oxfordshire, I focused much on Limbu families, also because it was not possible, under the scope of my MPhil dissertation, to scrutinise many communities, who often have separate religious beliefs and practices. As an observer and active member, I also studied the Nepali Community in Oxford (NCO), an organisation run by mostly ex-Gurkha residents for all Nepalis in Oxfordshire. I regularly took part in committee meetings and annual events, including the Dashain festival in autumn, Nepali New Year in April and summer barbecue. This gave me an opportunity to understand the perspectives of the wider community. I also conducted a semi-structured interview of 20 ex-servicemen, mostly those living in east Oxford, often in the company of their spouses and children.

A special case of migration

Before delving into the experiences of Oxford Gurkhas in their new homes, perhaps it will be useful to briefly introduce the history of Gurkha service and their recent struggle for the settlement right. This is a unique type of migration, partly because the ex-Gurkhas, many of them economically quite well-off in Nepal with savings and pensions from Gurkha service and other overseas jobs, are neither purely economic migrants nor refugees. Of course, part of the reason for coming to Britain was to ensure a better prospect for their children. Their migration is also a result of their organised legal and political campaign, since the early 1990s, at home and in Britain, to make the British government treat them on par with the British and other foreign nationals serving in the British army. They have always claimed that it is their 'right' to live and work in the UK with their families after retiring from the service for the 'sacrifice' of thousands of Gurkhas fighting for the British Empire, for minimal or no compensation.

The history of Gurkha service is intricately linked to that of Britain–Nepal relations. Historically, Nepal provided a key transit route for the Indian trade with Tibet and China, which the East India Company also wanted to exploit. While the company was expanding its sphere of influence throughout the length and breadth of the Indian subcontinent, in the 18th century, a king of Gorkha, a small mountain-town and principality, was launching a bloody campaign to annex the little kingdoms in the foothills of the Himalayas. The British were particularly threatened by the Gorkha king's attempts to take the three strategically important principalities in the Kathmandu Valley, ruled by Newar kings – their trade partners (Stiller 1973; Caplan 1995). At one point, the company sent troop reinforcement, under the command of Captain Kinloch, to help the king of Kathmandu, Jayaprakash Malla, thwart the imminent Gorkhali invasion. But the British were vanquished, together with the Newars, and the valley became a part of Gorkha kingdom. The new ruler, King Prithvi Narayan Shah, obviously unhappy with the British intervention, blocked trade routes to Tibet and China (Des Chene 1991; Caplan 1995: 13).

Initially, the company made an effort to gain the king's support through diplomatic means. The first British Residency was set up in Kathmandu, the capital of newly founded and bigger Nepal, in 1801. However, it had to be shut down four years later, as the king refused to cooperate. The king even proceeded with more military conquests in the region, expanding his territory. The Raj particularly objected to the expansion of the Gorkha kingdom southwards, along the northern edges of the fertile Gangetic plains, which they considered to be an encroachment upon their territory. The Raj feared that this could lead to the formation of an alliance between the Gorkhalis, Sikhs and Marathas to potentially force it out of the subcontinent (Des Chene 1991: 37). The company ordered an immediate withdrawal of the Nepali troops from the plains, but the king refused to comply because the fertile land was a lucrative source of wealth for the royal and noble families. The British launched war against Nepal in 1814. The two-year war had multiple impacts in Nepal's history, one of the important ones being the start of Gurkha service; it was in this war that the British observed an extraordinary fighting capability of Nepali men, particularly as an infantry for action in jungles and rugged terrains. They were so impressed with the combative skills of the Nepalis that a few Nepali defectors and prisoners of war were recruited into the British forces even before the war ended.

Despite the initial refusal of the Nepal government to allow its citizens to join the British army, the Raj always drew young Nepali men from certain ethnic groups – called the 'martial races' – into its Brigade of Gurkha by hook or by crook. The recruitment became popular also because many tribal people in the mountain villages saw it as an escape from crippling poverty. The hereditary, dictatorial Rana prime ministers, who were more powerful than kings, and who ruled Nepal from the mid-19th to the mid-20th century, 'traded' the Gurkhas for personal and national benefits – mainly in the form of arms, ammunition, money, honours and titles (Des Chene 1991: 68). Prime Minister Jang Bahadur Rana himself led a 10,000-strong Nepali troop to regain the state of Lucknow during the Mutiny of 1857 (Whelpton 2005: 46). Grateful, the British returned a part of the south-western plains to Nepal, which became the private estates of top Rana families. Over 200,000 Nepali young men were drawn to fight for the British in each World War; tens of thousands were killed or wounded. The families of the dead and the wounded did not get compensation; most of the survivors were sent back home without any benefit. Gurkha activists claim that at least 5,000 Gurkha veterans, who fought for the British in Malaya and the Falklands, are still living in acute poverty across Nepal. Although the Gurkha Brigade has been significantly reduced over the recent decades – only 3,500 men are serving now – they continue to play a crucial role in British military missions. They were deployed in Iraq, and are still serving in Afghanistan. The tradition of sacrifice for the British continues to the day.

Whereas much of the literature on the legendary soldiers, most of it written by the British officers who commanded them, has depicted them as extremely faithful and submissive, their traditional image has changed to some extent after they started clamouring for equal rights. Almost all the critical decisions affecting their profession, including the terms and conditions of service, were taken by the British government. Although it did consult with the Nepal government before taking some decisions, the servicemen had hardly any say in the matters affecting their careers. The 1947 Tripartite Treaty between the Nepalese, Indian and British governments, a key document setting out the terms and conditions of Gurkha service, is a fine example of this. Using this document – a compromise between the states following India's independence – the British government always treated Gurkhas poorly in comparison with British soldiers, and other nationals serving in its forces, particularly in terms of pay, pensions, benefits and other facilities.

One of the fundamental conditions of Gurkha service was that all retirees were to be discharged in Nepal, and would not be allowed to live or work in Britain, although other foreign nationals who served in their army did not face such bar. The Brown government was forced to abandon this long-held discriminatory policy in April 2009, following the popular Parliament vote — initiated and led by the Liberal Democratic Party — that supported unconditional settlement of all former Gurkhas and their families in Britain. Although the UK media rightly hailed Joanna Lumley and Nick Clegg for championing the Gurkha case, they did not mention the fact that this was the culmination of a decade-long struggle by the ex-servicemen through Gurkha Army Ex-Servicemen's Association (GAESO). The Gurkha activists challenged the British government's discriminatory policies in a series of court cases in London, besides launching effective political campaigns. No doubt, the support of the public figures was tremendously important for the ultimate victory, but it was the Gurkha activists themselves who actually initiated the movement and built it up over the years. This is, therefore, an extraordinary tale of transnational activism, a shining example of 'transnationalism from below' (Smith and Guarnizo 1998).

Although about 100 Gurkha families have settled in Oxford, it has not been one of the most attractive destinations for them, probably due to the fact that the city offers limited scope for the kind of job they want, i.e. private security. Other places such as Aldershot, Farnborough, Reading, Ashford and London have a much bigger Gurkha population. The flow of Gurkha migrants started in 2004, after the Blair government allowed the post-1997 retirees to settle in Britain. Obviously, thousands more of Gurkha families have poured in since the Parliament voted in April 2009, which allowed everybody, the new and the old, to live in Britain.

Almost all Gurkha families arrived with an Indefinite Leave to Remain (ILR), which means that they can live and work in Britain, or move out, if they choose. After living in the country for a certain minimum number of years, and fulfilling the general criteria set by the Home Office, they can apply to become British citizens. Indeed, quite a few have already acquired the citizenship. However, many are still unsure of whether to accept it, as it entailed the termination of the Nepalese one. Although the British passport was seen to be handy for living and working in Britain, many of them were anxious about severing their official ties with their motherland. They would, of course, be much more enthusiastic about acquiring it if Nepal adopted a policy of dual citizenship.

One of the problems encountered by some Gurkha families in Oxford, and possibly elsewhere in the UK, was that their adult children were not allowed to settle in Britain. The age-bar, perhaps justifiable according to the British culture, where children are expected to move out of parent's house at the age of 18, is deleterious to the popular Nepali practice of a joint family. Although a few had managed to, somehow, dodge the immigration system and get their older children through, others suffered the pain of separation. This is just one of the many problems Gurkha families face in their daily lives, some of which, not least those associated with ritual and worship, have been explored below.

'Not at home' at home

Chandra Limbu, an ex-Gurkha in his late forties, said:

> I have to not only keep visiting my place in Nepal but also do all I can to support it and my people. Even if I become very rich here and never go back, my *atman* or spirit will go back where it came from when I die. It cannot possibly hang around here because it will not get due respect and space in this country.

When I asked him whether he liked his house which he had bought the previous year, his answer was both yes and no. It was about the right size for his family of five, and that the garden and the overall design of the house were also good. The house was also close to other Nepali households. Yet, he did not quite feel that he belonged to the house. One of the reasons for this was that, although he owned the house in legal terms, he did not own in the ritual sense because although his family resided in the house, his deities and ancestral spirits did not.

Based on his study of a Limbu village in the 1970s, Philippe Sagant shows (1996) that the Limbus are required to perform a special ceremony for installing *Yuma* and other ancestor spirits in the house before the family moves in. A trained shaman and priest, called Phedangma, performs the ritual, which includes sacrificing a pig in the main pillar of the house. On top of this, 'the Limbu calendar requires that every household make annual sacrifices, one in November and one in April, to the goddess *Yuma*; twice a year to *Manguenna*, to deceased ancestors, and to *Nahangma*' (ibid.: 379).

The house-warming ritual is not easy to perform in the UK houses. Besides the unavailability of a Phedangma, a key problem is that the slaughter of animals and birds – a central part of many ritual performances of the Limbus and others – is not permitted inside the house, or indeed, anywhere outside licensed venues run by butcher shops.

In an edited volume, Gérard Toffin (ed) (1991) shows that many other castes or ethnic groups in Nepal hold a similar belief about deities dwelling in their houses. They need to be not only ritually installed, but also regularly worshipped for the well-being of the family, which partly depends on the harmonious relationship between people and their gods. In one of the chapters of the book, Corneille Jest shows that the Majhis, the fishermen in eastern and central Nepal, believe that the deities, residing in the house, could become malicious and cause death and destruction in the family if they were not worshipped regularly and properly (1991: 158). In another work, Robert Levy (1990) shows that the Newars of Bhaktapur (part of the Kathmandu Valley) believe that the deities could seek to draw human blood by causing destruction of the house, or through other accidents, if they are not worshipped regularly, with blood sacrifice. The Newars are similarly fearful of motor vehicles; they always sacrifice a chicken or goat before using them. At least some Limbus in Oxford are fearful that the *Yuma* could get annoyed for their apparent neglect, and bring harm to the family.

As Sagant observes, 'The house (of a Limbu) is the sanctuary, almost the definition, of cultural order. Beyond it there is almost nothing' (1996: 9). In other words, much of the Limbu rituals and other social activities take place within the extended family. Many Gurkhas in Oxford found this problematic. For one thing, many of their family and kin are in Nepal, and are very unlikely to be given the visa to travel to Britain for family events; whether they could actually afford such trips is another issue. Although most Gurkhas in Oxford are not directly related to each other, some of them have a few members of their family or kinship in the UK.

Part of the problem is that there is little free time; almost every Gurkha works 12-hour shifts – with frequent night duties – to meet the high cost of living. Nor does the travel come cheap. Even if they did manage to come together, the size of the house would not accommodate many people. Fairly strict health and safety regulations do not allow many people to share a house with limited space. One way of organising family get-togethers would be to hire public venues, which, of course, would cost a lot. Of course, it is possible to organise bigger events, such as the Dashain festival, where the cost is shared by hundreds of people, but not for smaller family events. In any case, holding rituals in a public venue would not be the same as doing it at home, as many functions are associated with deities residing in the house.

According to my informants, house-centred gathering was manageable in Nepal partly because many Gurkhas owned quite big houses. Even if the houses were small, guests could be easily accommodated in neighbours' houses, or in tents erected in open fields; this is not always possible in the UK. Often, related families in Nepal live in clusters, which is another advantage. This is not easy in the UK because people need to consider the availability of jobs and houses, schools and colleges for children, and many other things before deciding to settle in an area. Even if there was no problem of space in the house, conducting many rituals would not be easy; for instance, playing big drums and other instruments, singing or chanting loudly, and similar noise and crowding at home may not be tolerated by the neighbours. Karma Limbu, a Gurkha spouse, had to take a special permission from her neighbours before organising a small gathering of women at her house to worship an Indian saint, Sai Baba, in January 2010, although the function did not involve loud music or noise.

Death rites

On a number of occasions, I heard Gurkha spouses saying, 'Although we may live a materially richer life here, we will certainly die poorer'. One of the ways to understand the substance of this statement would be to see how their last rites are performed in Britain.

The Limbu death rites consist of mainly two parts – one performed immediately after death, and the other conducted within a year. Soon after the death, a shaman goes into trance, enabling the spirit of the dead, possessed in his body, to speak in his voice. The spirit reveals the cause of his death, his important life experiences, likes and dislikes, unfulfilled desires, and so on; family and friends engage in an emotional communication with it. The final ritual, called *khauma,* held within a year of death, brings together everybody in the kinship network – affinal and consanguinal – who support the family with free supply of meat, drinks, food and other things essential for the feasts. The fanfare, involving music, singing, dances and romantic encounters, takes place over several days and nights. A crucial part of the ritual involves sacrificing a pig or buffalo, together with food and home-brewed drinks, to the spirit of the dead. Such an elaborate funeral, conducted over several days and nights, is not performed for those who die an unnatural death; a brief funeral, however, requires the killing of a piglet in a cruel manner in the bush.

The Limbu custom states that the dead body should not be touched by a person from a different caste or ethnic background. The Oxford Limbus found out, from a few cases, that it is not possible to keep to this rule in

Britain, because the officials at the crematorium are the ones who wash the body and prepare it for cremation. The Limbus generally do not cremate their dead, unlike the Hindus, but not everybody can afford a burial. Given the costs, limited space in the house, ban on animal slaughter for ritual purposes, health and safety regulations, inability of many members of the family network to travel from Nepal, and above all the absence of a phedangma, a proper *khauma* looks almost unthinkable in the UK.

Celebrating the festivals

During the interviews, most Gurkhas said that they continued to celebrate Dashain, as well as the festival of *Deepawali* or Tihar – popular in many parts of the Indian subcontinent. In practice, however, I did not observe a fraction of the usual excitement and enthusiasm in the autumn festivals. The NCO organised a gathering and feast for all Nepalis on the occasion of the festival of Dashain, but it was, by and large, not much different from any other gathering, in the sense that there was no religious ritual performed. A few oil lamps, sprinkled with flowers, were burning on the stage, which may or may not be interpreted in religious terms, because such lamps can also be used purely for secular events. The programme was conducted in a semi-official way, involving speeches by official guests and the leader of the organisation, which also did not include any reference to associated rituals.

A majority of Nepalis who I interviewed also stated that they had not given up wearing the *tika* – red or white colours mixed with rice and worn on foreheads, as sacred marks symbolising blessings from deities and senior kin – in Dashain. In Nepali culture, the tika is an important symbol of unity and hierarchy among the members of the extended family. It is also an important religious and national symbol, and is used publicly. In reality, however, I did not see many Nepalis in Oxford wearing the marks. Many families, including the ones I shared the house with, did not use it at all. Some informants told me that they were discouraged to wear the marks, especially in public, for fear of being ridiculed by natives and others for what might appear to them, following an awkward practice of attaching raw rice on one's forehead. Although they valued the religious and national significance of the symbol, they were not enthusiastic to display it, in response to the possible racist tendencies of the local population. As a result, even those few who actually used the *tika* in private, rubbed it off before coming out in public.

Based on his observation of a Dashain celebration in a Limbu village, Sagant notes: 'One morning the festival (Dashain) opens to the sound of Damai horns. From then on it is one endless round of slaughtering goats and chicken, buffalo and pigs, and going from house to house drinking' (1996: 265). There have been many social, cultural and political changes in Nepal since the 1970s. Indeed, some activists of ethnic groups, marginalised from the state power, the Limbus included, have interpreted the Hindu festival as a form of legitimating the dominance of high castes on other Nepalis; some have called for the boycott of the festival, not least the tika, in order to symbolise their freedom (Hangen 2010). Despite this, the festival continues to be widely celebrated in Nepal, and tika and blood sacrifice are still the popular markers of the festival. Animal sacrifice is considered essential not only to please the deities, but also to ensure the supply of meat for feasts that run over 10 days. One of the reasons why Dashain had lost its charm in Oxford, and probably across the UK, was the ban on animal sacrifice.

Even those in Oxford who did not necessarily believe in sacrifice for gods, missed slaughtering animals at home on important occasions such as Dashain. Indeed, Nepalis of almost all faiths and traditions, including the Christians, kill animals and birds at home on important festivals or functions in Nepal. Oxford Gurkhas missed this so much that they had invented an ingenious way of getting around the system. They travelled to the farms in Didcot, or sometimes as far as Salisbury, where they would be offered whole pigs after killing them. They then spend several hours chopping the pig into pieces, cleaning the meat, and distributing portions of it to the interested households in the neighbourhood. Almost everybody claimed that self-prepared pork tasted much better than the readymade ones available in supermarkets.

Part of the Tihar festival involves the public performance of especial dances and festive chants, called *Deusi* and *Bhailo*. Groups of people go around houses, singing and dancing; the host family offers them food, drinks and some cash. A few youths, eager to revive the tradition in east Oxford, visited some Nepali homes; but the *Deusi* here was nothing like that in Nepal. Traditionally, chanting, singing and dancing are supposed to take place loudly and outside the house, in the forecourt, but they did not do it here as they were concerned about disturbing the neighbours. They squeezed into the house and chanted *Deusi* in a very low voice, very anxious to avoid the neighbours calling the police.

A Hindu temple like a church

Many Gurkhas said that they missed a house of worship in Oxford. Although many of them largely followed their own shamanistic traditions, the influence of Hinduism was also significant. Alan MacFarlane

(1997) has found the same about the Gurungs in western Nepal. Some Gurkhas said that they missed a Hindu temple, as there was none in Oxfordshire. This was interesting because, although there were two Hindu temples in the nearby town of Reading, nobody visited them. They said that they did not like the temples there because they hardly looked like a temple! Indeed, other Nepalis – including Hindu high castes – did not appear terribly keen to worship there. I visited one of the temples to see why it was not very popular among the Nepalis.

Most Hindu temples in Nepal are marked by the frequent ringing of bells, chanting of prayers, thick smoke from burning incense, rows of oil lamps producing a distinctive smell, and so forth. The statues or symbols representing the deities, placed in the heart of the temple, are often covered in flowers, rice, vermillion, coins, fruits, oil-lamps and other stuff offered by worshippers; indeed, many are drenched in sacrificial blood. Hardly any of this was seen in the Reading temple. The statue of Vishnu stood tall on the stage in front of the hall, but there was no representation of smaller deities, such as goddess Kali or Durga, popularly worshipped by lower- and middle-caste groups, such as the Limbus. The worshippers are not allowed to offer coins, rice, vermillion, food, clothes or other stuff to the deity; nor could they burn incense sticks or light oil-lamps owing to, as the priests explained, fire safety regulations. The venue itself could be easily converted into a church or mosque by removing the statues of the deities.

Of course, the temple was run by high castes of Indian origin, who are increasingly – thanks to the reform movements – moving towards a more congregational and non-violent form of worship. This could partly be the reason behind the type of atmosphere maintained in the temple, which, to many devotees from the lower and middle castes in Nepal, may not look Hindu at all. However, the priests explained that they had to impose many restrictions on what could and could not be done by the worshippers because of the strict guidelines based on health and safety, fire safety and other regulations. For instance, they would certainly like to have many bells, large and small, inside and outside the building, additional to the single one in a quiet corner of the hall. But the temple managers, anxious to avoid confrontation with the local authorities, decided to keep the temple very quiet. In fact, the temple was so quiet and unnoticeable that an onlooker in the street could not easily recognise it, except for the signboard. This is untypical of any Hindu temple in Nepal or India.

This chimes with the private protest of a Muslim in east Oxford for not being allowed to publicly perform their prayers, like in Islamic and some other states, using loudspeakers attached to the roofs of mosques.

If Britain truly respected the freedom and equality of religious faiths, he wondered, why it was only church bells that could be heard in public, loud and clear.

Ancestor worship

Ancestor worship is an important ritual of almost everybody in Nepal (MacFarlane 1997). As Chaitanya Subba, a prominent Limbu intellectual and ethnic activist, shows (1995), ancestor worship called *tongshing* is a central part of the Limbu religion, and it should be held every year, or at least once every three years. The Oxford Gurkha families also accepted this view and saw tongshing as one of their crucial functions – the one that not only pleases their ancestor spirits, but also revitalises the solidarity and cohesion within the kinship network.

The tongshing rituals, performed by a different brand of ritual experts called Yeba or Samba, include a central part, called *sambok phengma,* which involves the ceremonial slaughter of a piglet in the bush for the master spirits. Yeba invokes the spirits and embodies them, through possession, and accepts the sacrifice. Before the function draws to a close, the worshippers ask the spirits if they were content with the sacrifice and other offerings and seek their divine protection and blessing.

Dreams of sacrifice

One of the central themes running through the chapter is the concept of sacrifice, called *balidan* or *balichadaunu* in Nepali. Oxford Gurkhas, and possibly many others, understand balidan mainly in two contexts: the painful memory of their forefathers who died fighting for the British, and blood sacrifice – the *sine qua non* of many of their domestic and communal rituals. The historical sacrifice of Gurkha lives does not appear totally pointless now, at least for the fact that the Gurkha campaigners made an effective use of this to get many of their demands met. They would possibly not have won the right to settle in Britain if the British public had not remembered and honoured the extraordinary sacrifice. Commenting on the Parliament vote, journalist Vicky Woods wrote, 'The Gurkha rebellion . . . was the sunniest thing to come out of Parliament . . . an astonishing majority of people want them to be repaid their debt of honour' (*Daily Telegraph,* 1 May 2009). The *Guardian* said, 'The outcome is the result of hard work by Joanna Lumley, who has championed the Gurkhas . . . her strength came from having a good case' (30 April 2009). The *Sun* celebrated, 'The move comes as a major victory for *The Sun*'s crusade for Gurkha justice' (29 April 2009).

Ironically, the migration has deprived the Gurkhas of other kinds of sacrifice – blood sacrifice – thereby fuelling a sense of alienation from their ancestral spirits and deities, and therefore heightening the feeling of loss of their homeland. This ritual deficit, leading to a spiritual deficit, has resulted in a significant reduction in their sense of belonging in the country of residence, which was once their 'dreamland'. Before the Gurkha movement gained momentum, they could only dream of living in Britain; but the actual settlement has led to a different kind of dreaming – dreaming of reuniting with their ancestors and living relatives, and fulfilling the obligation to their deities with, of course, the blood sacrifice.

Conclusion

From the discussions so far, one should not get the impression that every Gurkha in Oxford, and indeed elsewhere in Britain, is bloodthirsty. This is not the case even in Nepal. Some Nepalis have, under the growing influence of Buddhism, taken to non-violent forms of worship. For some, bloodshed is no longer acceptable even in the holy festival of Dashain, where they make do with cucumbers, gourds, pumpkins and other vegetables or fruits as surrogate victims in the sacrifice for Durga (Gellner 2001: 75). Some Oxford Gurkhas are less bothered about not being able to worship their deities and spirits than others. There are, of course, some who miss rituals very much, but do not wish to express it. Yet, many Gurkhas do, to a certain extent, feel alienated from their cultural and religious milieu.

One of the impacts of the spiritual deficit has been the strengthening of their transnational ties: they find it necessary to remain in constant touch with their families or relatives back home for, among others, getting the deities and spirits worshipped on their behalf. Just as their people in Nepal expect financial support from them, they rely on the former to perform the necessary rituals on their behalf. They sponsor sacrificial goats and chickens in family events such as ancestor worship, *khauma*, housewarming, worship of Durga in Dashain, and so on. When somebody in the UK falls ill, he or she not only goes to see the general physician, but also contacts family or friends in Nepal for divine healing. My research reveals that many Gurkhas visit their original places once a year; almost every family travels to Nepal at least once in three years. They use their holidays not only to reconnect with their relatives and friends, but also to reunite with their deities and spirits. Many go to Nepal to organise important family rituals, such as weddings and funerals. Thus, the Gurkha families in Oxford, while not performing many rituals in their UK homes, ensure that they remain connected to their cultural and spiritual realms in Nepal.

Olwig (2007, 2009) has rightly stressed the need to scrutinise rituals of immigrant families to understand their connections and disconnections in their everyday life. Her latest article (2009) shows how the actual enactment of life cycle rituals – in this case, a funeral – creates the context for generating the sense of community among immigrants who come from the same places and who are related to each other. Building on her framework, I show here how it is not just the performance of rituals, but also the absence of common rituals that helps generate a sense of community among migrants. Similar experiences of serving in the foreign army, of not being able to perform many religious functions and other rituals properly, of having similar socio-economic status and of cherishing similar memories and dreams, have formed the key bases for the formation of a Gurkha community, distinct from other Nepalis and migrant groups, in Britain.

The Gurkhas, however, do not necessarily blame the British government or society for the difficulties they face here. Many accept that such problems are inevitable in an alien land. They are very unlikely to launch campaigns against the authorities. Their problems will probably not be discussed and debated widely, unlike the case of the *burqa*, at least in the near future. Yet the problems exist, and their lives continue to be affected.

I am also not suggesting that the Gurkhas do not conduct any ritual in Oxford at all. What I have tried to show is that many rituals cannot be performed in the UK properly, i.e. strictly according to the customary rules. I observed two funerals in Oxford; the mourners observed certain taboos for a few days; a few friends and relatives gathered for the funeral. Many parts of the ritual, such as bathing and shaving by the river or stream, were not held. There would perhaps be no problem even if they followed the procedures by the river, but they were not sure if it was allowed. They hoped to conduct the second, but very important, part of the funeral – the one involving feasts and dances – *khauma,* in their Nepal home, if possible, during their holidays later.

These problems, associated with their daily lives, should be problematised because, while migrants may not appear to mind so much, their sense of belonging to the host society or country will be reduced. Therefore, I concur with Olwig, Levitt, Gardner and Grillo and others in arguing that it is important to consider religious beliefs and practices of migrants at the level of households and families in order to get a better grasp of their integration in the receiving country. Whereas it may be easy to blame immigrants for continuing to look back to their original societies, and for not giving enough attention to the country of residence, it is necessary to see how many factors associated with the host society block their true integration. Immigrants want to integrate into the host society in their own terms. I argue, therefore, that it is important to consider the religious practices of migrant communities as one of the important indicators of their integration, along conventional markers such as employment, income, education and language proficiency.

Although they are recent arrivals, the Gurkha families are doing quite well – socially and economically. There has been no serious problem with their social behaviour. Many Gurkhas work as private security officers, and some as bus drivers; the unemployment rate is very low. Despite the long hours and frequent night shifts, their average income is around £25,000 per annum – similar to the UK national average. Together with the earnings of their spouses – working as cleaners on minimum wage – and of children in many cases, they are financially not in a bad shape. Over 60 per cent of them own a house; many others are in the process of buying one. Many have sold their houses and properties in Nepal to invest in the UK houses. Having worked for the British officers over a decade, most Gurkhas have no problem communicating in English, and are quite capable of selling themselves in job markets fairly quickly. Despite this, their sense of belonging to the British society is very low, as we saw above. This could not be understood properly without looking at their daily practices at the level of households and families.

As I showed earlier, this is a unique type of migration because of its links to the history of Gurkha service, the sacrifice of tens of thousands of young Nepali men fighting for the British colonial interests, and to the latest political and legal movements to make the UK pay its 'debt of honour'. The experiences of migrants are likely to change over time and over the generations (Foner 2002). It will be of great interest to observe them adapt, change and shape their identities.

Bibliography

Caplan, Lionel. 1995. *Warrior Gentlemen: "Gurkhas" in the Western Imagination*. Providence and Oxford: Berghahn Books.

Des Chene, Mary. 1991. 'Relics of Empire: A Cultural History of the Gurkhas, 1815–1987'. Unpublished PhD Thesis, Stanford University.

Foner, Nancy. 2002. 'Second-Generation Transnationalism: Now and Then', in Peggy Levitt and Mary C. Waters (eds), *The Changing Face of Home: The Transnational Lives of the Second Generation*. New York: Russell Sage Foundation.

Gardner, Katy and Ralph Grillo. 2002. 'Transnational Households and Rituals: An Overview', *Global Networks*, 2(3): 179–90.

Gellner, David. 2001. *The Anthropology of Buddhism and Hinduism: Weberian Themes.* New Delhi: Oxford University Press.

Hangen, Susan I. 2010. *The Rise of Ethnic Politics in Nepal: Democracy in the Margins.* London and New York: Routledge.

Jest, Corneille. 1991. 'How I Built My House; An Account by Sarkiman Majhi, Fisherman', in Gérard Toffin (ed), *Man and House in the Himalayas: Ecology of Nepal.* New Delhi and Bangalore: Sterling Publishers Private Limited.

Levitt, Peggy. 2003. ' "You know Abraham was really the First Immigrant": Religion and Transnational Migration', *International Migration Review*, 73(3): 847–73.

Levy, Robert I. 1990. *Mesocosm: Hinduism and the Organization of a Traditional Newar City in Nepal.* Berkeley, LA and Oxford: University of California Press.

Lewis, I. M. 1989. *Ecstatic Religion: A Study of Shamanism and Spirit Possession.* London and New York: Routledge.

Macfarlane, Alan. 1997. 'Identity and Change among the Gurungs (Tamu-Mai) of Central Nepal', in David N. Gellner et al. (eds), *Nationalism and Ethnicity in a Hindu Kingdom: the Politics of Culture in Contemporary Nepal.* Amsterdam: Harwood Academic.

Mauss, Marcel. 1990 [1922]. *The Gift: The Form and Reason for Exchange in Archaic Societies.* New York: Norton.

Olwig, Karen F. 2007. *Caribbean Journeys: An Ethnography of Migration and Home in Three Family Networks.* Durham, London and New York: Duke University Press.

Olwig, Karen F. 2009. 'A Proper Funeral: Contextualising Community among Caribbean Migrants', *Journal of the Royal Anthropological Institute*, 15(3): 520–37.

Sagant, Philippe. 1996 (*trans. Nora B. Scott*). *The Dozing Shaman: The Limbus of Eastern Nepal.* Delhi: Oxford University Press.

Smith, Michael P. and Luis Guarnizo. 1998. *Transnationalism from Below.* New Brunswick, NJ: Transaction Publishers.

Stiller, Ludwig F. 1973. *The Rise of the House of Gorkha: A Study in the Unification of Nepal.* New Delhi: Manjusri Publishing House.

Subba, Chaitanya. 1995. *The Culture and Religion of Limbus.* Kathmandu: K. B Subba.

Toffin, Gérard (ed.). 1991. *Man and House in the Himalayas: Ecology of Nepal.* New Delhi and Bangalore: Sterling Publishers Private Limited.

Tubergen, Frank van. 2006. *Immigrant Integration: A Cross-National Study.* New York: LFB Scholarly Publishing LLC.

Whelpton, John. 2005. *A History of Nepal.* Cambridge: Cambridge University Press.

19

CONCLUSION

Tanka B. Subba and A. C. Sinha

In this chapter, we wish to identify some of the important issues and challenges raised by the contributors to the volume. One such issue seen here is whether the Nepalis living outside Nepal are diasporic or constitute a diaspora. From the evidences provided by the contributors to this volume, it may be safer to say that the Nepalis vacillate between being a diaspora and being diasporic: in the former sense, they fulfil most criteria of a diaspora, if not all, and in the latter sense, they fulfil only one or two criteria of diaspora. This is primarily due to a varied history of migration, settlement, sources of livelihood, legal and political rights they have, imagination of their home country and so on.

One serious challenge for social scientists studying the Nepalis living outside Nepal is to neatly categorise them as short-term or long-term migrants, having or not having land and other immovable property in Nepal and the place of their migration, having or not having legal and political rights in Nepal and place of their migration, wanting or not wanting to return to Nepal, and so on. When a Nepalese youth leaves his village, he leaves with the intention and promise to return soon, but that often does not happen. Even if he succeeds in earning money, he may decide to start a new life in the place of migration rather than return to the place of his origin, where his wife and children may be waiting for him to return. And when he returns, he often finds it difficult to adjust with the people back home or get a job. Thus, he leaves again.

The other serious challenge for social scientists studying them is the extraordinarily varying circumstances in which they are found in more than 100 different countries of the world. The variation is huge even within a country such as India, where some are full citizens of the country and enjoy all the civil and political rights like any other citizen of the country. However, there are others who have no such rights and there are still others who have civil but no political rights. In Sikkim, they feel secure because they constitute about 75 per cent of the population and same is the situation in the hill areas of Darjeeling, but even in the nearby Siliguri subdivision of Darjeeling district, they do not feel secure, as they are, at times, taunted, beaten up, or when they assert themselves, they are asked to go to Nepal. Wherever they are in sizeable numbers, they feel physically secure, but where they are dispersed or are in minority, the legal and political rights they have can be violated by any mob constituting the local delinquent youths.

It is for the above reasons that we decided to retain both 'Gurkha' and 'Gorkha' and both Nepalese and Nepalis in this volume. The distinction between Gurkha and Gorkha is not just historical, i.e. the colonial usage being 'Gurkha' and the postcolonial 'Gorkha', but it is also contextual. For instance, when it comes to the Nepali soldiers in the UK or Nepali policemen in Singapore, they are even today referred to as 'Gurkha'. The difference is not even between the standard international usage and the vernacular because it is not rare to see the vernacular use of the word 'Gurkha' with a 'u', such as in *The Gurkha's Daughter* (2013) by Prajjwal Parajuly, a novelist from Sikkim. It is, therefore, not an issue of etic and emic usages either. 'Gorkha' is certainly how it is written in Devnagari script, but in English, it may also be seen as a symbol of protest against the colonial usage. The issue being that complicated we have let both 'u' and 'o' exist in this volume.

The continuous use of both 'Nepalese' and 'Nepalis' in this volume is for similar, but not the same reasons. While the former technically means the citizens and language of Nepal, the literature published in English on the Nepalis of Darjeeling, Sikkim and Bhutan by the Nepalis and other Indians alike use 'Nepalese' even today, while in the same breath, they claim separate identity from the Nepal Nepalis. We have used in this volume the spelling 'Nepalis', unless under quotes, because we think this usage frees them from any nationality tag. It is more a cultural term rather than a political or legal one. It may include the Nepalese, Gurkhas, Gorkhas, Nepali-speaking Indians, Nepali-speaking Bhutanese, Nepali-speaking Myanmarese, and so on. Some of them may even be citizens of more than one country.

On the whole, the book provides a curious mix of all possible diasporic situations that Nepalis could be in. It remains to be seen how the diasporic situations unfold for them in the United States of America, Australia, Canada, Denmark, The Netherlands, New Zealand, Norway and the Gulf countries, where they have settled more recently. What cultural adaptations they will go through and what kind of identities emerge ultimately are difficult even to speculate. What will be the role of social media such as Facebook and Twitter in giving them a common platform to express themselves and lobby together for their rights or for their survival? The new technologies will hold enormous prospects for them to communicate among themselves quickly and intensively, even if physically, they may be thousands of miles away from each other. Will the Nepali community eventually turn into, from an imagined community in the sense Benedict Anderson defined the word, an e-community or cloud-community? What will then happen to their rights and loyalties, beings and belongings, roots and rootedness? Only the future holds the answer.

The Nepali intellectual class, which is still small and thin and is more or less confined to Kathmandu and Darjeeling, has not exercised its minds seriously on these issues. Many members of this class are the first generation to be educated and exposed to the outside world. This exposure itself has caused a huge stress on them to look modern, cosmopolitan, secular, and above all, as people who are not only 'brave' and 'loyal' but also as people with some grey matter in their heads. They are trying to achieve in one generation what their counterparts in many communities took several generations to evolve and stabilise themselves intellectually.

One of the consequences of a community with an immature and unstable intellectual class is the often inconsistent and unrealistic demands made and positions taken by its political, literary and cultural organisations. There is no proper debate on their demands and the ways those demands could be articulated and achieved. The intellectual class is often alienated from the social and political movements. As a result, such movements find themselves difficult to sustain intellectually over a long time and often degenerate into violence and cultural insensitivity towards the minority communities living among themselves. Or there is stagnation, with no clear road map for forward movement. Lack of intellectual support also leads to blind support to often incompetent and ill-educated leaders, who cannot see the larger picture or who refuse to see such a picture because of their weakness for power and wealth. The trajectory of Nepali diaspora is remindful of such failures.

One other failure of a diasporic community devoid of a robust intellectual class is its inability to understand the different nuances of an identity movement. That identity is not unilayered or unilinear is rarely understood or articulated by the leaders who spearhead ethnic movements. They attribute all their failures to their ethnicity or the ethnicity of their adversary. And their adversary is, more often than not, the dominant host community. They have no strategies for negotiation and no established channels of communication with the leaders of the host community. In any crisis, the state apparatuses either support the dominant community or turn a blind eye to their crimes against the minorities. Yet, the Nepali diaspora has all its organisations limited to the members of its own community only, which in itself is a sign of an insecure diasporic community that fails to see that it is more important to secure itself from outside than from within.

Finally, the diasporic Nepalis must form a network across the world so that they know the comparative advantages and disadvantages of working in a globalised world. The few educated among them must serve as information providers for Nepalis working in other countries. By doing so they will be able to avoid physical and sexual exploitation of their men and women by their employers and avoid death in workplaces, as is reported from many Gulf countries almost on daily basis. When that happens, the dead bodies are sent back to Nepal. The dead bodies can neither repay the loans taken by them to go abroad for employment nor wipe the tears of their near and dear ones. One dead body is sent back to Nepal almost every day, and yet, the country is silent. The country is also silent about the Bhutanese refugees who continue to languish in Nepal for its failure to negotiate with the Government of Bhutan. While Nepal has always provided refuge to those who needed it, the diasporic Nepalis should expect nothing more than that and prepare themselves to eke out their living from wherever they are. Hence, it is all the more reason for them to keep in touch with each other, which is possible today, thanks to the social media and the affordable internet facilities even on mobile platforms.

GLOSSARY

balidan	sacrifice
basai sarai	long-term migration
bhadralok	gentlemen
bhalu	bear
bhanja	nephew
bhanji	niece
bhisti	traditional water carrier belonging to the Muslim community
bhumi puja	worship of land
bidesh	foreign land
bigha	a unit of land measurement (1 bigha=14,400 sq.ft)
burqa	Muslim women's veil
chai taret khuthakpa	seven years of devastation
chetana	awakening
chimi	member of national assembly
churpi	cottage cheese
daju	(lit.) elder brother, (fig.) porter
desh	motherland
dhami	shaman
dhoti	loin cloth
durban	door keeper, security man
durbar	palace
dzong	fort
ghebring	Buddhist shaman
ghumphir	wandering about
gonpa	Buddhist monastery
haat	market
hami	we

GLOSSARY

jahaji bhai/behen	ship-brother/-sister
janajati	tribe
jat	caste
jatiya kabi	national poet
jhankri	shaman
jyanmara	murderer
kancha	(lit.) youngest brother, (fig.) household servant
khauma	mortuary ritual
khukuri	curved knife with the blade inwards
khutti	cow shed
kodali	spade
lahure	soldier
lakhang	receptacle of worship
lhotshampa	Nepalis of southern Bhutan
maiti	natal home
mandal	headman
manguena	ancestor worship
mayang	outsiders
mulbasi	indigenous
nwaran	naming ceremony
padayatra	a journey on foot for a cause
pakhe	backward, rustic
pathsala	school
pathy	a unit of measurement equivalent to 3.7 kgs
patta	land certificate
phanek	lower wraparound
phedangma	shaman
ponjyo	Buddhist shaman
prabasi	one who lives outside one's country
puja	worship to god
sabai jatko phulbari	a flower garden of all castes
samaj sewa	social work
sapori	river island
sastra	holy scripture
satyug	Golden Age
sloka	rhyme
tapu	river island
tarai	flat land between the hills and the plains
thaluwa	local
thar	clan

GLOSSARY

tika	sacred mark on forehead
tongsing	ancestor worship
tsongdu	national assembly
yagna	sacred ritual by fire
yuma	grandmother

INDEX

Aaja Ramita Chha (Rai) 98, 103
Acharya, Bhanu Bhakta 96, 97
Afro-Trinidadians 15
Akil Bharatiya Adivasi Vikash Parisad (ABAVP) 122–3
All Assam Gorkha Students' Union (AAGSU) 170, 175, 177
All India Gorkha League 94
ancestor worship 286
Anderson, Benedict 95
'The Andhi Khola' (Bishta) 61
Anglo-Bhutan Treaty 235
Anglo-Burmese war 207
Anglo-Saxon migrants 3
anthropology 11, 85, 87, 149; literature 13
Aris, Michael 246
Aryan-looking Nepalis 225
Asom Gana Parishad (AGP) 177–8
Assam 4, 8, 170–4, 176–7, 179–82, 184, 188–9, 192–6, 198–9, 201, 204, 207–9, 213, 216, 244
Assameli-Nepalis 193–5, 201
Assamese 8, 172–4, 177, 192–3, 197, 199
Assamese movement 170
Assmann, Jan 82, 84

Bahuns 43–4, 93–4, 156, 158, 160, 163, 172, 174, 176
Bajhangi Tole 47, 48
Banerjee, Mamata 116, 122
Bangladeshis 176–7
barbarism 85
Basai sarai 34
Bell, Charles A. 235
Bentham, Geoffrey 210–12

BFF *see* Burma Frontier Force
Bhandari, Nar Bahadur 158
Bharatiya Gorkha Parisangh (BGP) 114, 122
Bhattarai, Baburam 64
Bhramar (Sinha) 97, 98
Bhutan 9, 17, 115, 117, 120, 144, 230–51, 254–5, 257, 292, 294; army of 247–8; citizens of 248–9, 255; government of 248–9; refugees 248–9, 251–7, 294
Bhutanese 236, 238–9, 241, 248
Bhutanese Refugee Children Forum (BRCF) 232
Bhutan, Lhotshampas case 230–45
Bhutia-Lepcha group 157
Bhutias 117, 134–5, 139, 156–7, 159–60
Bishta, Daulat Bikram 61
Blue Mimosa (Tamang) 62
BMP *see* Burma Military Police
Bodo movement 170
Bokakhat 8, 170–8, 180–3
Booker Prize 145, 147, 150–1
Brahmaputraka Cheuchau (Chhetri) 188–201
Brass, Paul 3
British Army 4, 65–7, 70, 72, 86, 93, 138, 223, 277–8
British government 65, 67, 72, 85, 277–8, 288
British Gurkhas 4, 66, 73
British India, province of 203, 205
Brubaker, R. 153, 171, 175, 178
Buddhism 154, 157–60, 163, 287

299

INDEX

Burma 4, 8, 25, 63, 203–13, 216–18; Gurkhas from 203–18
Burma Army (BA) 203, 205, 214–15
Burma Frontier Force (BFF) 203, 205, 207–9, 211, 213–15
Roy Burman, B.K. 157
Burma Military Police (BMP) 203, 205, 207–9, 214–15
Burmese 204–5, 208, 222

Campbell, W. L. 236
Carroll, Peter 67
CEDA *see* Centre for Economic Development and Administration
Centre for Economic Development and Administration (CEDA) 34
Centre for Nepal and Asian Studies (CNAS) 34
Chamling, Pawan 158
Chhetri, Dhan Bahadur 181
Chhetri, H. B. 117, 118, 120
Chhetri, Lil Bahadur 188–201
Chirol, Valentine 97
Chitwan Tharus 43
Chomsky, Noam 139
CNAS *see* Centre for Nepal and Asian Studies
Cohen, Robin 77, 95
Collett, Nigel A. 60
Communist Party of India (CPI) 113–14, 119, 122
Contemporary Nepal 44, 58
Craig, Tudor 217
Criminal Tribe Act 87
cultural collectives, idea of 226–7
cultural identity 101–2, 138–9, 163, 178

Dalit movements 41
Darjeeling 4, 7, 93–101, 113–25, 134–8, 142, 144–5, 209–10, 213, 216, 232–3, 238–9, 242–4, 247–8, 292–3; centre of Indian Nepalis 116–18; Dooars and Terai 118–19; as ethnoscape 119; place of ancestors 118; place of previous wealth 118; as promise 119–21; resistance movements in 142
Darjeeling Gorkha Hill Council (DGHC) 114

Dashain festival 101–2, 283–4, 287; *see also* festivals
death rites 282–3
demography, politics of statistics 240
denotified tribes 87
Deokota, Laxmi Prasad 97
Department of Foreign Employment (DFE) 19–20, 26, 29
Desai, Kiran 144, 147
Desai, Morarji 99
Dhakal, D. N. S. 238
diaspora 2–7, 9, 12, 16, 18–19, 34, 36–7, 40–1, 44, 46–8, 50, 76–84, 87–8, 184, 171–2, 175–8, 181–4, 197, 204, 221, 246–7, 291, 293–4; communities of 3, 5–6, 16–17, 224, 269–72, 293; consciousness 170–84; in Delhi 44–8; discourse on 76–9; idea of 2–3, 11, 77; imaginations of Darjeeling 108–25; junctions 11–17; Lhotshampas and 246–57; movements 12–13; mythical entrapment of 76–91; notion of 78–81, 171; scholars of 77–8; self 80–1, 83; societies 6, 93–105, 110, 171; in Switzerland 48–50
Dirks, Nicholas 85
Dooars 102, 116, 118–19, 124
dormant diaspora 182–3
Drukpas 232–3, 237, 239, 242
Dubois, W. E. B. 140
Dungel, Ramesh 246

eastern Nepal 33, 47, 203–4, 216, 230, 232, 239
ecological regions 23, 26–7, 29
Emic discourses 175; assimilation and political demands 177–8; distinction and identity 175–7
ethnic groups 3, 41, 43, 50, 69–70, 73, 101–3, 118, 137–8, 141, 153, 156–8, 160–3, 278
ethnic identity 134
ethnicity 31, 34, 41–2, 44, 108, 133, 153, 188, 293
ethnic politics 170
evacuees 212–15, 217–18
ex-Gurkha immigrants 274–89

INDEX

Far-West Nepal 48, 50
Foreign Employment Act 19, 27
foreign labour markets 29
foreign labour migration 19–20, 27–33
fragmented identity, of Indian Nepalis 131–42
Freire, Paulo 88
Frenkel, Ronit 150

Gay, Paul 60
Ghising, Subhas 100, 145
ghumphir 6, 18–19, 34–5
Giri, Agam Singh 98, 100
Giri, B. P. 150
Giri, Roshan 122
Glass, Timothy 59
Golay, Bidhan 109, 134, 178
Goojars 88
Gooroong, B. B. 155
Gopinath, Gayatri 79
Gorakhpur 4, 210–12
Gorkha Janamukti Morcha (GJM) 101–2, 108, 113–22, 125
Gorkhaland 101, 108–25, 142, 146, 177, 180, 243; deconstructing 122–3; demand 101–2, 114, 119, 184; Mâyel Lyâng, part of 123; as national security threat 123; power and class-consciousness, threat to 122–3; strategic imaginative geography 116; territorial administration 122
Gorkhaland movement 100, 109, 150
Gorkha National Liberation Front (GNLF) 100, 114, 116, 145, 148, 237
Gorkhas 42–4, 50, 56, 58, 70–2, 94, 96–104, 109, 117–23, 125, 145–7, 176–7, 222–6, 231, 292; of Darjeeling 7, 95; de-territorialised subjectivity of 109–10; of India 101, 121; parties 119, 122, 125; population 226; soldiers 5, 64, 70, 98, 222–3
Gorkhasthan 114–16, 117–21
Gorkhay Khabar Kagat 96
Government of Bhutan 247, 249, 255, 257, 294
Government of Burma 205, 210–13
Government of India 101, 204, 209, 211–13, 217, 239

Government of Nepal 18–19, 27, 29, 34, 43, 212, 224, 241, 248, 250–2, 254, 260, 278
graziers 93–4, 172–3, 189, 193, 196–8, 234
Greater Nepal 114, 121, 238, 248, 251, 255
Greene, Damian 274
GSG *see* Gurkha Security Guards
Gurkha Army Ex-Servicemen's Organisation (GAESO) 66
Gurkha Contingent (GC) 9, 260–5, 267, 269–71
Gurkha Evacuee Camp 213
Gurkhas 4, 7, 57–60, 62, 64–72, 84–90, 93, 203–5, 207–8, 216–18, 259–63, 265–71, 278–9, 281–9, 292; from Burma 203–18; children 264, 267, 270; community 68, 269, 288; displaced 204, 209–11, 216; evacuees 209, 213, 216–18; families 209–10, 259, 261, 263–9, 271, 276, 279, 289; and identity politics 55–73; Justice Campaign 7, 59, 66–71; in Oxford 275, 280, 281, 287; recruitment of 72, 204–7, 259–60; refugees 210–13; regiments 4, 57, 59, 71, 84, 176, 236; retired 4, 68, 261, 266–8; rifles 207, 212, 236; Singaporean identity, sustaining 267–9; tradition 55, 60, 62–4, 72; *see also* Nepalis
The Gurkha's Daughter (2013) 292
Gurkha Security Guards (GSG) 65–6
Gurkha service 277–9; history of 276–7, 289
Gurkha soldiers 4–5, 55–6, 66–7, 70, 72, 138, 205, 207, 217; women and children and dependents of 203, 208
Gurung, Bimal 108, 119
Gurung community 8, 154, 159, 161
Gurung cultural identifications 153–63
Gurung, Gopal 69, 70, 158
Gurung, Gorman 60
Gurungs 7, 35, 69–70, 93–4, 96, 145, 153–61, 163, 176, 231; of Nepal 154
Gurung village religious practices 160–2
Gyawali, Surya Bikram 96

INDEX

Hami Nepali 40–50
Hangen 69, 284
Henry, Schwarz 97
Hidden Facts in Nepalese Politics (1985) 69, 158
Hind Swaraj 88
Hinduism 42–3, 154, 158, 161–2
Hindu temples 264, 284–5
homeland, ancestral 111, 113, 116, 118
human movement 11–12; *see also* Nepali migration
Hutt, Michael 145

identity-crisis 120, 122, 125
identity politics 55, 111
imaginative geographies 108–14, 116–17, 119, 121, 123–4; Gorkhaland as 113–14; regionalisation and 110–13
immigrants 2–3, 43, 94, 97–8, 139, 275, 288–9; ex-Gurkha 274
Imphal 206, 209, 222, 224
INA *see* Indian National Army
India-born Gurkhas 4
All India Gorkha League 94, 99
Indian Army 56, 85–6, 121, 207, 236
Indian Gorkhas 7, 93–105, 114, 117, 120; early phase (1815–90) 93–5; second phase (1890–1947) 95–9; third phase (1947–) 99–105
Indian government 87, 99, 120–1
Indian Identity 14, 175, 183–4
Indian National Army (INA) 222–3
Indian National Congress 97, 236, 238
Indian Nepalis 8, 103, 109–10, 117, 123, 134, 138–42, 144, 170–2, 175, 177–8, 180, 182–4, 232, 243; fragmented identity of 131–42; issues of identity facing 138–40; portrayal of 144–52
Indians 2–3, 13–16, 64, 100, 103, 135, 138, 142, 145, 177, 180–1, 206, 208, 235–6, 238
Indian Tea Association (ITA) 209
Indigenous Lepcha Tribal Association (ILTA) 123
Indo-Nepalese Friendship 5
Indo-Nepal Treaty of Peace and Friendship 180
The Inheritance of Loss (2006) 144, 149

International Labour Organization (ILO) 1
international migration 1, 26–7, 29, 35, 181; women's participation in 29, 31
International Office of Migration (IOM) 251
IOM *see* International Office of Migration
irregular migrants 48–50
Iser, Wolfgang 149
ITA *see* Indian Tea Association

Janajati 69–71, 159
Jennings, Francis 227
Jews 2, 3, 9, 12, 76
Joint Verification Team (JVT) 249–50

Kami 44
Kansakar, V.B.S. 34–5
Kathmandu Valley 42–3
Kemp, W. N. R. 212
Kennedy, Robert E. 235
Khas Kura 94
Khudunabari Camp 249–50, 255
Koirala, Dharanidhar 96
Kunraghat 210–11, 213, 215–16
Kurseong 114–15, 216

labourers 3, 6, 14, 93; indentured 6, 13–15
labour migrants 27, 29
Lacan, Jacques 80
Lama, Migi 161
landlords 181, 190, 193, 200
language movement 96, 99, 117, 142
Lepchas 114, 117–18, 123, 139, 156–7, 159–60
Levy, Robert 281
Lewis, I. M. 275
Lhotshampas 9, 230–48, 254–6; apprehension of 243; aspirations, Bhutanese response 232–3; in Bhutan 240–1, 243; culture and 231–2, 244–5; denial, history of 255–6; ethnic assimilation of 236–7; ethnic catharsis and expulsion of 237–40; identity, future of 242–3; in India 241, 244–5; Nepali diaspora 246–57; population 240–2; refugees 230, 239,

241, 246–55; thriving settlements, malarial jungle 233–5; in Western destinations 241–2
Limbus 69–70, 93–4, 96, 101, 154, 157, 160, 176, 280–6
Lumley, Joanna 67, 286

MacFarlane, Alan 284–5
McLeod, John 104
Manipur 8–9, 139, 206, 208, 210, 221–6, 228; short history 222–4; socio-economic scenario 225–6
martial races 4, 59, 69–70, 85–6, 88–90, 124, 260, 262–3, 278
Mauss, Marcel 275
memories, shared 111, 113, 116, 118–19, 242
mercenaries 5, 64–6, 69–71, 84, 147; debate 64–6
migrants, international 1, 26–7, 36
Mishra, Vijay 80, 99
Misra, P. K. 6
Mongol National Organisation (MNO) 59, 69–71
Morris, C. J. 236
Motihari camp 204, 211–18
Mount Vernon Camp 260, 263–4, 267–70
Mulbasi Mongol Rastriya Yuwa Sabha 69
Myitkyina 203, 205, 207–8
mythical entrapment 76–91

Nasreen, Taslima 144
National Assembly of Bhutan 237–8
national emblem 56–7
national identity politics 69–71
national immigration policy 267
Nepal: camps in 230; citizens of 103, 109, 120, 267; international migration in 35; links to 171, 179, 184; practices related to 179–82; repatriation to 266–7, 270
Nepalese *see* Nepalis
Nepali migration: contemporary internal movement 24, 26; of foreign labour 27–33; historical trend 24; international 26–7; paradigm shifts in 33–4; patterns of 24–33; reversible and irreversible forms of 35; special case of 276–80; territorial mobility and diaspora 34–6
Nepalis 4–8, 24, 26–7, 29, 31, 33–4, 36, 48–9, 96, 99–103, 138–40, 145–7, 172–8, 180–2, 191–3, 196–8, 223–6, 230–7, 244, 246–8, 278–9, 283–7, 291–4; in Bokakhat 171–2, 174–7, 181; citizenship 181, 183; community 145, 149, 193, 196, 200, 223–5, 256, 293; culture 247, 250, 283; diaspora *see* diaspora; families 179, 196; geographical and social composition 174–5; households 174, 280; identity 157, 184, 270; language 18, 34, 94, 96, 100, 117, 237; literature 63, 97, 100; of Manipur 8–9, 221–7; migrants 19, 26, 33, 50, 173, 175, 197, 201; migration 6, 18–37, 188–9, 191, 206, 232; narratives 61–4; origin 9, 137, 170, 244; population 78, 118; settlement 172–5; of southern Bhutan 246–7, 296; speakers 99–100
Nepali Sahitya Sammelan 96
Nepali-speaking Indians 103, 292
Nepal Janajati Mahasangh 69
Nepal Nepalis 171, 175, 177, 180, 292
Newars 42–3, 50, 96, 156, 158, 163, 277, 281
Non-Resident Bhutanese (NRB) 257
Non-Resident Nepalese (NRN) 36
Nepali diaspora, notion of 76
NRB *see* Non-Resident Bhutanese

Olwig, Karen Fog 275
Other Backward Classes (OBC) 154, 156–8, 225
Oxford Gurkhas 276, 284, 286–7

Parajuly, Prajjwal 292
Pokhara 64, 158–9, 161, 261, 268
political regionalisations 111
postcolonial discourse 59–61, 63–5
Pradhan, C. K. 148
Pradhan, E. D. 119, 121
Pradhan, Kumar 96
Pradhan, Paras Mani 96

Radhakrishna, Meena 85
Rai, Indra Bahadur 98, 102

INDEX

Rai, R. B. 117, 120
Rai, Shiv Kumar 62
Rao, Anjali 147
refugee camps 211, 230, 237, 240–1
refugee community 249–51, 255
refugees 2, 203, 206, 208–9, 212–13, 218, 230, 239, 244, 247–52, 255, 257, 276
rehabilitation 204, 209–11, 217
rejected diaspora 178
religious practices 43, 158, 160–2, 231, 274–5, 289
religious specialists 158, 161
remittances 1, 5, 35, 55, 72–3
repatriated Gurkhas 261, 267–8
repatriation 230, 250–1, 257, 259–72
resistance movements, in Darjeeling 142
rights, political 142, 291–2
Rimpoche, Guru 246
riots 259–72
ritual practices 274–89
Royal Government of Bhutan (RGB) 230, 237–9, 241, 247, 249–50
Royal Government of Nepal (RGN) 230, 239
Rushdie, Salman 144

sacrifice, dreams of 286–7
Safran, William 2, 77, 95, 269
Sagant, Philippe 280
Said, Edward 109, 112
Sarki 44
Scheduled Tribes (ST) 153–7, 159, 162
self-identification 162–3
SGA *see* Sikkim Gurung Buddhist Association
Shah, Prithvi Narayan 41, 42
Sheffer, Gabriel 79
Shuval, Judith 2
Sikkim 4, 7, 93, 114–15, 117, 153–61, 163, 232–3, 238, 240, 242, 244, 248, 250, 291–2
Sikkimese Gurungs 153–5, 157–9, 162
Sikkim Gurung Buddhist Association (SGA) 153–6; conflict within 154–7
Singaporeans 259, 261, 265, 268
Singapore government 259, 261, 263–5, 267, 269

Singapore Gurkha Contingent (SGC) 259
Singapore Gurkha Pensioners' Association (SGPA) 266–7
Singapore Gurkhas 9, 259–72; diaspora 269–70
Singapore Police Force 9, 260–2, 265
Sinha, Rupnarayan 97, 98
Smith, Anthony 111
social identity 90, 103
southern Bhutan 9, 230, 233, 235, 237–8, 246–7, 252, 254, 256
statehood demand 113, 116, 121–2, 124
statehood movements 110–13
strategic imaginative geographies 7, 112–13, 116
Subba, Jai Bahadur 118
Subba, Manprasad 104
Switzerland 7, 41, 48–50, 251

Tamang, Parijat 62
Tamsang, Lyangsong 114
Terai 116, 118–19, 124
territorial mobility 34–6
Thakuri 44
Thapa, Remika 104
Titley, John 66
Toffin, Gérard 281
Tölölyan, Khachig 2
tongshing 286
traditional marriages 14–15
Transport Management 19, 21–3, 27–8, 30
Treaty of Segowli 93, 188, 207
Trinidad 13–15, 17

Unified Nepal Nationalist Front 121
United Nations High Commission of Refugees (UNHCR) 230, 238–9, 248, 254
Upper Assam 201, 206, 208–9, 213
Upper Burma 204, 206–9

Van Hear, Nicholas 2
Vansittart, Eden 86
Village Development Councils (VDC) 45

INDEX

West Bengal 100, 108, 114, 116–20, 136, 150, 237–8, 244
Wittgenstein, Ludwig 78
women 29, 34, 46, 48, 200, 203, 208–10, 282, 294; in foreign labour markets 29
Wood, E. 206
Woods, Vicky 286

Wooldridge, Ian 65
worship, ancestor 286–7

Yangang 159–62
youth bulge 20

Žižek, Slavoj 80